The Cambridge Companion to
Comparative Family Law

Families and family law have faced significant challenges in the face of rapid changes in social norms, demographics and political expectations. *The Cambridge Companion to Comparative Family Law* highlights the key questions and themes that have faced family lawyers across the world. Each chapter is written by internationally renowned academics experts, and focuses on which of these themes are most significant to their jurisdictions.

In taking this jurisdictional approach, the collection will explore how different countries have tackled these issues. As a result, the collection is aimed at students, practitioners and academics across a variety of disciplines, interested in the key issues faced by family law around the world and how they have been addressed.

Shazia Choudhry is Professor of Law at Queen Mary, University of London. Her research interests lie in the fields of European and UK human rights law, and in particular gender-based violence. She has published a number of articles and chapters, as well as two books, *European Human Rights and Family Law* (2010 with J. Herring) and *Rights, Gender and Family Law* (2009 with J. Herring and J. Wallbank). In addition to her publications, her work has included her appointment as Specialist Adviser to the Joint Parliamentary Committee on Human Rights Inquiry into Violence against Women (2014–15); and acting as an expert for the UNFPA, the European Commission and the Council of Europe.

Jonathan Herring is Vice Dean and Professor of Law at the Law Faculty, Oxford University and Fellow in Law at Exeter College, Oxford University. He has written nearly 100 books on family law, medical law, criminal law and legal issues surrounding care and old age. His books include *Medical Law and Ethics* (2018); *Family Law* (2018); *Childhood, Vulnerability and the Law* (2018); *Vulnerable Adults and the Law* (2016); *Caring and the Law* (2014); *Older People in Law and Society* (2009); *European Human Rights and Family Law* (2010 with Shazia Choudhry); *Criminal Law* (2018). He has also written for the general public *The Woman Who Tickled Too Much* (2009) and *How to Argue* (2012).

Cambridge Companions to Law

Cambridge Companions to Law offers thought-provoking introductions to different legal disciplines, invaluable to both the student and the scholar. Edited by world-leading academics, each offers a collection of essays which both map out the subject and allow the reader to delve deeper. Critical and enlightening, the *Companions* library represents legal scholarship at its best.

The Cambridge Companion to European Private Law
Edited by Christian Twigg-Flesner

The Cambridge Companion to International Law
Edited by James Crawford and Martti Koskenniemi

The Cambridge Companion to Comparative Law
Edited by Mauro Bussani and Ugo Mattei

The Cambridge Companion to Human Rights Law
Edited by Conor Gearty and Costas Douzinas

The Cambridge Companion to Public Law
Edited by Mark Elliott and David Feldman

The Cambridge Companion to International Criminal Law
Edited by William A. Schabas

The Cambridge Companion to Natural Law Jurisprudence
Edited by George Duke and Robert P. George

The Cambridge Companion to Comparative Family Law
Edited by Shazia Choudhry and Jonathan Herring

The Cambridge Companion to
Comparative Family Law

Edited by

Shazia Choudhry
Queen Mary, University of London

Jonathan Herring
University of Oxford

CAMBRIDGE
UNIVERSITY PRESS

University Printing House, Cambridge CB2 8BS, United Kingdom

One Liberty Plaza, 20th Floor, New York, NY 10006, USA

477 Williamstown Road, Port Melbourne, VIC 3207, Australia

314–321, 3rd Floor, Plot 3, Splendor Forum, Jasola District Centre, New Delhi – 110025, India

79 Anson Road, #06–04/06, Singapore 079906

Cambridge University Press is part of the University of Cambridge.

It furthers the University's mission by disseminating knowledge in the pursuit of education, learning, and research at the highest international levels of excellence.

www.cambridge.org
Information on this title: www.cambridge.org/9781107167537
DOI: 10.1017/9781316711750

© Cambridge University Press 2019

This publication is in copyright. Subject to statutory exception and to the provisions of relevant collective licensing agreements, no reproduction of any part may take place without the written permission of Cambridge University Press.

First published 2019

Printed and bound in Great Britain by Clays Ltd, Elcograf S.p.A.

A catalogue record for this publication is available from the British Library.

Library of Congress Cataloging-in-Publication Data
Names: Choudhry, Shazia, editor. | Herring, Jonathan, editor.
Title: The Cambridge companion to comparative family law / edited by Shazia Choudhry, Queen Mary, University of London; Jonathan Herring, University of Oxford.
Description: Cambridge , United Kingdom ; New York, NY : Cambridge University Press, 2018. | Includes index.
Identifiers: LCCN 2018035157 | ISBN 9781107167537
Subjects: LCSH: Domestic relations. | Domestic relations (Islamic law)
Classification: LCC K670 .C43 2018 | DDC 346.01/5–dc23
LC record available at https://lccn.loc.gov/2018035157

ISBN 978-1-107-16753-7 Hardback
ISBN 978-1-316-61805-9 Paperback

Cambridge University Press has no responsibility for the persistence or accuracy of URLs for external or third-party internet websites referred to in this publication and does not guarantee that any content on such websites is, or will remain, accurate or appropriate.

Contents

	List of Contributors	*page* vii
	Acknowledgements	viii
	Introduction Shazia Choudhry and Jonathan Herring	1
1	Contemporary Issues in Family Law in England and Wales Rosemary Hunter	19
2	Family Law in the United States: Freedom and Inequality Theresa Glennon	48
3	Human Rights in the German Family Law Context Bettina Heiderhoff	77
4	Australian Family Property Law: Current Issues and Challenges Belinda Fehlberg and Lisa Sarmas	106
5	Towards the Constitutionalization of Family Law in Latin America Nicolás Espejo and Fabiola Lathrop	128
6	The Nuclear Norm and the Free-Form Family: Irreconcilable Paths in Swedish Family Law? Pernilla Leviner	158
7	South African Family Law and the Chimera of Diversity Anne Louw	180
8	The Post-Divorce Child Support System in China: Past, Present and Future Lei Shi	203

9	The Problem with Personal Law in India Farrah Ahmed	225
10	The Postcolonial Fallacy of 'Islamic' Family Law Abdullahi Ahmed An-Na'im	254
	Index	280

Contributors

Farrah Ahmed, University of Melbourne
Abdullahi Ahmed An-Na'im, Emory University, USA
Shazia Choudhry (Queen Mary, London)
Nicolás Espejo, Universidad Católica de Chile
Belinda Fehlberg, University of Melbourne
Theresa Glennon, Temple University, USA
Bettina Heiderhoff, University of Munster
Jonathan Herring (University of Oxford)
Rosemary Hunter, University of Kent
Fabiola Lathrop, Universidad de Chile
Pernilla Leviner, Stockholm University
Anne Louw, University of Pretoria
Lisa Sarmas, University of Melbourne
Lei Shi, Southwest University of Political Science and Law

Acknowledgements

The editors are very grateful to the contributors for their excellent contributions to this volume. We have also greatly appreciated the support and work of the team at Cambridge University Press, especially Laura Blake, and of Jim Diggins, for his work on the index.

Introduction

Shazia Choudhry and Jonathan Herring

Introduction

It has become almost a cliché to say that family law is in a state of turbulence. The long-established cornerstones of family law: marriage, parenthood, childhood and even family itself are crumbling before our eyes, or at least becoming complex and contested concepts. Family lawyers are asking questions which our forebears would never have foreseen: what is a parent? Can a child have three or more parents? What is the position if a woman carries a baby using an egg from her daughter? Should we allow a group of four people to marry?

Some of these changes are a result of technological developments which have meant that children can be created in family forms that are far more diverse than in the past. However, the greatest impact has been dramatic changes in social attitudes and social conditions. The most significant has been the changing position of women. The traditional role of wife and mother which was so central to women's lives in the past and their position in family law is now adopted by fewer women. The 'ideal of motherhood' still hangs over family law and can still be found in the many aspects of it, but it grates with the reality of family life for many women. That said, family law has still struggled in many countries to respond to the changing norms of family life for women and in particular to develop legal responses which are not based on an assumption of traditional married life. That challenge is made more complex by the variety of family forms, meaning that a single model of family law becomes difficult.

With these challenges come many possibilities. Family lawyers are now required to think more deeply and richly about what it means to be a family; what is at the heart of parenthood; and what family law is trying to do. Rather than relying on external formalities (e.g. marriage; birth certificates) as a proxy for the deeper values being promoted, the law must seek to explore what those values are.

In this book we encouraged leading family lawyers from a range of jurisdictions to explore what issues they thought were the major ones facing family law today. We gave some broad indications of the kind of issues we thought might be raised, but left it to each author to identify what they thought were the key ones in their jurisdictions. In this introduction we seek to bring out some of the common themes.

Gender

All the chapters in this collection make references to gender. This is not surprising. Traditionally in many societies families were seen as the world of women. Family life was seen as structured around clearly defined gendered roles: the husband as breadwinner, the wife as homemaker; the father as disciplinarian and decision maker; the mother as carer. One of the most significant changes in the twentieth century was the dismantling of these roles, or at least partial dismantling. While the concepts of equal sharing of childcare and equal access to the labour market are promoted in most, if not all societies, they are the subject of idealised rhetoric, rather than reality. There has certainly been significant changes in the employed work lives of the average men and women. The division of household and family labour has been harder to shift. This means that while most family law systems now seek to promote equality between men and women, what equality means is still hotly debated.

It might be thought that it would be rare to find family laws which overtly discriminate against women nowadays. However, as Farrah Ahmed notes in Indian law (Chapter 9), through its use of personal law, depending on the religious category into which one is deemed to fall, some rules overtly discriminate on the grounds of sex. This might be justified on the basis that if an individual chooses to follow a religion that sets up different roles for men and women, then this choice should be respected. However, even accepting that premise, which we would not, Ahmed explains how often Indian law assigns a religion to an individual which does not reflect their self-identified religion. The differences in treatment under Indian law can be significant. She notes:

By giving women weaker rights to inheritance and weak powers of marriage, divorce, adoption, and guardianship, most personal laws leave them with fewer options and less power over their own lives. Without such rights, women are denied valuable options, including the many options closed by a lack of money.[1]

But such overt distinctions between men and women are now rare in family law. In Chapter 5, Nicolás Espejo and Fabiola Lathrop, looking at family law in South America, see the equalising of the rights of mother and fathers in family law as an important development, promoting 'a more egalitarian distribution of child rearing in family life'.[2] Certainly few would decry the fact that under most family law jurisdictions mothers and fathers have equal responsibilities to care for their children. However, as already indicated the term equality is problematic. Feminist scholars have done much to highlight the way that equal treatment of those unequally positioned does not promote equality. Fehlberg and Samas give a good example using the issue financial orders on divorce (Chapter 4). It might be claimed that an equal division of assets on divorce would promote fairness or equality, but if the relationship has impacted on the parties' capacity for earning income the equality would be short-lived. There would not then be in the long term a fair sharing of the economic disadvantages generated by the marriage.

A similar issue relates to childcare. In Chapter 3, Heiderhoff explains that it is common for a couple to agree on a 50:50 sharing of childcare following relationship breakdown in Germany, in Chapter 1, Hunter explains that in England in court-resolved disputes there is strong pressure to ensure as much contact with both parents as possible. Yet in both Germany and England we are still well short of an equal sharing of childcare while the relationship is intact. Indeed, in many jurisdictions there is a notable disjunction between the considerable efforts put into enforcing shared care post-separation, with the minimal efforts in ensuring shared care during the relationship. A notable exception is Sweden where, as Leviner (Chapter 6) mentions, parents each get individual paid leave, which they must use or lose. That provides a powerful encouragement for both parties to be involved in childcare.

A more profound challenge to gender difference may be found in the discussion of Nicolás Espejo and Fabiola Lathrop of a series of cases on intersex children. The South American courts have been more progressive than in many other jurisdictions in arguing for the right to registered as intersex and for acknowledging the rights of children with intersex bodies

---

[1] Page 237.   [2] Page 132.

to determine for themselves what surgery, if any, they wish to receive and gender identity to adopt. These decisions demonstrate the breaking down of the binary model of sex being either male or female. As a broader range of sexual identities and sexualities are developed, the male–female divide, that has been so powerful in family law, becomes problematised.[3] Of course, even if there is growing acknowledgement that sexual fluidity is a biological truth and gender fluidity becomes more common as a social identity, it remains to be seen how far gender norms and patriarchal forces will operate. Certainly, the traditional feminist analysis of patriarchy will need to become far more sophisticated than a straightforward story of men's power over women's. The current work by black feminist scholars on intersectionality has begun that work.[4]

One area where there can be particular tensions between family law and gender concerns religious understandings of marriage and we turn to that issue next.

Religion

It is, perhaps surprising, how often religion is mentioned in the chapters which follow. One of the major changes in social attitudes and practice in the latter part of the twentieth century, mentioned previously, is attitudes towards religion. In many countries formal religious observance has declined. Yet religion still, undoubtedly, has enormous social and personal significance in many countries.

Religion and family law have a long history in many jurisdictions. In England family law was largely administered by the ecclesiastical (church) courts until the nineteenth century, and in India, as Farrah Ahmed's chapter discusses, Indian law is still largely a set of religious laws (Chapter 9). Even in countries which seek an overtly secular family law, it is difficult to avoid any reference to religious practices or concepts.

The overlap between religion and legal understandings of family relationships partly flows from an overlap between the terminology and

---

[3] J. Herring, 'Making family law less sexy ... And more careful', in R. Leckey (ed.), *After Legal Equality: Family, Sex, Kinship* (Abingdon, UK: Routledge, 2014), pp. 25–41.
[4] K. Crenshaw, 'Mapping the margins: Intersectionality, identity politics, and violence against women of color' (1991) 43 *Stanford Law Review* 1241.

concepts. Given the influence of religion on the way people organise and structure their family lives, a legal intervention which sought to ignore religion would be based on a false understanding. Yet, as religious practice, at least in the context of formal religion, become far less prevalent in many countries and as religious values far from underpinning the legal system in some cases are in direct opposition to it, the relationship between law and religion has become more complex. Ahmed explains that in India it is the belief that family law is about personal law that means the law should reflect the religious views of the individual, hence there are separate family laws for Hindus, Buddhists, Sikhs, Jains, Muslims, Parsis, Jews and Christians. This is certainly a challenge to western concepts of law built on the concept of 'one law for all'. However, as we shall see under the heading 'Autonomy' below, that concept is under challenge from other sources apart from religion. What is notable about the Indian approach is that, by contrast with English family law, there is no attempt to impose a single religious vision of what family life should be or at least privileged certain religious forms of family life, but rather an attempt to acknowledge a wide range of alternate religious understandings.

A further difficulty identified by Ahmed is that if an attempt is made to match the legal regulation and religious beliefs of an individual, the question then arises as to which religious rules to apply. As she notes, Indian law tends to identify a person's religion, rather than allow them to self-identify. She explains that this means that Sikhs, Buddhists and Jains can be regarded as Hindu, although they would never describe their religion in that way. This might undermine any claim that the law is simply seeking to allow an individual to select what form of legal regulation if any they wish to apply. However, one can see the difficulty that can arise if an individual is simply permitted to select their religion. An individual's religious beliefs may change over time making it difficult to identify the correct regulation to apply. Further, it will be rare, even for a firm believer, to adopt all of particular religious group's teaching. If we seek to match the regulation to an individual's religious beliefs (by contrast with their membership of a religious group), the task for legal intervention becomes very difficult. If, however, as seems to happen in some cases in India an individuals is deemed a member of a religious group and rules to which they do not adhere apply to them, this becomes hard to justify. Even if one's religion is correctly identified, it becomes the state which then determines the regulations that should apply to that religious group. Hence, even

Indian law which might be seen as an attempt to acknowledge and treasure religious diversity, in some respects ends up undermining respect for individual religious beliefs. Ahmed claims that in Indian law respect for choice is illusionary. Indeed, she claims that for women the use of 'personal law' is autonomy reducing, rather than autonomy enhancing.

One solution, proposed by Ahmed, is to have general family law that applies to everyone, but permit specific detailed regulations on secondary matters to be left to individual religious preferences. Hence, in English law, the precise form of a marriage ceremony can be determined by the preferences of certain religious groups, although only a tightly defined group. However, as Ahmed's chapter demonstrates there are considerable difficulties that such a partial accommodation can generate.

Notably critics of attempts to use state law to uphold religious principles in the area of family law include religious groups themselves. In Chapter 10, Abdullahi Ahmed An-Na'im questions the very possibility of having the state enforce Muslim law: 'since it is enacted and enforced by the state, this field of state law does not qualify as being "Islamic" by any clear and verifiable criteria of what it means to be Islamic'.[5] One might imagine similar points being made from the perspectives of other religions where what is 'in the heart' and spiritual truths are what matters and these are, in their nature, outside the scope of a formal legal assessment.

A second reason for scepticism of state-enforced religious regulation from a religious perspective is that as Abdullahi Ahmed An-Na'im states 'arbitrary selectivity fails to account for the normative and social cohesion of each school in its broader social context'.[6] If the state were to decide to affect some aspects of religious law (e.g. only in the area of family law), but not other aspects of religious law, this would create all kinds of difficulties.

Another issue raised by the use of opting into religious regulation is whether such a choice can ever be free. Hunter writing on the English position of the use of religious tribunals is concerned that 'there is evidence that women feel pressured into taking this route by their communities and feel they have little choice in the matter'.[7]

The easiest route might be thought to make family law a religion-free zone and leave religious matters entirely to religious bodies and individuals. This is the kind of approach that is promoted in South Africa, as discussed by Louw (Chapter 7), where religious and customary marriages

---

[5] Page 254.   [6] Page 271.   [7] Page 26.

are not formally recognised by law. Looking at the issue of customary family law and marriage she notes that 'a distinction is drawn between so-called "official customary law", as applied by the courts and state bodies, and "living customary law", represented by the current customary practices of the people whose customary law is in question'.[8] In other words, if the law decides to ignore customary or religious law, that does not mean individuals will. If they continue to abide by religious regulation and see the state regulation as irrelevant to them, then they will fall outside the law's scope.

Alternative Dispute Resolution

Many family law systems offer some form of alternative dispute resolution (ADR) as an option to be used instead of court resolution. There are multiple reasons behind this shift. One is certainly cost. Given the increasing numbers of cases of family breakdown leading to disputes in many jurisdictions, the expense involved in providing traditional court-based resolution has meant that cheaper forms of ADR are used. However, there is more behind the move to ADR than this.

One factor is the growing complexities of issues that are raised on family breakdown. Family breakdown problems are not restricted to traditional legal issues concerning division of assets or care of children, but can highlight mental health issues; psychological difficulties; religious concerns; debt counselling; and educational problems. Without seeking to resolve some of these broader issues legal interventions may well be ineffective. A court order determining child arrangements may well only succeed if the parties are able psychologically to resolve the broader issues around it. Traditional courtroom settings are often not appropriate to deal with the complex emotional difficulties that can arise, although increasingly courts are required to deal with these.[9]

A further factor is that ADR is seen as more consistent with the broader push towards autonomy mentioned below. It enables parties to use the values that they live by to resolve their disputes, rather than have

---

[8] Page 183.
[9] J. Eekelaar and M. Maclean, *Family Justice: The Work of Family Judges in Uncertain Times* (Oxford: Hart, 2013).

generalised values that the law uses. Farrah Ahmed suggests this may be particularly appropriate in the Indian context for couples of religious faith. They may seek to use ADR to ensure that the religious and practical issues around their dispute are resolved. She sees this as preferable to the court-based system in India, which she explains can seek to determine the religion of the individuals, which may not match their self-identification. It would mean that only those who choose to use religious ADR would be subject to its terms, rather than the current system in India where religious personal laws apply to an individual, whether they wish them to or not. It would also have the advantage of the couple seeking to precisely define the nature of their religious belief, if for example, they hold a minority view within a religion they could seek ADR that reflected that. However, as already mentioned, questions are raised over the extent to which individuals embedded in a religious community can choose not to participate in a religious-based ADR if that is promoted by the leadership of the religion.

Ahmed, however, acknowledges the difficulty with ADR is that it can allow discriminatory results. If the views of the couple, be they religious based or not, are discriminatory, is it appropriate that the legal system allows a system of dispute resolution that is sexist? One answer to that, as Ahmed proposes, would be 'to introduce safeguards that would prevent the enforcement of such discriminatory norms'.[10] Abdullahi Ahmed An-Na'im also calls for 'state legislation and regulation should reflect the religious/cultural values and practices of the communities they govern, that must be with due regard to constitutional and human rights requirements of equality and non-discrimination'. The Canadian Supreme Court in *Miglin* v. *Miglin*,[11] looking at a spousal separation agreement assessed whether the agreement was entered into freely and whether it complied with the objectives of Canadian family law. It might be very difficult to know whether or not discriminatory norms were used in an ADR settlement which was in its nature private.

Outside the context of religious ADR, there are, as Hunter notes, real concerns about the very common situation that the parties do not have equal bargaining power. She writes 'the more vulnerable party is likely to find the process traumatic, the chances of settlement are low, and any outcome reached is likely simply to reflect the power imbalance between the parties'.[12]

---

[10] Page 244. [11] *Miglin* v. *Miglin* [2003] 1 SCR 303. [12] Page 42.

Hunter also raises a major practical problem: few couples seem keen to take up ADR. It is, perhaps not surprising, that at the point of relationship breakdown the last thing someone wants is to spend time in a room with their ex-partner.

Marriage

Marriage in some jurisdictions has been at the heart of marriage, but as an institution it is facing challenges in many parts of the globe. These have taken several forms.

First, there are disputes over access to marriage. In particular whether marriage should be restricted to opposite-sex couples or whether it should be available to same-sex couples. Further, there are arguments over whether it should be open to more than one person. Increasingly marriage has been extended to same-sex couples. In many jurisdictions this has been through the intervention of the courts, for example *Obergefell* v. *Hodges*[13] in the US and *Minister of Home Affairs* v. *Fourie* (*Doctors for Life International and Others*, amici curiae); *Lesbian and Gay Equality Project and Others* v. *Minister of Home Affairs* (*Fourie*)[14] in South Africa. In others including England and Wales this has been through legislation.[15]

Second, there are issues around the regulation of couples living together in relationships, but do not formalise these through the concept of marriage. In many jurisdictions there has been a sharp increase in the number of unmarried cohabitants. Traditionally many family law regimes have made minimal recognition for unmarried couples. One justification is that couples have chosen to avoid marriage and its legal regime, and it would be contrary to their autonomous wishes to impose regulation upon them. This argument is certainly open to question. One can query how many of those who do not marry are aware of the legal significance of their status. It may be that they falsely believe the law will protect them even if they are not married, or that they never actively think through the issues and make a choice. Certainly, the idea that many cohabitants pour over a family law textbook and having considered the alternative legal regimes opt for cohabitations seems absurd. Further, it seems wrong to assume that even

---

[13] *Obergefell* v. *Hodges*, 135 SCt 2584   [14] 2006 (1) SA 524 (CC).
[15] Marriage (Same Sex Couples) Act 2013.

if a couple have rejected marriage, they therefore do not want any form of legal regime at all. It is not surprising that some jurisdictions have sought ways of providing some kind of legal protections, even if short of marriage. Another justification is that it would undermine marriage if couples who were not married were given the advantages of marriage. Hunter provides a powerful response to such an argument: 'the legitimate aim of promoting marriage is clearly not being achieved by leaving cohabitants – and just as importantly, the children of cohabitants – less well provided for following the breakdown of their relationship'.[16]

Third, there is the challenge of whether marriage is in its nature a patriarchal or outdated institution, or whether it can adapt to modern life and values. Whichever side you take on that question there is still the question of whether the law should provide alternatives to marriage for those who do take the view that it is inherently patriarchal or undesirable. In England and Wales, as Rosemary Hunter discusses, the status of civil partnership was originally created for same-sex couples who sought the legal privileges of marriages, but were denied access to matrimony itself. Now that in England and Wales same-sex couple can marry, civil partnership has become, at least for some, an alternative status to marriage that does not carry the religious and gendered overtones that it used to. It is not currently open to opposite-sex couples, although as Hunter states that may happen in the future. It is an interesting debate because civil partnership and marriage carry for practical purposes the same set of legal rights and obligations. The difference lies primarily in the name and whether it is seen to symbolise.

Anne Louw notes that under the South African law at the solemnisation of a civil union the authorised officer must ask the parties whether they wish to call their union a marriage or civil partnership. This can be taken to make clear that for the state there is no difference between the two.

Fourth, there is the rise in divorce rates. Many jurisdictions have seen an increase in divorce rates. This creates difficulties for marriage. Perhaps the primary claim for privileging marriage over other forms of relationships is the argument it promotes stability in relationships. Increasingly marriage seems better promoted in legal terms as offering an effective framework for resolving disputes when the relationship breaks down, than as providing a scaffolding for a lifelong relationship.

---

[16] Page 32.

Finally, it is worth noting that while it is often assumed that family law is in the business of promoting marriage, Glennon refers to issues in the US which may be seen as discouraging marriage. Looking at the context of welfare provision she notes these can create 'penalties' for marrying, meaning that the 'financial implications of a decision to marry may render access to marriage more theoretical than realistic'. As she implies, it is ironic that at the same time as the law is extending the scope of couples who can marry, it is restricting it in practical terms.

What the future will be for marriage in law will be remains to be seen. In part this might depend on the extent to which it is able to break free from its patriarchal and religious origins. It is interesting to note that Pernilla Leviner, discussing the progressive Swedish law, notes that while Swedish law has opened up a range of choices to live in 'non-traditional ways', many of the reforms are still premised on the nuclear family. So, the norm of a family as traditional nuclear form still holds sway even as legal systems seek to widen the concept of families. She writes 'the nuclear family is reproduced – even in reforms designed to give more individuals the chance to have children, etc., because family constellations, twoness and genetics continue to be given priority'.

Financial Orders

It is notable that for some chapters relatively little mention is made of financial issues, while in others they are a major theme. It may be that for many couples there are simply not enough assets for meaningful orders to be made and so making financial orders cannot be a major theme in modern family law. Glennon highlights how in the US there has been a clear shift towards a 'clean break' divorce so that there are no ongoing financial responsibilities between the parties. Indeed, she describes alimony payments as an 'infrequent event'.[17] The arguments that tend to be used in favour of the clean break are based around autonomy. Both parties are then left free to enter new relationships or take on new economic ventures free from concerns that doing so will impact on alimony payments. However, Glennon is concerned about the decline of alimony in the US and summarises in this way: 'Financially stronger spouses often leave the marriage with greater

[17] Page 66.

assets and little, if any, ongoing financial liability to the less financially independent spouse. This arguably enhances the freedom and autonomy of the former spouse who avoids extended financial responsibility at the expense of the less economically powerful spouse.'[18]

It is notable that in other jurisdictions there seems a greater engagement with financial issues. Indeed, Fehlberg and Sarmas focus their chapter on Australian family law on financial remedies. They favour a shift away from examining the contributions of the parties to the marriage to 'prioritise the provision of suitable housing for children aged under 18, followed by consideration of the parties' material security'. The contributions focus tends to support an equal division of the assets. Courts are very likely to determine that both parties contributed equally to a marriage, albeit maybe in different ways. However, where one party is in employment and the other has had their career impacted by childcare or other family caring responsibilities this may leave them unable to meet their housing and material needs. Doing this may, however, require alimony payments in cases where there are limited available assets on divorce. This also seems to be the approach taken in Germany where Heiderhoff explains the law is based on *Zugewinngemeinschaft* where by 'the gains accrued during marriage by each spouse will then be compared, and the spouse who gained more property during marriage will have to share his or her surplus with the other one'. However, alimony payments may be required to respond to spousal needs related to childcare, sickness or age.

Domestic Abuse

Domestic abuse is prevalent in many families. Most jurisdictions have moved beyond the view that domestic abuse is simply a private matter that should not be the business of the state, and have now put in force a range of legal protections that can be accessed. However, few would claim that their jurisdiction has 'solved' the problems with domestic abuse. The reasons for this are varied.

The first is the issue of funding. Rosemary Hunter, looking at the context of England and Wales, notes that while there has been the creation of new criminal offences and legal remedies designed to combat domestic abuse,

---

[18] Page 98.

these are 'symbolic gestures' and are not matched by public funding for 'the provision of resources to tackle domestic abuse or provide safety for its victims'.[19]

Second, as Hunter also highlights, there is a conflict between taking domestic abuse seriously and the strong push towards ensuring that children maintain contact with both parents following separation. She is concerned that this means that in private litigation concerns over domestic abuse are minimised.

Third, domestic abuse is a complex phenomenon. It reflects, reinforces and is reinforced by patriarchy. It also inters with other social forces such as racisms, classism, poverty and disablism.[20] This means that an effective intervention requiring challenging deeply entrenched attitudes towards women and other powerful stereotypes.

Autonomy

In many jurisdictions there has been an increasing emphasis on autonomy in family law. Glennon notes that in the past decade a feature of US family law has been 'individual freedom and family pluralism'. The argument in favour of autonomy is that couples should be able to choose for themselves the kind of legal regime they wish for their family life and what form of resolution is most appropriate when there are legal disputes. This can be seen in the increased use of ADR; the promotion of contractual devices (e.g. premarriage contracts) to regulate relationships; and the reduction in 'moralising' in family law. As Hunter notes autonomy is commonly presented as an 'unqualified good'. How can anyone be against free choice? There are however, reasons to express concern.[21]

First, we might question the degree to which there is choice. Premarriage contracts, for example, are commonly sought by would-be husbands to protect their assets. Brides-to-be are in a difficult position. If they refuse, this might jeopardise the relationship as it might imply they are marring for money or predicting the relationship will end in divorce. Further it will be

---

[19] Page 34.
[20] J. Herring, 'The Istanbul Convention: Is domestic abuse violence against women?', in G. Douglas, M. Murch and V. Stephens (eds.), *International and National Perspective on Child and Family Law* (Cambridge: Intersentia, 2018).
[21] J. Herring, *Relational Autonomy and Family Law* (London: Springer, 2014).

impossible to predict what the position of the parties will be decade before hand. They can hardly be taken to have consent for a legal solution to a scenario they have not foreseen. Although premarriage contracts are increasingly justified in the name of autonomy, there are good reasons to be concerned about them. Glennon summarises these neatly:

> The autonomy of the financially powerful spouse is upheld at the expense of the financially vulnerable spouse, who often contributed more to household labour and childcare. This contract-friendly approach also favours decisions made prior to marriage and ignores life-changing decisions or events that happen during the marriage. It treats family caregiving as irrelevant to family dissolution unless the parties themselves valued caregiving in their initial agreement.[22]

Second, as Hunter notes, the emphasis on autonomy typically relates to the autonomy of adults to determine the financial consequences at the end of the relationship or the arrangements for the children. However, these can have a significant impact on the life of the child. The child's autonomy is commonly overlooked in these arguments. Lei Shi looking at Chinese law (Chapter 8) provides a fine example. He is critical of the option there of parents deciding not to pay for child support. While allowing couples to opt out of child support payments may enhance the autonomy of adults, it does so at a cost for children.

The pressure for increased weight on autonomy might be seen more generally as an increased individualisation. Some sociologists believe family life is being affected by an increase in individualisation, with personal development being a key aspect of people's lives. Elisabeth Beck-Gernsheim explains the individualisation thesis in this way:

> On the one hand, the traditional social relationships, bonds and belief systems that used to determine people's lives in the narrowest detail have been losing more and more of their meaning ... New space and new options have thereby opened up for individuals. Now men and women can and should, may and must, decide for themselves how to shape their lives – within certain limits, at least.
>
> On the other hand, individualization means that people are linked into [social] institutions ... these institutions produce various regulations ... that are typically addressed to individuals rather than the family as a whole. And the crucial feature of these new regulations is that they enjoin the individual to lead a life of his or her

---

[22] Page 60.

own beyond any ties to the family or other groups – or sometimes even to shake off such ties and to act without referring to them.[23]

She argues that in family life the traditional obligations to a family or spouse is being replaced with informal relationship with loser obligations. People wish to be free to move on from relationships they no longer find fulfilling and make new relationships. Hence we have easier divorce and fewer financial orders on divorce. Pernilla Leviner finds this reflected in Swedish family law. She notes 'An interesting contradiction lies in this Swedish idea that the welfare of the individual is to be protected by the state rather than by the family. Individualism is strongly emphasised at the same time as there is a significant acceptance of control of the individual by the state.'[24] This is interesting because individualism is commonly associated with a withdrawal of state interference in individual choices, whereas under the Swedish model the state intervenes to enable individualism.

However, not all family law systems are dominated by talk of individualism. Nicolás Espejo and Fabiola Lathrop's discussion of South American family law which they note is seen by some as increasingly based on constitutional law principles and international human rights norms, what they call 'the evolution of the constitutionalisation of family law'.[25] This kind of language might been as antagonistic to a more autonomy-focused approach. The more family law regulation is seen as based on deep human rights, the harder it may be to claim that someone can 'opt out' of these rights. It may be, as Nicolás Espejo and Fabiola Lathrop suggest that the turn to constitutional principles is necessary to create a sufficiently strong legal argument to break free from the traditional understandings of family and family law concepts. They may also be seen as necessary to create what might be politically controversial changes to permit same-sex marriage and assisted reproductive parenthood. Notably both of these can be seen as autonomy enhancing.

In relation to Germany, Heiderhoff also sees as a key aspect of German family law a 'distinct attachment to the human rights in the constitution'.[26] As she notes, the most significant reforms in German family law have not been though legislative amendment but decisions of the German Federal Constitutional Court. These are welcomed: 'It has led to a legal framework

---

[23] E. Beck-Gernsheim and U. Beck, *Individualization* (London: Sage, 2002), p. ix.
[24] Page 160.   [25] Page 133.   [26] Page 77.

that grants a high degree of equal treatment, autonomy in familial matters, a space of protection and freedom for families and a highly developed understanding of fair procedure and the right to be heard.'[27] Notably here it is through the protection of constitutional rights for individuals by the state that individual choice is enhanced.

A further aspect of autonomy is an increased reluctance of the courts to set down general principles about how people should behave or what family life should be like. This is problematic because commonly family law is based on a wide discretion based on concepts of welfare or justice. A good example is the broad discretion which is commonly found in family law to make decisions based on what is in the welfare of a child or is 'just and equitable'. The last phrase was recently considered by the High Court in Australia, in *Stanford* v. *Stanford*,[28] considered by Fehlberg and Sarmas. There it was said:

The expression 'just and equitable' is a qualitative description of a conclusion reached after examination of a range of potentially competing considerations. It does not admit of exhaustive definition. It is not possible to chart its metes and bounds.

Such comments are increasingly common in several jurisdictions where the courts wish to preserve discretion. While this approach might have been more appropriate at a time with well-established community standards, in societies where there is an increasing range of diversity it becomes harder to maintain the idea that there are generally accepted norms of what is just and fair in family life.

Maybe that argument is over-egged. In the English Court of Appeal Mumby LJ[29] thought it was possible to identify what a reasonable ordinary parent would want for their children:

First, we must recognise that equality of opportunity is a fundamental value of our society: equality as between different communities, social groupings and creeds, and equality as between men and women, boys and girls. Second, we foster, encourage and facilitate aspiration: both aspiration as a virtue in itself and, to the extent that it is practical and reasonable, the child's own aspirations. Far too many lives in our community are blighted, even today, by lack of aspiration. Third,

---

[27] Page 81.
[28] (2012) 247 CLR 108. The case has been applied to de facto property disputes (*Watson & Ling* [2013] FamCA 57).
[29] *Re G* [2012] EWCA Civ 1233, para. 80

our objective must be to bring the child to adulthood in such a way that the child is best equipped both to decide what kind of life they want to lead – what kind of person they want to be – and to give effect so far as practicable to their aspirations. Put shortly, our objective must be to maximise the child's opportunities in every sphere of life as they enter adulthood.

Of course, not everyone will agree with those sentiments, indeed the father in that case did not, but Mumby LJ was not claiming that everyone would agree with this comments, but that they reflected widespread community norms. The more autonomy is emphasised and with it the idea it is for each person to fashion their understanding of what a good family life is like, the harder it will be for statements about fairness in families or the welfare of children.

Parenthood

The definition of parenthood and the nature of parental rights has become the site of considerable controversy. Traditionally parenthood was marked through marriage and birth. Most legal systems established the woman who gave birth as the mother of the child and her husband as the father.

This has come under challenge from three sources. First, with the declining popularity of marriage the allocation of paternity through marriage became more problematic. The alternative of using the naming of the father on birth registration as an alternative is common, but that still leaves many children without a father and particularly without the financial support that can be attached to paternity.

Second, the possibility of genetic testing means there is no need to rely on the presumptions that were said to underpin the presumption that the husband was the father of any child being born. The new understanding of genetics also created claims about the need for the child to know their genetic origins, which is conceptually distinct from any paternity questions, even though they often get merged together. As Heiderhoff notes in German law there has been increased claims by the biological fathers and a powerful lobby in favour of their rights.

Third, a strong argument could be made for regarding as parents those who are in the closest relationship with the child or who have undertaken the greatest amount of care for the child. An argument in favour of this view is that it reflects a shift from seeing parental rights flowing from a quasi-ownership claim over a child, to one where the parent is making decisions on the child's behalf and which are designed to promote the welfare of the child. In short, that the person who cares for the child regularly is in a better position to determine what will promote a child's welfare, than a parent with simply a blood connection. As Glennon notes one benefit of this approach is that it enables non-traditional families to claim parentage rights as the 'one mother one father' model is not required if parent follows from care, rather than blood. These have also been required to respond to cases involving assisted reproduction, where those who donate material are not intended to be parents and would be discouraged from being donors if they were treated as having legal responsibilities towards the child.

Children's Rights

Given the significant work in the area of children's rights, it is notable that these receive relatively little attention in the chapters. It may be that in many jurisdictions so much work has been done over the turn of the century on children's rights that other issues are now receiving attention or that the concept of children's rights has become so endemic it needs little discussion. Nicolás Espejo and Fabiola Lathrop see children's rights and particularly the United Nations Convention on the Rights of the Child as having significant impact on South American family law. Elsewhere these have little impact. Lei Shi, writing on Chinese law, suggests courts typically resolve disputes over child arrangements based on preserving the status quo rather than any assessment of children's rights and interests. Of course, doing that might be seen as the quickest (and therefore cheapest) and least controversial way of resolving such fraught disputes.

Contemporary Issues in Family Law in England and Wales

Rosemary Hunter

Introduction

Although the United Kingdom is a unified jurisdiction for many purposes, this is not the case for family law. Both Scotland and Northern Ireland have their own separate systems of family law. This chapter therefore focuses on family law in England and Wales.

The following discussion of key issues facing family law in England and Wales is organised around four of the themes identified by the editors of this volume: marriage, family finances, family violence and neglect, and autonomy and family law. I have added divorce alongside marriage, as divorce has, somewhat surprisingly, recently re-emerged as an area of contestation in this jurisdiction. I have also introduced a fifth theme – access to justice – as this is one of the major issues currently facing the family law system in England and Wales.

The other themes identified by the editors appear as cross-cutting issues throughout the discussion. Cultural and religious diversity is an issue having a particular impact on marriage and divorce. Informal relationships are a particular issue in relation to family finances. Human rights and child arrangements on separation appear particularly in relation to family violence and neglect, and human rights have also been raised in the context of marriage and access to justice. Finally, gender issues are pervasive in family law and appear throughout the discussion.

Marriage and Divorce

This section introduces four contemporary controversies concerning marriage and divorce in England and Wales. Although the law in these areas is well established, concerns about its operation have led to calls for reform. These are based, first, on perceptions that the law is out of date, as is the case with the formalities required for a valid marriage, and the grounds for divorce. Second, there are concerns that the law produces injustice for particular groups, as is the case with civil partnerships and the granting of religious divorces by sharia councils. Two of these issues – civil partnerships and grounds for divorce – involve the substantive law, while the other two relate to procedural aspects.

The Future of Civil Partnerships

Civil partnerships were introduced in England and Wales in 2005 in response to pressures for the formal recognition of same-sex relationships. The Civil Partnership Act 2004 provided a same-sex alternative to marriage, which substantially mirrored the legal provisions relating to marriage and produced a status that amounted to 'marriage in all but name'.[1] The lack of the name of marriage, however, remained symbolically significant. While many same-sex couples entered civil partnerships,[2] campaigners continued to argue that equality for gay men and lesbians required access to marriage on the same terms as heterosexual couples, and that a separate status could never be equal.[3] In 2013, the Coalition government passed the Marriage (Same Sex Couples) Act, which amended the Matrimonial Causes Act 1973 to remove the former requirement that, for a valid marriage, the parties had to be respectively male and female.[4] Those who had entered civil partnerships since 2005 were given the option of remaining in a civil partnership or converting their civil partnership to marriage.[5]

This left the question of the future of civil partnerships – should they be phased out, or remain available as an alternative to marriage? So long as they remained available, same-sex couples had two options for formalising their relationships, whereas heterosexual couples only had the option of marriage. This, in turn, led to calls for civil partnerships to be opened up to heterosexual couples, on grounds of equality, and on the basis that some heterosexual couples might prefer the more 'modern' status of civil

---

[1] *Wilkinson* v. *Kitzinger* [2006] EWHC 2022 (Fam) [88] (Potter P.).
[2] From 21 December 2005 until the end of 2016, almost 65,000 civil partnerships were formed in England and Wales: Office of National Statistics, *Civil Partnerships in England and Wales: 2016* (2017), figure 1.
[3] See e.g. *Wilkinson* v. *Kitzinger* [2006]; and the website of the Equal Love campaign: http://equallove.org.uk
[4] Matrimonial Causes Act 1973, s. 11(c), repealed by the Marriage (Same Sex Couples) Act 2013, Sched. 7, cl. 27.
[5] Marriage (Same Sex Couples) Act 2013, s. 9.

partnership, one which was not heavily freighted with gendered expectations and patriarchal tradition.[6]

In early 2014 the government conducted a review of civil partnerships. The consultation received a large number of responses to an online survey setting out options for the future. Only one third of respondents thought civil partnerships should be abolished, just over half thought civil partnerships should continue to be available in the future, but over three quarters thought civil partnerships should not be extended to heterosexual couples.[7] The demographics of respondents, however, were highly unrepresentative, with almost 60 per cent aged 55 or over.[8] Religious objections to providing heterosexual couples with an alternative to marriage also featured prominently among narrative responses.[9] The government decided to make no immediate changes and to 'wait and see' what proportion of civil partnerships would be converted to marriages.[10] Waiting and seeing would not, of course, provide any indication of the level of demand for heterosexual civil partnerships.

That demand was pursued by a heterosexual couple, Rebecca Steinfeld and Charles Keidan, who brought an action under the Human Rights Act 1998, arguing their inability to enter a civil partnership constituted discrimination in the enjoyment of their rights to family life under articles 8 and 14 of the European Convention on Human Rights.[11] As described by Arden LJ, Ms Steinfeld and Mr Keidan:

are a young couple in a committed long-term relationship. They wish to formalise their relationship, but they have deep-rooted and genuine ideological objections to marriage based upon what they consider to be its historically patriarchal nature. They consider that the status of civil partnership would reflect their values and give due recognition to the equal nature of their relationship.[12]

All three Court of Appeal judges found that the bar on civil partnerships did constitute discrimination against heterosexual couples. However, two of the three (Arden LJ dissenting) considered that maintenance of that discriminatory position was currently justified as the government continued

---

[6] See e.g. equalcivilpartnerships.org.uk, especially equalcivilpartnerships.org.uk/why-does-it-matter
[7] Department for Culture, Media and Sport, *Civil Partnership Review (England and Wales): Report on Conclusions* (2014), 8–11.
[8] *Ibid.*, 24.   [9] *Ibid.*, e.g. 9, 12.   [10] *Ibid.*, 21.
[11] *Steinfeld and Keidan* v. *Secretary of State for Education* [2017] EWCA Civ 81.
[12] *Ibid.* [5].

to evaluate the ongoing viability of civil partnerships. However, they warned that the government's 'wait and see' policy could not continue indefinitely, and the discrimination must be eliminated 'within a reasonable timescale'.[13] In the meantime, private member's bills were introduced into Parliament in July 2016 and again (following the 2017 general election) in July 2017, which would extend the Civil Partnership Act to heterosexual couples.[14] Finally, after defeat in the Supreme Court on the question of justification,[15] the government announced in October 2018 that heterosexual couples will be granted access to civil partnerships.

No-Fault Divorce

Unlike many other western countries, England and Wales has never managed to eliminate complaints of marital fault from its divorce law. The Matrimonial Causes Act 1973 provides for a single ground for divorce, that 'the marriage has broken down irretrievably'.[16] However, irretrievable breakdown must be evidenced by one of five possible facts, three of which are fault-based: adultery, unreasonable behaviour or desertion.[17] The other two facts are based on separation: two years' separation if both parties consent to the divorce, or five years' separation if one of the parties does not consent.[18] The consequence is that the fault-based facts allow for a much quicker divorce than the separation facts, which has advantages, for example, in relation to the finalisation of the parties' financial affairs.[19] In practice, the largest proportion of divorce petitions are based on unreasonable behaviour.[20] An attempt to reform the law in the mid 1990s, among other things to remove any requirement to make allegations of fault, failed for a variety of reasons.[21]

---

[13] *Ibid.* [161] (Beatson LJ).
[14] Civil Partnership Act 2004 (Amendment) Bill 2016–17, Civil Partnership, Marriages and Death (Registration Etc.) Bill 2017–19, introduced by Tim Loughton MP.
[15] R *(on the application of Steinfeld and Keidan)* v. *Secretary of State for International Development* [2018] UKSC 32.
[16] Matrimonial Causes Act 1973, s. 1(1).   [17] *Ibid.*, s. 1(2)(a), (b), (c).
[18] *Ibid.*, s. 1(2)(d), (e).
[19] This not only facilitates the parties moving on with their separate lives, but also has tax advantages.
[20] Office of National Statistics, *Divorces in England and Wales: 2016*, 6.
[21] Family Law Act 1996, Part II. The legislation was enacted but never brought into force and was eventually repealed. See e.g. H. Reece, *Divorcing Responsibly* (Oxford: Hart, 2003); C. Fairbairn, *No-Fault Divorce* (House of Commons Library Briefing Paper No. 01409, 2017) 10–13.

While lawyers and divorcing parties have to some extent learned to live with the peculiarities of the current divorce law, it does have several undesirable consequences. First, it creates perverse incentives to invent or massage facts to meet the legal requirements. Allegations are taken at face value unless the other party contests them (which occurs only rarely).[22] Where the parties are agreed in wanting a divorce, the construction of the divorce petition almost inevitably involves some level of collusion in arriving at a mutually liveable statement of alleged fault on the part of one of the parties.[23] Indeed, in the case of *Ripisarda* v. *Colladon*, the court held that perjury as to the court's jurisdiction to grant a divorce would render the divorce void, but perjury as to the basis for granting a decree would not suffice to make a divorce decree void on the basis of fraud.[24]

Second, there is a risk, albeit a small one, that the facts alleged will not be considered by the court to constitute a sufficient basis to establish that the marriage has broken down irretrievably. In the recent high-profile case of *Owens* v. *Owens*, the Supreme Court upheld a judge's refusal to grant a divorce on the basis that, although it was clear the parties' marriage had completely broken down, the facts alleged in the wife's divorce petition lacked substance and did not reveal behaviour which the wife could not reasonably be expected to live with.[25]

Third, the requirement to allege fault in order to obtain a timely divorce undermines efforts otherwise made to encourage parties to determine post-separation arrangements amicably and cooperatively in their own interests and those of their children. As discussed below, there is a strong policy emphasis in England and Wales on parties resolving post-separation matters between themselves without resort to court or even lawyers. By contrast, the need for one party to blame the other for the breakdown of the marriage can exacerbate tensions and lead to animosity and adversarialism. In light of this, lawyers generally attempt to 'tone down' the allegations in a divorce petition so as to avoid as far as possible giving offence to the other side. But a fine line must be trodden between minimising offence and minimising the risk of a petition

---

[22] Fewer than 2 per cent of divorces are contested: L. Trinder, D. Braybrook, C. Bryson, L. Coleman, C. Houlston and M. Sefton, *Finding Fault? Divorce Law and Practice in England and Wales: Full report* (London: Nuffield Foundation, 2017) 56, n. 120. See also L. Trinder and M. Sefton, *No Contest: Defended Divorce in England and Wales* (London: Nuffield Foundation, 2018).
[23] Trinder et al., *Finding Fault?*, 38–72.
[24] *Ripisarda* v. *Colladon: in the matter of 180 irregular divorces* [2014] EWFC 35.
[25] *Owens* v. *Owens* [2018] UKSC 41.

being rejected.[26] Furthermore, limitations on the availability of legal aid, as also discussed below, mean that more parties are left to formulate divorce petitions without the assistance of lawyers to negotiate the minefield of fault.

As a consequence, there have been persistent calls for divorce law reform in recent years from a range of family justice system actors, including judges, practitioner organisations, academics and politicians.[27] In September 2018 the government finally responded with a consultation on divorce reform, packaged as a measure to 'reduce family conflict'.[28] Arguably, however, there is no need for further consultation, which merely introduces more delay when the case for reform is already compelling.[29]

In the meantime, changes are being effected from a different direction, with an emphasis on efficiency rather than justice. A major review of the family justice system in 2011 argued that scarce judicial time was wasted on reviewing divorce petitions, which could be done more efficiently by court administrators.[30] In response, the handling of routine divorce petitions has been centralised to a small number of courts, where they are dealt with by legal advisers who conduct minimal scrutiny as to the sufficiency of alleged facts.[31] Further, forthcoming digitisation of the divorce process as part of the 'courts modernisation' programme will mean that divorce petitions are completed and lodged online. Although the online system is still being designed, it is intended to be more than simply an electronic version of the current divorce petition. How – or whether – allegations of fault will survive the digital revolution will soon be revealed.

Marriage Formalities

Another anachronistic element of English and Welsh divorce law are the steps required to create a valid marriage. An ongoing legacy of the fact that England and Wales has an established church is the existence of both religious and civil marriages. But the only religious marriages recognised by the Marriage Act 1949 are those of the Church of England, and Jewish

---

[26] See Trinder et al., Finding Fault?, 103–18.   [27] See Fairbairn, No-Fault Divorce, 14–20.
[28] Ministry of Justice, Reducing Family Conflict: Reform of the Legal Requirements for Divorce (2018).
[29] See Fairbairn, No-Fault Divorce, 24–5.
[30] Family Justice Review, Final Report (2011) 173–4 and Annex H.
[31] Legal Advisers are legally trained court officials who advise lay benches of magistrates on the law. They may be analogised to court clerks, judicial associates or registrars in other jurisdictions. On the process of scrutiny, see Trinder et al., Finding Fault?, 62–72.

and Quaker marriages.[32] Marriages conducted in any other place of worship and/or in accordance with the rituals of any other faith are regarded as civil marriages. The requirements for a civil marriage include the giving of prescribed notice,[33] and the conduct of the ceremony in a registered building, in the presence of an authorised person, and including a specified form of words.[34] A marriage may not be conducted outdoors or in a private home, for example, or in accordance with any unrecognised religious ritual.

If the parties wilfully disregard the formal requirements for the formation of a marriage, the marriage will be void.[35] However, the courts have also developed the category of 'non-marriage' to describe the situation where the parties have undergone 'some questionable ceremony or event [which] while having the trappings of marriage' failed fundamentally to comply with the legal requirements.[36] Thus, for example, an Islamic ceremony performed in a private house,[37] a Hindu ceremony performed in a restaurant[38] and a ceremony in the Moroccan embassy in accordance with Moroccan law[39] have all been classified as non-marriages. The issue has become particularly salient in England and Wales in relation to unregistered Muslim marriages, where a *nikah* ceremony is conducted in the home of one of the parties or in an unregistered mosque, and never followed by a civil ceremony. In the eyes of English law, the marriage does not exist. In recent research on religious tribunals, around half of the marriages observed were unregistered *nikah* marriages.[40] Reasons for non-registration include lack of awareness of the need for separate registration, failure to get around to doing so, not wishing to engage with secular marriage for religious or cultural reasons, the marriage being polygamous (although this is said to be rare) or deliberate evasion of the financial consequences of marriage and divorce.[41] The problems created for women in particular when it comes to divorce and post-divorce financial arrangements are discussed further below. Notably, if a marriage is void it

---

[32] Marriage Act 1949, Part II and s. 26.   [33] *Ibid.*, s. 27.   [34] *Ibid.*, s. 44.
[35] Matrimonial Causes Act 1973, s. 11(a)(iii).
[36] Hudson v. Leigh [2009] EWHC 1306 (Fam) (Bodey J.).   [37] AM v. AM [2001] 2 FLR 6.
[38] Gandhi v. Patel [2002] 1 FLR 603.   [39] Dukali v. Lamrani [2012] EWHC 1748 (Fam).
[40] G. Douglas, N. Lowe, S. Gillat-Ray, R. Sandberg and A. Khan, *Social Cohesion and Civil Law: Marriage, Divorce and Religious Courts* (Cardiff University, 2011) 39.
[41] *The Independent Review into the Application of Sharia Law in England and Wales* (Home Office, Cm 9560, 2018) 14.

remains possible for one of the parties to apply for financial orders, but in the case of a non-marriage, financial orders are not available.

In 2014 the government asked the Law Commission to review the law relating to how and where people can marry. In December 2015 the Law Commission issued a scoping paper covering the range of potential issues for review, including questions around preliminaries to a marriage, the marriage ceremony and registration of marriages.[42] However, in 2017 the government decided that 'now is not the right time to develop options for reform to marriage law'.[43] Separate recommendations in 2018 for reforms to ensure the registration of Muslim marriages[44] have not yet received a formal response.

Sharia Councils

Religious divorce is a necessity for those who consider civil divorce to be insufficient in the eyes of God and/or of their community. And for those with only a religious and no civil marriage, religious divorce is the only kind of divorce possible. Although religious divorces are dealt with by a variety of faith bodies, including Roman Catholic and Jewish tribunals, it is the practices of Muslim divorce which have attracted the greatest public attention. In the Sunni Muslim community in England and Wales, bodies known as sharia councils have developed in local areas to deal with matters of religious law, and especially family law. Council members are generally self-appointed volunteers who are scholars and respected persons in the local community, almost always men. They take varying approaches and are not nationally or regionally coordinated. Their primary function is issuing religious divorces for women whose husbands will not agree to a divorce. On the one hand, therefore, they offer a benefit in assisting women to escape their marriages, and the great majority of the petitions they receive are from women. On the other hand, there is evidence that women feel pressured into taking this route by their communities and feel they have little choice in the matter. Councils will usually try to encourage reconciliation before determining if grounds exist for termination of the marriage, and they may also assist in negotiations over children and

---

[42] Law Commission, *Getting Married: A Scoping Paper* (2015).
[43] Dominic Raab MP, Minister of State for Justice, letter to the Law Commission, 11 September 2017, available at www.lawcom.gov.uk/project/marriage-law
[44] Home Office, *Independent Review into Sharia Law*, 17–18.

property. There are concerns that in the process, the issue of domestic abuse, as well as civil law norms regarding post-divorce child arrangements and property division may be ignored.[45]

Public debates on sharia councils have accused them of both oppressing women and illegitimately setting up a parallel legal system. Thus, for example, the media persistently refer to them as 'Sharia courts'. The prominent black and minority women's organisation Southall Black Sisters argues that abused Muslim women need to be accorded equality and human rights rather than to be rendered vulnerable to further abuse by patriarchal religious power.[46] A series of private member's bills have been introduced into the House of Lords seeking to prevent sharia councils from discriminating against or coercing women and from making false claims about the legal status of their rulings.[47] The House of Commons Home Affairs Committee launched an inquiry into the operation of sharia councils in Britain in 2016 which was abandoned due to the 2017 general election, and in the same year the Home Office established an independent review of the application of sharia law in England and Wales. This review reported in February 2018, although it was widely boycotted by women's human rights organisations unhappy with the terms of reference and appointments of advisers.[48] The review identified both good practices of sharia councils and bad practices which discriminated against women and failed to safeguard women and children from abuse.[49] The majority of members recommended regulation of sharia councils by the establishment of a state body to promulgate and monitor the implementation of a code of

---

[45] See S. S. Ali, 'Authority and authenticity: Sharia councils, Muslim women's rights and the English courts' (2013) 25(2) *Child and Family Law Quarterly* 113; S. Bano, *Muslim Women and Sharia'h Councils: Transcending the Boundaries of Community and Law* (Basingstoke: Palgrave Macmillan, 2013); S. Bano (ed.), *Gender and Justice in Family Law Disputes: Women, Mediation and Religious Arbitration* (Lebanon, NH: Brandeis University Press, 2017); Home Office, *Independent Review into Sharia Law*; D. Pearl and W. Menski, *Muslim Family Law* (3rd edn, London: Sweet & Maxwell, 1998).

[46] See e.g. Southall Black Sisters, 'Further supplementary written evidence submitted by Southall Black Sisters' to Home Affairs Committee Sharia Councils Inquiry (10 January 2017) at www.parliament.uk/business/committees/committees-a-z/commons-select/home-affairs-committee/inquiries/parliament-2015/inquiry6/publications

[47] Arbitration and Mediation Services (Equality) Bill 2016-17. For discussion, see R. Grillo, *Muslim Families, Politics and the Law: A Legal Industry in Multicultural Britain* (Farnham: Ashgate, 2015).

[48] See Home Office, *Independent Review into Sharia Law*, Annex C.   [49] *Ibid.*, 15–16.

practice.[50] The government, however, immediately rejected this recommendation on the basis that it would confer legitimacy on sharia councils and support perceptions of a parallel legal system. It also noted that legislation was already in place to protect the rights of women and prevent discriminatory practices, and sharia councils must abide by this law.[51]

Family Finances

In England and Wales, parties to a marriage maintain their own separate property. Assets acquired during the marriage are jointly owned if the parties so specify, but this is not an automatic consequence of the marriage. On divorce, however, all of the parties' individual as well as their jointly owned property becomes available for redistribution according to a discretionary scheme which seeks to achieve overall fairness between the parties in the circumstances of each case.[52] Two current controversies concerning post-separation financial arrangements are first, the relative merits of discretion versus bright-line rules for property division; and, second, the fact that the discretionary scheme is available only to married couples and does not extend to cohabitants. As indicated above, for this purpose, parties to unregistered 'non-marriages' are treated as cohabitants.

Rules versus Discretion

While an equal split of marital assets following separation has a superficial appeal, the result is often post-divorce poverty for women and the children for whom they remain primary carers.[53] The gender division of labour which still prevails in most heterosexual families[54] – even if somewhat

---

[50] Ibid., 19–22.
[51] Secretary of State for the Home Department, 'Written statement on faith practices', Hansard HC, 1 February 2018, col. 30WS.
[52] Matrimonial Causes Act 1973, s. 25; *White* v. *White* [2000] UKHL 54.
[53] See e.g. L. Weitzman, *The Divorce Revolution: The Unexpected Social and Economic Consequences for Women and Children in America* (New York: Free Press, 1985). For more recent US figures: United States Census Bureau, 'Divorce rates highest in the South, lowest in the Northeast, Census Bureau reports' (CB11-144, 2011), available at www.census.gov/news room/releases/archives/marital_status_living_arrangements/cb11-144.html
[54] The extent to which it also operates in same-sex families is not yet clear – see e.g. C. Bendall, 'Some are more "equal" than others: Heteronormativity in the post-*White* era

modified by women working part-time and men taking a more active parenting role – leaves most couples in an unequal financial position at the end of the marriage. The breadwinner (usually the man) has maintained his income, earning capacity and pension savings throughout the marriage and is thus in a position to recover or indeed improve his financial position post-divorce. The homemaker (usually the woman), on the other hand, has lost income, earning capacity and pension savings, and is often in a position of continuing economic dependency, whether on her former husband or the state, in order to maintain herself and her children.[55] However, the overall financial position of families varies enormously, and judicial discretion enables these differences to be catered for. The exercise of discretion is governed by some fundamental principles: marriage is seen as a partnership of equals and there is no discrimination between financial and non-financial contributions to the welfare of the family.[56] Meeting the future needs of the children and then of the adults are the first considerations.[57] Relationship-generated economic disadvantage is to be compensated where possible.[58] Equal sharing is desirable – especially where assets exceed needs – but may be departed from in the interests of fairness.[59]

Two criticisms are made of this regime of property division. One is that women do too well out of it. This argument is typically made by wealthy businessmen and those who represent them. The argument is that privileged wives who have enjoyed a life of ease and luxury should not be handed a half share of the assets accumulated by their ex-husbands through their arduous business labours. The excessive generosity of the law has allegedly made London the divorce capital of Europe (or the world!)

---

of financial remedies' (2014) 36(3) *Journal of Social Welfare and Family Law* 260; R. Leckey, 'Must equal mean identical? Same-sex couples and marriage' (2014) 10(1) *International Journal of Law in Context* 5.

[55] See H. Fisher and H. Low, 'Who wins, who loses and who recovers from divorce?', in J. Miles and R. Probert (eds.), *Sharing Lives, Dividing Assets: An Interdisciplinary Study* (Oxford: Hart, 2009) 227; H. Fisher and H. Low, 'Recovery from divorce: Comparing high and low income couples' (2016) 30(3) *International Journal of Law, Policy and the Family* 338.

[56] *White* v. *White* [2000].

[57] Matrimonial Causes Act 1973, s. 25(1); *Miller* v. *Miller, McFarlane* v. *McFarlane* [2006] UKHL 24.

[58] *Miller, McFarlane* [2006].

[59] *White* v. *White* [2000]; *Miller, McFarlane* [2006]; *Charman* v. *Charman* [2007] EWCA Civ 503.

as women (or their lawyers) who bring proceedings in England and Wales know they will do better there than in many other jurisdictions.[60] This argument has provided at least part of the impetus for the legal recognition of prenuptial agreements discussed below. The other criticism is that discretionary property division results in an unacceptable level of uncertainty of outcomes,[61] making litigation either more likely (because each party's 'best alternative to a negotiated agreement' is unclear) or riskier (because who knows how a judge might decide?).

These arguments appear to be somewhat exaggerated, since the vast majority of property cases that reach a court involve settlements achieved by negotiation between the parties and/or their lawyers and embodied in consent orders.[62] Litigation is also more likely to end in settlement than in adjudication,[63] and cases that proceed to appellate level tend to involve very large sums in dispute.[64] Having recently considered the question of whether a statutory formula for property division should be introduced, the Law Commission concluded that no change in the law was needed, although it suggested the production of further guidance on how to determine parties' future needs, especially for the benefit of the growing numbers of litigants in person in the family courts (as discussed below).[65]

Nevertheless, the argument persists that the uncertainty and unpredictability of the law impedes out-of-court settlement of property disputes, especially where parties cannot afford legal representation. A further series of private member's bills introduced over successive parliaments by Baroness Ruth Deech have sought to reform the law to create greater certainty, in order to facilitate mediation and reduce litigation and its associated costs.[66] The bill would provide for equal division of property

---

[60] See e.g. F. Gibb, '"Meal ticket for life deals" must be stopped, urge law chiefs', *The Times* online, 20 November 2017.

[61] See e.g. House of Lords Library, *In Focus: Divorce (Financial Provision) Bill [HL]: Briefing for Lords Stages* (2017) 1, available at http://researchbriefings.parliament.uk /ResearchBriefing/Summary/LIF-2017-0004; Law Commission, *Matrimonial Property, Needs and Agreements* (2014) 5.

[62] E. Hitchings, J. Miles and H. Woodward, *Assembling the Jigsaw Puzzle: Understanding Financial Settlement on Divorce* (University of Bristol, 2013) 33.

[63] *Ibid.*

[64] The unrepresentative nature of these cases is stressed in E. Hitchings and J. Miles, 'Financial remedies on divorce: The need for evidence-based reform' (London: Nuffield Foundation Briefing Paper, 2018).

[65] Law Commission, *Matrimonial Property*, 5–6.

[66] The latest version is the Divorce (Financial Provision) Bill [HL] 2017–19.

and pensions acquired during the marriage, binding prenuptial agreements, and time-limited maintenance. But although these are the headline provisions, each element is hedged about with a series of exceptions relating to the needs of children, conduct which has adversely affected financial resources, serious financial hardship, and a range of other factors.[67] The net result, arguably, would be no more certain than the current law. It would simply institute a different starting point. The tendency of bright-line rules such as 50/50 division of marital property to create greater injustices means that discretion remains the utilitarian preference.

Cohabitants

England and Wales, like many other western jurisdictions, has seen a steady decline in the rate of marriage since the early 1970s and a corresponding rise in cohabitation as an alternative to marriage.[68] In many areas of law, cohabitation and marriage are treated as functionally the same, for example in relation to social welfare, social housing, immigration, and parenting. In relation to property, however, the law maintains a formal distinction. While divorcing couples are governed by the property regime described above, couples separating from cohabitation are subject to the general rules of property law. General property law does not enable redistribution of assets following separation, it merely determines the property rights of the parties at that point. This is particularly problematic in the situation where the family home is in the sole name of one of the parties. A cohabiting primary caregiver may find herself at the end of a relationship with continuing care of her children but with little income and no housing.

The Law Commission conducted an inquiry into the financial consequences of relationship breakdown after cohabitation in 2005-7 and made recommendations designed to ameliorate some of the hardships and injustices faced by former cohabitants.[69] The Commission did not suggest equalisation of the position of cohabitants and married couples, but rather suggested a new statutory regime to apply to cohabitants who met the eligibility requirements (related to the length of the relationship or whether there were children) on an opt-out basis. The focus of remedies would be on

---

[67] Divorce (Financial Provision) Bill [HL] 2017-19, cl. 2-6.
[68] Office of National Statistics, *Families and Households: 2017* (2017) 4.
[69] Law Commission, *Cohabitation: The Financial Consequences of Relationship Breakdown* (2007).

the parties' contributions during the relationship, with the aim of achieving a fair sharing of the enduring economic benefits and disadvantages of the relationship. The major rationale for treating married and cohabiting couples differently was the fact that cohabiting couples had not made the same financial commitments to each other as had married couples. The ability to opt out was also designed to respect couples' autonomy.[70] Yet research has shown that the 'choice' not to get married may be that of only one of the parties, not necessarily both, and also that such choices are rarely made by reference to or in full knowledge of the financial consequences.[71]

Neither the Labour government that received the report nor the Coalition government that succeeded it evinced any interest in enacting the Law Commission's proposals. Any reforms that might be perceived to undermine marriage were considered politically unfeasible. Indeed, the Labour government funded a publicity campaign to alert cohabitants to the legal disadvantages of cohabitation and to encourage them to get married in order to protect themselves financially.[72] This made little difference. When it comes to intimate relationships, people tend not to act as 'rational maximisers' but take an optimistic view of the future.[73]

In the absence of legislative reform, some efforts have been made by the courts to adapt property law to the situation of former cohabitants. This has seen the rise of the common intention constructive trust as the primary means by which cohabitants' shares in the family home may be determined more fairly than their strict legal position may indicate. The UK's highest court has developed the principles relating to common intention constructive trusts in two leading cases, *Stack* v. *Dowden*[74] and *Jones* v. *Kernott*,[75] led by Lady Hale, a family law expert and the only woman member of the Court at the time. Among other things, these principles recognise non-financial contributions to

---

[70] *Ibid.*, 1.
[71] A. Barlow, S. Duncan, G. James and A. Park, *Cohabitation, Marriage and the Law: Social Change and Legal Reform in the 21st Century* (Oxford: Hart, 2005); G. Douglas, J. Pearce and H. Woodward, *A Failure of Trust: Resolving Property Disputes on Cohabitation Breakdown* (Cardiff University, 2007); R. Probert, *The Changing Legal Regulation of Cohabitation* (Cambridge University Press, 2012) 200–20, 262–4; R. Tennant, J. Taylor and J. Lewis, *Separating from Cohabitation: Making Arrangements for Finances and Parenting* (Department of Constitutional Affairs Research Report 7/2006).
[72] See A. Barlow, C. Burgoyne and J. Smithson, *The Living Together Campaign: An Investigation of Its Impact on Legally Aware Cohabitants* (Ministry of Justice Research Series 5/07, 2007).
[73] *Ibid.*   [74] *Stack* v. *Dowden* [2007] UKHL 17.   [75] *Jones* v. *Kernott* [2011] UKSC 53.

the property and to the relationship generally in quantifying the parties' shares of the beneficial ownership, and therefore go some way towards equalising the position of cohabiting homemakers and primary carers with their breadwinning partners. Some commentators have seen this as representing the familialisation of property law, a process which 'retunes' property law principles developed in the context of commercial relationships to cater to the specific needs of family members, thereby 'challeng[ing] the doctrinal purity of property law',[76] and for that reason disapproved by many orthodox property lawyers.[77]

One significant remaining drawback of property law, however, is that where a home is in the sole name of one of the parties rather than in joint names, either an express intention to share the beneficial ownership of the property or financial contributions to the purchase price are required in order to give rise to a constructive trust.[78] Arguably, this problem is more academic than real, since most cohabiting couples now acquire property in joint names, and this is a more obvious and straightforward means of protecting one's interests than getting married.[79] A second drawback is that property law only applies to property. It does not extend, for example, to other assets such as pensions,[80] and it does not provide a basis for any claim to ongoing income support. Fundamentally, it is focused on past contributions rather than future needs. In these respects, therefore, it is much more limited than the regime applying to formerly married couples.

This area has been the subject of yet another series of private member's bills, which aim to implement the scheme proposed by the Law Commission a decade ago.[81] As with most of the other bills noted above it appears to have little chance of enactment. Arguably, too, with the passage of time and the increasing normalisation of cohabitation as an alternative form of long-term relationship, the maintenance of distinct regimes for cohabitants and married couples appears less and less justified.

---

[76] A. Haywood, '"Family property" and the process of "familialization" of property law' (2012) 24 *Child and Family Law Quarterly* 284; T. Etherton, 'Constructive trusts: A new model for equity and unjust enrichment' (2008) 67 *Cambridge Law Journal* 265; M. Pawlowski, 'Imputing beneficial shares in the family home' (2016) 22(4) *Trusts and Trustees* 377.
[77] See summary and references in Haywood, 'Family property', 303.
[78] *Lloyds Bank* v. *Rosset* [1991] 1 AC 107
[79] R. Auchmuty, 'The limits of marriage protection in property allocation when a relationship ends' (2016) 28 *Child and Family Law Quarterly* 303.
[80] Douglas *et al.*, *Failure of Trust*, 77–8.
[81] The latest version is the Cohabitation Rights Bill [HL] 2017–19, Part 2.

Family Violence and Neglect

Policy attention to child abuse and neglect and family violence in recent years has followed somewhat conflicting trajectories. There has been a perceived need by the state to be seen to be 'doing something' in these areas, while at the same time wishing to maintain the overriding goal of minimising public sector spending. This has resulted in a preference for symbolic gestures such as criminalisation and child protection performance targets rather than the provision of real resources to tackle abuse and provide safety for its victims. At the same time there is a disconnect between taking abuse seriously in public law domains (criminal law and child protection) and the pro-contact culture in private family law proceedings, which has led to allegations of domestic abuse being ignored or minimised in such cases.[82]

The Criminalisation of Forced Marriage and Domestic Abuse

Forced marriage has been recognised as a form of domestic violence and a violation of human rights,[83] yet the government remained ambivalent about the regulation of forced marriage. A regime of civil injunctions to prevent forced marriages and protect those who had been forced into marriage was enacted in 2007 but was initiated by a private member's bill rather than by the then Labour government.[84] The government did attempt a form of indirect regulation via immigration law by increasing restrictions on spousal visas, but the motivations for this initiative were dubious[85] and the regulations were struck down as 'a colossal interference' with the right to respect for family life.[86] Consultations conducted in 2000 and 2005-6 canvassed the idea of making it a criminal offence to force

---

[82] See e.g. M Hester, 'The three planet model: Towards an understanding of contradictions in approaches to women and children's safety in contexts of domestic violence' (2011) 41 *British Journal of Social Work* 837.

[83] See e.g. House of Commons Home Affairs Committee, *Domestic Violence, Forced Marriage and 'Honour'-Based Violence*, 6th report of Session 2007-8 (HC 263-1, 2008); A. Gill and S. Anitha (eds.), *Forced Marriage: Introducing a Social Justice and Human Rights Perspective* (London: Zed Books, 2011).

[84] Forced Marriage (Civil Protection) Act 2007, inserting a new Part 4A into the Family Law Act 1996.

[85] See e.g. R. Hunter, 'Constructing vulnerabilities and managing risk: State responses to forced marriage', in S. FitzGerald (ed.), *Regulating the International Movement of Women: From Protection to Control* (Abingdon: Routledge, 2011) 11.

[86] *R (Quila and another) v. Secretary of State for the Home Department* [2011] UKSC 45 [32] (Lord Wilson).

someone into marriage, but the majority of respondents opposed the creation of a criminal offence on the grounds that it was likely simply to drive the practice underground and make it harder to tackle.[87]

Nevertheless, the Coalition government returned to the issue of criminalisation in 2011.[88] Independent research among NGOs again produced a majority opposed to criminalisation,[89] but the government pressed on. The chief arguments in favour of criminalisation relied on the deterrent effect of criminal law and sending a strong message that forced marriage would not be tolerated.[90] Two new offences of forced marriage were created in Part 10 of the Anti-Social Behaviour, Crime and Policing Act 2014.[91] There are a range of practical problems in enforcing this legislation, however, and convictions have remained rare.[92] For example, young women are reluctant to bring criminal charges against their families, and risk retaliation, estrangement from their families and isolation from their communities if they do so.[93] Research following the introduction of forced marriage civil protection orders showed that women seeking to avoid or escape forced marriages need substantial material support and services,[94] which have been less forthcoming than 'law in the books'. Education and prevention work in communities is

---

[87] P. Uddin and N. Ahmed, *A Choice by Right: The Report of the Working Group on Forced Marriage* (Home Office, 2000); Foreign and Commonwealth Office and Home Office, *Forced Marriage: A Wrong Not a Right* (2005); A. Gill and S. Anitha, 'The illusion of protection? An analysis of forced marriage legislation and policy in the UK' (2009) 31 *Journal of Social Welfare and Family Law* 257, 260–1.

[88] Home Office, *Forced Marriage Consultation* (2011).

[89] A. Gill, *Exploring the Viability of Creating a Specific Offence for Forced Marriage in England and Wales: Report on Findings* (University of Roehampton, 2011).

[90] Home Office, *Forced Marriage – A Consultation: Summary of Responses* (2012); N. Pearce and A. Gill, 'Criminalising forced marriage through stand-alone legislation: Will it work?' (2012) 42 (May) *Family Law* 534.

[91] Anti-Social Behaviour, Crime and Policing Act 2014, s. 121(1) (offence to use violence, threats, or any other form of coercion to cause someone to enter a marriage without their free and full consent) and s. 121(3) (offence to practice any form of deception with the intention of causing a person to leave the UK intending them to be subject to a forced marriage outside the UK).

[92] e.g. L. Fisher, 'Forced marriage law is failing', *The Times* online, 15 August 2017.

[93] See e.g. *Forced Marriage Cops* (Channel 4 documentary, 2015) available at www.youtube.com/watch?v=SPeepNAD4fM

[94] Ministry of Justice, *One Year on: The Initial Impact of the Forced Marriage (Civil Protection) Act 2007 in Its First Year of Operation* (2009); Pearce and Gill, 'Criminalising forced marriage through stand-alone legislation'; L. Tickle, 'Criminalising forced marriage fails to protect girls', *Guardian* online, 22 September 2015.

also underfunded.[95] Partly this is a structural issue of public sector management: central government can legislate, while responsibility for the commissioning and funding of services in England and Wales has been decentralised to local authorities, which have been subject to major funding cuts in recent years.

The area of domestic abuse more generally has seen a similar pattern of de-funding or underfunding of domestic abuse services, including refuge accommodation,[96] combined with 'being seen to do something' in the form of a new criminal offence. While perpetrators of abuse could be charged under general laws concerning offences against the person, there was no specific crime of domestic violence until s. 76 of the Serious Crime Act 2015 introduced the crime of controlling or coercive behaviour in an intimate or family relationship. This law importantly recognises the coercive control dynamics of domestic abuse, going beyond the simplistic notion that the only serious form of harm in a domestic context is physical violence, but action under the law has been just as limited and disappointing as in relation to forced marriage.[97] Longstanding problems with the policing and prosecution of domestic abuse have not been fully addressed,[98] suggesting that government reliance on the criminal justice system as the primary means to prevent abuse and hold abusers accountable[99] is misplaced. And, once again, while the government has articulated national expectations for local service provision,[100] the funding necessary to give effect to these expectations is severely limited.

---

[95] See Hunter, 'Constructing vulnerabilities and managing risk'.

[96] See e.g. House of Commons Home Affairs Committee, *Domestic Violence*, 71-4; L. Buchanan, 'Women's refuges budgets slashed by nearly a quarter over past seven years', *Independent* online, 16 October 2017; J. Grierson, 'Women's lives at risk from changes to funding for refuges, say charities', *Guardian* online, 26 November 2017.

[97] In the year ending December 2016 there were five cautions, 155 prosecutions and fifty-nine convictions for coercive and controlling behaviour: Office for National Statistics, *Domestic Abuse in England and Wales: Year Ending March 2017* (2017) 40.

[98] HM Inspectorate of Constabulary and Fire & Rescue Services, *A Progress Report on the Police Response to Domestic Abuse* (2017); H. Summers, 'CPS accused of failing domestic violence victims after woman loses eye in attack', *Guardian* online, 27 January 2017; C. Bishop, 'Why it's so hard to prosecute cases of coercive or controlling behaviour', *The Conversation*, 31 October 2016.

[99] HM Government, *Ending Violence Against Women and Girls: Strategy 2016-2020* (2016).

[100] Home Office, *Violence Against Women and Girls: National Statement of Expectations* (2016)

The Crisis in Public Law

A major review of the family justice system in 2011 concluded that the system lacked coordination and efficiency, and in particular, that child protection proceedings took an unacceptably long time to conclude from the child's perspective.[101] Such proceedings took an average of forty-eight weeks in (lower level) Family Proceedings Courts and sixty-one weeks for more complex cases in the county courts.[102] The Family Justice Review recommended that they should be concluded in a maximum of twenty-six weeks. This extremely challenging target required significant changes of practice in terms of new procedural guidance, strict judicial case management, pre-proceedings preparation of cases and minimising the number of hearings and the use of expert assessments and reports. While the average duration of hearings is now close to twenty-six weeks, this is still some distance from a maximum duration of twenty-six weeks.[103] Nevertheless, the twenty-six-week maximum was enshrined in primary legislation by the Children and Families Act 2014.[104]

At the same time, a moral panic over failures of child protection services to identify children at risk of significant harm and to prevent child deaths led to a substantial increase in the number of applications to family courts for formal care and supervision orders.[105] The result has been a sense of crisis in the courts, with the pressures to reduce case processing times combined with a burgeoning case load.[106] Emerging evidence suggests courts have responded by changing the kinds of orders they are making. With less time to obtain opinions from independent experts and to assess various options for children's welfare, courts are tending to make more 'wait and see'-type orders rather than definitive interventions. Children are more likely to be left in the care of their parents or transferred to the care of

---

[101] Family Justice Review, *Final Report* (2011).   [102] *Ibid.*, 91.
[103] Ministry of Justice, *Family Court Statistics Quarterly, England and Wales, July–September 2017* (2017) 3: the average duration of public law cases in July–September 2017 was twenty-eight weeks, with 59 per cent of cases dealt with within twenty-six weeks.
[104] Children and Families Act 2014, s. 14, amending the Children Act 1989, s. 32.
[105] Official statistics measure the number of children involved in proceedings rather than the number of cases. There was a 75 per cent increase in the number of children involved in child protection proceedings between 2000 and 2016, with an increase of 18 per cent between 2011 and 2016: Ministry of Justice, *Family Court Statistics Quarterly, England and Wales: Annual 2016 Including October–December 2016* (2017) 8.
[106] See Family Rights Group, *Care Crisis Review: Options for Change* (London: Family Rights Group, 2018).

another family member, subject to supervision, rather than being transferred to the care of the local authority. As the researchers who detected this trend observe, this was not an intended outcome of the reforms and 'it is not clear that there is an evidence base' for this change.[107] Whether changing the pattern of orders has produced better or worse outcomes for children remains to be determined.

Taking Abuse Seriously in Child Arrangements Cases

The Children Act 1989 states that in decisions concerning children's upbringing, the child's welfare shall be the court's paramount consideration.[108] The Family Justice Review rejected the suggestion that this should be supplemented by a presumption that children's welfare would best be promoted by spending equal time with each parent following separation.[109] Fathers' rights groups continued to lobby strongly, however, and the government announced that it would introduce a presumption concerning children's contact with both parents. Protracted wrangling over the wording of the presumption ultimately resulted in 2014 in a complex and convoluted provision which, paraphrased, states that courts are to presume that the involvement of each parent in the life of the child will further the child's welfare, unless there is evidence that the parent's involvement will put the child at risk of suffering harm.[110] Arguably, this does little more than codify the previous law, which always included at least an 'assumption' that it was in children's best interests to maintain contact with both parents.[111]

The courts' strong orientation towards maintaining direct contact between children and non-resident parents[112] creates problems in cases involving abusive parents – in practice, almost always abusive fathers.

---

[107] J. Masson, J. Dickens, K. Bader, L. Garside and J. Young, 'How is the PLO working? What is its impact on court process and outcome? The outcomes of care proceedings for children before and after care proceedings reform study interim report', *Family Law Week*, 17 February 2017; J. Masson, J. Dickens, K. Bader, L. Garside and J. Young, 'Achieving positive change for children? Reducing the length of child protection proceedings: Lessons from England and Wales (2017) 41 *Adoption and Fostering* 401.

[108] Children Act 1989, s. 1(1).   [109] Family Justice Review, *Final Report* (2011) 21 [109].

[110] Children Act 1989, s. 1(2A), (2B), (6) and (7).

[111] See e.g. *Re R (A Minor) (Contact: Biological Father)* [1993] 2 FLR 762; *Re M (Contact: Welfare Test)* [1995] 1 FLR 274; *Re O (Contact: Imposition of Conditions)* [1995] 2 FLR 124; *Re L (Contact: Domestic Violence)* [2000] 2 FLR 334; *V v. V (Contact: Implacable Hostility)* [2004] 2 FLR 851.

[112] See e.g. *Re C (Direct Contact: Suspension)* [2011] EWCA Civ 521 [47] (Munby P.); *Re K (Children)* [2016] EWCA Civ 99.

Despite extensive evidence of the seriously detrimental effect on children of witnessing or being exposed to domestic abuse, or having their primary carer subjected to abuse,[113] there is no countervailing presumption that an abusive parent should be disqualified from direct or unsupervised contact. Rather, the Court of Appeal has ruled that allegations of domestic abuse which might affect the court's decision about contact must first be adjudicated to determine their veracity. Subsequently, proven allegations must be weighed alongside all other factors going to the question of the child's welfare in order to make a final decision.[114] Research has consistently shown, however, that contact continues to trump safety, despite the formulation of detailed guidance specifying how courts should proceed in cases with allegations of abuse before, during and after 'fact-finding hearings'.[115] Allegations may be dismissed as 'historic' or otherwise deemed irrelevant to the question of contact; fact-finding hearings are avoided or curtailed; and findings may have few consequences.[116] It is rare

---

[113] J. L. Edleson, 'The overlap between child maltreatment and woman battering' (1999) 5 *Violence Against Women* 134; L. Harne, *Violent Fathering and the Risks to Children: The Need for Change* (Bristol: Policy Press, 2011); P. Jaffe, J. Johnston, C. Crooks and N. Bala, 'Custody disputes involving allegations of domestic violence: Towards a differentiated approach to parenting plans' (2008) 46 *Family Courts Review* 500; L. Kelly, N. Sharp and R. Klein, *Finding the Costs of Freedom: How Women and Children Rebuild Their Lives after Domestic Violence* (London: Solace Women's Aid, 2014); K. Kitzman, N. Gaylord, A. Holt and E. Kenny, 'Child witnesses to domestic violence: A meta-analytic review' (2003) 71 *Journal of Consultative Clinical Psychology* 339; A. Mullender and R. Morley, *Children Living with Domestic Violence* (London: Whiting & Birch, 1994); L. Radford and M. Hester, *Mothering Through Domestic Violence* (London: Jessica Kingsley, 2006); C. Sturge and D. Glaser, 'Contact and domestic violence – the experts' court report' (2000) 30 *Family Law* 615.

[114] *Re L (Contact: Domestic Violence)* [2000] 2 FLR 334.

[115] A. Barnett, 'Contact at all costs? Domestic violence and children's welfare' (2014) 26 *Child and Family Law Quarterly* 439; A. Barnett, '"Like gold dust these days": Domestic violence fact-finding hearings in child contact cases' (2015) 23 *Feminist Legal Studies* 47; M. Coy, K. Perks, E. Scott and R. Tweedale, *Picking up the Pieces: Domestic Violence and Child Contact* (London: Rights of Women, 2012); M. Harding and A. Newnham, *How Do County Courts Share the Care of Children between Parents? Full Report* (Nuffield Foundation, 2015); J. Hunt and A. Macleod, *Outcomes of Applications to Court for Contact Orders after Parental Separation or Divorce* (London: Ministry of Justice, 2008); R. Hunter and A. Barnett, *Fact-finding Hearings and the Implementation of the President's Practice Direction – Residence and Contact Orders: Domestic Violence and Harm* (Family Justice Council, 2013); A. Perry and B. Rainey, 'Supported, supervised and indirect contact orders: Research findings' (2007) 21 *International Journal of Law, Policy and the Family* 21; Women's Aid, *Nineteen Child Homicides* (Bristol: Women's Aid, 2016).

[116] Hunter and Barnett, *Fact-finding Hearings*; Barnett, 'Contact at all costs?'; 'Like gold dust these days'.

for contact to be refused altogether, and if supervised contact at a contact centre is ordered, it will usually be time-limited. The notion that contact should be safe and beneficial for children[117] is defeated by the assumption that contact is always beneficial for children, and human rights-based arguments justifying restrictions on contact[118] have gained little traction. A recent parliamentary report and hearing on domestic abuse, child contact and the family courts called, among other things, for specialist training for all judges and court welfare officers on all aspects of domestic violence, and for expert safety and risk assessments to be carried out in all cases involving an abusive parent.[119] None of its recommendations have yet been implemented. Even a proposed minimal legislative change to restrict direct cross-examination of victims of domestic abuse by their abusers in family court proceedings[120] was discontinued due to the 2017 general election, and has not yet been reintroduced.

Autonomy and Family Law

The rhetoric of autonomy has played an increasingly prominent role in family law policy in recent years. As Sharon Thompson has observed, however, and as noted above in relation to cohabitation, there is a tendency to *presume* autonomy rather than to question whether it actually exists, and if so, who is exercising it.[121] Autonomy is promoted as an unqualified good without critical scrutiny as to its (often gendered) operation and its effects, particularly for children. The two major areas in which autonomy has been promoted are in relation to out-of-court dispute resolution and prenuptial agreements.

---

[117] Sturge and Glaser, 'Contact and domestic violence'; Family Procedure Rules Practice Direction 12J, paras. 27, 38–40.

[118] S. Choudhry and J. Herring, 'Righting domestic violence' (2006) 20 *International Journal of Law, Policy and the Family* 95; S. Choudhry and J. Herring, 'Domestic violence and the Human Rights Act 1998: A new means of legal intervention?' [2006] Public Law 752. And see J. Birchall and S. Choudhry, *"What About My Right Not to be Abused?" Domestic Abuse, Human Rights and the Family Courts* (London: Women's Aid and Queen Mary University of London, 2018).

[119] All Party Parliamentary Group on Domestic Violence, *Domestic Abuse, Child Contact and the Family Courts* (2016); 'Domestic abuse victims in family law courts', HC Hansard, 15 September 2016, vol. 614, col. 1081.

[120] Prisons and Courts Bill 2016–17, cl. 47.

[121] S. Thompson, *Prenuptial Agreements and the Presumption of Free Choice: Issues of Power in Theory and Practice* (Oxford: Hart, 2015).

The Promotion of Family Mediation

While alternative dispute resolution has long been an integral part of the family justice system, traditionally it took the form of out-of-court negotiations between solicitors, aiming to broker a resolution on behalf of their clients.[122] As Alison Diduck has observed, however, the 'A' in ADR has increasingly come to stand for 'autonomous' dispute resolution,[123] with parties expected to settle post-separation issues between themselves without the assistance of either courts or lawyers. The preferred dispute resolution route in the eyes of policymakers is now family mediation, with a neutral mediator assisting the parties to reach agreement about arrangements for their children and finances. One of the key claimed benefits of mediation is that parties are able to make decisions that best suit their individual circumstances rather than having matters taken out of their hands by lawyers, or having standardised arrangements imposed on them by a judge who knows little about their family. Further, it is assumed that agreements reached between the parties will be more likely to 'work' and hence be more durable than those imposed following litigation.

This positive picture is complicated, however, by the fact that actual demand for mediation among the divorcing and separating population remains low.[124] Despite increasingly coercive measures to encourage people to discover the benefits of mediation, including requiring applicants to consider mediation prior to commencing court proceedings,[125] and cutting legal aid for all forms of family dispute resolution other than mediation,[126] the take-up of family mediation remains disappointing.[127] A recent study comparing mediation with lawyer-led family dispute

---

[122] See e.g. H. Genn, *Paths to Justice: What People Do and Think about Going to Law* (Oxford: Hart, 1999) 115.

[123] A. Diduck, 'Justice by ADR in private family matters: Is it fair and is it possible?' (2015) *Family Law* (May) 616.

[124] See R. Hunter, 'Inducing demand for family mediation – Before and after LASPO' (2017) 39 *Journal of Social Welfare and Family Law* 189.

[125] Children and Families Act 2014, s. 10; Family Procedure Rules Practice Direction 3A – Family Mediation Information and Assessment Meetings.

[126] Legal Aid, Sentencing and Punishment of Offenders Act 2012. Here, the autonomy agenda dovetails neatly with the public sector cost-cutting agenda noted above.

[127] See Family Mediation Task Force, *Report of the Family Mediation Task Force* (Ministry of Justice, 2014); Hunter, 'Inducing demand for family mediation'; Ministry of Justice and Legal Aid Agency, *Legal Aid Statistics Quarterly, England and Wales, July to September 2017* (2017) 8.

resolution options – solicitor negotiations and collaborative law – found that while mediation has obvious strengths and benefits, it is not suitable for all parties or cases, and the exclusive policy emphasis on mediation is not justified.[128] In particular, mediation is problematic in cases where the parties are not able to participate in the process on an equal footing, including where one of the parties is not emotionally ready to mediate, and where there is a history of domestic abuse.[129] Where such cases enter mediation, the more vulnerable party is likely to find the process traumatic, the chances of settlement are low, and any outcome reached is likely simply to reflect the power imbalance between the parties.[130] While the dominant party may be exercising their autonomy, that of the other party is seriously undermined. More generally, disputes between separating couples are characterised by gendered norm conflicts, which may simply be incapable of autonomous resolution.[131]

The other potential casualty of parental autonomy is consultation with children. In court proceedings, children's wishes and feelings must be ascertained and taken into account. But none of the forms of out-of-court family dispute resolution routinely includes input from children or acknowledges children's rights to be heard. Child-inclusive mediation, while available in theory, is rarely conducted. By focusing on party autonomy rather than, say, family autonomy, the voice of the child is marginalised and muted.[132]

Prenuptial Agreements

Traditionally, the law in England and Wales held prenuptial agreements to be unenforceable on the basis that by contemplating the possibility of divorce, they undermined the notion of marriage as a lifetime commitment

---

[128] A. Barlow, R. Hunter, J. Smithson and J. Ewing, *Mapping Paths to Family Justice: Resolving Family Disputes in Neoliberal Times* (Basingstoke: Palgrave Macmillan, 2017).

[129] *Ibid.*, chs. 5–7; R. Hunter, A. Barlow, J. Smithson and J. Ewing, 'Mapping paths to family justice: Matching parties, cases and processes' (2014) 44 *Family Law* (Oct.) 1404.

[130] Barlow *et al.*, *Mapping Paths*. Whereas these kinds of experiences have been highlighted as problematic in relation to sharia councils, there has been much less public concern expressed about the potentially oppressive operation of 'mainstream' mediation.

[131] *Ibid.*, ch. 8.

[132] See J. Ewing, R. Hunter, A. Barlow and J. Smithson, 'Children's voices: Centre-stage or sidelined in out-of-court dispute resolution in England and Wales?' (2015) 27 *Child and Family Law Quarterly* 43; Family Mediation Task Force, *Report*, 27.

and so were contrary to public policy.[133] This position came under increasing pressure in the context of wealthy businessmen seeking to protect their assets after the decision in *White* v. *White* (discussed above),[134] and also in the context of greater exposure of the English courts to international marriages and the more common practice of prenuptial agreements in overseas jurisdictions. One such case coming before the UK Supreme Court in 2010 changed the law.

Radmacher v. *Granatino*[135] concerned a German heiress and her international banker husband, who had signed a prenuptial agreement prior to their marriage in Germany. Having moved to England and divorced there, the enforceability of the prenuptial agreement came before the English courts. The Supreme Court ultimately decided that 'the court should give effect to a [pre- or post-] nuptial agreement that is freely entered into by each party with a full appreciation of its implications, unless in the circumstances prevailing it would not be fair to hold the parties to their agreement.'[136] In reaching this decision, the court emphasised the importance of respecting the parties' autonomy to decide how their own financial affairs should be regulated.[137] There was a strong dissent, however, from Lady Hale, who emphasised other values, particularly the duties and obligations of marriage and gender equality.[138] In essence, the court split between commercial law thinking – that people should be bound by their contracts – and family law thinking – the need to protect financially weaker or more vulnerable parties, and it was no coincidence that this philosophical split was also a gender split. If the developing law on constructive trusts represents the familialisation of property law, it might be said that this development in relation to prenuptial agreements signalled a shift towards the contractualisation of family law.

Thompson's feminist critique of prenuptial agreements, however, explains why these agreements are not like business contracts. They are not the result of arm's length, self-interested, win–win bargaining between equal parties but almost always involve gendered power imbalances. She notes that these power imbalances must be ignored in order for prenuptial agreements to function, and therefore it is not a case of *the parties* exercising their autonomy, but of *one party* doing so. She advocates an approach that

---

[133] *N* v. *N (Divorce: ante nuptial agreement)* [1999] 2 FCR 583 (Fam Div).
[134] e.g. *Crossley* v. *Crossley* [2008] 1 FLR 1467 (CA).   [135] [2010] UKSC 42.
[136] Ibid., para. 75.   [137] Ibid., para. 78.   [138] Ibid., paras. 132, 137.

would promote and guarantee rather than presume individual autonomy by, for example, looking for mutual benefit and mutual empowerment, and not overlooking its opposite.[139]

While the decision in *Radmacher* clearly fails to go this far, it does at least incorporate prenuptial agreements under the general umbrella of fairness between the parties. Thus, in both *Radmacher* itself and subsequent cases, prenuptial agreements have been varied to ensure that the needs of the parties' children and the financially weaker party are catered for,[140] or in some instances have been disregarded altogether on grounds of fairness.[141] The Law Commission has recommended legislative reform to enable 'qualifying nuptial agreements' to be enforced as contracts without judicial scrutiny as to fairness, but nevertheless also considered that it should not be possible to contract out of providing for the financial needs of both parties and any children.[142] Thus, in this area, a slightly more nuanced approach to autonomy has thus far prevailed.

Access to Justice – the Crisis in Private Law

The final and perhaps the most worrying contemporary issue in family law in England and Wales concerns the ability of divorcing and separating couples to access the family justice system. As noted above, while England and Wales previously had a relatively generous legal aid scheme for family law matters, public sector austerity measures introduced by the 2010–15 Coalition government included severe cuts to legal aid, such that for most family law parties, legal aid remains available only for mediation. As I have argued elsewhere, access to mediation does not constitute access to justice.[143] In particular, the withdrawal of legal aid for legal representation has left many divorcing and separating people floundering, trying to negotiate a complex and uncoordinated terrain of web-based information,

---

[139] Thompson, *Prenuptial Agreements*, chs. 5–6.
[140] e.g. *V* v. *V* [2011] EWHC 3230 (Fam); *Luckwell* v. *Limata* [2014] EWHC 502 (Fam); *SA* v. *PA (Premarital Agreement: Compensation)* [2014] EWHC 392 (Fam).
[141] e.g. *GS* v. *L* [2011] EWHC 1759 (Fam); *Kremen* v. *Agrest (No. 11) (Financial Remedy: Non-disclosure: Post-nuptial Agreement)* [2012] EWHC 45 (Fam); *Gray* v. *Work* [2015] EWHC 834 (Fam).
[142] Law Commission, *Matrimonial Property*, chs. 5–6.
[143] R. Hunter, A. Barlow, J. Smithson and J. Ewing, '"Access to what?" LASPO and mediation', in A. Flynn and J. Hodgins (eds.), *Access to Justice and Legal Aid: Comparative Perspectives on Unmet Legal Need* (Oxford: Hart, 2017) 239.

unbundled services and do-it-yourself offers, in the absence of the traditional source of support, i.e. expert, individualised advice from a solicitor.[144]

Contrary to the government's expectations that people would exercise their autonomy and choose mediation to resolve family law disputes, the immediate effect of the legal aid cuts has been a significant rise in the number of people appearing in court as litigants in person.[145] This has placed enormous burdens on the court system, as well as on litigants themselves, since self-representation is highly stressful and rarely effective.[146] There has been little systematic effort to adjust court procedures to cater for litigants in person as the 'new normal', with the experience for the litigant very much depending on which judge and (if relevant) which lawyer on the other side they happen to encounter.[147]

Legal aid does remain available for victims of domestic violence, however those seeking legal aid are required to produce one of the enumerated forms of 'evidence' of domestic violence.[148] The regulations concerning evidence were initially extremely narrow, so that many victims of violence found themselves unable to obtain the necessary documentation.[149] Following successful judicial review proceedings,[150] the regulations have been widened, but difficulties remain.[151] In particular, there is an overemphasis on physical violence, while abuse in the form of coercive control

---

[144] See e.g. Ipsos Mori Social Research Institute, *The Varying Paths to Justice: Mapping Problem Resolution Routes for Users and Non-Users of the Civil and Administrative and Family Justice Systems* (Ministry of Justice, 2015); R. Lee and T. Tkacukova, *A Study of Litigants in Person in Birmingham Civil Justice Centre* (CEPLER Working Paper 02/2017, University of Birmingham, 2017); Low Commission, *Tackling the Advice Deficit: A Strategy for Access to Advice and Legal Support on Social Welfare Law in England and Wales* (London: Legal Action Group, 2014); L. Trinder, R. Hunter, E. Hitchings, J. Miles, R. Moorhead, L. Smith, M. Sefton, V. Hinchly, K. Bader and J. Pearce, *Litigants in Person in Private Family Law Cases* (Ministry of Justice, 2014).

[145] Ministry of Justice *Family Court Statistics Quarterly*, 5.

[146] Trinder *et al., Litigants in Person*; Lee and Tkacukova, *Study of Litigants in Person*.

[147] Trinder *et al., Litigants in Person*; J. Mant, 'Litigants in person and the Family Court: The accessibility of private family justice after LASPO' (Preliminary PhD research findings, University of Leeds, 2018).

[148] Civil Legal Aid (Procedure) Regulations 2012, Reg. 33 and Sched. 1.

[149] Rights of Women, Women's Aid and Welsh Women's Aid, *Evidencing Domestic Violence: A Barrier to Family Law Legal Aid* (2013).

[150] *R (Rights of Women) v. Lord Chancellor and Secretary of State for Justice* [2016] EWCA Civ 91.

[151] See F. Syposz, *Research Investigating the Domestic Violence Evidential Requirements for Legal Aid in Private Family Disputes* (Ministry of Justice, 2017).

is unlikely to give rise to the kind of documentation required. Moreover, even if a victim is able to obtain legal aid, her abuser will not be eligible, and may use the opportunity of his own self-representation to continue to harass her through repeated court applications and, as discussed above, by directly cross-examining her in court. While judges do have discretion to control and prevent abusive questioning, the available research indicates their general unwillingness to exercise that discretion robustly.[152]

Moreover, many other forms of personal and circumstantial vulnerability besides domestic violence may render it extremely difficult for a litigant to advocate for their own interests in court. The legal aid cuts were accompanied by provision for funding in 'exceptional' cases in which failure to extend legal aid would constitute a breach of the applicant's human rights.[153] However, the human rights criteria were also initially interpreted extremely narrowly and few awards were made,[154] until successful litigation forced the Legal Aid Agency to take a more inclusive approach.[155] The proportion of applications granted rose from under 10 per cent in October–December 2013 to 54 per cent in July–September 2017.[156] Still, the number of applications remains relatively low and the scheme fills only a very small part of the 'LASPO gap'[157] created by the cuts. The problem of access to justice remains one of the biggest challenges facing the family justice system. While a 'post-implementation review' of the Legal Aid, Sentencing and Punishment of Offenders Act 2012 is currently underway, frequent ministerial changes and the distraction caused by Brexit have impeded policy attention to this area and made it difficult to predict future directions.

---

[152] N. Corbett and A. Summerfield, *Alleged Perpetrators of Abuse as Litigants in Person in Private Family Law: The Cross-Examination of Vulnerable and Intimidated Witnesses* (Ministry of Justice Analytical Services, 2017).
[153] Legal Aid, Sentencing and Punishment of Offenders Act 2012, s. 10.
[154] Ministry of Justice and Legal Aid Agency, *Legal Aid Statistics in England and Wales 2013-2014* (2014) 26-7; House of Commons Justice Committee, *Impact of Changes to Civil Legal Aid under Part I of the Legal Aid, Sentencing and Punishment of Offenders Act 2012*, 8th report of session 2014-15 (HC311, 2015) 14-20; House of Commons Public Accounts Committee, *Implementing Reforms to Civil Legal Aid*, 36th report of session 2014-15 (HC 808, 2015).
[155] *Gudanaviciene* v. *Director of Legal Aid Casework* [2014] EWCA Civ 1622; *Director of Legal Aid Casework* v. *IS* [2016] EWCA Civ 464.
[156] Ministry of Justice and Legal Aid Agency, *Legal Aid Statistics Quarterly (2017)*, 10.
[157] R. Hunter, 'Exploring the "LASPO gap"' (2014) 44 *Family Law* (May) 660. And see E. Marshall, S. Harper and H. Stacey, *Family Law and Access to Legal Aid* (Public Law Project, 2018).

Conclusion

Several unifying strands emerge from the above account of contemporary issues in family law in England and Wales. Family law policy is marked by commitments to the value of marriage, to private ordering and to minimising public sector spending. In family law practice children's contact with both parents is highly valued but human rights, freedom from domestic abuse and gender equality, while not ignored, are less clearly prioritised. Arguments from efficiency, rationalisation and modernisation currently tend to have more purchase than arguments from equality and justice. In the last five years governments have enacted significant reforms in the areas of child contact, child protection, domestic violence offences, dispute resolution and legal aid funding, but have resisted reform in the areas of civil partnerships, marriage regulation, no-fault divorce, cohabitation and domestic violence as it relates to arrangements for children after parental separation. Family law responds well to a diverse and pluralistic society when providing for post-divorce financial arrangements, but less well when it comes to cultural and religious diversity and diversity of family forms. It is a site on which strongly held values collide. As a result, it seems family law is likely to remain an area of controversy and contestation for the foreseeable future.

2 Family Law in the United States: Freedom and Inequality

Theresa Glennon

1 Introduction

The trajectory of family law in the United States (US) over the last fifty years may be described as one of increasing individual freedom and family pluralism. Individuals are now more free to enter intimate relationships or to have children without interference by the state. This form of liberty is widely accepted in the US, which prides itself on being a highly individualistic society.[1] There have also been significant gains in freedom and autonomy through increased access to state-sanctioned institutions, such as marriage and legally recognised parent–child relationships. Access to legal recognition is a somewhat more 'positive' form of liberty, since state action provides legal protections for family relationships. The gains in these two forms of liberty may obscure the rejection of a stronger version of positive liberty, which would involve active state support and intervention to protect both liberty and equality in family contexts.[2] Instead of protecting equality, shifts in the legal regulation of intra-family disputes have bolstered the freedom of economically more powerful members of families at the expense of those who are more vulnerable. Furthermore, in the US, relative to other economically developed countries, there is less support for public assistance to enable families to thrive.[3] The US has largely rejected calls for economic support to empower individuals to make decisions about fundamental issues such as procreation, cohabitation, marriage and divorce without facing serious economic impediments

---

[1] J. Nedelsky, *Law's Relations: A Relational Theory of Self, Autonomy, and Law* (New York: Oxford University Press, 2011) 39–45; N. J. Hirschmann, *The Subject of Liberty: Toward a Feminist Theory of Freedom* (Princeton University Press, 2003) 4–6.

[2] Nedelsky, *Law's Relations*, 316; Hirschmann, *Subject of Liberty*, 142–3.

[3] M. Eichner, *The Supportive State: Families, Government, and America's Political Ideals* (New York: Oxford University Press, 2010) 5–6; C. Huntington, *Failure to Flourish: How Law Undermines Family Relationships* (New York: Oxford University Press, 2014) 111–13.

or harm.[4] Instead the use of family law to privatise support for dependents has greatly increased the struggles of middle and lower-income families.

US adults now face fewer legal barriers to entering intimate relationships of their choice and to determining the extent of their rights and responsibilities within those relationships. Family, labour and public benefits law, however, privilege marital relationships over cohabiting relationships. Within both marital and cohabiting relationships, family law tends to enhance the freedom of those with greater market power at the expense of those with less power. Family law has been less effective at assuring intra-couple financial and caregiving support or protecting partners who sacrificed their own individual economic development to provide caregiving or support for their partner's education or career. In addition, the family formation choices readily accessible to those with higher levels of education and income may not be available to many US residents with lower levels of education and income.[5] For members of society with less education and income, choices regarding family structure may be driven by financial constraints; their families struggle in the face of harsh economic circumstances.

These concerns extend to parent–child relationships as well. Although legal changes and advances in assistive reproductive technologies (ARTs) have afforded greater freedom to create parent–child relationships for some, legal impediments or financial barriers have foreclosed those options for others. Divorced and unwed parents have faced increased state intervention into and control over their lives. Lower-income parents have most often been subjected to this greater judicial and administrative oversight, through child custody and child support laws and social welfare law.[6]

Thus, while new realms of freedom related to family life have emerged, the benefits of these freedoms have not been equally distributed within or among families. Without a supportive economic, social and legal structure

---

[4] A. L. Alstott, 'Neoliberalism in U.S. family law: Negative liberty and laissez-faire markets in the minimal state' (2014) 77 *Law and Contemporary Problems*, 25-6.

[5] S. Rand, 'The real marriage penalty' (2015) 18 *University of the District of Columbia Law Review* 99.

[6] J. E. Hasday, *Family Law Reimagined* (Cambridge, MA: Harvard University Press, 2014) 200-2, 210-20; D. Hatcher, 'Forgotten fathers' (2013) 93 *Boston University Law Review* 908-10; J. Murphy, 'Revitalizing the adversary system in family law' (2010) 78 *University of Cincinnati Law Review* 911-14.

for the families being created now, the well-being of those family members, and thus, of the larger society, may be undermined. While family law may be suited to address intra-family inequalities, it is unlikely to be able to address the broader economic and social stresses reshaping the lives of most families in the early twenty-first century. Scholars and policymakers concerned about family well-being must not only evaluate current family law doctrines, but must look beyond, to the laws of market labour and social welfare, if they wish to address the significant challenges facing families today.

The chapter provides an overview of the demographics of the modern US family, highlighting the increased social and economic stratification in family structures. It examines the broadened zone of privacy for intimate adult relationships, which has, however, left in place a governmental structure privileging marital over non-marital families. The chapter considers a concurrent legal trend that de-emphasises the intimate adult relationship as a site of support, particularly upon relationship termination, thereby reinforcing the power of family members with greater economic resources. It further examines the broadened sphere of freedom for developing parent–child relationships along with the legal and economic hurdles faced by some to creating or gaining recognition of those relationships. The chapter highlights increases in state regulation of parent–child relationships and financial support through child custody and child support law, which most powerfully controls the lives of lower-income families. Finally, the chapter suggests that those concerned with the well-being of families and their children may need to look beyond the traditional boundaries of family law. The legal regulation of the labour market and public benefits deserves to be examined for its effect on the ability of people to enter into and sustain satisfying and supportive family relationships.

2 Changing Demographics of the US Family

No brief overview of changing demographics of the family in a pluralistic, diverse society such as the US can do justice to the complexity of families in the US. This overview focuses primarily on the experiences of families as related to income and educational levels and leaves in the background important differences regarding religion, race, ethnicity, immigration status, sexuality and gender. While the intersections of these differences are crucial to a full understanding of how social and economic issues affect different communities, the factors of income and education tracked by this overview display a strong correlation with changes in family structure that have cut across groups over the last half-century.[7]

2.1 Trends in Marriage, Cohabitation and Childbearing

A lower percentage of adult Americans are currently married than in any earlier era in US history. As of 2016, just over one-half of adult Americans were married.[8] This low rate of marriage, however, does not evenly affect all educational and income groups. Instead, the growing gap in marriage rates tracks the degree of income inequality in the US. At the end of the nineteenth century, another period of dramatic income inequality, men in professional, technical and managerial occupations had significantly higher marriage rates than did men in service occupations. That gap narrowed along with decreasing income inequality in the years following the Second World War. As income inequality has again re-emerged, so too has the significant gap in marriage rates for these two groups of male workers.[9] Unlike the late nineteenth century, however, today's declining marriage rates among less skilled workers have not discouraged childbearing. Instead, changed societal norms have contributed to growing rates of cohabitation and non-marital childbearing among adults with less than a college education.[10] While almost all women who graduate from college have their children within marriage, women without a college education have fewer than one-half of their children in the context of marriage.[11]

---

[7] M. J. Carlson and P. England, 'Social class and family patterns in the United States', in M. J. Carlson and P. England (eds.), *Social Class and Changing Families in an Unequal America* (Stanford University Press, 2011) 2; M. Cancian and R. Haskins, 'Changes in family composition: Implications for income, poverty, and public policy'. (2014) 654 *The ANNALS of the American Academy of Political and Social Science* 32.

[8] US Census Bureau, America's Families and Living Arrangements: 2016 Adults (A table series), table A1.

[9] A. J. Cherlin, *Labor's Love Lost* (New York: Russell Sage Foundation, 2014) 16–22.

[10] *Ibid.*, 20.

[11] A. J. Cherlin, E. Talbert and S. Yasutake, 'Changing fertility regimes and the transition to adulthood: evidence from a recent cohort' (2016) 81 *American Sociological Review* 749–70 (survey of women born between 1981 and 1985 conducted in 2011).

Differences in marriage rates are linked not just to rates of cohabitation, but also to dramatic differences in the outcomes of cohabitation. While the majority of college-educated women marry the individuals with whom they cohabit, fewer than one-third of women without a high school diploma see their cohabiting relationships develop into marriages.[12] These divergent rates of transitioning from cohabitation to marriage do not seem to be tied to differences in the intention to marry, which is consistent across educational levels. Rather, this distinction appears to be linked to economic and other barriers that disproportionately prevent non-college educated adults from meeting the higher standards for financial security and relationship quality prior to marriage imposed by the societal norms of today.[13]

These changes have led to increased family instability among less-educated and moderately educated adults. About one-half of cohabiting unions break up within five years of the birth of a child.[14] Similarly, divorce rates among moderately educated and less-educated adults are up to two times higher than for those with college educations.[15] Overall, while the US experiences a high rate of turnover in household and family lives through divorce, separation and re-partnering, this turnover affects so many people with less than a college education that they can be described as the norm.[16]

Serial relationships by divorced and separated parents have resulted in increased multi-partner fertility and family complexity. Fewer than one-half of US children live with coresident married parents in their first marriage, a decrease of more than one-quarter since 1960.[17] The rate of multi-partner fertility has also increased, and more children live with half-siblings, step-siblings or children with whom they are unrelated. There has been a rise in families in which 'marriage and legal ties, living arrangements, fertility, and parenting are not coterminous, that is, when roles and

---

[12] J.C-L. Kuo and R. K. Raley, 'Diverging patterns of union transition among cohabitors by race/ethnicity and education: Trends and marital intentions in the United States' (2016) 53 *Demography* 932–3.
[13] *Ibid.*   [14] Cherlin, *Labor's Love Lost*, 167.
[15] US Bureau of Labor Statistics, 'Marriage and Divorce: Patterns by Gender, Race, and Educational Attainment' (October 2013) *Monthly Labor Review*, table 3, p. 6 (for those born between 1957 and 1964).
[16] Cherlin, *Labor's Love Lost*, 167.
[17] G. Livingston, 'It's no longer a "Leave It to Beaver" world for American families – but it wasn't back then, either', *Pew Research Center Fact Tank* (30 December 2015) (statistics are not yet available on married same-sex couple families).

relationships diverge from the simple nuclear family scheme'.[18] Increased family complexity can contribute to families' economic difficulties, especially because such increases are concentrated among the most economically vulnerable. For example, non-resident fathers may not have the resources to financially support or remain in contact with children of different mothers. Parents in complex families experience greater difficulty providing the safe, secure and nurturing relationships children need to thrive, and emotional support for children may vary as parents re-partner.[19] This family complexity may 'represent[] an important aspect of the "diverging destinies" of children in different socioeconomic groups'.[20] Rather than receiving support to aid in these challenges, however, lower-income, complex families receive less support and are subject to greater state intervention and control.

2.2 Changes in US Employment, Financial Stress and the Family

Lower marriage rates among adults with moderate or low-education levels are correlated to low wages for men with less than a college diploma. Despite substantial increases in wage work by women, it is clear that 'men's ability to fill the provider role remains a consistent requirement for [opposite-sex] marriage across the class spectrum'.[21] In the US, men are increasingly unable to fulfil this provider role unless they have at least a college degree – a degree held by only one-third of adult males.[22] Unemployment rates for those with a high school diploma or less are significantly higher than for those with a college diploma.[23] As middle-class jobs, and in particular the manufacturing jobs dominated by men,

---

[18] L. Tach and K. Edin, 'The compositional and institutional sources of union dissolution for married and unmarried parents in the United States' (2013) 50 *Demography* 1799.

[19] P. R. Britto *et al.*, 'Nurturing care: Promoting early childhood development' (2017) 389 *The Lancet* 91.

[20] M. J. Carlson and D. R. Meyer, 'Family complexity: setting the context' (2014) 654 *ANNALS of the American Academy of Political and Social Science* 9 (quoting S. McLanahan, 'Diverging destinies: how children are faring under the second demographic transition' (2004) 42 *Demography* 607).

[21] S. Sassler, S. Roy and E. Stasny, 'Men's economic status and marital transitions of fragile families' (2014) 30 *Demographic Research* 72.

[22] C. L. Ryan and K. Bauman, 'Educational attainment in the United States: 2015', *Current Population Reports* (March 2016) 2.

[23] Bureau of Labor Statistics, *Employment Projections, Unemployment Rates and Earnings by Educational Attainment* (2016).

have diminished, men without a college education are increasingly unable to fulfil their historic and current provider role.[24] Over a thirty-year period, the earnings of men with a college diploma or post-college degree increased substantially, while the earnings of male high school graduates and high school dropouts declined by more than one-tenth and almost one-quarter, respectively.[25] In contrast, women's median gains in earnings over the last forty years, most striking for women with a college degree, increased women's ability to raise their children without financial help from their children's fathers.[26] The role of gendered expectations appears to remain strong. Some economic research indicates that women are less likely to marry men who do not earn more than them.[27] Marriages in which husbands lack full-time employment face a greater risk of divorce than do marriages in which the husband is employed full-time.[28]

Almost one-half of US households cope with financial insecurity. This makes it difficult for families to deal with the stresses life brings, such as major car or house repairs, unemployment, hospital visits or loss of a spouse or partner.[29] These environmental stressors undermine family members' health and ability to cope with further hardships.[30] Low-income couples live with significant environmental stressors, such as 'unemployment, non-standard work hours, unsafe neighborhoods, inadequate transportation, accumulating debts, and a relative absence of supportive social networks'.[31] Some evidence indicates that reducing

---

[24] Cherlin, *Labor's Love Lost*, 122–6, figure 5.1.
[25] D. Autor, 'Skills, education, and the rise of earnings inequality among the "other 99 percent"' (2014) 344 *Science* 849, figure 6 (statistics for 1980 to 2012); Cherlin, *Labor's Love Lost*, 16 (in 1996 average 30-year-old man with high school degree earned 20 per cent less than the comparable man in 1979).
[26] Cancian and Haskins, 'Changes in family composition', 37–8.
[27] D. Autor, D. Dorn and G. Hanson, 'When work disappears: Manufacturing decline and the falling marriage-market value of men', National Bureau of Economic Research, Working Paper 23173 (2017).
[28] A. Killewald, 'Money, work, and marital stability: Assessing change in the gendered determinants of divorce' (2016) 81 *American Sociological Review* 716.
[29] Pew Charitable Trusts, 'Are American families becoming more financially resilient?', *Issue Brief* (April 2017), 3–5
[30] R. Rebouché and S. Burris, 'Social determinants of health', in I. G. Cohen, A. K. Hoffman and W. M. Sage (eds.) *The Oxford Handbook of U.S. Healthcare Law* (Oxford University Press, 2016).
[31] L. A. Neff and B. R. Karney, 'Acknowledging the elephant in the room: How stressful environmental contexts shape relationship dynamics' (2017) 13 *Current Opinion in Psychology* 107.

financial stresses may improve the quality and stability of marital relationships, and perhaps would reduce their high risk of dissolution.[32] Parental employment insecurity and family financial insecurity, which now affect 60 per cent of US families, also affect child development, reducing the ability of parents to purchase high-quality childcare as well as educational and other activities that foster children's cognitive and emotional development.[33]

3 Intimate Adult Relationships: More Privacy, Less Support

Intimate adult relationships have gained increasing protection from state intrusion. These protections have increased the autonomy of adults to enter into a wide range of intimate relationships beyond marriage as well as state-sanctioned marital relationships. They also allow marital partners greater freedom to determine most aspects of their financial obligations to each other. Increased autonomy and privacy, however, have not translated into increased entrance to marriage. Shifts in cultural norms and economic opportunities have decreased entrance to marriage, and marriage may reduce, rather than increase, financial support available from government programmes. In addition, this increase in autonomy and privacy for intimate adult relationships has been accompanied by decreased support obligations at divorce and limited support obligations for non-marital relationships, leaving less economically powerful members of those relationships less protected upon family dissolution.

3.1 Privacy Protections for Intimate Adult Relationships

Contemporary legal protections for intimate adult relationships represent a dramatic break in the nation's treatment of these relationships. Indeed, the US has a history of criminalising sexual activity between consenting adults. States criminalised sexual conduct such as fornication, sodomy,

---

[32] *Ibid.*, 109.
[33] D. J. Hernandez and J. S. Napierala, 'Children's experience with parental employment insecurity and family income inequality', Foundation for Child Development (6 February 2017), www.fcd-us.org/childrens-experience-parental-employment-insecurity-family-income-inequality

adultery and 'open and notorious cohabitation'.[34] On top of these were criminal laws prohibiting the sale and use of contraceptives, as well as charges of 'bastardy' for non-marital relationships that led to the birth of children.[35]

Privacy for decisions regarding childbearing is now largely protected through the repeal of these criminal statutes and through interpretations of a constitutional right to privacy. As social norms changed, many states eliminated or stopped enforcing these criminal statutes.[36] A federal constitutional right to privacy was derived from a line of US Supreme Court cases that first recognised a right of access to contraception for marital partners, in *Griswold* v. *Connecticut*, and then extended this right to unmarried individuals, in *Eisenstadt* v. *Baird*.[37] Later cases involving the right to abortion determined freedom for procreative decisions to be a liberty interest protected under the Due Process Clause of the Fourteenth Amendment.[38]

For many years, it remained unclear whether the 'zone of privacy' protections for decisions regarding procreation would be extended to choices regarding intimate sexual relationships outside marriage. In *Lawrence* v. *Texas* in 2003, Justice Kennedy, speaking for the court, identified privacy for sexual relationships as inherent to the dignity and liberty guarded by the Due Process Clause. He recognised that the criminalisation of sexual acts had 'far-reaching consequences, touching upon the most private human conduct, sexual behavior, and in the most private of places, the home'.[39] Thus, while statutes criminalising non-marital sexual relationships persist in many states, enforcement of these statutes is now likely to be unconstitutional.[40] Nonetheless, the history of criminalisation of non-marital sexual relationships, and the stigma that arose

---

[34] J. Sweeny, 'Undead statutes: The rise, fall, and continuing uses of adultery and fornication criminal laws' (2014) 46 *Loyola University Chicago Law Journal* 127–8; R. A. Posner and K. B. Silbaugh, *A Guide to America's Sex Laws* (University of Chicago Press, 1996) 98–110.

[35] Sweeny, 'Undead statutes', 162 n. 32; M. Dudziak, 'Just say no: Birth control in the Connecticut Supreme Court before Griswold v. Connecticut' (1991) 75 *Iowa Law Review* 918–20.

[36] Sweeny, 'Undead statutes', 136.   [37] 381 US 479, 484–5 (1965); 405 US 438, 453 (1971).

[38] *Roe* v. *Wade*, 410 US 113 (1973); *Planned Parenthood of Southeastern PA* v. *Casey*, 505 US 833 (1992).

[39] 539 US 558, 567 (2003).

[40] M. Murray, 'Rights and regulation: The evolution of sexual revolution' (2016) 116 *Columbia Law Review* 583–4.

therefrom, may help explain the continuance of staunchly differential civil legal treatment of marital and non-marital relationships.[41]

Individuals and couples have sought not just decriminalisation for their relationships – they have also sought legal recognition. The US Supreme Court has recognised an increasing zone of freedom for decisions of *whom* to marry. From *Loving* v. *Virginia* in 1967, in which the Supreme Court prohibited bans on interracial marriage, to *Obergefell* v. *Hodges* in 2015, which required states to permit marriage by same-sex couples, the Supreme Court has expanded the right of individuals to choose their marital partners as a fundamental liberty interest under the Fourteenth Amendment.[42]

Despite the expanded freedom to choose marital partners and the removal of specific hurdles to marriage, certain constraints on marriage remain, including prohibitions of plural marriage, incest and, in some states, marriage by first cousins.[43] Nor do parties have a right to public assistance in support of their marriage, and states may even exclude or reduce access to certain benefits for those who choose to marry. For example, persons who became disabled as children risk losing their social security disability payments if they marry.[44] Many other government benefit programmes, such as health insurance, income support and tax credits, impose similar 'penalties' on those who marry, policies that most strongly affect lower-income families.[45] For some, the financial implications of a decision to marry may render access to marriage more theoretical than realistic.

Those who are unable or do not wish to marry are likely to be excluded from any state recognition of their relationships, recognition that might allow them to access workplace or government benefits, or that could afford them economic remedies upon dissolution of their relationships. Advocates for same-sex couples, faced with a prohibition on marriage, had developed and gained recognition, at least in some states, for their relationships. These included enforcement of private agreements regarding matters such as cohabitation and selection of healthcare decision makers, and, for some jurisdictions, the development of alternative forms of relationships, such as domestic partnerships, that garnered state recognition of

---

[41] Ibid.　[42] *Loving* v. *Virginia*, 388 US 1(1967); *Obergefell* v. *Hodges*, 576 US ___ (2015).
[43] See e.g. 23 Pennsylvania Consolidated Statutes §§1304(e), 3304.
[44] Rand, 'The Real Marriage Penalty', 93, 97, 124.　[45] Ibid., 93–5.

a bundle of rights and responsibilities.[46] Functional couple relationships gained recognition.[47] Large companies began to extend benefits to cohabiting partners in addition to marital partners of their employees. Some of these private and state mechanisms were available to and used by opposite-sex couples as well. These advances in the recognition of non-marital relationships, however, may be diminished in light of *Obergefell*'s requirement that same-sex couples be given access to marriage, leaving behind both same-sex and opposite-sex couples who do not marry.[48]

3.2 The Diminishing Role of Marriage as a Site of Support

Divorce has become more likely to bring about a 'clean break' from financial obligations based on marriage.[49] While the definition of marital property available for distribution at divorce has expanded in most jurisdictions, few couples accumulate many assets during their marriage. Almost all courts have refused to regard one spouse's increased human capital – often the family's greatest accomplishment – as a marital asset.[50] Financially stronger spouses often leave the marriage with greater assets than the less financially independent spouse, and little, if any, ongoing financial liability to that spouse.[51] This arguably enhances only the freedom and autonomy of the economically powerful spouse.

Present in about one-quarter of all divorces in the twentieth century prior to the advent of no-fault divorce, alimony has become an infrequent event, with one study finding alimony awarded in fewer than one in ten divorces.[52] Permanent alimony has become even more unusual. Recently, some states have adopted strict limits on alimony. Texas, for example, permits alimony only if the marriage lasted more than ten years and the

---

[46] M. Murray, 'Paradigms lost: How domestic partnership went from innovation to injury' (2013) 37 *New York University Review of Law & Social Change* 294-6.
[47] M. Murray, 'Obergefell v. Hodges and nonmarriage inequality' (2016) 104 *California Law Review* 1249-50.
[48] *Ibid.*, 1242-9.
[49] M. C. Regan, *Alone Together: Law and the Meanings of Marriage* (New York: Oxford University Press, 1999) 141.
[50] E. Aloni, 'The puzzle of family law pluralism' (2016) 39 *Harvard Journal of Law and Gender* 339-40.
[51] A. B. Kelly, 'Navigating gender in modern intimate partnership law' (2012) 14 *Journal of Law and Family Studies* 42.
[52] J. G. McMullen, 'Spousal support in the 21st century' (2014) 29 *Wisconsin Journal of Law, Gender & Society* 6.

recipient is too disabled to work. Similarly, Massachusetts limits alimony to a specific statutory duration for marriages lasting less than twenty years.[53] Alimony also comes with controls over its recipients' relationships, as states terminate alimony payments upon proof that the recipient is cohabiting or married, regardless of whether the new relationship provides any financial support.[54] Given the diminished post-dissolution assistance provided to dependent, caregiving spouses upon divorce, one might expect them to use premarital or marital agreements to protect their interests. Nonetheless, few such agreements are drafted to provide financial security to the usually female stay-at-home or reduced-market-labour parent.[55]

Diminished *inter se* obligations of marital partners have not, however, reduced their position as shared economic partners in their relationship to outside creditors. Marriage continues to create obligations to outside creditors through the doctrine of necessaries and other statutes requiring support within marriage.[56] Under the doctrine of necessaries, a creditor may sue one spouse for payment for services or goods provided to the other spouse.[57] This doctrine is most often invoked in the context of medical expenses for those without health insurance, or whose health insurance fails to cover all expenses. Common practices by marital partners such as sharing credit cards, cosigning auto loans and mortgages, or other joint assumptions of debt can likewise make it difficult for one to terminate marital debts towards outsiders even if one's former spouse retains the benefits gained by the debts. Spouses' financial obligations to outsiders make marriage a riskier undertaking for those with lower incomes who are less able to deal with additional debt.

3.3 The Turn to Contract in Marital and Cohabiting Relationships

Historically, entering marriage meant entering a status, the terms of which could not be altered by the parties. However, private agreements between the parties regarding financial matters at the time of separation or divorce

---

[53] *Ibid.*, 6–7.
[54] C. L. Starnes, *The Marriage Buyout: The Troubled Trajectory of U.S. Alimony Law* (New York University Press, 2014) 111–16.
[55] Aloni, 'Puzzle of family law pluralism', 342–5.
[56] J. E. Hasday, 'Intimacy and economic exchange' (2005) 119 *Harvard Law Review* 503.
[57] A. B. Kelly, 'Money matters in marriage: Unmasking interdependence in ongoing spousal economic relationships' (2008) 47 *University of Louisville Law Review* 152.

are now accepted. Beginning in the 1970s, state legislatures and courts have increasingly recognised and given effect to such agreements whether they are entered into at all phases of marriage – before, during or upon the dissolution of marriage.[58] The use of premarital and marital agreements is reported to be on the rise.[59] Today, all states permit parties to enter into premarital agreements regarding inheritance upon death or property upon separation or divorce, and almost all states permit parties to enter into premarital agreements regarding support or alimony.[60] The trend is to focus judicial concern on procedural safeguards, including access to counsel, and to limit judicial scrutiny concerning the substantive fairness of those agreements at the time of enforcement.[61]

The 'paradigmatic' situation in which premarital agreements have been used and enforced involves an older man with substantial assets marrying a younger woman with few, if any, assets.[62] These agreements generally prevent the dependent spouse – almost always a woman, in the reported judicial opinions – from equitable distribution of most, if not all, property acquired during the marriage.[63] They also typically eliminate or greatly constrain access to post-divorce spousal support. These premarital contracts have been upheld even in contexts that include lengthy marriages, children, homemaker spouse status, physical abuse or other marital misconduct, or post-divorce impoverishment of the dependent spouse.[64] The autonomy of the financially powerful spouse is upheld at the expense of the financially vulnerable spouse, who often contributed more to household labour and childcare. This contract-friendly approach favours decisions made prior to marriage and ignores life-changing decisions or events that happen during the marriage. It treats family caregiving as irrelevant to family dissolution unless the parties themselves valued caregiving in their initial agreement. This approach to contractual freedom, thus, may undermine marriage's crucial roles in encouraging spouses to put familial interests ahead of their own separate interests, protecting dependency and

---

[58] B. H. Bix, 'Private ordering and family law' (2010) 23 *Journal of the American Academy of Matrimonial Lawyers* 260–6.
[59] B. A. Atwood and B. H. Bix, 'A new uniform law for premarital and marital agreements' (2012) 46 *Family Law Quarterly* 313.
[60] Aloni, 'Puzzle of family law pluralism', 332.   [61] *Ibid.*, 333.
[62] Atwood and Bix, 'New uniform law for premarital and marital agreements', n. 31.
[63] J. T. Younger, 'Lovers' contracts in the courts: Forsaking the minimum decencies' (2007) 13 *William and Mary Journal of Women and the Law* 349, 419–20.
[64] *Ibid.*, 421–2.

providing ongoing support for or rehabilitation of a dependent spouse who made greater contributions to the family's caregiving needs during the marriage.[65]

Some states extend the right to contract to already married partners.[66] Some states, however, have refused to enforce inter-spousal contracts, under which one spouse offers to pay the other for domestic services, including housework and childcare. Those courts have treated these contracts as unenforceable, because 'marital support' is supposed to be freely given, not part of a bargained-for exchange.[67] This exception to spouses' ability to contract diminishes their freedom to construct their marital relationship as they wish and runs against the general acceptance of marital contracts. Like the deferential review of premarital agreements, this exclusion of interspousal contracts for domestic services often works to the detriment of the spouse (usually the wife) who labours in the home rather than in the marketplace, by permitting the marketplace labourer to control the finances upon which both spouses depend.[68]

For cohabitants, the background 'status' assumption is that no shared property or other financial obligations arise from the relationship.[69] This approach is supported by the view that it respects the autonomy of individuals who choose not to marry.[70] Indeed, studies show that unless the couple has a shared child, cohabiting couples are much less likely to pool their resources than are married couples. However, unmarried partners who share a biological child combine their resources at rates similar to marital partners.[71]

Cohabiting couples may contract into financial obligations, although it is likely uncommon. Cohabitation contracts, for services other than sexual services, are generally valid and enforceable.[72] Only a small number of states have adopted a functional approach to cohabiting relationships, whereby financial obligations at dissolution are based on a judicial

---

[65] *Ibid.*, 422; Aloni, 'Puzzle of family law pluralism', 360–1.
[66] B. H. Bix, 'Private ordering and family law', 267; B. A. Atwood, 'Marital contracts and the meaning of marriage' (2012) 54 *Arizona Law Review* 25.
[67] Hasday, *Family Law Reimagined*, 69–70.   [68] *Ibid.*, 86–7, 92.
[69] A. L. Estin, 'Ordinary cohabitation' (2001) 76 *Notre Dame Law Review* 1391.
[70] M. M. Mahoney, 'Forces shaping the law of cohabitation for opposite sex couples' (2005) 7 *Journal of Law and Family Studies* 200–1.
[71] Kelly, 'Navigating gender in modern intimate partnership law', 20–3.
[72] *Marvin v. Marvin*, 557 P.2d 106 (Calif. 1976); Kelly, 'Navigating gender in modern intimate partnership law', 44.

determination that the cohabiting relationship has been the functional equivalent of a marriage or a domestic partnership and so should likewise receive due consideration upon dissolution.[73] In the context of cohabitation, as in the context of marriage, courts are loathe to enforce contracts for domestic services, finding that those are generally provided without the expectation of compensation.[74]

Divorce law's reduced role in providing financial support after dissolution, its enforcement of contracts related to marriage and its presumption that cohabitation excludes obligations absent a contract are all described as successes for individual autonomy. These successes, however, call into question the family as a site of interdependence and ongoing support between the adults who have formed either a marital or coresidential family. These trends generally increase the autonomy and power only of more economically privileged partners, even in marriages that have not opted out of the default rules governing divorce, at the expense of values such as interdependence and substantive equality between former partners.[75] The law of both marital and coresidential families rewards the partner who labours in the market economy over the partner who labours in the family economy.[76]

4 The New Parent–Child Relationship

The last fifty years have brought both profound changes to the freedom of individuals to build and maintain parent–child relationships outside of the traditional marital family, as well as greater freedom by men to reject marital fatherhood. The freedom to parent one's children is central to many individuals' definitions of family autonomy. However, those who are not married to the mother may have difficulty gaining recognition as parents. Same-sex partners have also faced barriers, as have others who have entered into *in loco parentis* relationships with children. Finally, not all those who experience biological or structural infertility have access to

---

[73] Hasday, *Family Law Reimagined*, 85; W. A. Reppy, Jr., 'Choice of law problems arising when unmarried cohabitants change domicile' (2002) 55 *SMU Law Review* 277.
[74] A. Antognini, 'The law of nonmarriage' (2017) 58 *Boston College Law Review* 33.
[75] Aloni, 'Puzzle of family law pluralism', 360–2.
[76] D. A. Widiss, 'Reconfiguring sex, gender, and the law of marriage' (2012) 50 *Family Court Review* 210–11; Antognini, 'Law of nonmarriage', 61.

reproductive technologies. As some barriers have fallen, others, particularly those based on economic power or non-marital same-sex relationships, remain.

Parent–child relationships prevent divorced or separated parents from achieving the 'clean break' from each other favoured by divorce law, as these parents are prevented from fully disengaging with their children's parents once the adult–adult relationship ends. Mandatory post-dissolution engagement through coparenting, shared legal custody and restrictions on relocation impose significant restraints on the autonomy of at least one parent. Further limits on that freedom arise from mandatory economic support for children, support that can significantly constrain parents' choices about their own lives. These state interventions affect those with lower incomes most powerfully.

4.1 Broadening the Base for Developing Parent–Child Relationships

The law of parentage has long relied on the marital relationship to define parental rights and obligations. Through the centuries, when a married mother has given birth to a child, the legal presumption has been that her husband is the father.[77] More recently, the advent of genetic testing and the resulting legal changes have made it easier for many husbands to overcome this presumption where the legal fiction does not accord with biological facts. Thus, in many states, husbands now have the choice, at least shortly after the child's birth, to accept legal parenthood or to seek to disestablish the presumption.[78] Post-*Obergefell*, the marital presumption may eventually be extended to the same-sex spouse of the birth parent, easing the hurdles to dual parenthood faced by many same-sex couples.[79]

Legal recognition of the relationships for unwed biological fathers with their children has expanded dramatically. Until the mid-twentieth century, few unwed fathers were permitted to seek to build relationships with their children, even if they were required to provide economic support for those children through 'bastardy' proceedings. More

---

[77] T. Glennon, 'Somebody's child: Evaluating the erosion of the marital presumption of paternity' (2000) 102 *West Virginia Law Review* 562–4.

[78] *Alisha C. v. Jeremy C.*, 808 NW2d 875, 888–9 (Neb. 2012).

[79] D. NeJaime, 'Marriage equality and the new parenthood' (2016) 129 *Harvard Law Review* 1240–9.

typically, courts refused unwed fathers parenting time to prevent their involvement in their children's lives from furthering the shame and stigma such children would face.[80] Until the 1970s, this societal shame and stigma was also a powerful force used to make many young women, generally white and middle class, give up their children for adoption rather than face the life of an unwed single mother. Adoption law encouraged that decision by providing very little time after a child's birth for the mother to reconsider her choice, and by excluding fathers entirely from the mother's rushed deliberation. While some women willingly chose this path, many others, faced with risk of poverty or social and familial isolation, had it forced upon them.[81] In many instances, both expecting parents were forced to marry in so-called 'shotgun' marriages, to prevent the expected child from being 'illegitimate'.[82]

Diminished societal shaming and increased recognition of the constitutional rights of all parents has resulted in greater freedom for biological, non-marital parents to develop legally recognised relationships with their offspring. Beginning in the early 1970s, a series of successful constitutional challenges was brought against statutes that excluded children born outside marriage from the benefits granted to children with married parents. While the reasoning in those cases focused on the 'innocence' of the children involved, they had the effect of 'legitimating' those parent–child relationships.[83] Unwed fathers, too, gained recognition. In *Stanley v. Illinois*, the Supreme Court upheld the right of an unwed father to a hearing on his fitness to raise his children upon the death of their mother.[84] A second case struck down a law that gave only married fathers the right to contest the adoption of their child.[85] These cases established the principle that an unwed father may, under some circumstances, have protected rights in his relationship with his child.

---

[80] L. J. Harris, 'The basis for legal parentage and the clash between custody and child support' (2009) 42 *Indiana Law Review* 616–18.

[81] A. Fessler, *The Girls Who Went Away: The Hidden History of Women Who Surrendered Children for Adoption in the Decades Before Roe v. Wade* (New York: Penguin, 2007); C. A. Bachrach *et al.*, 'Relinquishment of premarital births: Evidence from national survey data' (1992) 24 *Family Planning Perspectives* 27, table 1.

[82] G. A. Akerlof, J. L. Yellen and M. L. Katz, 'An analysis of out-of-wedlock childbearing in the United States' (1996) 111 *Quarterly Journal of Economics* 278.

[83] S. Mayeri, 'Marital supremacy and the constitution of the nonmarital family' (2015) 103 *California Law Review*, 1277.

[84] *Stanley* v. *Illinois*, 405 US 645 (1972).   [85] *Caban* v. *Mohammed*, 441 US 380 (1979).

The freedom of unwed genetic fathers to claim rights in their relationships with their children, however, is not absolute. The Supreme Court has found that biological connection alone between father and child is not enough, but merely 'offers the natural father an opportunity ... to develop a relationship with his offspring ... [i]f he grasps that opportunity and accepts some measure of responsibility for the child's future'.[86] Still, even where an unwed father has grasped that opportunity, the Constitution will privilege the husband's claim to his wife's child over those of an unwed genetic father who had developed a relationship with his child.[87]

The last thirty years also saw the development, in some states, of legal theories to support the extension of parental rights to other 'parents', including same-sex partners of biological or adoptive parents, stepparents and others who may stand *in loco parentis* to a child. Recognition of these relationships was based on the concept of functional or social parenthood, supporting parental rights for individuals who had, with the consent of the legal parent, developed a parent–child relationship with the child in question. These newly acknowledged parent–child relationships, however, did not gain recognition in every state, nor did they always stand on an even playing field with biological or adoptive parent–child relationships.[88] Moreover, some fear that, post-*Obergefell*, states may remove some of these protections and make it harder for non-marital same-sex partners of the children's biological or adoptive parents to gain such recognition if states now limit such relationships to married same-sex couples.[89]

New freedoms to create parent–child relationships have also emerged through the use of ARTs. Today, third-party donor gametes may be used to create parent–child relationships between artificially conceived children and not only a genetically unrelated but marital parent, but also, in some states, a genetically unrelated and non-marital parent as well.[90] Some states now permit parent–child relationships grounded in surrogacy, either

---

[86] *Lehr* v. *Robertson*, 463 US 248, 262 (1983).
[87] *Michael H.* v. *Gerald D.*, 504 US 905 (1992).
[88] L. J. Harris, '*Obergefell*'s ambiguous impact on legal parentage' (2017) 92 *Chicago-Kent Law Review* 55, 61–6.
[89] M. Murray, '*Obergefell* v. *Hodges* and nonmarriage inequality', 1253–4.
[90] T. Glennon, 'UK and US perspectives on the regulation of gamete donation', in M. Richards, G. Pennings and J. B. Appleby (eds.), *Reproductive Donation: Practice, Policy and Bioethics* (New York: Cambridge University Press, 2012), 90, 104–6.

through silent acquiescence or formal statutory or case law recognition.[91] Recognition of these relationships is largely based on the concept of intentional parenthood, that is, by determining whether the individual claiming parental rights intended to serve as a parent in an ART context such as surrogacy or gamete donation, with the consent of the other legally recognised parent. For many, however, ART is unaffordable. In the US, in contrast to many European countries, little provision is made to financially assist those who need ARTs due to medical or structural infertility, sending many into debt or completely excluding those desiring children from achieving their dream of parenthood.[92]

4.1.1 State Intrusion into the Parent–Child Relationship

Recognition of parentage and parental rights, however, does not fall wholly on the side of freedom and autonomy. Parents must often share parenting time and consult one another before making major decisions on behalf of their children. Their own freedom of movement may also be limited through restrictions on relocation with their children. Men and boys who claim that they were 'conscripted' into biological fatherhood through sexual assault or theft of their sperm, or those who thought they were merely donating sperm for others to serve as parents, experience fatherhood not as a form of freedom, but as a source of unwanted financial responsibility.[93] Even those who accept financial responsibility for their children may find that the obligations impose unexpected constraints on their own lives.

4.2 Post-Dissolution Child Custody

Historically, post-dissolution parenting was given only to one parent. For many years, fathers were granted all parental rights to their children upon divorce. By the mid-twentieth century, however, states adopted doctrines, such as the tender years doctrine, that shifted post-dissolution parental care almost exclusively to mothers. Fathers who sought to maintain

---

[91] M. A. Field, 'Compensated surrogacy in the age of Windsor' (2014) 89 *Washington Law Review* 1160–6.

[92] A. B. Carroll, 'Cracks in the cost structure of agency adoption' (2011) 39 *Capital University Law Review* 443–53.

[93] M. Higdon, 'Marginalized fathers and demonized mothers: A feminist look at the reproductive freedom of unmarried men' (2015) 66 *Alabama Law Review* 517–23.

relationships were often limited only to a visiting relationship. Under both of these legal trends, only one parent was tasked with making legal parenting decisions regarding education, medical treatment and religious affiliation for the child after dissolution.

Beginning with the 1970s, however, gender-based presumptions regarding child custody were discarded as violations of constitutional norms concerning gender equality, and the tender years presumption was abandoned.[94] More recently, arguments that children need both parents, as well as an outspoken and effective fathers' rights movement, have ushered in a new era of shared legal and physical custody.[95] Shared legal custody is now the norm.[96] While no national data is collected on joint physical custody, it is no longer unusual or discouraged. State custody laws commonly favour ensuring that children maintain significant ties with both parents and give positive consideration to the parent who is most likely to assist children in maintaining ties to their other parent.

Higher divorce rates, increased non-marital childbearing and greater use of joint legal and physical custody have increased the judiciary's involvement in the lives of post-dissolution families. This is especially true for lower-income families, who have higher rates of relationship dissolution and less access to attorneys who can help settle their disputes out of court.[97] Custody decision-making by courts is no longer a one-time event, but an ongoing process of directing the lives of post-dissolution families. Child custody disputes may begin in infancy and involve courts in the lives of families for eighteen years or more. Shared legal custody may bring parents back to court to resolve disagreements between the parents about educational, medical and religious issues. Shared physical custody that involves considerable interaction between parents may lead to multiple requests for modification or enforcement of existing orders. Parents with complex families may face these court processes for multiple children with different parents over the course of many years.[98]

---

[94] J. H. DiFonzo, 'Dilemmas of shared parenting in the 21st century: How law and culture shape child custody' (2015) 43 *Hofstra Law Review* 1003, 1004–7.
[95] J. Carbone, *From Partners to Parents: The Second Revolution in Family Law* (Columbia University Press, 2000) 181–5; J. E. Crowley, *Defiant Dads: Fathers' Rights Activists in America* (Cornell University Press, 2008) 34–8, 56–9.
[96] Carbone, *From Partners to Parents*, 181–94.
[97] J. C. Murphy and J. B. Singer, *Divorced from Reality: Rethinking Family Dispute Resolution* (New York University Press, 2015) 60–82.
[98] Ibid., 62–3, 77–9.

State court efforts to maintain shared parenting of children can lead to significant intrusions on the lives of parents, most often the primary custodial parents who continue mainly to be mothers. Parents engaged in conflict may be required to pay for and attend sessions with coparent counsellors or parent coordinators. Survivors of domestic violence, also most commonly women, may be forced by custody orders into ongoing contact with their abusers, creating opportunities for the abuser to continue efforts to control or harass them.[99] States also protect parent–child relationships by preventing custodial parents from moving away from the other parent with the children. Mothers are most frequently the parents who are prevented from relocating with their children for work, relationships, education or proximity to extended family.[100]

4.3 Financial Support for Children

Child support orders are common in the context of divorce or separation, and approximately one-half of custodial parents have child support orders in place, although approximately only 50 per cent of those with orders actually receive child support payments.[101] Custodial parents with incomes adequate to support their children may choose to forgo the support payments in order to avoid further interaction with the courts. The freedom to make this choice may be important to custodial parents who wish to maintain a positive relationship with the other parent, or to cut ties with the other parent for safety or other personal reasons. However, the government insists that low-income custodial parents who need financial assistance from the state seek child support, whether they wish to or not. The only exception to this obligation is if they are able to convince the relevant state agency that filing a petition for child support would place them at risk of physical harm from someone who has abused them. Low-income parents thus may not be able to avoid becoming adversaries in court or being in touch with abusive former partners. These state

---

[99] J. G. Greenberg, 'Domestic violence and the danger of joint custody presumptions' (2005) 25 *Northern Illinois University Law Review* 411–12.
[100] T. Glennon, 'Still partners? Examining the consequences of post-dissolution parenting' (2007) 41 *Family Law* Quarterly 119.
[101] T. Grall, 'Custodial mothers and fathers and their child support: 2013', *US Census Bureau Current Population Reports* (2016).

requirements may also undermine fragile but positive coparenting arrangements.[102]

Parents who live apart may also find their life choices limited by their court-imposed financial obligations to their children. These obligations are imposed disproportionately on men due to their generally lower share of custodial time and relatively higher incomes.[103] Lower-income fathers may struggle to pay child support as they face bouts of unemployment or earn wages that leave little for the support of anyone besides themselves.[104] Parent obligors who are incarcerated may be unable to stop their obligation from increasing during their incarceration and find that the child support obligation they face upon release is onerous. This debt may prevent successful re-entry into society, or place a heavy burden on those striving to reintegrate. Once behind on payments, obligors face draconian penalties, including wage garnishment, loss of occupational licences needed to earn a living and jail time. While some of these obligors have the ability to pay, most are 'dead broke' rather than the 'deadbeats' of popular imagination and political rhetoric. Child support enforcement is largely targeted at the most economically vulnerable, less educated men who have faced the greatest labour market hardships in the last fifty years. Wilfully blind to the economic hardships these obligors face, courts routinely incarcerate child support obligors who are in arrears, regardless of evidence that many obligors are simply too poor to pay, or that they are unable to obtain employment despite the rosy predictions of judges that they can get a job anytime they want.[105]

Filial responsibility statutes, which make adult children liable for certain debts of their parents, such as nursing home debts, as well as 'reverse' filial responsibility statutes in some states, which make parents liable for the debts of their indigent or disabled adult children, also impose financial hardships on middle- and lower-income families.[106] These statutes may deprive struggling nuclear families of the hard-earned money they need to

---

[102] D. L. Hatcher, 'Forgotten fathers' (2013) 93 *Boston University Law Review* 909.
[103] Grall, 'Custodial mothers and fathers and their child support'.
[104] A. Cammett, 'Deadbeats, deadbrokes, and prisoners' (2011) 18 *Georgetown Journal on Poverty Law and Policy*, 140-1.
[105] N. D. Zatz, 'A new peonage?: Pay, work, or go to jail in contemporary child support enforcement and beyond' (2016) 39 *Seattle University Law Review* 934.
[106] D. Harkness, 'What are families for? Re-evaluating the return to filial responsibility laws' (2014) 21 *Elder Law Journal* 332-3.

stabilise and advance their economic futures. Rather than spreading the costs of support for elderly parents or indigent or disabled adult children more broadly, these statutes concentrate this responsibility on those least able to afford it.

Child support obligations may prevent obligors from improving their economic futures. They are permitted to lower their child support obligations only when confronted by 'involuntary' reductions in income. Decisions to decrease their earnings or to achieve important personal goals by returning to school or developing new businesses or careers, however, are viewed as voluntary reductions in income that do not reduce child support obligations.[107] Wealthier parents often have the capacity to do both. However, many lower-income child support obligors are unable to finance their child support obligation while attending school or starting a new, risky business, so child support obligations can prevent them from advancing, leaving them stuck in dead-end jobs or unstable work settings. Lower-income parents who pay child support for children on welfare may not even have the reward of seeing their children benefit from their payments. All or most of the money they pay may be siphoned off by the government to offset its welfare costs, or may be used to reduce the overall benefits received by the family, leaving the custodial parent and children in the same position financially as if the child support obligor had paid nothing.[108]

Even the child custody or child support court processes disadvantage lower-income families, who must often navigate complex proceedings without the advice of attorneys.[109] *Pro se* litigants are at a great disadvantage in adversary proceedings. Even with newer, non-adversarial processes such as mediation, low-income parties' lack of access to legal information and advice may make it difficult for them to reach agreement, or may lead them unknowingly to undermine their rights regarding important matters. Lower-wage parents or survivors of domestic violence may not know how to effectively protect their parenting rights. Courts with large low-income populations face massive dockets and delays that further undermine the

---

[107] L. Becker, 'Spousal and child support and the "voluntary reduction of income" doctrine' (1996–7) 29 *Connecticut Law Review* 647, 647–61.

[108] D. L. Hatcher, 'Don't forget dad: Addressing women's poverty by rethinking forced and outdated child support policies' (2012) 20 *American University Journal of Gender, Social Policy and the Law* 775, 780–1.

[109] Murphy and Singer, *Divorced from Reality*, 68–9.

rights of these families. Court hearings can also lead to job loss, as many lower-wage workers are not protected from termination or losing pay for days on which they are obligated to appear in court.[110] Between child custody and child support issues, judicial intervention into the lives of lower-income parents and their children is both commonplace and disruptive.

5 Inequality among Families

The intra-family inequalities discussed in this chapter often fall within the traditional realms of family law. However, inequality among families cannot be addressed solely by family law reforms. Too many families simply lack the financial resources or stable employment necessary for them to thrive. As more US families lose access to well-paying, secure jobs, it has become clear that changes to traditional areas of family law are not enough, by themselves, to shore up these fragile families. Where no one within a household has significant income or assets, redistribution of those assets through family law is unlikely to achieve the financial stability that might empower families to care for themselves and their chosen family relationships. Scholars and policymakers have suggested looking beyond the borders of family law, to areas such as labour market regulation and public benefits law, to enable families to meet their needs.[111]

5.1 Labour Market Challenges for Families

Labourers in the US increasingly work for low wages insufficient to support a family, and endure working conditions that undermine their ability to take care of their families. Many parents face employment insecurity that creates unexpected interruptions in income.[112] Although almost three-quarters of single parents work, most of them work in the low-

---

[110] *Ibid.*, 71–6.
[111] J. Carbone and N. Cahn, *Marriage Markets: How Inequality Is Remaking the American Family* (New York: Oxford University Press, 2014) 145–67.
[112] Hernandez and Napierala, 'Children's experience with parental employment insecurity and family income inequality'.

wage labour market.[113] Approximately one-quarter to one-third of US workers do not make enough to support a family of four above the poverty threshold.[114] The erosion of the legal minimum wage places many who work full-time well below the poverty line. In addition to receiving low wages, these workers are unlikely to have other employment arrangements or benefits that provide key assistance to families, nor do they earn enough to pay for childcare. The growth of the 'gig economy' has placed even more workers outside even basic labour protections.[115]

Most workers need to juggle work and family responsibilities, but the jobs held by low-wage workers are not structured to provide the schedule predictability or flexibility essential to deal with their family's needs.[116] Thus, low-wage workers often have schedules that are both rigid and unpredictable. Their hours may be changed with little or no notice, making it impossible to commit in advance to medical appointments or parent–teacher conferences. They may have mandatory overtime, their hours may abruptly be cut or they may even be laid off during slow periods for their employer. They are unlikely to control their break time, and they often have to work overnight or on weekends. Unpredictable and non-standard work hours make it difficult to find childcare or to meet the needs of ageing parents.[117] This lack of control hits hardest single parents, who have fewer resources to draw on to assist with children or parents.

Low-wage workers generally also lack paid leave time to care for their own or a family member's illness or for maternity or paternity care. They often also lack vacation days, retirement benefits or health insurance.[118] Without benefits like these, families face formidable challenges with even just being able to bond with newborn infants, address basic health concerns, support children's educational growth, meet the needs of ageing

---

[113] P. Loprest et al., Office of the Assistant Secretary for Planning & Evaluation, US Department of Health & Human Services, 'Who are low-wage workers?', *ASPE Research Brief* (2009) 1, https://aspe.hhs.gov/pdf-report/who-are-low-wage-workers

[114] T. Jones, 'A different class of care: The benefits crisis and low-wage workers' (2017) 66 *American University Law Review* 702–3.

[115] V. DeStefano, 'The rise of the "just-in-time workforce": On-demand work, crowdwork, and labor protection in the "gig-economy"' (2016) 37 *Comparative Labor Law & Policy Journal* 479–80.

[116] Jones, 'Different class of care', 706.

[117] *Ibid.*, 716; N. Ruan and N. Reichman, 'Hours equity is the new pay equity' (2014) 59 *Villanova Law Review* 35.

[118] Jones, 'Different class of care', 706–7.

parents and protect themselves from poverty upon retirement.[119] Low-income families have even greater needs for these benefits as their wages are inadequate to allow them to purchase these important aids for themselves.

5.2 The Two-Tiered World of Public Benefits

Many US families receive public benefits, including both social insurance programmes, like social security retirement benefits and unemployment compensation, and programmes designed to address poverty, such as Temporary Assistance for Needy Families (TANF) and the Earned Income Tax Credit (EITC). Spending on social insurance programmes based on work dwarfs programmes that target those living in poverty. These latter programmes, moreover, generally involve stingier benefits and greater state intrusion into the family than those programmes that primarily aid middle- and upper-income families. Programmes addressing poverty operate on an assumption that poverty is caused by individual moral failings, not broader social and economic structural forces. Therefore, those seeking assistance are viewed sceptically and required to prove that they are justified in seeking assistance.[120]

Thus, while applications for social security family benefits, widely available to the larger US population, involve little more than proof of family relationship, applications for public benefits for low-income families, such as TANF, require extensive documentation, frequent proof of continued eligibility and numerous behavioural requirements and restrictions. Federal law not only requires recipients to work, but also permits states to impose 'individual responsibility plan[s]' requiring TANF recipients to take classes on parenting and money management and to have their children vaccinated and attend school regularly. These requirements might sometimes conflict. For example, the work requirements may undermine parents' ability to ensure their children's attendance at school or to attend their own classes, leaving them vulnerable to the loss of benefits. They allow states to impose family caps to dissuade recipients from having more children. Various restrictions on public assistance and intrusions on private family life related to receipt of such assistance have been upheld as constitutional. These great efforts on the part of recipients yield little

[119] *Ibid.*, 712–14. [120] Alstott, 'Neoliberalism in U.S. family law', 39.

benefit as payments are extremely low. Because payments are so low, many ultimately find ways to subsist without this small amount of support.[121]

In recent years, the provision of financial assistance to the families of low-wage workers has become primarily a function of the tax system. The EITC is now the largest programme distributing financial assistance to low-wage workers in the US, yet it remains insufficient to lift recipients, all engaged in paid labour, to an adequate living standard.[122] Because it aids only those with wage income, moreover, it also fails to reach the nation's poorest citizens.[123]

Neither public benefits nor innovative tax programmes currently address the challenges many US families face as a result of dramatic changes in the economy that put family economic security out of reach for so many. Like legal regulations related to market labour, these programmes should be examined to determine how better to support the essential work of all families, no matter what forms they take.

6 Conclusion

Over the last fifty years there have been significant gains in the autonomy of individuals to create intimate adult relationships. These have been accompanied by legal recognition of broader freedoms to choose marital partners, and to develop parent–child relationships outside opposite-sex marital relationships or through the use of innovations in ARTs. However, shifts in family law doctrines privilege economically more powerful marital partners to the detriment of those whose family care contributions came at the expense of their own economic independence. Expanded rights to develop parent–child relationships have also been paralleled by increased intrusions into post-dissolution family life through the child custody system, as well as by greater privatisation of the support of children, which has resulted in onerous child support orders that many obligors are unable to afford.

---

[121] *Ibid.*, 28; Hasday, *Family Law Reimagined*, 208–20.
[122] Alstott, 'Neoliberalism in U.S. family law', 40.
[123] H. C. Tahk, 'The tax war on poverty' (2014) 56 *Arizona Law Review* 803.

Inequality among families leaves many vulnerable to economic stresses that undermine, and prevent many from having real choices in, their family relationships. It will take more than changes to family law doctrine to ensure that US families thrive, requiring consideration of further adjustments to other areas of law, including the law of labour markets and of social welfare.

Further Reading

M. F. Brinig, *From Contract to Covenant: Beyond the Law and Economics of the Family* (Harvard University Press, 2000).

J. Carbone, *From Partners to Parents: The Second Revolution in Family Law* (Columbia University Press, 2000).

J. Carbone and N. Cahn, *Marriage Markets: How Inequality Is Remaking the American Family* (New York: Oxford University Press, 2014).

A. J. Cherlin, *Labor's Love Lost* (New York: Russell Sage Foundation, 2014).

S. Coontz, *Marriage, a History: From Obedience to Intimacy or How Love Conquered Marriage* (New York: Viking Penguin, 2005).

J. E. Crowley, *Defiant Dads: Fathers' Rights Activists in America* (Cornell University Press, 2008).

N. E. Dowd, *The Man Question: Male Subordination and Privilege* (New York University Press, 2010).

M. Eichner, *The Supportive State: Families, Government, and America's Political Ideals* (New York: Oxford University Press, 2010).

A. Fessler, *The Girls Who Went Away: The Hidden History of Women Who Surrendered Children for Adoption in the Decades before Roe v. Wade* (New York: Penguin, 2007).

M. Garrison and E. S. Scott (eds.), *Marriage at the Crossroads: Law, Policy, and the Brave New Worlds of Twenty-First-Century Families* (New York: Cambridge University Press, 2012).

S. Golombok, R. Scott, J. B. Appleby, M. Richards and S. Wilkinson (eds.), *Regulating Reproductive Donation* (Cambridge University Press, 2016).

M. B. Goodwin (ed.), *Baby Markets: Money and the New Politics of Creating Families* (New York: Cambridge University Press, 2010).

J. E. Hasday, *Family Law Reimagined* (Harvard University Press, 2014).

N. Hirschmann, *The Subject of Liberty: Toward a Feminist Theory of Freedom* (Princeton University Press, 2003).

C. Huntington, *Failure to Flourish: How Law Undermines Family Relationships* (New York: Oxford University Press, 2014).

E. F. Kittay, *Love's Labor: Essays on Women, Equality, and Dependency* (New York: Routledge, 1999).

J. A. Levine, *Ain't No Trust: How Bosses, Boyfriends, and Bureaucrats Fail Low-Income Mothers and Why It Matters* (Berkeley, CA: University of California Press, 2013).

L. C. McClain, *The Place of Families: Fostering Capacity, Equality, and Responsibility* (Harvard University Press, 2006).

L. C. McClain and Daniel Cere (eds.), *What Is Parenthood?: Contemporary Debates about the Family* (New York University Press, 2013).

J. C. Murphy and J. B. Singer, *Divorced from Reality: Rethinking Family Dispute Resolution* (New York University Press, 2015).

J. Nedelsky, *Law's Relations: A Relational Theory of Self, Autonomy, and Law* (New York: Oxford University Press, 2011).

J. T. Oldham and M. S. Melli (eds.), *Child Support: The Next Frontier* (4th edn, University of Michigan Press, 2003).

M. C. Regan, Jr., *Alone Together: Law and the Meanings of Marriage* (New York: Oxford University Press, 1999).

Family Law and the Pursuit of Intimacy (New York University Press, 1993).

C. L. Starnes, *The Marriage Buyout: The Troubled Trajectory of U.S. Alimony Law* (New York University Press, 2014).

Human Rights in the German Family Law Context

3

Bettina Heiderhoff

Introduction: Constitutionalisation

If, by way of introduction, a central feature of German family law had to be identified, it would have to be its distinct attachment to the human rights in the Constitution (in German: *Grundgesetz* (GG), which translates to Basic Law). Not only have the special rules on the protection of marriage, family and of parental responsibility in Art. 6 GG had a substantial impact on private family law, but so too have Art. 3 GG (equality and equal treatment) and certainly Art. 2 sec. 1 GG, which protects free development of personality and private autonomy.

One might assume that this causes German family law to be particularly static. In fact, the opposite is true. The decisions of the German Federal Constitutional Court (in German: Bundesverfassungsgericht (BVerfG)) have had enormous influence not only on the interpretation of existing law, but also on its reform. The vast majority of changes that have been made to family law since the Second World War have been imposed by the BVerfG.[1] Almost as a rule, amendments have only been implemented after the existing rules had been declared unconstitutional by the court. The German Parliament has always been rather reserved towards family law reforms. In reforming the law, the legislator has demonstrated a tendency to limiting itself to the minimum of absolutely necessary adjustments. This has provoked new decisions by the BVerfG, and led to further reluctant reforms. Thus, the constitutionalisation has not made family law static, but, on the contrary, might be considered the motor of progress in family law. It must be acknowledged, though, that there are some major exceptions, one of which is the Reform of the Child Law of 1998.

---

[1] A list of abbreviations can be found at the end of this chapter.

Human Rights and Family Law Reforms

In the post-war era, equal treatment of men and women, which is regulated in Art. 3 sec. 2 GG, was the issue that triggered a complete restructuring of the matrimonial property regime and the parental rights of fathers. When the GG came into force in 1949, a period of almost four years was prudently reserved for the transformation of the new constitutional standards into family law. Sadly, the period expired without action, and it was the BVerfG that had to declare the old rules void in 1953. For five years, the lawmaker struggled to make new laws that were not discriminatory towards women, in particular towards wives. On 1 July 1958, the new law finally came into force, undeniably still containing some discriminatory rules. Its core element was the community of accrued gains. The distinguishing feature of this matrimonial property regime is the separation of property during marriage. The spouse that has no or little income (historically typically the wife) does not directly receive a share of the other spouse's income, but gets compensated after the divorce (for details, see p. 97).

Later, other aspects of equal treatment became more important. Non-discrimination of children born out of wedlock (Art. 6 sec. 5 GG) was only achieved in the late 1990s. In 1970, the Law of the Status of Children Born out of Wedlock (in German: *Nichtehelichengesetz*, a response to a decision by the BVerfG) came into effect. This clarified that such children are, in fact, related to their father. The distinction between children born in and out of wedlock was not abandoned until the Reform of 1998, which, by and large, equalised their legal positions. At the same time, it was clarified that the unmarried mother had full parental responsibility for the child. Before, the old law had already been 'turned into ruins'[2] by various decisions of the BVerfG.

Several decisions by the BVerfG dealt with discriminatory regulations regarding transsexuals. Most importantly, it was determined that an existing marriage does not end with the 'sex change' of a spouse[3] and that a transsexual has the right to have their gender identity recognised by civil status law without undergoing any operations.[4]

---

[2] D. Coester-Waltjen, *Familienrecht* (6th edn, Munich: Beck, 2010), 573.
[3] ECLI:DE:BVerfG:2008:ls20080527.1bvl001005.
[4] ECLI:DE:BVerfG:2011:rs20110111.1bvr329507; ECLI:DE:BVerfG:2011:rk20111027.1bvr202711.

In the twenty-first century, homosexual relationships and parentage have been at the centre of attention. When the Civil Act (in German: *Lebenspartnerschaftsgesetz* (LPartG)) was introduced in 2001, some Christian Democratic state governments (including Bavaria) applied to the BVerfG for judicial review. In particular, the BVerfG was asked to clarify whether Art. 6 sec. 1 GG allows for an institution such as civil partnership to exist alongside traditional marriage.[5] The BVerfG held that the particular protection of marriage in Art. 6 sec. 1 GG does not 'prevent the legislature from providing rights and duties for the same-sex civil partnership that are equal or similar to those of marriage. The institution of marriage is not threatened by any risk from an institution that is directed at persons who cannot be married to each other.' Since then, the court, following this path, has demanded on several occasions that equal treatment of same-sex couples must be respected. Against this background it may seem surprising that political voices, including Chancellor Angela Merkel, uttered doubts about the constitutionality of same-sex marriage when it was introduced in 2017. This is based on a reading of Art. 6 sec. 1 GG that assumes that the provision, while giving room for a same-sex partnership other than marriage, reserves the institution of marriage itself to heterosexual couples (for details see p. 95).

Even after the introduction of same-sex marriage, discussions continue regarding various issues relating to same-sex relationships, such as the extension of the *pater est* rule to cover women who are in registered relationships or married with the mother (*mater est* rule).

Currently, however, the largest construction site in family law probably concerns the rights of the father who is not married to the mother of the child. The question of when he can obtain legal paternity if the child already has a legal father is a matter of great discussion. The current solution is based on a judgment of the BVerfG from 2003.[6] It does not grant the biological father the right to contest the paternity of the legal father as long as there is a social and family relationship between the legal father and the child. Further, the matter of how the unmarried father can get shared parental responsibility with the mother is not entirely settled. Following a decision of the BVerfG demanding it,

[5] ECLI:DE:BVerfG:2002:fs20020717.1bvf000101.
[6] ECLI:DE:BVerfG:2003:rs20030409.1bvr149396.

the father now has the possibility to request shared parental responsibility in court.[7]

The ECtHR was at the forefront of strengthening the rights of the so-called merely biological father.[8] Only following a decision of the ECtHR were contact rights between the biological father and the child introduced. The new law does, however, restrict these rights to cases in which contact is in the child's best interest.

The relationship between the ECHR and the GG may best be described as complementary. Where the human rights in the ECHR require stricter protection than the rights contained in the GG, they will be applied by the BVerfG in its review of the constitutionality of state acts.[9] The national courts must take account of the decisions of the ECtHR.[10]

Concluding this introduction, a short examination of Art. 2 sec. 1 GG is necessary. The free development of personality and, more broadly, the freedom of action extensively influence private law in general. They are considered the basis of private autonomy. The general personality right derives from both Arts. 1 (human dignity) and 2 sec. 1 GG. Part of this is the right to know one's own data, comprising the right to know the identity of one's own genetic parents and offspring. This has caused a lot of controversy in recent years. Fathers, mothers and children all have the right to have genetic parentage tested (§ 1598a of the Civil Code, in German: *Bürgerliches Gesetzbuch* (BGB)). It is also established that a child conceived after donor insemination has the right to know the identity of the donor. However, major issues remain unclear. The legislator is currently working on a law to protect the donor from maintenance claims. Whether the child also has the right to obtain a genetic sample from a third person whom it assumes to be its father is one of the open questions. The existing law only foresees this right within the proceedings for court determinations of paternity. If the child does not wish the person concerned to become their legal father, they have no right to such an isolated paternity test. In 2016, the BVerfG stressed the difference from cases involving sperm donors in a decision on this matter. In the sperm donor cases, the

---

[7] ECLI:DE:BVerfG:2003:ls20030129.1bvl002099.
[8] Anayo v. *Germany*, no. 20578/07, 21 December 2010; *Schneider* v. *Germany*, no. 17080/07, 15 September 2011.
[9] F. Klinkhammer, 'Wer gehört zur Familie?' ZfPW 1/2015: 5–29, 5ff.
[10] ECLI:DE:BVerfG:2005:rk20050405.1bvr166404; ECLI:DE:BVerfG:2015:rk20150519.2bvr 117014.

information requested by the child already exists. Here, by contrast, the child is asking to have new genetic data of another person generated. This person may or may not turn out to be the father. The BVerfG decided that it is not unconstitutional to deny a right of the child to have such data produced. The GG gives leeway to the lawmaker to balance the rights of children to learn who their genetic parents are with the rights of the alleged father to not have his genetic data generated and shared.[11]

Summary and Preview of the Chapter

The constitutionally influenced amendments roughly sketched above are sometimes anticipated, sometimes received and almost always actively accompanied by the scientific community. The family courts adopt them and integrate them in practice. This way, there is always movement in the law. Additionally, family law scholars are far from agreeing on all issues – different solutions are favoured in particular for the matters of parentage and parental responsibility in patchwork and rainbow families. Consequently, a report on German family law can always only be a snapshot and will also necessarily be subjective.

Overall, what can at least be said with certainty is that the constitutionalisation has been immensely beneficial to family law. It has led to a legal framework that grants a high degree of equal treatment, autonomy in familial matters, a space of protection and freedom for families and a highly developed understanding of fair procedure and the right to be heard.

In the following main part of this chapter we will deal with two core subjects: the parent–child relationship and the couple's relationship.

In the first section, which will in particular cover legal parenthood and parental responsibility, our particular attention will remain on human rights. We will have to scrutinise in more detail how the undebated significance of the child's well-being is connected to the child's human rights. While the focus on the well-being of the child is the central guiding principle in child law and is constantly growing more important, the GG does not expressly include the protection of the child's well-being (see p. 93).

Individual subtopics of this first section will be legal parentage, parental responsibility and contact rights with separated parents, the role of the

---

[11] ECLI:DE:BVerfG:2016:rs20160419.1bvr330913.

biological father and the removal of parental responsibility in cases of abuse. At the end of this part, we will see how children can be involved in court proceedings and mediation.

The second section of the chapter will then address the law of relationships, and in particular the financial compensation after the termination of a relationship. Here, the aspects of autonomy and gender become more dominant. It will be seen that while German law leaves considerable room for autonomous decisions, this is rarely taken advantage of. Couples often rely on the statutory provisions, even though these contain gaps, especially regarding unmarried couples.

Parenthood

Parenthood as Status

In Germany, the question of who has the status of a legal parent of a child is regarded as a fundamental element of all family rights. Parental responsibility, maintenance rights and obligations, inheritance rights and to a large degree also contact rights depend on the legally recognised parent–child relationship. Therefore, the rules on parentage are of great importance. With a birth rate of less than 1.5, it does not come as a surprise that the major issues have shifted from fathers wanting to avoid parentage to fathers – and mothers – fighting to be legal parents.

Motherhood

Dogma of the Birth Mother

Until 1998, the law did not regulate who the legal mother of a child is. Only when it became clear that reproductive medicine makes it possible that birth mother and genetic mother are not the same person, the legislator introduced a new rule stipulating that the woman who gives birth to a child is its (legal) mother. The intention was to avoid surrogacy arrangements.[12]

Methods of reproductive medicine involving egg transfer, such as egg donation and surrogacy, are illegal in Germany.[13] While liberalisation is

---

[12] BT-Drs. 13/4899, 82, 13 June 1996.
[13] § 1 Embryo Protection Law, in German: *Embryonenschutzgesetz*.

carefully discussed, the most practical issue concerns female same-sex partners that want to have children together.

Becoming Co-mothers

Currently, women can become co-mothers by way of adoption. If one partner gives birth to the child, adoption by the other partner is possible – however, it is subject to the consent of the father. In recent years, family courts were very involved with constellations in which the intended mothers tried to overcome this impediment. It is important to note that it is difficult for female same-sex couples in Germany to have a medically assisted, anonymous sperm donation performed. The main reason for this lies in the legal framework. The law does not provide for an option to exclude definitively the risk of maintenance duties for the sperm donor.

The Federal High Court (in German: Bundesgerichtshof (BGH)) had to decide two particularly interesting cases. In the first and more common case, the mother submitted that the private sperm donor had waived all rights as a father and did not want to be involved in the adoption procedure. The BGH decided that the father must still be informed before the adoption procedure is started in such cases.[14] Only when he specifically decides not to assert his rights in the procedure is the adoption possible. As of yet it is unclear how the courts will decide a case if the birth mother simply claims that she does not know the identity of the genetic father. It must be assumed that an adoption can be performed if the court is convinced of the truth of that claim.

In the second, more elaborate case, the birth mother, who had made use of a private sperm donation, asked a second man to acknowledge paternity for the child and thereby take the position of the legal father.[15] The purpose of this is that the man who thereby becomes the legal father can then consent to the adoption of the child by the mother's female partner. The BGH stopped this method and reinstalled the legal position of the private sperm donor.

Recently scholars have been suggesting that the law needs to allow for there being more than two parents for the child in these cases. It is debated whether this is in accordance with the Constitution. The BVerfG will

---

[14] BGH, NJW 2015, 1820.   [15] BGH, NJW 2013, 2589.

certainly make very clear that more than two parents can – if at all – only be allowed if this is in the best interest of the child.[16]

Fatherhood

Mix of Principles

Establishing legal paternity has always been much more complicated because of the lack of the distinct bond created by giving birth. Not even the strongest supporter of bloodline theories would suggest defining paternity merely genetically, even though it would be possible today. The reason for this is that the law of descent aims at determining a father who will presumably further the child's well-being. At this point, however, we face a basic misunderstanding, or at least a contentious point, in the German debate on the law of descent. Some scholars vehemently deny that the child's well-being is a principle in the law of descent. They worry that such a principle could imply that state authorities may claim the right to choose the person best suited as parent of a child. Such an understanding of the principle of the child's well-being would certainly infringe human rights and must be strictly rejected. However, the general rules of parentage are clearly designed to give the child a safe and supportive father.[17]

Social Father versus Genetic Father

The most intense conflict within the law of descent is the conflict between the man who already has the status of legal father, and the man who is the genetic father of the child; a question that is once again debated and answered on the basis of Art. 6 GG.

Up until 2003, it was completely impossible for the biological father to contest the paternity of the legal father. The BVerfG decided in 2003 that this legal situation was not compatible with Art. 6 sec. 2 GG.[18] Consequently, the law was changed, enabling the biological father to contest the paternity of the legal father in cases in which the latter does

---

[16] A careful indication of this kind was made in ECLI:DE:BVerfG:2013:ls20130219.1bvl000111 para. 51; a different tone was struck in ECLI:DE:BVerfG:2003:rs20030409.1bvr149396 paras. 61ff. – however, this decision dealt with a social and a biological father and the court considered the constellation to be fraught with role conflicts and strife.
[17] ECLI:DE:BVerfG:2003:rs20030409.1bvr149396.   [18] *Ibid.*

not actively take over the father role. The individual prerequisites of the contestation are as follows: every man claiming to be the biological father is allowed to contest the legal paternity (except for the anonymous sperm donor). The contestation must take place within two years of gaining knowledge of the fact that the legal and the biological father are not identical. Finally, and most importantly, the legal father must not have a 'social and family relationship' with the child. As soon as such a relationship exists, the contestation is blocked. In case of a successful contestation, the man is directly determined to be the father in the same proceedings.

This statutory situation still provokes criticism. In regard to some rather exceptional cases in which the law leads to problematic results, these objections are indeed justified. In particular, this pertains to cases in which the biological father had already tried to gain legal paternity at the birth of the child but failed due to the assumption by the court that there was already a social and family relationship with the legal father (typically the mother's husband, but it could be a new partner, who has acknowledged paternity with her consent) and the child. Various solutions have been suggested. Some authors would like to abolish the prerequisite of the nonexistence of the social and family relation (with additional suggestions of shortening the time period to one year),[19] while others would like to just change the time limits and let the two years begin only after the apparent end of the social and family relationship with the legal father. Still others would prefer a specific decision by the court between the two potential fathers. A working group in the ministry of justice released suggestions for legislation in summer 2017.

While there are good legal reasons for strengthening the rights of the biological father to a certain degree, one should not overlook that the debate has been strongly influenced by a lobby of biological fathers that can get emotional. What is often forgotten is that this is about the well-being of the child, not about a power struggle between two fathers. Keeping this in mind, it seems reasonable to change the law just slightly, in order to avoid a blockade of those biological fathers who seek recognition of their paternity right at the birth of the child and show serious interest in the

---

[19] T. Helms, 'Rechtliche, biologische und soziale Elternschaft – Herausforderungen durch neue Familienformen', in Verhandlungen des 71. Deutschen Juristentages Essen 2016 (Munich: Beck, 2016), vol. I, 44ff.

child's development. An individual review of the cases in order to avoid abuse seems advisable.

Position of the Biological But Not Legal Father

The merely biological father currently still has a very weak position. Traditionally, he did not have any right to have the paternity verified by a genetic sample, nor did he have any rights towards the child. Recently, this has changed significantly.

As previously mentioned, limited contact rights for the biological father were introduced after a judgment of the ECtHR. Paternity needs to be proved in court proceedings. To this end, a genetic test will be carried out in case of doubt. This was somewhat revolutionary and seemed to weaken the whole system based on status. However, under the new rule, the contact right of the biological father is subject to the child's best interest. Only if the contact serves the best interests of the child, will the contact right be granted. The courts quickly developed an understanding of this rule that avoided ordering genetic tests in most cases. They investigated the child's best interests first and regularly denied it when the child did not even know of the existence of the biological father or when the parents strongly opposed the contact. In a decision from October 2016, the BGH set the foundation for a change of procedure.[20] In it, the BGH carefully weighed the rights of the biological father and those of the legal parents and established that the refusal of the parents alone cannot be decisive, but that the court must generally also personally hear the child. If the child has sufficient age and maturity and there are no other obvious obstacles for contact, the child must be informed that it has a biological father who is not its legal father and that the biological father wants to have contact. In case the parents do not inform the child, the judge may arrange for the child to be informed by other means (e.g. through an expert). The BGH did not have to deal with the chronology of events as the biological parentage was undisputed. It can be expected, however, that the decision will lead to courts from now on first investigating whether the claimant is actually the biological father of the child. Otherwise, informing the child seems unnecessarily unsettling and excessive. This way, at least such men would have the opportunity to clarify parentage in court who, as § 1686a BGB demands, have shown interest in the child from the beginning.

---

[20] ECLI:DE:BGH:2016:051016BXIIZB280.15.0.

Child Arrangements on Separation

Model of Joint Parental Responsibility

In order to understand how custody is arranged in the case of a separation of the parents, it is necessary to examine the distribution of custody before the separation.

Generally, both parents jointly exercise parental responsibility. This implies that they must agree on all matters concerning the child, such as choice of school, religion, sports, medical treatment and investment of the child's assets. The law provides for the option to apply to the family court in case an agreement cannot be reached in a relevant matter (§ 1627 BGB).

Unmarried Parents

When the father is not married to the mother of the child, joint parental responsibility does not automatically apply. On the contrary, both parents must formally declare that they want to exercise parental responsibility jointly. Otherwise, the mother has sole parental responsibility. In 2013, a new rule was added to the law allowing the father to apply for joint responsibility at the family court. So far, this has been the final point in a long development: after the declaration on joint parental responsibility had been introduced in 1998, the BVerfG found it to be in accordance with Art. 6 GG in a judgment from 2003.[21] In retrospect, this decision should possibly better be regarded as a positive evaluation of progress. In it, the BVerfG required the legislator to examine whether the declaration of parental responsibility really allowed all unmarried fathers to obtain joint parental responsibility. A subsequent investigation showed that the mother agreed to such a declaration in only about 50 per cent of the cases. In 2009, the BVerfG declared the rule unconstitutional because it contained no possibility for the father to obtain joint parental responsibility in court.[22] The decision was well received by legal scholars.[23] The ECtHR had almost at the same time also declared that the 'general exclusion of

---

[21] ECLI:DE:BVerfG:2003:ls20030129.1bvl002099.
[22] ECLI:DE:BVerfG:2010:rs20100721.1bvr042009 para. 24.
[23] Klinkhammer, 'Wer gehört zur Familie?', 14ff.; D. Coester-Waltjen, 'Commentary on Art. 6 GG', in I. von Münch and P. Kunig (eds.), *Grundgesetz-Kommentar* (6th edn, Munich: Beck, 2012) vol. I, 542–626, 592.

judicial review of the initial attribution of sole custody to the mother according to § 1626a (2) of the Civil Code' violates Art. 14 in conjunction with Art. 8 of the ECHR.[24] In contrast to the BVerfG, the ECtHR emphasised the principle of equal treatment.

Only in 2013 did the current law come into effect. While many voices in legal literature had demanded introducing joint responsibility from birth – requiring no court proceedings – the legislator chose another path: when the mother does not agree to joint responsibility, the father has to apply to the court for it. At least a simplified and faster procedure was implemented for this purpose. The BGH, however, has already stated that in these proceedings, as in all child related proceedings, the interests of all factors speaking for and against joint responsibility will necessarily have to be carefully weighed against each other.[25]

One cannot deny that the new law is paradoxical, compelling the father to commence court proceedings against the mother in order to be granted joint responsibility together with her. It is hardly surprising that such court proceedings are often unsuccessful for the father.[26] Arguably, the recent statutory changes may at least have the positive side effect that the number of declarations of joint responsibility is rising. There are no reliable statistics in this regard yet, though.

Parental Responsibility after Separation

Until the reform in 1998, the law stipulated that after a divorce only one parent could carry the parental responsibility. It was statistical information that triggered a change. Empirical studies had revealed that over half of the fathers who lost paternal responsibility after a divorce had no contact with the child anymore one year after the divorce.[27] Thus, continuing joint responsibility after a separation or divorce was established as the statutory rule. Only when one parent applies for it, the court decides whether the applicant should be granted sole responsibility, pursuant to § 1671 BGB. The only criterion is the well-being of the child.

---

[24] *Zaunegger* v. *Germany*, no. 22028/04, 3 December 2009; commentary by M. Coester, 'Sorgerechtliche Impulse aus Straßburg', NJW 8/2010: 482-5, 482ff.
[25] ECLI:DE:BGH:2016:150616BXIIZB419.15.0.   [26] See e.g. KG, FamRZ 2011, 1661.
[27] BT-Drs. 13/4899, 13 June 1996, 62.

The actual problem in this area is that some parents fight long and intense battles regarding parental responsibility and the right of contact. There are estimations that about 10 per cent of parents are such 'high-conflict parents'.[28] Even if one parent is granted sole responsibility, the fight is not over. Typically, one parent (often the mother entitled to responsibility) continuously impedes or denies the other parent contact with the children. These are cases that are difficult to regulate legally. In the last decade, many models that are designed to prevent an escalation before it happens have been regionally implemented or tried out. The Cochemer Model[29] was particularly noteworthy, in which all professions involved sat down with the parents to find a solution. Today this approach has been developed further in many areas. Youth welfare offices try out different types of dialogue to enable the parents to communicate productively regarding the child. Mediation is also often offered. However, in many cases the court ends up having to take drastic measures. The denial of contact is sanctioned with a fine or even administrative detention.[30] In cases in which the child has a sufficiently close relationship to the parent that is not yet entitled to responsibility, and that parent is prepared to act, the parental responsibility can be transferred from the parent that is denying contact to the other parent.[31] This, however, is often not an option, because the children do not have a close enough relationship to the other parent.

Shared Care Arrangement: 50:50

In the majority of cases, parents can communicate well enough after getting a divorce and recognise and respect the well-being of their children. There can still be disputes, however. The most important question,

---

[28] See S. Walper, J. Fichtner, Zwischen den Fronten, 'Psychosoziale Auswirkungen von Elternkonflikten auf Kinder', in S. Walper, J. Fichtner and K. Normann (eds.), *Hochkonflikthafte Trennungsfamilien* (2nd edn, Weinheim Basel: Juventa, 2013) 91–110, 95.

[29] See e.g. M. Noll, 'Das Cochemer Modell – zum Wohle der Kinder', in C. Müller-Magdeburg (ed.), *Verändertes Denken – zum Wohle der Kinder* (Baden-Baden: Nomos, 2009) 21–4, 21ff.

[30] § 89 of the Act on Procedures in Family Matters and Miscellaneous Matters, in German: *Gesetz über das Verfahren in Familiensachen und in den Angelegenheiten der freiwilligen Gerichtsbarkeit* (FamFG).

[31] D. Schwab, *Familienrecht* (25th edn, Munich: Beck, 2017) 364ff.

which one of the parents the child will live with and how much and at what times it visits the other parent, often has to be decided by a court. This type of situation triggered a fundamental dispute as to whether courts can decide that a child moves regularly between the two parents (50:50 shared care). The BVerfG decided that parents at least do not generally have a right to this arrangement.[32] Most courts reject it.[33] This is reassuring, as it cannot be denied that the 50:50 model often serves the interests of the parents and suggests that both have a right to equal participation in the child. It can easily be forgotten that the well-being of the child has to be the goal of every model for allocation of parental responsibility after a separation.

Still, the 50:50 shared care arrangement is now used often in Germany. This results from both parents agreeing on it. When the cooperation works well, and the external circumstances are fitting, the parties often give it a positive evaluation. Sometimes difficult follow-up questions arise for the courts regarding support payments and potential social benefits.

Contact Rights

In Germany, the contact rights are regulated separately from parental responsibility matters.[34] A parent who does not live with the child has the right and the obligation to maintain contact with the child pursuant to § 1684 BGB. Further contact rights exist for close relatives and persons that have a social and family relationship with the child.

The duration and type of contact of the parent who does not live with the child is decided by the courts. The decision depends on the child's well-being, but also on organisational feasibility. The law about how to deal with problems regarding the contact right is quite detailed. For instance, there is an option for supervised contact sessions and there is even the option to appoint a so-called contact guardian, who may, for example, organise the meetings or accompany the child from one parent to the other.

As mentioned, each parent also has the duty to spend time with the child. If a parent refuses to maintain contact with the child, the above-mentioned instruments – even administrative detention – may be applied for

---

[32] ECLI:DE:BVerfG:2015:rk20150624.1bvr048614.
[33] See e.g. OLG Hamm, NJW 2012, 398; OLG Munich, FamRZ 2013, 1822.
[34] §§ 1684ff. BGB

enforcement. This becomes relevant where a parent who has a good relationship with the child refuses to observe regular appointments or longer holiday arrangements, even if this could be important for the everyday life of the child. However, the duty to contact also has its constitutional limits. When a father has never met the child and completely rejects contact because he fears problems with his family, then weighing the constitutional rights of the father and the child against each other can lead to the result that contact is not enforceable.[35]

Family Violence and Child Neglect

Violence within the Family

There is a general law on the protection against violence in families in Germany (Protection against Violence Act, 2002, in German: *Gewaltschutzgesetz*). The central measures contained in this Act are protection orders and the allocation of a family home. This law will not be dealt with in this chapter. It is often seen as tort law rather than family law, even though these cases come before the family courts. The Act does not apply to violence against children.[36]

Endangerment of the Child

Progressive Measures

The provisions on measures in case of child abuse, neglect[37] or, as the German law says, 'endangerment of the child' show once more, and more than all other regulations in German family law, the strong influence of the basic right of the parents (Art. 6 sec. 2 GG) to exercise parental responsibility without outside interference. The judge fulfils the function of a 'guardian' that the state has been given by Art. 6 sec. 2 GG.

Therefore, the rules do not only seek to take a child out of its family and place it in a home or a foster family. They cover all measures taken to support or protect the child, beginning with the simple instruction to seek public assistance, such as benefits of child and youth welfare and healthcare. This may seem peculiar to a non-German audience, because it would

---

[35] ECLI:DE:BVerfG:2008:rs20080401.1bvr162004.   [36] § 3 of the *Gewaltschutzgesetz*.
[37] §§ 1666, 1666a BGB.

seem like the child protection authorities should be in charge of such matters. However, under the German Constitution, any intervention in parental rights is strictly reserved for the family court. Even seemingly small restrictions such as instructions to apply for a certain benefit – and in fact, the substitution of any declaration given by a parent in the context of parental responsibility – cannot be executed by administrative bodies such as the child protection offices.

The removal of parental responsibility, be it fully or partially, is the last resort in a chain of instruments. Measures that entail a separation of the child from its parents are admissible only if there is a current or imminent danger that cannot be countered in another way, not even through intense public support. The decision to take the child from its parents is subject to constant review. As soon as circumstances permit, the child is returned to the parents.

In recent years, the BVerfG has decided a series of cases regarding § 1666 BGB. These almost always dealt with family courts violating a parent's constitutional right in Art. 6 sec. 2 GG by taking away parental responsibility without adequately clarifying why there was supposedly a current significant danger for the child and that no other less invasive means were available.[38] This has led to great uncertainty in the practice of the family courts, because it gave the impression that the BVerfG had declared the removal of the child from the family as unconstitutional as such in the concrete and partly extreme cases it had decided. Gabriele Britz, judge at the constitutional court, later emphatically explained in an article that the BVerfG was in fact mainly concerned that the correct procedure was complied with.[39] One can only hope that no unnecessary suffering was caused to children of abusive parents through this misunderstanding.

When a child is endangered by its family, but the court does not make a decision protecting the child pursuant to § 1666 BGB, the child is generally also entitled to lodge a constitutional complaint. In a decision from December 2016, the BVerfG clarified that the guardian *ad litem* may represent the child.[40]

---

[38] ECLI:DE:BVerfG:2016:rk20160120.1bvr274215.
[39] G. Britz, 'Kindesgrundrechte und Elterngrundrecht: Fremdunterbringung von Kindern in der verfassungsrechtlichen Kontrolle', FamRZ 10/2015, 793–8, 793.
[40] ECLI:DE:BVerfG:2016:rk20161205.1bvr256916.

This high esteem for parental rights may be understood better if one takes into account that it has two roots. First and foremost, lawyers apply the findings of child psychology and assume that the separation from the parents is so detrimental to the child and has such a negative impact on its development that it will often be less harmful for the child's well-being to grow up with its own, albeit deficient, parents. Additionally, there are historical reasons. The danger of the state arrogating the right to select suitable parents for a child was a reality not only during the National Socialist Period until 1945, but also in the German Democratic Republic until 1989.

Forced Adoption

Adoption without consent of the parents is extremely restricted in Germany. There are narrow rules under which the consent of a parent may be substituted by the court. In short, first, the parent must either have 'persistently grossly violated' their duty to the child or they must be completely indifferent to the child. Second, it is necessary that it would be 'disproportionately disadvantageous' to the child if the adoption did not take place. These adoptions hardly ever happen, although foster families are constantly pointing out how beneficial the stabilisation of the foster relationship by way of adoption would be for the well-being of the child. The constitutional protection of the parental rights excludes a broader practice.[41]

Rights of the Child

It may seem troubling from the outside that the legal position of the child is not expressly stipulated and that the GG does not contain a specific article on children's rights. In particular, the right to apply for protection against or separation from its parents is not regulated. This follows the logic of the Constitution, which is built on the idea that it is the parents' task to protect the rights and the well-being of their children. The child is fully entitled to all human rights in the GG,[42] but the state only supports the child in enforcing these rights where the parents fail to do so to an extent that endangers the child.

---

[41] BVerfG, FamRZ 1968, 578.   [42] *Ibid.*

It is often stressed that the child, even if it had a right to apply for protection against its own parents, would still need to be supported by state bodies. A decision by the BVerfG of 2008 led to a short-lived debate about whether the child can claim its constitutional rights directly against its parents.[43] By now it has become clear that this is not possible.[44] Rather, it is the state that must protect the constitutional rights of the child, also towards the parents.

While the lack of explicit rights does not seem to have led to a worrying lack of protection overall, there has long been a discussion in Germany regarding the integration of an explicit provision on children's rights into the GG. So far, all political initiatives in this regard have been unsuccessful.[45]

Procedure

The role of the child in family proceedings is rather elaborate in Germany. In particular, it is seen as an essential and indispensable element of the proceedings that the judge obtains a direct impression of the child. The judge must talk to the child to try to determine their best interests, their attachments and wishes.[46] These hearings take place with children as young as 3. Normally, the family courts have special rooms for the hearings, in order for the children to feel less intimidated. It is, however, important that the judge is not meant to rely on his or her own impressions alone. In most cases, a guardian *ad litem* is appointed to speak for the child. This happens in particular when the interests of the child cannot be fully represented by their parents because the parents are involved in the court proceedings themselves. Expert witnesses are appointed where a more thorough investigation of the child's psychological and general development is needed. Regulations on the quality and professional qualification of court experts are currently undergoing legislative reform.

---

[43] M. Jestaedt, 'Das Recht des Kindes auf Pflege und Erziehung durch seine Eltern', in D. Coester-Waltjen, V. Lipp, E. Schumann and B. Veit (eds.), *Alles zum Wohle des Kindes?* (Göttingen: Juristische Schriften, 2012) 13–37, 25ff.

[44] F. Wapler, *Kinderrechte und Kindeswohl* (Tübingen: Jus Publicum, 2015) 173.

[45] For details, see A. Röthel, B. Heiderhoff (eds.), 'Mehr Kinderrechte? Nutzen und Nachteil', (Frankfurt a.M., 2018).

[46] ECLI:DE:BVerfG:2008:rk20080627.1bvr031108.

Still, many judges and lawyers call for more expertise within the court itself. It has been suggested that experts in child development (psychologists or psychiatrists) should be added to the panel or to ensure that the judges that are placed in the family courts are more specifically trained.

Marriage and Informal Relationships

Marriage, Registered Partnership, Cohabitation and Divorce

Turning to the law of relationships, it is worth beginning with constitutional rights yet again. Marriage is protected under Art. 6 sec. 1 GG. This provision is understood to grant different types of protection to marriage. It not only protects the individual spouses from state intervention in their marriage, but marriage is also protected as an institution. Historically, this was typically interpreted to mean that the legislator had to ensure that marriage was prioritised over other forms of relationship.[47] As has been mentioned above, the BVerfG has meanwhile expressly and repeatedly stated that it violates the principle of equal treatment laid out in Art. 3 GG to favour marriage over other equivalent partnerships (same-sex civil partnerships) for no objective reason.[48] However, the court has still not overhauled its 2001 decision in which it had made equally clear that marriage is not open to same-sex couples.[49] Opinions in academia are currently divided on this point. The notion that the concept of marriage in the Constitution is transformable and adapts to changes in society seems compelling. The popularity of the opposite view appears to be declining and, so far, no complaint to the BVerfG has been lodged.[50]

Interestingly, the right to get a divorce is also derived from Art. 6 sec. 1 GG. This is because only when one has the right to end a marriage that is no longer functional can there be freedom to start a new genuine marriage.

In Germany, divorce is highly formalised.[51] It is conducted through a court order. Both spouses are obliged to be represented by legal counsel. Only in a consensual divorce, in which all contentious issues are sorted out beforehand, can the couple be represented by one common lawyer. Divorce requires the

---

[47] BVerfG, NJW 1957, 417.   [48] ECLI:DE:BVerfG:2012:rs20120619.2bvr139709.
[49] ECLI:DE: BVerfG:2002:fs20020717.1bvf000101.
[50] D. Kaiser, 'Gleichgeschlechtliche Ehe – nicht ganz gleich und nicht für alle', FamRZ 2017, 1889ff.
[51] See N. Dethloff, *Familienrecht* (32nd edn, Munich: Beck, 2018) 177ff.

conjugal community of the spouses to have been terminated and that the couple has spent the past year living apart (§ 1567 BGB). If only one spouse applies for a divorce and they are unable to prove that the conjugal community of the spouses has definitively ended, the period that has to be spent living apart can go up to three years.

Same-Sex Couples

As has been seen, same-sex marriage was introduced in Germany in 2017. This happened in great haste for reasons of electoral strategy and was, at least in regard to some parts, ill-prepared. Follow-up legislation seems necessary for several issues. However, it is clear that as of 1 October 2017 new civil partnerships cannot be concluded. Under § 20a LPartG, couples living in a civil partnership can choose to convert it into a marriage. Some shortfalls of the civil partnership, such as the impossibility for partners to adopt children together, have now automatically been overcome.

Cohabitation

There are no specific rules for cohabitation ('factual relationships'). For one thing, this is because only marriage is protected in the GG. It is commonly thought that the legislator is prohibited from creating a second institution that would compete with marriage and would serve couples that want to make a binding commitment.[52] There might still be room, though, for some general rules concerning obligations between the partners and the termination of factual relationships. That such laws have not yet been created is often justified by the argument that partners in a factual relationship seek precisely the freedom of living outside of a statutorily regulated structure.[53] This line of argument is only moderately convincing.

Presently, the general rules of the law of obligations and property law govern the division of assets at the end of cohabitation. In 2008, the BGH changed its established jurisprudence and set out that the 'doctrine of frustration' and the rules on unjust enrichment were also applicable in these cases.[54] As a result, a partner who has paid significant amounts of money to the other partner in the expectation that the relationship would continue can seek recourse under

---

[52] ECLI:DE:BVerfG:2002:fs20020717.1bvf000101 para. 103.
[53] See Dethloff, *Familienrecht*, 254.   [54] BGH XII ZR 39/06.

certain circumstances. Many details remain unclear at the time being.[55] It is clear, however, that there are no maintenance obligations between the partners.

Financial Claims at the End of Marriage: Maintenance and Sharing of Accrued Gains

The German system strictly distinguishes between two types of claims at the end of marriage: those securing maintenance (alimony) and those arising out of the marital property regime. Alimony must be paid when one spouse is not able to earn an adequate livelihood in certain, statutorily precisely regulated cases. Claims arising out of marital property regimes are completely independent from this. It is, therefore, theoretically possible that one spouse has to pay alimony while the other is obligated to pay equalisation of accrued gains under the rules of the marital property regime. In reality, until this day, it is typically one spouse, often the husband, that earns well during marriage and acquires property, while the other spouse, usually the wife, gives up their job or at least advances their own career less actively. In these cases, the latter receives equalisation of accrued gains on the one hand and alimony on the other, each according to specific rules described in greater detail below.

Next to alimony and equalisation of accrued gains, there is a third important institution. The adjustment of pension rights is an integral part of all divorce proceedings.[56] All state and private pension rights that have been acquired during marriage are shared at the divorce, such that both spouses obtain equal pension rights.

Community of Accrued Gains for Marriage and Registered Partnership

Overview

The community of accrued gains – *Zugewinngemeinschaft* – is a marital property regime with a confusing name. In fact, it describes a system of separated property, quite unlike the regimes of community of acquisitions

---

[55] For details, see: http://ceflonline.net/wp-content/uploads/Germany-IR.pdf.
[56] For an overview, see A. Dutta, 'Marital agreements and private autonomy in Germany', in J. Scherpe (ed.), *Marital Agreements and Private Autonomy in Comparative Perspective* (Oxford University Press, 2012) 158–99, 162ff.

that are very common on the European continent. When a couple gets married, the spouses' assets remain separate. Unlike the name of the regime suggests, gains accrued during the marriage do not become joint property. Nor are the spouses even significantly restricted as to how they manage and dispose of their assets. It is only when the *Zugewinngemeinschaft* is terminated due to divorce, death of one spouse or a marital agreement, that its effect become apparent: the gains accrued during marriage by each spouse will then be compared, and the spouse who gained more property during marriage will have to share his or her surplus with the other one.

Most couples in Germany accept this default regime. Prenuptial agreements are possible[57] but rare and are mainly concluded when one spouse owns a company or is partner in a company.

It should be mentioned that it is very common for spouses in Germany to jointly own property (in particular, the family home). The rule on the division of household goods in § 1568b BGB even contains the statutory presumption that household goods acquired during the marriage become joint property. However, this happens entirely outside of the matrimonial property regime. When household goods are purchased, the acquisition of property follows the general rules of property law. The spouses are free to agree on joint property,[58] and this is what they generally do. When real estate is purchased by the spouses, they only acquire joint property when this is agreed on in the contract and recorded in the land register.

Basic Ideas and Criticism

The traditional idea behind the system of the community of accrued gains much resembles the idea of other forms of matrimonial property regimes that include elements of real community of property. At its core, it pursues the goal that both partners obtain an equal share in everything that is gained during the marriage.[59] The manner in which the accrued gains are calculated is very generous. This shows that, despite the rejection of community property, the idea of equal participation is actually rather strong.

Though there are no current reform projects underway concerning the *Zugewinngemeinschaft*, voices demanding a general change in the system are growing louder. In 2012, an initiative by the Federal Ministry of Family Affairs, Senior Citizens, Women and Youth was undertaken under the

---

[57] See for limitations ECLI:DE:BVerfG:2001:rs20010206.1bvr001292 para. 3.
[58] Dethloff, *Familienrecht*, 119.   [59] *Ibid.*, 117 f.

ironic title 'Who is afraid of the *"Errungenschaftsgemeinschaft"?*' (the Swiss version of the community of acquired gains).[60]

The criticism appears to have two central points: first, the crucial element of splitting the accrued gains only after the so-called community has ended is questioned. The idea that the assets remain entirely separate during marriage – when the couple typically feels like a unity – is almost paradoxical. Many, if not the majority, of German couples do not realise that their assets are entirely separate. As has been shown, they generally want to acquire goods together. But at the time of divorce, when the marriage has broken down and negative feelings prevail, it will typically cause frustration and incomprehension that the gains must now be shared. The spouse with larger gains will often even try to conceal their gains.

If the death of one spouse leads to the end of the marriage, these frustrations do not occur. In the typical case, the surviving spouse will obtain half of the assets, based on a combination of succession and marital law. Whether this is too much or too little is a highly debated question.[61]

On a more general level, some authors have pointed out that the idea of sharing the accrued gains may not always suit modern marriages, in which both spouses work – in particular when they have no children.

All in all, one cannot overlook that the *Zugewinngemeinschaft* is not psychologically convincing, nor does the general population even understand the system.

Details

Effects during Marriage

The community of accrued gains hardly has any effect during the marriage. There are only two restraints for the spouses concerning disposal. The first one concerns the disposition of the 'assets as a whole' (§ 1365 BGB), which includes the disposition of a single item as long as its value exceeds 90 per cent of the total assets.[62] The second concerns the disposition of household objects (§ 1369 BGB). The disposal of both types of goods is only possible

---

[60] G. Brudermüller, B. Dauner-Lieb and S. Meder, (eds.), *Wer hat Angst vor der Errungenschaftsgemeinschaft?* (Göttingen: V&R Unipress, 2013).
[61] For more detail, see Coester-Waltjen, *Familienrecht*, 432ff.; A. Röthel, 'Ist unser Erbrecht noch zeitgemäß?', in *Verhandlungen des 68. Deutschen Juristentages Berlin 2010* (Munich: Beck, 2010), vol. I, 52ff.
[62] Dethloff, *Familienrecht*, 120.

with the consent of the other spouse. The underlying purpose of these rules is the preservation of the living conditions of the couple, which should not be jeopardised by the decision of just one of the spouses. Additionally, § 1365 BGB is generally considered to aim at securing the possible compensation claims that one of the spouses may have at the end of the property regime.[63]

Effects and Procedure at the End of the Marriage

At the end of the marriage, in a first step, the accrued gains of the spouses are ascertained and compared. Each spouse can demand disclosure from the other under § 1379 BGB. In a second step, the difference between the values of the assets the spouse owned when they entered into the marriage and the value of their assets at the end of it is determined. The accrued gains are calculated by simply subtracting the original assets from the final assets (§ 1373 BGB). The increase in value in both spouses' assets is then compared in order to measure the difference. Finally, the spouse whose assets have increased in value less during the time of the marriage is entitled to claim payment of half of the difference in gains of the other. As a result, both spouses participate equally in the gains that were accrued by either of them during the marriage.[64] The compensation is paid in money; no items are transferred. It is one of the main characteristics of the *Zugewinngemeinschaft* that interference with property rights is kept to a minimum.[65]

§ 1374 BGB gives some guidelines as to which assets are to be considered initial assets, while § 1375 BGB contains the rules for assessing the final assets. Under § 1374 sec. 1 BGB, the original or 'initial' assets are defined as the assets that belong to a spouse at the beginning of the matrimonial property regime. More importantly, § 1374 sec. 2 BGB stipulates that any acquisition by succession or by donation during the marriage must also be regarded as part of the original assets. As a result, these legacies or gifts are not considered part of the accrued gains as calculated under the simple method of subtraction described above.[66]

The final assets generally comprise all assets held by the spouse at the termination of the community of accrued gains. Only in exceptional cases is a certain amount added to the existing assets. The value of

---

[63] Coester-Waltjen, *Familienrecht*, 376.   [64] Schwab, *Familienrecht*, 91.
[65] Dethloff, *Familienrecht*, 118.   [66] *Ibid.*, 132ff.

dispositions by one spouse that were made gratuitously, to squander property or to intentionally disadvantage the other spouse is added to the final total of assets of the spouse who made the dispositions (§ 1375 sec. 2 BGB).

The allocation of household goods and of the family home is not regulated within the framework of the matrimonial property regime. Rules concerning those assets can be found in § 1568a (for the family home) and § 1568b BGB (for movables). These provisions ensure that the spouse who depends more on the items – taking the best interests of the children living in the household into account – may generally demand that the other spouse transfer these items to them.[67] However, the transfer of property of a house or apartment may only be mandated in cases of hardship. In any case, a suitable financial compensation is due.

Maintenance after Divorce (Alimony)

After a marriage ends, the principle of personal responsibility is applicable. Alimony is only owed after a divorce when a specific statutory claim is applicable. One of the most important cases regards childcare.

It can be observed that the wording in the regulation of support for childcare for a divorced parent is almost identical to the provisions regarding support for childcare for a parent taking care of a child born out of wedlock. In both cases, the caretaking parent may claim support during the first three years. After that she (or he) must start working again, except under special circumstances. This parallelism was demanded by the BVerfG, because it deemed the length of support payments to the caretaking parent to have an indirect effect on the child. The equal treatment of children born in and out of wedlock could only be guaranteed if the parent's right to support was identical.[68]

Further claims for maintenance can result from sickness or high age. The so-called top-up maintenance is also important (§ 1573 sec. 1 sentence 2 BGB). A spouse can claim such maintenance when he or she does not have sufficient income despite having returned to work. What is considered sufficient is not specified in absolute numbers in the law of alimony, but rather depends on the marital standard of living (§ 1578 BGB). Thus, it depends on the amount of income that the couple had while being together.

---

[67] Schwab, *Familienrecht*, 213.   [68] ECLI:DE:BVerfG:2007:ls20070228.1bvl000904.

If one spouse stopped working during the marriage and resumes working after the marriage has ended, the actual income earned by the other spouse is – in some cases – increased by a fictitious amount that the unemployed spouse could have earned. It is clear that the spouse responsible for maintenance will often not be able to pay the 'sufficient' support in full. A chart containing the minimum living wages that any maintenance debtor may keep for himself is regularly updated and provided to courts and lawyers. Currently, the minimum monthly amount for the debtor to keep for himself is €1,200. This amount is dynamic and responds to increases in income.

Child maintenance is regarded as a separate matter. It is part of maintenance for relatives. Here, the central rule stipulates that direct relatives owe each other maintenance payments – this also includes children's obligation towards their parents. Often, this can turn into quite a liability once the parents are old and in need of care. Parents have increased obligations towards their minor children. The minimum monthly amount for the parent to keep is lower and there is an obligation to earn the necessary money, if possible. Siblings do not have maintenance claims against each other.

Epilogue: Gender and Autonomy

Much has now been said on the constitutionalisation of family law, on children's rights, parents' rights and on equal treatment. In the final part of this chapter, we will shift the perspective and investigate two remaining fundamental issues. How does German family law deal with gender and with autonomy? Both are intrinsically linked.

Starting with autonomy, one will realise that modern family law aims to leave room for autonomy. The abolition of incapacitation in 1992 is symbolic of this. Nowadays, the law aspires to support adults who are unable to safeguard their own affairs while preserving as much autonomy as possible. Still, many issues, such as parentage and adoption, remain firmly in state hands. An examination of the constitutional right of parents to exercise parental responsibility in Art. 6 sec. 2 GG, in regard to the autonomy contained therein, shows that the scope of freedom for parents is extensive. At its core, Art. 6 sec. 2 GG is intended to give parents freedom in exercising their parental responsibility. To what degree the parent's freedom also includes physical interventions has been much discussed lately. In 2012, a law was introduced that expressly allows the circumcision of boys, as long as it is performed following state-of-the-art medical practice. Currently, the issue of gender reassignments of the child and the role of courts and parents in this process are beginning to be debated.[69] No matter which subject is at stake, the main objective of parental responsibility must always be the well-being of the child. Autonomy ends where the child is acutely endangered.

There has to be even more leeway where there is no child involved is in need of protection and only the relationship of two grown-ups is affected, as is the case with marriage or same-sex civil partnership. Against this background it is noteworthy that a divorce requires one year of separation and can only be declared by a court. There are also limiting stipulations within marriage. While the barring for persons of same sex has now been abolished, the fact that three people cannot enter into one marriage is a limitation. In 2017, the strict legal age of 18 for marriage was introduced. Further, according to the majority opinion, the obligation to marital fidelity cannot be contractually waived.

The way in which the law deals with cases where the spouses' bargaining positions are unequal deserves closer inspection. If one is to understand the issue of gender in a broad sense, so that it also includes the relationship of men and women, then this is not only an issue of autonomy, but also a gender issue. It is generally said that German family law is based on a gender-neutral statutory concept. In theory, this is a convincing approach. However, it does not come without complications, as there are areas in which women are de facto in need of more protection than men.[70]

The development of content control of prenuptial agreements is instructive. The BVerfG declared the jurisprudence of the BGH unconstitutional, which said that prenuptial agreements where valid even when they severely disadvantaged one spouse.[71] The court particularly stressed the spouses' inequality at the time of the conclusion of the contract: 'A position of inferiority is to be assumed whenever an unmarried pregnant woman is confronted with the alternative of either caring for the expected child on her own or of involving the child's father in the care by marrying him, even

---

[69] A. Röthel, 'Autonomie im Familienrecht der Gegenwart', JZ (Juristenzeitung) 2017 116ff.
[70] H. Saygin, *Geschlechtergerechtigkeit unter dem Deckmantel der Leitbildneutralität* (Frankfurt am Main: Peter Lang, 2016).
[71] ECLI:DE:BVerfG:2001:rs20010206.1bvr001292.

if this comes at the price of a prenuptial agreement with him that severely disadvantages her.' The court substantiated the problem with sociological studies regarding the situation of single mothers. Does this diminish the spouses' autonomy? In Germany, the decision is generally regarded to do the exact opposite: the court's goal was to strengthen the woman's autonomy. Art. 2 sec. 1 GG includes freedom of contract. This (also) means substantive freedom of contract – the opportunity to agree on what is actually wanted. If one party does not have this freedom because she is in an inferior negotiation position and thus does not have influence on the content of the contract, the law must assist this contractual party. In regard to autonomy, it must be considered an improvement that the content of prenuptial agreements is examined when one spouse was in an inferior negotiating position.[72]

Finally, we should take a quick look at the obvious questions of gender categories in the narrow sense. Trans- and intersexuality is of particular relevance here. While the laws on transsexuality (Act on Transsexuals, in German: *Transsexuellengesetz* = TSG) have already had some time to develop, and were, in fact, amended several times in order to comply with fundamental rights, intersexuality is a younger topic and important questions remain to be answered.

As far as transgenderism is concerned, the milestone decision of the BVerfG from 2011,[73] abolishing the necessity of an operation, has already been mentioned above. To this day, the law is criticised by some, however, because it still demands court proceedings in which the transperson must submit two expert statements confirming that he or she has been under the 'compulsion' to live as the other gender for at least three years, pursuant to §§ 9 sec. 3, 4 sec. 3 TSG.

Regarding intersexuality, the personal statute law had been changed in 2013, allowing the gender indication to be left blank. It is also possible to have the indication erased later. While the BGH had rejected the possibility for persons who do not identify as either male or female to register a third gender.[74] The BVerfG overhauled this judgment in 2017, holding that the German law infringes the general right of personality protected by Art. 2 sec. 1 GG by only giving the choices male, female or opting for the option 'no entry'.[75] The court argued that gender identity is of paramount

---

[72] Dutta, 'Marital agreements', 174ff. [73] ECLI:DE:BVerfG:2011:rs20110111.1bvr329507.
[74] ECLI:DE:BGH:2016:220616BXIIZB52.15.0.
[75] ECLI:DE:BVerfG:2017:rs20171010.1bvr201916.

importance for a person's self-conception as well as for how a person is perceived by others. The legislator must therefore either entirely dispense with information on gender or provide for a third positive option by the end of 2018. Renouncing gender categories completely (concerning such terms as husband, wife, father and mother as legally relevant terms) has occasionally been discussed in doctrine and could be a great step forward. However, this would be rather revolutionary and seems politically unlikely.[76]

In summary, we can see that the modernisation of German family law is advancing under the influence of the GG and the BVerfG interpreting it, and while it has not exactly been a steady process, it has overall been quite continuous.

Abbreviations

AG	Amtsgericht
BGBl.	Bundesgesetzblatt
BGH	Bundesgerichtshof
BT-Drs.	Bundestagsdrucksache
BVerfG	Bundesverfassungsgericht
FamRZ	*Zeitschrift für das gesamte Familienrecht*
KG	Kammergericht
NJW	*Neue Juristische Wochenschrift*
OLG	Oberlandesgericht
ZfPW	*Zeitschrift für die gesamte Privatrechtswissenschaft*

---

[76] The current proposal suggests the word "*divers*" (BT-Drs. 19/4669).

4 Australian Family Property Law

Current Issues and Challenges

Belinda Fehlberg and Lisa Sarmas*

1 Introduction

There are several reasons why it seems important to focus on Australian family property law now. In May 2017, the Australian Federal Attorney General announced a major review of the family law system, to be undertaken by the Australian Law Reform Commission. The inquiry is now underway, and the final report is due by 31 March 2019. The Inquiry's widely cast terms of reference include 'the underlying substantive rules and general law principles in relation to ... property'.[1] Inclusion of property is significant given that Australian family property law has not been the subject of major law reform proposals since 1999.[2] Lack of law reform attention has been striking – and concerning given that the adverse economic consequences of separation and divorce for women in the short and longer term continue to be identified by Australian empirical research (section 3.1),[3] and are known to be particularly

---

* Thanks to Shazia Choudhry, John Eekelaar, Rosemary Hunter, Rae Kaspiew, Mavis Maclean, Jo Miles, Patrick Parkinson and Lisa Young for valuable conversations, suggestions and feedback throughout the course of writing this chapter.
[1] George Brandis, Attorney General for Australia, 'Transforming the family law system', media release, 9 May 2017 and 'First comprehensive review of the Family Law Act', media release, 27 September 2017. At the time of writing, a Discussion Paper had been released (Australian Law Reform Commission, Review of the Family Law System, Discussion Paper No 86 (2018)) stating that, 'on balance, the ALRC did not consider that the case had been made out for a shift from a discretionary system to a prescriptive system before further research is undertaken about property division on relationship breakdown' (p 61). The ALRC suggested amendments to improve the clarity of the legislation and to clarify the relevance of family violence to property settlements and to the future needs of those experiencing family violence (pp 61–64).
[2] Commonwealth of Australia, *Property and Family Law: Options for Change. A Discussion Paper* (Canberra: Commonwealth of Australia, 1999). On earlier proposals for reform, see Margaret Harrison, 'Matrimonial property reform' (1992) 31 *Family Matters* 18.
[3] e.g. Davis De Vaus, Matthew Gray, Lixia Qu and David Stanton, 'The economic consequences of divorce in Australia' (2014) 28 *International Journal of Law, Policy and the Family* 26.

serious for some groups of women, especially mothers with dependent children (but also older divorced mothers whose children are no longer dependent: a smaller group that has received less research focus),[4] victims of family violence[5] and women leaving low asset relationships.[6] While private transfers alone cannot be expected to fully resolve post-separation poverty[7] ('people who divorce have substantially lower incomes, assets, and employment rates pre-divorce than people who remain married',[8] two households will be more expensive to run than one, and commonly pre-separation family arrangements will result in one party having a much reduced income earning capacity), property division in Australian family law remains an important strategy for reducing post-separation financial disadvantage.[9] Clearly, in order to maximise the potential of this strategy, law and the family law system[10] need to be

---

[4] Susan Feldman and Harriet Radermacher, *Time of* Our Lives: Building Opportunity and Capacity for the Economic and Social Participation of Older *Australian* Women (Melbourne: Lord Mayor's Charitable Foundation, 2016)21-2; Bruce Smyth and Ruth Weston, *Financial* Living Standards *after* Divorce: A Recent Snapshot, Research Report no. 23 (Melbourne: Australian Institute of Family Studies, 2000). In Britain, see Mike Brewer and Alita Nandi, *Partnership Dissolution: How Does It Affect Income, Employment and Well-being?* (ISER Working Paper Series, paper no. 2014-30, University of Essex, Institute for Social and Economic Research, 2014).

[5] Grania Sheehan and Bruce Smyth, 'Spousal violence and post-separation financial outcomes' (2000) 14 *Australian Journal of Family Law* 102; Emma Smallwood, *Stepping Stones*: Legal Barriers to Economic Equality after Family Violence (Melbourne: Women's Legal Service Victoria, 2015); Rae Kaspiew and Lixia Qu, 'Property division after separation: Recent research evidence' (2016) 30 *Australian Journal of Family Law* 1. See also *A Better Family Law System to Support and Protect Those Affected by Family Violence*, Report of the Parliamentary Inquiry into a Better Family Law System to Support and Protect Those Affected by Family Violence, Standing Committee on Social Policy and Legal Issues, House of Representatives (Canberra: Parliament of Australia, 2017) ch. 5.

[6] It should be noted that most separating spouses and de facto partners have low or modest property to divide (section 3), and receipt of a just and equitable share of available property remains important in a context where every dollar counts. This issue is currently the focus of an Australian research project: Women's Legal Service Victoria, 'Small claims, large battles: Improving access to justice for women with small property claims in family law', Project being conducted 2016-17 and funded by Victorian Legal Services Board.

[7] Raising questions regarding the extent of individual ('local'), partner ('horizontal') and State ('vertical') responsibility: Joanna Miles, 'Responsibility in family finance and property law' in Jo Bridgman, Heather M Keating and Craig Lind, *Regulating Family Responsibilities* (Farnham: Ashgate, 2011) 92.

[8] De Vaus *et al.*, 'Economic consequences of divorce in Australia', 42.

[9] Belinda Fehlberg, Christine Millward and Monica Campo, 'Post-separation parenting arrangements, child support and property settlement: Exploring the connections' (2010) 24 *Australian Journal of Family Law* 214.

[10] While not our focus in this chapter, it is clear that many women in Australia cannot pursue property settlements due to paucity of legal aid for family property matters and absence of

accessible and responsive. After many years of significant research, policy and law reform focus on post-separation parenting law and process[11] (including the relevance of family violence and abuse in this context,[12] along with the operation of the Child Support Program),[13] it is timely to also reflect on the operation of the current Australian family property regime.

In this chapter, we therefore focus on the broad discretion under Australia's Family Law Act 1975 (Cth) (FLA) to reallocate interests in property of spouses and separating de facto partners.[14] We look at previous empirical research on the discretion's operation and consider options for change. We identify that there is an absence of up-to-date empirical research data on the discretion's operation, and that there is potential risk and possibly limited effect associated with legislative reform in this area. Yet the consistent empirical research finding that women, particularly mothers with dependent[15] children, experience significant economic disadvantage post-separation leads us to see some merit in legislative reform to address this concern and thus increase the likelihood of outcomes that are more fundamentally consistent with the key legislative

---

avenues other than courts and lawyers for resolving cases involving low assets: see Women's Legal Service Victoria, 'Small claims, large battles'.

[11] Following amendments in 2006 to encourage separated parents to share the care of children: Family Law Amendment (Shared Parental Responsibility) Act 2006 (Cth). See further, B. Fehlberg, R. Kaspiew, F. Kelly, J. Millbank and J. Behrens, *Australian Family Law: The Contemporary Context* (2nd edn, Oxford University Press, 2015) 192-6, 201-4.

[12] *Ibid.*

[13] Most recently, see Parliament of Australia, House of Representatives Committees, Standing Committee on Social Policy and Legal Affairs, *From Conflict to Cooperation: Inquiry into the Child Support Program* (Canberra: Parliament of Australia, 2015); *Australian Government response to the House of Representatives Standing Committee on Social Policy and Legal Affairs report: From Conflict to Cooperation - Inquiry into the Child Support Program*, tabled in the House of Representatives 5 September 2016.

[14] 'De facto relationship' for the FLA is defined as a couple (different sex or same sex), who are not legally married to each other, are not related by family, and have had 'a relationship as a couple living together on a genuine domestic basis' (s. 4AA(1)). For financial orders, the FLA also requires a de facto relationship of at least two years' duration, a child of the relationship or that a party has made substantial contributions such that a failure to make an order would lead to serious injustice (s. 90SB). See further Fehlberg *et al.*, *Australian Family Law*, 20-2, 91-8, 495-6.

[15] Which we define as children of the parties aged under 18, and children of the parties aged over 18 who are completing their education or have a mental or physical disability (consistent with FLA s. 66L which provides for court-ordered maintenance for children over 18 in these circumstances). While the current financial provisions of the FLA refer only to children of the parties aged under 18 (e.g. ss. 72(1) and 75(2)), we consider that an extension paralleling s. 66L is warranted.

requirement that 'The court shall not make an order ... unless it is satisfied that, in all the circumstances, it is just and equitable to make the order' (FLA s. 79(2)/90SM(3)).

2 Existing Framework

The starting point for Australian family property law is a separate property regime, under which no automatic co-ownership arises from being married or in a de facto relationship.[16] Under the FLA, judges have considerable power to reallocate interests in property of spouses and of separating de facto partners.[17] First, 'property' is defined broadly, to mean property to which the parties, or either of them, 'are entitled, whether in possession or reversion' (FLA s. 4(1)) and has been given a broad construction by the family law courts.[18] Second, the jurisdiction of courts under the FLA extends to all of the property of the parties at the date of the trial, whether acquired before their relationship began, during their relationship or after their relationship ended.[19] Third, the discretion to alter interests of the

---

[16] In contrast to an immediate (or full) community property regime, in which 'property defined as being matrimonial and acquired during marriage is immediately and automatically owned equally by husband and wife throughout the marriage, and each takes an equal share if the marriage ends' (Harrison, 'Matrimonial property reform', 19).

[17] The requirement of relationship breakdown in the case of de facto partners (but not spouses: *Stanford* v. *Stanford* (2012) 247 CLR 108) reflects the terms of the referral of powers from the state to the Commonwealth, which provided the basis for the federal Parliament to legislate in 2009. A referral of power was required due to the marriage-focused content of the federal Parliament's legislative power under s. 51 of the Constitution: Commonwealth of Australia Constitution Act (The Constitution), s. 51 (xxi), (xxii), (xxxvii).

[18] The case often cited for this point is *In the Marriage of Duff* [1977] FLC 90–217: the Full Court of the Family Court of Australia (the Full Court) gave its support to a broad definition of 'property' found in *Jones* v. *Skinner*, an old English case: 'Property is the most comprehensive of all terms which can be used inasmuch as it is indicative and descriptive of every possible interest which the party can have' ((1835) 5 LJ Ch 90 cited in *In the Marriage of Duff*, 133). The Full Court considered that 'property' for the FLA extended to real and personal property, and choses in action (i.e. property that comprises a bundle of rights but has no physical form – e.g. company shares).

[19] This is in contrast to the more limited definition of matrimonial property in many other jurisdictions, including Scotland, New Zealand and British Columbia. In Scotland, for example, 'matrimonial property' for the purposes of the 'sharing principle' (but not the remaining four principles) does not include property acquired by the parties before their relationship began (unless acquired 'for use by them as a family home or as furniture or

parties in their property is cast very broadly. Specifically, the legislation provides that, 'In property settlement proceedings, the court may make such order as it considers *appropriate* ... altering the interests of the parties to the marriage in the property' (s. 79(1)(a) (spouses); s. 90SM(1)(a) (de factos)). The FLA further provides that, 'The court shall not make an order under this section unless it is satisfied that, in all the circumstances, it is *just and equitable* to make the order' (s. 79(2) (spouses), s. 90SM(2)(a) (de factos)) (emphases added).

The legislation includes some guidance regarding the exercise of discretion, by means of a checklist of factors that 'the court shall take into account' in 'considering what order (if any) should be made' (s. 79(4) (spouses); s. 90SM(4) (de factos)). The list refers first to contributions (financial and non-financial, direct and indirect) made by or on behalf of the parties to property of either or both of them (including property they have ceased to own since making the contribution) and to the welfare of their family. The list then refers to additional factors relating to the parties' respective futures (in particular, s. 79(4)(e), incorporating s. 75(2) (spouses); s. 90SM(4), incorporating s. 90SF(3) (de factos); these factors are also relevant to spousal and de facto maintenance, which can be ordered if the respondent has the capacity to pay and the applicant (usually female) is unable to support herself adequately (s. 72(1) (spouses); s. 90SF(1) (de factos)). Responsibility for care of children of the parties under age 18 is included as a factor relevant to the parties' financial futures.

The physical structure of the legislation thus *encourages* (but does not *require*) contributions to property to be considered first (an encouragement reinforced by the inclusion of two property-related contributions, followed by only one in relation to contributions to the welfare of the family), followed by needs (mainly through reference to the additional factors). Our point here is that the ordering of the list encourages a perception that contributions to property are the first concern, a point backed up by jurisprudence: judgments most commonly involve consideration of contributions before needs. Express consideration of compensation for costs of investing in the relationship or to enable loss sharing more broadly is possible but much rarer.[20] The form of the legislation is thus in marked contrast to the position in England and Wales under the Matrimonial Causes

---

plenishings for such home'), after their cohabitation ended, or 'by way of gift or succession from a third party' (Family Law (Scotland) Act 1985, ss. 9 and 10).

[20] *Waters & Jurek* [1995] FamCA 101.

Act 1973, where one list of factors applies to determine property and spousal maintenance disputes and the needs of minor children are the 'first consideration' to which the court must have regard (s. 25(1)); matters relating to the parties' futures, their contributions, and questions of fault are also to be considered (s. 25(2)).

In 2012 in *Stanford* v. *Stanford*,[21] the High Court of Australia underlined the breadth of the s. 79 discretion, encouraging increased uncertainty regarding how it would be exercised from case to case. The Court emphasised the centrality of the requirement in FLA s. 79(2) that it must be 'just and equitable' for a court to make a property settlement order, while also conveying the amplitude of that expression:

The expression 'just and equitable' is a qualitative description of a conclusion reached after examination of a range of potentially competing considerations. It does not admit of exhaustive definition. It is not possible to chart its metes and bounds.[22]

Stanford reminded family law courts of the requirement to determine whether it is just and equitable to make *any* order departing from existing interests in property (although the High Court indicated that 'in many cases' involving separation the requirement would be 'readily satisfied', as 'there is not and will not thereafter be the common *use* of property by the husband and wife' (Court's emphasis)).[23] The High Court also underlined that the 'just and equitable' requirement is fundamental to *the* property orders (if any) that are made. More broadly, at least in decisions of the Full Court of the Family Court of Australia (Full Court), *Stanford*'s emphasis on the centrality of the 'just and equitable' requirement has discouraged the use of formulaic approaches that may risk predetermining the outcome.[24] The impact of the latter message has been seen, for example, in the Full Court's abandonment of the 'doctrine of special skill' (which accorded

---

[21] (2012) 247 CLR 108. The case has been applied to de facto property disputes (*Watson & Ling* [2013] FamCA 57).

[22] *Ibid*. [36].

[23] *Ibid*. [42]. So far, *Stanford* has had greatest impact in less usual fact scenarios, for example a spousal relationship that had not broken down (*Stanford* v. *Stanford* (2012)), representations by a husband to a wife during their relationship that the property is hers along with delay in pursuing his property claim (*Bevan & Bevan* [2013] FamCAFC 116), and relationships without children in which parties have maintained separate finances, and one has made significantly greater contributions than the other (*Watson & Ling* [2013] FamCA 57; *Elford & Elford* [2016] FamCAFC 45).

[24] See further, Fehlberg *et al*., *Australian Family Law*, 548–73.

special recognition to 'stellar' income earners in cases involving very high assets),[25] and increased ambivalence regarding formulaic approaches where property has been dissipated by a party before trial[26] and in relation to property acquired pre and post-relationship.[27]

Before *Stanford*, the suggestion had sometimes been made that fundamental legislative reform to limit the breadth of the discretion afforded by s. 79 should be considered.[28] Detailed consideration of the possibility of legislative reform last occurred at the governmental level in 1999,[29] when the federal Attorney General's Department released a discussion paper suggesting two options for reform of family property law, the first involving the introduction of a legislative starting point of equal contributions and the second involving a starting point of equal sharing of property accumulated by spouses during their marriage. Neither proposal gained much support so no fundamental change to property division under the FLA occurred.

Following *Stanford*, discussion regarding the breadth of discretion afforded by s. 79/90SM has again been evident.[30] In 2014 the Productivity Commission, an independent Commonwealth review and advisory agency on federal government microeconomic policy and regulation, looked briefly at family property law and recommended a presumption of equal sharing in its report *Access to Justice*

---

[25] *Hoffman & Hoffman* [2014] FamCAFC 92, para. 52: '[T]here is no principle or guideline (or indeed anything else emerging from s. 79), that renders the direct contribution of income or capital more important – or "special" – when compared against indirect contributions and, in particular, contributions to the home or the welfare of the family.'

[26] *Bevan & Bevan* [2013], para. 79; cf. *Vass & Vass* [2015] FamCAFC 51, paras. 135–40.

[27] *Dickons & Dickons* [2012] FamCAFC 154, paras. 20-2; *Marsh & Marsh* [2014] FamCAFC 24, paras. 62–7, 107.

[28] e.g. Patrick Parkinson, 'Unfinished business: Reforming the law of property division' (2000) 14(4) *Australian Family Lawyer* 1.

[29] Commonwealth of Australia, *Property and Family Law: Options for Change*. Change along similar lines was proposed in 1987 and 1992. See further Harrison, 'Matrimonial property reform' and Parkinson, 'Unfinished business'. See also: Rosemary Hunter, 'Decades of panic' (2005) 10 *Griffith Review* (pages not numbered), https://griffithreview.com/edition-10-family-politics/decades-of-panic

[30] See in particular Patrick Parkinson, 'Why are decisions on family property so inconsistent?' (2016) 90 *Australian Law Journal* 418. In terms consistent with his pre-*Stanford* concerns, Parkinson argues that the law on family property in Australia is 'plagued with uncertainty at its very core' for reasons including 'the lack of objects and principles in the legislation'. He concludes that 'The best option is statutory reform' (p. 523).

Arrangements.[31] It is possible that renewed interest post-*Stanford* was a temporary 'blip' as the implications of the decision were digested. However, the many years that have passed since fundamental property law reform was last considered in Australia, the impact of *Stanford*, at least in the Full Court, and the review into the family law system now being conducted by the Australian Law Reform Commission[32] suggest value in reflecting on the current operation of the discretion and whether there is a case for change.

3 The Overarching 'Just and Equitable' Requirement (s. 79(2)): Are 'Just and Equitable' Outcomes Being Achieved?

As noted in section 2, the High Court in *Stanford* emphasised that the 'just and equitable' requirement must be satisfied before the court can make *any* order altering property interests and further, that this requirement informs *the* orders made (if any). The Court provided very little guidance as to the substantive meaning of 'just and equitable', but it is clear that the requirement will not be satisfied by reference merely to the factors set out in s. 79(4)/90SM(4). Indeed, it is not essential that these factors be considered at all in determining the threshold question whether it is 'just and equitable' for any order to be made.[33]

It is perhaps surprising that the content and meaning of the 'just and equitable' requirement is relatively undeveloped in Australian family law jurisprudence. The answer partly lies in the pre-*Stanford* tendency to conclude that it was just and equitable to make an order under s 79(2) if matters referred to in s 79(4) were evident – an approach the High Court rejected: 'The requirements of the two sub-sections are not to be conflated.'[34] In our view, further development and articulation of the 'just and equitable' requirement provides an existing legislative basis for

---

[31] Productivity Commission, *Access to Justice Arrangements: Volume 2*, Inquiry Report No. 72 (Canberra: Australian Government, Productivity Commission, 2014) 874. The Commission made no reference to *Stanford*.
[32] Brandis, 'Transforming the family law system'; and 'First comprehensive review of the Family Law Act'.
[33] *Chapman & Chapman* [2014] FamCAFC 91, para. 25.
[34] *Stanford* v. *Stanford* (2012), para. 35.

the development of principled and appropriate family property law outcomes.

A sensible first step in attempting to articulate the substantive content of the 'just and equitable' requirement is to consider what the available empirical research evidence tells us about the economic consequences of separation and divorce on the basis of the law as it stands, and the relevance of law to those outcomes. To that end, we first look at the broader socio-economic context in which Australian family property law operates, before considering what existing research tells us about property division in the separating population. We then consider research on approaches of family lawyers to property division, and the available research on adjudicated property cases. A key theme to emerge is that we lack current empirical data about the relevance and impact of the current legislation in the way property is divided in all these contexts. However, the available empirical data demonstrates the significant economic disadvantage experienced by women after separation – particularly mothers with dependent children – and suggests that their interests are attracting insufficient attention in Australian family property law, a pattern which also has negative consequences for children.

3.1 The Socio-economic Context

The broader empirical context for our analysis, which focuses on the operation of family property law, is ongoing empirical work indicating disproportionate poverty rates for women and children in Australia,[35] and adverse economic consequences of separation and divorce for women, particularly women with dependent children. Indeed, the most recent data[36] suggests that this overall pattern has not changed since the 1980s,

---

[35] Australian Council of Social Service, *Poverty in Australia 2016*; De Vaus et al., 'Economic consequences of divorce in Australia'.

[36] While there is US research suggesting that over time the position for women experiencing relationship separation has improved for reasons including women's increased paid employment after having children and after relationships end, most is some years older than the Australian research discussed in our chapter. We also note recent UK research finding that after separation, 'the costs of divorce have been mitigated for women over time and more recent divorces have not led to the same falls in household income as earlier divorces' (Hayley Fisher and Hamish Low, 'Who wins, who loses and who recovers from divorce?', in Joanna Miles and Rebecca Probert (eds.), *Sharing Lives, Dividing Assets* (Oxford: Hart, 2009) 255). However, in this and a more recent article Fisher and Low find

the consistent finding in Australia (and other western countries, including the United Kingdom) being that 'the financial impact of divorce is greater for women than it is for men'.[37]

More broadly, a 2016 report *Poverty in Australia* conducted by the Australian Council of Social Service found that women are more likely than men to live in poverty as a result of their 'lower employment rates and lower wages ... and a greater caring role both for children and for other family members'.[38] The report also found that 'poverty in lone parent households has increased from 25.7% in 2003-04 to 29.1% in 2013-14'[39] and that the percentage of children living in poverty in Australia is increasing (17.4 per cent), with 40.6 per cent of children in sole parent households living in poverty.[40] The authors of the report concluded that

> that the financial impact of divorce continues to be greater for women than for men, that women's recovery is mainly the result of re-partnering (with women's likelihood of re-partnering being less than men's) and that, 'There is no significant response in labour supply for men or for women' (Hayley Fisher and Hamish Low, 'Recovery from divorce: Comparing high and low income couples' (2016) 30 *International Journal of Law, Policy and the Family* 338, 339). For US examples, see Matthew McKeever and Nicholas H. Wolfinger, 'Shifting fortunes in a changing economy: Trends in the economic well-being of divorced women', in L. Kowaleski-Jones and N. H. Wolfinger (eds.), *Fragile Families and the Marriage Agenda* (New York: Springer, 2005) 127-57; Sanford L. Braver, Jenessa R. Shapiro and Matthew R. Goodman, 'The consequences of divorce for parents', in Mark A. Fine and John H. Harvey (eds.), *Handbook of Divorce and Relationship Dissolution*, New Jersey: Lawrence Erlbaum, 2005); Christopher R. Tamborini, Kenneth A. Couch and Gayle L. Reznik, 'Long-term impact of divorce on women's earnings across multiple divorce windows: A life course perspective' (2015) 26 *Advances in Life Course Research* 44.

[37] Fisher and Low, 'Recovery from divorce', 338. See further, Richard Neely, 'The primary caretaker parent rule: Child custody and the dynamics of greed' (1984) 3 *Yale Law and Policy Review* 168, 179; A. Sørenson, 'Estimating the economic consequences of separation and divorce: A cautionary tale from the United States', in Lenore Weitzman and Mavis Maclean (eds.), *The Economic Consequences of Divorce: The International Perspective* (Oxford: Clarendon Press, 1991); Ruth Weston, 'Changes in household income circumstances' in Peter McDonald (ed.), *Settling Up: Property and Income Distribution in Australia* (Sydney: Prentice-Hall of Australia, 1986) 100. See also Gavin Wood, Chris Chamberlain, Alpherin Babacan, Mike Dockery, Grant Cullen, Greg Costello, Andi Nygaard, Alice Stoakes, Marc Adam and Kate Moloney, *The Implications of Loss of a Partner for Older Private Renters* (Report No. 16, Melbourne: Australian Housing and Urban Research Institute, 2008) 41, 89 (finding that after relationships end, women are also more likely than men to lose home ownership status, 'a finding that seems contrary to popular perception').

[38] Australian Council of Social Service, *Poverty in Australia 2016*, 32.   [39] Ibid., 19.
[40] Ibid., 22.

The high rate of poverty experienced by children in lone parent households is a result of high rates of poverty among lone parent households overall.[41]

Most lone parent households are female-headed: in Australia, '[t]here were 780 thousand single mother families in June 2012, making up the vast majority of one parent families (81%)'.[42]

While lone parent households do not always arise from parental separation, nearly half (48 per cent in 2015) of divorces in Australia involve children aged under 18, and following divorce most children live for most of the time with their mothers (97 per cent).[43] There is therefore a close connection between women's and children's poverty and the negative economic consequences of divorce for women and children, and this has been identified over many years now in Australian research. This includes recent analysis by Davis De Vaus and colleagues of data from the first ten years of an ongoing panel survey of Australian families, 'to estimate the impact of divorce (a term they used to include de facto separation) on income and assets'[44] for separating men and women aged under 55 years. De Vaus and colleagues found that women experienced a fall in income post-divorce while men experienced a significant increase:

For women who divorce, equivalent household income fell sharply from $36,200 pre-divorce to $27,900 at the first interview after divorce. It then increased steadily to be $41,300 after 6 years (an increase of 14 per cent over the 7-year period). While this represents a recovery in real income after a short-term post-divorce decline, these women fell behind their married counterparts who did not divorce (who had an increase in real income of 19 per cent). For men who divorced, equivalent household income increased in the year after divorce and grew by 29 per cent over the 7-year period, a much faster rate of growth than that experienced by couples who remained together (whose income increased by 18 per cent in real terms over this period).[45]

De Vaus and colleagues found that the negative impact of divorce on women's income was significantly exacerbated when women lived with

---

[41] *Ibid.*, 23.
[42] Australian Government, Australian Bureau of Statistics, 'One parent families', 6224.0.55.001 – Labour Force, Australia: Labour Force Status and Other Characteristics of Families, June 2012.
[43] Laurie Brown, 'Divorce: For richer, for poorer', AMP.NATSEM Income and Wealth Report Issue 39, December 2016, 5.
[44] De Vaus *et al.*, 'Economic consequences of divorce in Australia'.
[45] *Ibid.*, 33–4 (footnote omitted).

dependent children. They found that for these women the initial drop in income post-separation was 'substantially larger' and that while their position improved over time (for reasons including their increased paid employment post-separation, re-partnering, and receipt of government benefits) 'the recovery in income is much slower and the gap in income 6 years after separation is still substantially greater than it was pre-separation'.[46] While this research suggests (in contrast to recent analysis in the UK context by Hayley Fisher and Hamish Low)[47] that women's increased workforce participation after divorce has an impact in alleviating financial disadvantage, it also finds (consistent with Fisher and Low)[48] that significant disparity continues.[49]

The finding that women and children bear the brunt of economic disadvantage post-separation was once again confirmed in Australia in 2016, in the 'Divorce: For richer, for poorer', AMP.NATSEM Income and Wealth Report (NATSEM Report), which looked at the financial impact of divorce using economic modelling of longitudinal data collected from 2001 to 2014.[50] The NATSEM Report found, in relation to divorces involving couples with no dependent children under 16 living with them, that '[o]verall, divorced women are worse off than both divorced men, and married women',[51] on the basis of analysis of income, home ownership, household asset, debt, and superannuation data. In contrast, the report found that '[d]ivorce has little impact on the employment status and income of men [without dependent children] aged 25–64 years'.[52] The report further found that the negative financial consequences of divorce are 'most marked for mothers'[53] with consequent negative flow-on effects for children:

Nearly half of all divorces each year involve children. Divorced mothers experience financial hardship more than couple families or families headed by a father who has been divorced. And with 97 per cent of divorced households headed by divorced mothers in Australia, Divorce: For richer, for poorer shows divorce has a negative impact on the financial wellbeing of children of divorced families.[54]

While there is very little research on the extent to which property settlements can reduce women's economic disadvantage after separation,

---

[46] Ibid., 34.　[47] Fisher and Low, 'Recovery from divorce'.　[48] Ibid.
[49] See also above n. 36.　[50] Brown, 'Divorce: For richer, for poorer'.　[51] Ibid., 6.
[52] Ibid., 6.　[53] Ibid., 24.　[54] Ibid., 25.

research on the impact of the payment of child support suggests this would be so.[55]

Of course, women's economic disadvantage relative to men does not solely result from relationship separation: it is a function of a range of systemic factors, including the ongoing gender pay gap between men and women in Australia (hitting a record high of 18.8 per cent in February 2015),[56] which is then reflected in men's much higher superannuation savings compared to women's (especially mothers') superannuation savings,[57] both of which are in turn reflective of direct and indirect discrimination, stereotypes about what men and women 'should' do, and ongoing social and cultural expectation that women will tailor their workplace participation around their domestic, child-care and other informal care commitments.[58] As these systemic disadvantages operate to the benefit of the community – and in particular to the significant economic benefit of men as a group[59] – it follows that they are disadvantages which should be more equitably shared between men and women, including on relationship breakdown.

All of this suggests the wisdom of legislative amendment that de-emphasises the current contributions-based focus and addresses the economic disadvantage faced by women and children. However, as the next section makes clear, our lack of current empirical knowledge regarding the relevance and impact of the current legislation to family law property settlements, along with research underlining the significant role of non-legislative matters in influencing property settlement, makes the position considerably more complicated.

---

[55] Christine Skinner, Kay Cook and Sarah Sinclair, 'The potential of child support to reduce lone mother poverty: Comparing population survey data in Australia and the UK' (2017) 25 *Journal of Poverty and Social Justice* 79.

[56] Sarah Sedghi, 'Gender pay gap hits record high, prompting calls for government action' (*ABC News*, Melbourne, 27 February 2015).

[57] David Hetherington and Warwick Smith, *Not So Super, for Women: Superannuation and Women's Retirement Outcomes* (Per Capita Australia Limited in partnership with Australian Services Union, 2017): 'The superannuation system is systematically biased against half the population. Women are simply not being assisted by super towards a reasonable standard of living in retirement. Women's superannuation balances at retirement are 47% lower than men's. As a result, women are far more likely to experience poverty in retirement in their old age. Superannuation is failing women' (p. 6). Similar patterns have been identified in England and Wales (Hilary Woodward with Mark Sefton, *Pensions on Divorce: An Empirical Study* (Cardiff Law School, 2014) 5).

[58] Australian Government, Workplace Gender Equality Agency, 'What is the gender pay gap?' (available at: www.wgea.gov.au/addressing-pay-equity/what-gender-pay-gap).

[59] See for example: Deloitte Access Economics, *The Economic Value of Informal Care in Australia in 2015* (Deakin, ACT: Carers Australia, 2015).

3.2 Property Division Outcomes in the Broader Separating Population

The research on property division in the broader separating population – and particularly recent research by the Australian Institute of Family Studies – suggests an absence of clear or discernible patterns in, and reasons for, the way property is divided after separation, yet also a majority perception that outcomes are 'fair'.

There is no requirement in Australia to obtain court orders for property (or parenting). By far, the majority of property division on separation occurs outside the formal adjudication context.[60] Recent Australian Institute of Family Studies research conducted by Lixia Qu and colleagues, involving telephone interviews conducted with 10,000 separating parents, found that the majority described 'discussions' as their main pathway for resolving property issues (39.5 per cent), with a further 18.5 per cent responding that there had been 'no specific process'.[61] The researchers found that lawyers were described by a significant minority of respondents as their main pathway for resolving property issues (29.1 per cent), but very few described courts as their main pathway (7 per cent).[62] Private settlement was thus the norm, although with greater use of formal pathways (especially lawyers) as the value of the parties' property increased. Reasons for these patterns include that property pools are usually low or modest,[63] and a paucity of legal aid or other free or inexpensive legal advice for financial disputes.[64] Taxation relief on transfer of assets available to separating couples who formalise their property settlements means that consent orders are often sought and made,[65] which partly explains the use of lawyers by a significant minority in this context.

---

[60] Fehlberg et al., *Australian Family Law*, 476–9.
[61] Lixia Qu, Ruth Weston, Lawrie Moloney, Rae Kaspiew and Jessie Dunstan, *Post-Separation Parenting, Property and Relationship Dynamics after Five Years* (Melbourne: Australian Institute of Family Studies, 2014) 98, table 6.9.
[62] *Ibid.*
[63] *Ibid.*, 93, table 6.2: Qu and colleagues found that among their sample, 19.6 per cent had no assets, 1.3 per cent had only debts, 18.5 per cent had assets of less than AUD$40,000 and 10 per cent had assets of more than AUD$500,000.
[64] Belinda Fehlberg, Christine Millward, Monica Campo and Rachel Carson, 'Post-separation parenting and financial settlements: Exploring changes over time' (2013) 27 *International Journal of Law, Policy and the Family* 359. See also Productivity Commission, *Access to Justice Arrangements*.
[65] Parties who wish to avoid state tax (stamp duty) on transfer of real property, and federal tax (capital gains tax) on the transfer of certain assets (in essence, investments) need to

In relation to outcomes Qu and her colleagues found that:

On average, based on both fathers' and mothers' reports, mothers received 57% of assets and fathers received 43%. The most common division reported was a share for the mother of between 40% and 59% (one-third), and about a quarter of parents reported a higher share for the mother of between 60 and 79%.[66]

While this suggests a general pattern of mothers receiving the majority share of property, closer analysis indicated a more complex story, due to differential reporting between mothers and fathers: 'On average, fathers estimated 65% going to the mother, compared with mothers' estimates of 49%.'[67] There was thus no clear indication that mothers were receiving a major share of what was usually modest property, at the end of relationships averaging ten years' duration, during and following which mothers were usually majority time parents (across all three waves – parent interviews were conducted in 2008, 2009 and 2012 – around three-quarters of children were in the care of their mother for the majority of nights or all nights per year; that is, 66–100 per cent of nights).[68] Similarly, longitudinal qualitative research by Fehlberg and colleagues conducted between 2009 and 2011 found no clear link between parenting arrangements and property settlement, although 'as a group, mothers in our sample fared worse than fathers in relation to share of property received relative to their level of care of children: about two thirds of our mothers received a smaller percentage of property than their percentage of care'.[69]

This is unsurprising given that the current legislation does not prioritise the needs of children and their carers. Perhaps, then, legislative reform to encourage this may be a good idea. However, the position is complicated by the fact that Australian empirical studies have consistently found that a range of factors not referred to in the legislation influence property settlements on relationship separation,[70] and that this is the case whether

---

obtain court orders or enter a binding financial agreement. See further Fehlberg *et al.*, *Australian Family Law*, 483.

[66] Qu *et al.*, *Post-Separation Parenting*, Executive Summary, xvii.   [67] *Ibid.*, 102.
[68] *Ibid.*, 79, table 5.1.   [69] Fehlberg *et al.* 'Post-separation parenting arrangements', 230.
[70] For England and Wales, see Emma Hitchings, Joanna Miles and Hilary Woodward, *Assembling the Jigsaw Puzzle: Understanding Financial Settlement on Divorce* (University of Bristol, 2013).

or not family law professionals and processes are accessed.[71] For example, Qu and colleagues noted that:

[T]he evidence suggests the strongest influences on the proportionate share of property were: the size of asset pools, the dynamics surrounding the separation (who initiated separation, who left the house), a history of family violence/abuse and care-time arrangements. The influence of the effects of a history of family violence/abuse and the role played in the separation decision on the shares received by each [parent] were mediated by who left the house at separation. There was no association between property division and children's age.[72]

The full range of factors that the research indicates are likely to impact on financial settlements are thus not reflected in the checklist of factors in s. 79(4)/90SM(4), in particular: who left the family home, who initiated separation, being a target of family violence or abuse, and the quality of the post-separation relationship. It is also not clear whether the legislation is being used at all, or whether the combined effect of broad discretion and the checklist of factors limit its utility.

As a result, the 'extent to which law does or does not influence the behaviour and actions of people who do not engage with the formal legal system and even those who do'[73] is at best variable and unclear,[74] notwithstanding continued heavy use in Australia of legislative amendment (at least in the parenting context) as a mechanism for attempting to influence the behaviour of separating parents outside the courts.[75] There is a distinct possibility that legislative reform will be misunderstood or ignored altogether.

---

[71] See Fehlberg et al., 'Post-separation parenting arrangements', 229–36; Fehlberg et al., 'Post-separation parenting arrangements and financial settlements', 397–401.

[72] Qu et al., *Post-Separation Parenting*, 105; Fehlberg et al., 'Post-separation parenting arrangements and financial settlements'.

[73] Matt Harvey, Maria Karras and Stephen Parker, *Negotiating by the Light of the Law* (Sydney: Themis Press, Law and Justice Foundation, 2012) 4.

[74] For example, Ira Ellman, 'Why making family law is hard' (2003) 35 *Arizona State Law Journal* 699; John Eekelaar, 'Uncovering social obligations: Family law and the responsible citizen', in Mavis Maclean (ed.), *Making Law for Families* (Oxford: Hart, 2000) 9–28; John Dewar, 'Can the centre hold?: Reflections on two decades of family law reform' (2010) 24 *Australian Journal of Family Law* 139; Rae Kaspiew, Matthew Gray, Lixia Qu and Ruth Weston 'Legislative aspirations and social realities: Empirical reflections on Australia's 2006 family law reform' (2011) 33 *Journal of Social Welfare and Family Law* 397.

[75] See for example FLA ss. 65DAC and 65DAE, which direct parents regarding consultation in relation to major long-term issues and other issues.

Qu and colleagues' research also explored the extent to which parents considered that their property division was fair, both at the time it was finalised and at the time of interview. They found that the majority considered the result was fair at both points, although significant minorities (especially fathers) thought it was unfair:

> There were three main themes from parents' comments of unfairness: the perception that a fair outcome required an even split; inadequate consideration of the respondents' contributions during the relationship, with many comments suggesting values attaching greater weight to income-earning and financial contributions than homemaker contributions; and inadequate apportionment of liability debts and the inclusion of resources provided by the parents' own families (e.g., their own parents or grandparents) in the asset pool. Other comments include the assertion that the system is biased against men (fathers' reports), and that it is unable to handle one party behaving dishonestly in disclosures relating to property and financial resources.[76]

The themes identified in the above passage suggest a perception of a substantial minority – mainly fathers who reported receiving a minority share of the property – that financial contributions are given insufficient weight. The researchers observed that '[a]t a conceptual level, the responses reinforce ... that fairness is an inherently subjective concept. It was evident that a range of issues, including personal values and expectations of the relationship, influenced perceptions of unfairness.'[77]

In summary, research on property outcomes in the broader separating population suggests that most separating parents consider that 'fair' results are being achieved, but that outcomes do not clearly provide for a greater share to mothers – even though they are the usual primary carers of children before and after separation – over fathers. Yet fathers are nevertheless more likely than mothers to think outcomes are unfair. Importantly, this pattern is consistent with previous research finding 'that divorced men were more likely than divorced women to say they were poor or very poor. This is despite the fact that divorced men had higher incomes than divorced women and were less likely to experience financial hardships',[78] and conversely, women's greater satisfaction with their post-separation financial

---

[76] Qu et al., *Post-Separation Parenting*, Executive Summary, xvii.   [77] *Ibid.*, 112.
[78] Australian Institute of Family Studies, media release, 'The long-lasting financial impacts of divorce for women' (Australian Institute of Family Studies, Melbourne, 8 July 2009).

circumstances despite their greater poverty.[79] It is a pattern that should warn us of the dangers of accepting subjective claims of economic disadvantage at face value when considering reform. It is also possible that encouragement of shared parenting has fuelled formal equality discourse, including a perception that equal division of property is 'fair' – a point we return to in section 3.3. Finally, and unsurprisingly, previous research also confirms that a range of factors not referred to in the legislation will be relevant when property is divided (a reality not confined to family property law, or indeed to family law). Overall, the research suggests the challenges of – but need for – legislation that focuses our attention on post-separation economic disadvantage of women and their dependent children as an issue fundamental to our definition of 'just and equitable' outcomes.

3.3 The Impact of Family Lawyers

There is very little recent research to inform our understanding of how s. 79/90SM is being interpreted and applied by family lawyers. The main research – that of John Wade,[80] and Rosemary Hunter and colleagues[81] – was conducted, respectively, in the early 2000s and late 1990s, well before a number of significant family law changes in Australia, including the 2006 shared parenting amendments (the relevance of which is discussed in the next paragraph), the inclusion of de facto financial disputes in the FLA from 1 March 2009, and superannuation (or pension) splitting reform from 2002 (allowing splitting at the accumulation (pre-retirement) phase).[82] In summary, this research is consistent with that involving the broader separating population, in that it suggests outcomes do not substantively favour mothers (as the usual primary carers of children before and after separation) over fathers, along with the relevance when dividing property of a range of factors not referred to in the FLA.

---

[79] Smyth and Weston, *Financial Living Standards after Divorce*, 14–17.
[80] John Wade, 'Arbitral decision-making in family property disputes – Lotteries, crystal balls, and wild guesses' (2003) 17 *Australian Journal of Family Law* 224; Rosemary Hunter, with Ann Genovese, Angela Melville and April Chrzunowski, *Legal Services in Family Law* (Sydney: Justice Research Centre, Law Foundation of NSW, 2000).
[81] Hunter *et al.*, *Legal Services in Family Law*, 162.
[82] Although the research suggests that women's property settlements have not increased since this change: Grania Sheehan, April Chrzanowski and John Dewar 'Superannuation and divorce in Australia: An evaluation of post-reform practice and settlement outcomes' (2008) 22 *International Journal of Law Policy and the Family* 22.

More recently, interviews with family lawyers conducted as part of the Australian Institute of Family Studies Evaluation of the 2006 shared parenting amendments[83] suggested that post-amendment there has been a reduction in the share of property received by mothers. About half of the 319 family lawyers surveyed in 2008 said that property settlements had changed in favour of fathers and that the average property division allocated to mothers had decreased by about 7 per cent (from 63 per cent to 57 per cent) post-2006.[84] This appears to represent a shift away from the position that had developed from the mid 1990s, when more significant adjustments on the basis of the additional factors (i.e. factors relating to the parties' respective financial futures: section 2) began to be made.[85] It was not unusual to see adjustments of around 10-15 per cent in favour of mothers with children living with them, on the basis of care of children of the marriage along with reduced income earning capacity due to parenting and homemaker responsibilities during marriage, in combination with their enhancement of the husband's economic position, which sometimes allowed the mother and children to stay in the family home. The researchers suggested several reasons for this apparent change, including that bargaining dynamics/trade-offs may have been affected by the shared parenting amendments (e.g. mothers trading away property to resist shared time claims by fathers) and that shared time arrangements reduced the likelihood and extent of adjustments to take account of the parties' different economic positions. These findings have so far not been accompanied by any systematic empirical analysis of reported cases or court files to determine whether lawyers' observations are in fact being played out in reality. The reports of lawyers are certainly concerning, given the empirical evidence discussed in section 3.1 regarding the economic disadvantage of women and children.

3.4 Property Division Outcomes in Adjudicated Cases

There is limited recent empirical research analysing property cases decided by family law courts, either pursuant to consent orders or adjudication. As a result, we do not know how the legislation is being applied by courts.

---

[83] Rae Kaspiew, Matthew Gray, Ruth Weston, Lawrie Moloney, Kellie Hand, Lixia Qu and Family Law Evaluation Team, *Evaluation of the 2006 Family Law Reforms* (Melbourne: Australian Government, Australian Institute of Family Studies, 2009) 225.
[84] *Ibid.*   [85] e.g. *Waters & Jurek* [1995], per Fogarty J.

Previous research conducted in 2004 and 2005 by Helen Rhoades and colleagues on adjudicated property outcomes suggested that a settled approach existed in standard cases that accorded with a 'norm' involving modest assets accumulated over the course of a relationship of reasonable duration due to the joint efforts of the parties.[86] Rhoades found that within the Family Court of Australia, property division was approached differently in cases involving assets of modest value compared with cases involving high assets. Her analysis of sixty unreported Family Court judgments found that the detailed examination of the parties' contributions that occurred in high asset cases rarely occurred outside that context. Rather, the approach of judges in cases involving modest assets was usually to treat the contributions of spouses as 'roughly equal' and to focus on the needs of the spouses and their dependent children. Rhoades further found that 'judges regularly abandoned the requirement to consider the parties' contributions in favour of a needs-based approach where there were limited assets and dependent children to house'.[87] However, these findings were based on research conducted before the 2006 shared parenting amendments, before de facto financial disputes were brought within the FLA in 2009, and well before *Stanford*. More recently, Christopher Turnbull conducted an exploratory quantitative analysis of 200 first-instance property settlement determinations made between July 2012 (so before the High Court's decision in *Stanford*, on 15 November 2012) and June 2015. The cases analysed represented an estimated 7 per cent of financial judgments over that time, were mainly decisions of the Federal Circuit Court, and were all cases where there were children of the marriage or de facto relationship. While acknowledging variations in decision-making processes, Turnbull found that '[t]he overall mean result was 54% to mothers and 46% to fathers.'[88] As Turnbull acknowledges, there is much we do not know about the impact of these changes. At present, all we have is the suggestion that the 2006 shared parenting amendments appear to have led to a reduction in the likelihood and extent of s. 75(2) adjustments (section 3.3), in the face of ongoing empirical evidence of women's post-separation financial disadvantage (section 3.1).

---

[86] Helen Rhoades, 'Equality, needs and bad behaviour: The "other" decision making approaches in Australian matrimonial property cases' (2005) 19 *International Journal of Law, Policy and the Family* 194.
[87] Ibid., 194.
[88] Christopher Turnbull, 'Family Law Property Settlements: An Exploratory Quantitative Analysis' (2018) 7 *Family Law Review* 215, 228.

In summary, our analysis in section 3 suggests that there is considerable diversity in – and much we do not know about – property division outcomes across the broader separating community, including among those who receive legal assistance, and in adjudicated cases. This is consistent with John Dewar's observation that the Australian family law system is:

> a system polarised by pathways, by the dispositions of parties to agreement, by associated disparities of bargaining power, and disparities in access to legal advice and processes. The fundamental features of horizontalisation and the relative autonomy of multiple sites of interpretation are intensified in ways that seem to have more diverse results – positively in some cases, but negatively in others.[89]

While diverse outcomes are precisely what we would expect in a 'horizontalised' system and in the context of a discretionary legislative framework (no two families are the same), it is concerning that the interests of women and children appear to be attracting, if anything, decreasing attention in the context of the disproportionate poverty rates for women and children in Australia and the particularly adverse economic consequences of separation and divorce for them (section 3.1).

4 Next Steps?

Our analysis suggests the need for further Australian empirical research to inform understanding of how the broad discretion under s. 79/90SM is being interpreted and applied, particularly by lawyers and courts, and that a wide range of factors extending well beyond the s. 79(4)/90SM checklist influence both property outcomes and the socio-economic context in which they occur.

Given these challenges, we would suggest that any proposal for legislative amendment should be approached with caution in the absence of a solid research base. What *is* clear, however, is the research evidence regarding women's and children's economic disadvantage post-separation. On this basis, we would suggest that, if legislative reform were to be considered, it should aim to address this disadvantage.

Achieving consensus on reform of this nature is, however, likely to prove difficult, if not impossible in the current social and legal context of family law in Australia, in which debate continues to be polarised along gender lines.

---

[89] Dewar, 'Can the centre hold?', 147.

The history – and indeed the form – of the Australian shared parenting amendments reflect this tension, promoting both shared parenting outcomes and protection from harm in a manner that reflected the competing claims of fathers' groups and groups concerned to protect women and children from family violence.[90] In the current context, any departure from the predominantly 'contributions focused' model which currently exists would be likely to meet significant opposition.

Difficulty and opposition should not, however, inhibit the putting forward of reform proposals that are more likely to achieve just and equitable outcomes and that are intelligible and relevant to the range of actors in family law. In this spirit – and on the basis of current empirical evidence – we have elsewhere[91] suggested an approach that prioritises children's housing needs, followed by the material and economic security of parties, followed by compensating for any losses and lastly, equal division of any surplus in the absence of exceptional circumstances.

Yet we would also emphasise that introducing further legislative guidance may not of itself lead to more just and equitable outcomes without encouragement of social and cultural change supporting the principles implemented – a factor that is also of key relevance to judicial interpretation of law.[92] In the end, the key issue surrounds achieving greater consensus on what family property law is for.[93] In this regard, the ongoing – and apparently increasing – challenge is to achieve greater understanding and recognition of the economic consequences of separation and divorce for women and children in a social environment that prefers to believe that gender equality has been achieved, despite clear evidence to the contrary.

---

[90] Richard Chisholm, *Family Courts Violence Review* (Sydney: Family Court of Australia, 2009).

[91] Belinda Fehlberg and Lisa Sarmas, 'Australian family property law: Just and equitable outcomes?' (2018) 32 Australian Journal of Family Law 81.

[92] See, for example, Stanley Fish, *Is There a Text in This Class?: The Authority of Interpretive Communities* (Cambridge, MA: Harvard University Press, 1992): interpreters are not constrained by the 'text' but also are not free to read into the text whatever they like, as they are constrained by their tacit awareness of what is possible and not possible to do. The source of this tacit awareness is the relevant interpretive community – in the case of judges, primarily the legal, but also the broader, community, whom they seek to persuade that they have decided the case correctly. The constraint on interpretation is therefore the persuasiveness of any particular interpretation, in the first instance, to the legal interpretive community and then more broadly, to the community at large.

[93] A. L. Diduck, 'What is family law for?' (2011) 64 *Current Legal Problems* 287.

5 Towards the Constitutionalization of Family Law in Latin America

Nicolás Espejo and Fabiola Lathrop*

1 Introduction: the Constitutionalization of Family Relations

This chapter seeks to address several key rulings handed down by Latin American courts on three issues with a direct impact on family law: sexual orientation, gender identity and filiation. In doing so, we attempt to highlight the emergence of an embryonic process that could be labelled as the *constitutionalization of family relations* or the progressive adjudication of constitutional rights in the field of family law.

Driven by a wave of constitutional reforms that took place during the 1990s and early 2000s, Latin American constitutions began to recognize a series of principles, rules and obligations directly applied to family life. Among others, these constitutions recognize several principles, such as the 'integral protection of the family',[1] the 'special rights/duties of parents toward their children'[2] and the 'equality between children born in and out of wedlock'.[3] Some constitutions recognize, moreover, the rights of parents to 'choose the education of their children',[4] as well as the 'inviolability of the home' and the 'intimacy' of family life.[5] Others texts omit these specific rights for parents and recognize, instead, the rights of children to 'be free from abuse and violence'.[6]

---

* Professor Lathrop acknowledges the support of the academic activities abroad programme of the School of Law, Universidad de Chile.
[1] Federal Constitution of Argentina, Art. 14 *bis*; Constitution of Colombia, Art. 42.
[2] Federal Constitution of Brazil, Art. 229; Constitution of Costa Rica, Art. 53, Constitution of Paraguay, Art. 53; Constitution of Colombia Art. 42 (inc. 4).
[3] Constitution of Peru, Art. 6; Constitution of Uruguay, Art. 42; Constitution of Costa Rica, Art. 53; Constitution of Colombia, Art. 42.
[4] Constitution of Chile, Art. 19, N° 10; Constitution of Peru, Art. 13.
[5] Constitution of Chile, Art. 19, N° 5, Constitution of Ecuador, Art. 23.8; Constitution of Colombia, Art. 42.
[6] Federal Constitution of Brazil, Art, 227; Constitution of Colombia, Art. 44; Constitution of Uruguay, Art. 41.

These norms have created a particular 'landscape' of three different models of constitutional conceptions of family in Latin America:[7] (a) *a restrictive* model (where only 'natural' men and women are recognized as having the right to marry or enter into *de facto* civil partnerships);[8] (b) *an intermediate* model (where the Constitution provides protection for all forms of family, but only recognizes marriage between a man and a woman);[9] and (c) *a broad model* (where the Constitution establishes an expansive mandate for the 'integral protection of the family', leaving room for all forms of family, marriage or civil partnership).[10]

These constitutional reforms have been complemented by a series of legal modifications in Latin America designed to respond to a plethora of changes in the structure, composition and expectations of family members, inter alia reforms in the field of divorce, the recognition of 'consensual unions' or de facto couples, same-sex marriages, shared custody between parents, restrictions on corporal punishment against children and the legal obligation to satisfy the best interests of the child in any judicial proceeding. Although different in their nature and scope, these progressive reforms have also prompted the emergence of new academic debates in the field of family law, particularly those aimed at integrating a human rights approach into family relations.

1.1 A New Jurisprudence on Family Relations

Accordingly, a growing part of the jurisprudence has to call attention to the analysis of the ways in which Latin American constitutions define and regulate family life, as well as the implications for the constitutional rights of family members.[11] Inspired by what some have framed as the

---

[7] We take this typology from M. Herrera's, 'La Familia en la Constitución 2020, ¿Qué Familia?', in R. Gargarella (coord.), *La Constitución en 2020: 48 propuestas para una sociedad igualitaria* (Buenos Aires: Siglo Veintiuno Editores, 2011) 85–94.

[8] Art. 112 of the Constitution of Honduras.

[9] Art. 226 of the Constitution of Brazil and Art. 67 of the Constitution of Ecuador.

[10] Art. 14 *bis* of the Federal Constitution of Argentina.

[11] G. J. Bidart Campos, '*El derecho de familia y los nuevos paradigmas, in X Congreso Internacional de Derecho de Familia*', Mendoza, Argentina, 20 al 24 de septiembre de 1998, Vol. 5, 1998 *(Ponencias profesores invitados)* 16–22; Manuel Chávez Asencio, *Derecho de Familia y Relaciones Jurídicas Familiares* (7th edn, Mexico: Ed. Porrúa, 1998); A. Gil Domínguez, M. V. Famá and M. Herrera, *Derecho constitucional de familia* (Buenos Aires: Ediar, 2006), vol. I.

'constitutionalization of law',[12] family law and child law specialists have begun to incorporate a dogmatic analysis that directly relates to constitutional principles, rules and precedents.[13] Based on this approach, some authors have begun to challenge the foundations of the dogmatic that justified the regulation of family life in terms of both an organic conception of the family and an inegalitarian recognition of individual rights for all family members (particularly, women and children).

Among this emerging jurisprudence, works can be identified that highlight the impact of constitutional reforms on the regulation of families in civil and family law[14] as well as those that focus on the primary impact of international human rights law (widely incorporated in the constitutions of Latin America) on family law.[15] Similarly, some authors are now delving into such issues as the transformation of the biological grounding of parenthood, a matter particularly salient to the granting of parental responsibility.

Academic concerns about the transformations in the allocation of parental rights in the region have largely been fuelled by same-sex

---

[12] L. Favoreau, *Legalidad y constitucionalidad. La constitucionalización del derecho*, trans. Magdalena Correa Henao (Bogotá: Universidad Externado de Colombia, Instituto de Estudios Constitucionales Carlos Restrepo Piedrahita, 2000); L. R. Barroso, *El neoconstitucionalismo y la constitucionalización del derecho. El triunfo tardío del derecho constitucional en Brasil* (Instituto de Investigaciones Jurídicas, Universidad Nacional Autónoma de México, 2008); L. Ferrajoli, 'El paradigma normativo de la democracia constitucional', in Marcilla Córdoba, Gema, *Constitucionalismo y garantismo* (Bogotá: Universidad Externado de Colombia, 2009).

[13] E. Soto Kloss, 'La familia en la constitución política' (1994) 21–2 *Revista Chilena de Derecho* 217–29; N. Lloveras and M. Herrera (eds.), D. Benavides Santos and A. M. Picado (coords.), *El derecho de familia en Latinoamérica 1. Los Derechos Humanos en las relaciones familiares* (Córdoba: Nuevo Enfoque Jurídico, 2010); A. Álvarez Pertiz, 'Constitucionalización del derecho de familia' (2011) 7 *Revista Jurídicas CUC* 27–51.

[14] E. A. Zannoni, *Derecho de Familia* (3rd edn, Buenos Aires: Ed. Astrea, 1998) 22ff.; J. Parra Benítez, 'El carácter constitucional del derecho de familia en Colombia' (1996) 97 *Revista Facultad de Derecho y Ciencias y Políticas*, 47–52; M. L. Calvo Carvallo, 'Familia y Estado: Una perspectiva constitucional' (2000) 15 *Revista Uruguaya de Derecho de Familia* 163–65; J. C. F. J. de la Fuente Linares, 'La protección constitucional de la familia en América Latina' (2012) Rev. IUS 6–29, available at: www.scielo.org.mx/scielo.php?script=sci_arttext&pid=S1870-21472012000100005

[15] M. Beloff, 'Quince años de la vigencia de la Convención Sobre los Derechos del Niño en Argentina' (2008) 10 *Justicia y Derechos del Niño* 11–44; N. Lloveras and M. J. Salomón, 'Los derechos humanos en las relaciones familiares del S. XXI: Los caminos de la jurisprudencia argentina', in Lloveras *et al.*, *El derecho de familia*, 73–115.

unions/marriages and assisted reproduction techniques.[16] Based on the emergence of new family configurations recognized by the law, as well as the growing use of these technologies, part of the jurisprudence has called for a departure from mere 'biological parenthood'.[17] Adopting a tack similar to that of the current configurations of parenthood in both England and Wales[18] and the European system of human rights,[19] these authors have recommended a shift away from natural/biological/adoptive parenthood and the recognition of a broader understanding of parenting. In the case of assisted reproduction techniques, this appears to suggest the recognition of a type of parenthood derived from procreation, as witnessed by their use.[20]

Alternatively, other scholars have focused on the dogmatic transformations in children's autonomy, the exercise of their rights and the incorporation of the best interests of the child as the paramount or primary consideration in all matters affecting them. These works range from an analysis of the incorporation of the United Nations Convention on the Rights of the Child into domestic law,[21] to a critique of prevalent constitutional interpretations on moral and political autonomy of

---

[16] Especially, in the Colombian and Argentinean cases. See the recent decision of the Colombian Constitutional Court (August 2014) that rejects the decision to deny the adoption of a child, based on the homosexuality of the petitioner. The petitioner was the partner of the child's mother. Corte Constitucional de Colombia, *SENTENCIA SU-617/14*. In the case of Argentina, these debates are prompted by the enactment of Law N° 26.618 (2010) which recognizes every person's right to marry, regardless of their sex (Art. 2°).

[17] A. Kemelmajer de Carlucci, M. Herrera and E. Lamm, 'Los criterios tradicionales de determinación de la filiación en crisis', in M. Gómez de la Torre Vargas (ed.) and C. Lepin Molina (coord.), *Técnicas de Reproducción Humana Asistida: Una mirada transdiciplinaria* (Santiago: Abeledo Perrot/Thomson Reuters, 2013) 127–63; D. Jarufe Contreras, Las filiaciones 'no biológicas' derivadas de la aplicación de técnicas de reproducción humana asistida (TRHA), in Gómez de la Torre Vargas and Lepin Molina, *Técnicas de Reproducción*, 67–104.

[18] See House of Lords, *Re G (Children)* [2006] UKHL 43. Particularly, Baroness Hale's famous recognition of three forms of natural parenthood: genetic, gestational and psychological.

[19] European Court of Human Rights, *Lebbink* v. *The Netherlands*, Application No. 45582/99 (2005) 40 EHRR 18, para. 37; *Görgülü* v. *Germany*, Application No. 74969/01 (2004).

[20] Kemelmajer de Carlucci *et al.*, 'Criterios tradicionales de determinación de la filiación en crisis', 130. For a contrary opinion, see H. Corral, 'Maternidad subrrogada: Sobre la pretensión de formalizar la filiación mediante la adopción o recepción de su práctica en el extranjero, *ibid.*, 165–88.

[21] E. García-Méndez and M. Beloff, *Infancia, Ley y Democracia en América Latina*, Prefacio by L. Ferrajoli, Segunda (ed.) (Bogotá: Editorial Temis-Ediciones Depalma, 1999), vol. I

children,[22] to those who have attempted to refine the meaning and interpretative use of the best interests of the child.[23] Regardless of some differences in perspective, these authors have defended the moral and legal proposition that children are rights-holders and that these rights establish limits to both state and parental authority, that children have a progressive or dynamic autonomy, and that their voice must be heard and taken into account.

Lastly, in the field of parental rights and duties, the new doctrine of family law in Latin America has provided substantial support for a transformation of both statutes and adjudication, providing a more egalitarian distribution of child-rearing in family life. In some cases, the doctrine has focused on the historical justifications in favour of the organic family, to highlight the power relations exercised by men over women and children alike.[24] In other cases, the new doctrine has concentrated on the need to acknowledge new legal institutions that might strengthen co-responsibility between parents (such as shared custody)[25] as well as in the effects of divorce and separation on the spouses and on the welfare of the child.[26]

---

[22] D. Lovera and A. Coddou, 'Niño, adolescentes y derechos constitucionales: De la protección a la autonomía', in *Justicia y Derechos del Niño, N° 11* (Santiago: UNICEF, 2009) 11–54.

[23] M. Cillero, 'El interés superior del niño en el marco de la convención internacional sobre los derechos del niño', in *Justicia y Derechos del Niño, N° 1* (Santiago: Universidad Diego Portales, 1999) 46–63; Jaime Couso, 'El niño como sujeto de derechos y la nueva justicia de familia. Interés superior del niño, autonomía progresiva y derecho a ser oído' (2006) 3–4 *Revista de Derechos del Niño* 145–66; Domingo Lovera, 'Razonamiento judicial y derechos del niño: de ventrílocuos y marionetas' (2008) 10 *Justicia y Derechos del niño* 45–62; R. Garrido, 'El interés superior del niño y el razonamiento jurídico' (2013) *Anuario de Filosofía y Teoría del Derecho* 115–47.

[24] I. C. Jaramillo, 'Familia', in C. Motta and M. Sáez (eds.), *La mirada de los jueces. Género en la jurisprudencia latinoamericana* (Bogotá: Siglo del Hombre Editores, Washington College of Law, Center for Reproductive Rights, 2008), vol. I, 267–361. For a historical analysis of the conception, legal debates and reform of the family in Colombia, see I. C. Jaramillo, *Derecho y familia en Colombia* (Bogotá: Editorial Universidad de Los Andes, 2013).

[25] F. Lathrop, *Custodia compartida de los hijos* (Madrid: La Ley, 2008); A. Kemelmajer de Carlucci, 'La guarda compartida. Una visión comparativa', in *Revista de Derecho Privado, Instituto de Investigaciones Jurídicas UNAM* (special edn, 2012), 181–6.

[26] N. Espejo and F. Lathrop, 'Dissolution of marriage in Latin America: Trends and challenges', in J. Eekelaar and R. George (eds.), *Routledge Handbook of Family Law and Policy* (New York: Routledge, 2014) 133–7. A more general presentation on parental responsibility is in N. Espejo and F. Lathrop (coords.), *Responsabilidad Parental* (Santiago: Thomson Reuters, 2017).

1.2 Neo-constitutionalism and Constitutional Courts

The constitutionalization of family relations is, in a way, an extension of a specific form of constitutional interpretation, such as the one famously developed by Ronald Dworkin (arguing that the Constitution protects all the rights required by the best conception of the political ideals laid down in it -even if some of those rights are not formally or expressly recognised by that text).[27] The role of courts in finding rights not expressly enshrined in constitutions has been a major issue in the scholarly discussion in civil law countries – under the label of 'neo-constitutionalism'. In the neo-constitutional paradigm judges are paramount, since the legal system must be guaranteed in all its parts through jurisdictional mechanisms. Just as the Constitution of neo-constitutionalism is an 'invasive' or 'meddling' constitution, the judicial task also has to do with many aspects of social life (such as family relations). In this sense, neo-constitutionalism generates an explosion of judicial activity and entails or requires some degree of judicial activism, largely superior to what has been observed previously.[28]

As noted above, the emerging constitutionalization of family relations in Latin America can be observed through a careful reading of several key rulings handed down by constitutional courts on three issues with a direct impact on family law: sexual orientation, gender identity and filiation. Rulings in Argentina, Brazil, Chile, Colombia and Mexico provide particular insight.

The authors view both legislation and constitutional precedent[29] in these countries as good examples of the evolution of the constitutionalization of family law and believe that over the course of the past two decades these

---

[27] R. Dworkin, *Freedom's Law: The Moral Reading of the American Constitution* (Cambridge, MA: Harvard University Press, 1996) 72–81.

[28] M. Carbonell (ed.), Teoría del neoconstitucionalismo. *Ensayos escogidos* (Madrid: Trotta-UNAM, Instituto de Investigaciones Jurídicas, 2007); P. Comanducci, *Formas de (neo) constitucionalismo: un análisis metateórico*, 16 Isonomía 89, 100–1 (2002). The authors would like to thank Dr Domingo Lovera for his remarks on neo-constitutionalism in jurisprudence.

[29] In Latin American legal systems, judicial precedents or decisions do not have the same legal value as in the common-law tradition. The normative value of judicial decisions in Latin America depends on several factors, including the jurisdiction where they were adopted (for example, constitutional jurisdiction or civil). The main *proviso* here is that e.g. decisions, perhaps except for those emanating from constitutional courts, often lack the binding power of statutory regulations.

countries have developed a constitutional conception of justice in a fashion that has influenced the regulation of family relations. Due to space constraints, we are unable to refer to every major ruling. Nonetheless, we believe that we have selected the most representative cases and facets, taking special care to include the rights of children in our analysis (matters of gender identity and filiation).

Argentina appears to lead some of the main doctrinal debates in matters of family law (with a Constitution promulgated in 1995). In fact, the nation enjoys the most modern civil legislation in the region, thanks to a new National Civil and Commercial Code that came into force in 2015 following previous attempts at reform over the course of several decades to update Argentina's regulations to reflect progress in precedent. In fact, the country's uniform, generalized case law has allowed Argentina to unreservedly supersede the Civil Code of 1876.

Unlike the Argentinean case, the Chilean Civil Code harks back to 1855. While that code stood as the source of inspiration for much of the Latin American civil codification process of the nineteenth century, that body of law and the country's Constitution, passed in 1980, remain firmly anchored in nineteenth-century criteria in the areas of patrimonial regimes for marriage and civil unions, notwithstanding substantive reforms commencing in the 1990s. For its part, Mexico, like Brazil, is a federal nation, and thus presents a special diversity of civil legislation. Although the Federal Civil Code dates back to 1928 (and the Constitution to 1917), some twenty local Civil Codes coexist with that legislation. This situation makes the study of Mexican law uniquely complex, which is why the precedent emanating from that nation's Supreme Court in constitutional matters is particularly helpful in shedding light on uniform criteria. Moreover, in recent years the court has issued rulings that reinterpret the individual state's civil regulations, providing further insight.

For its part, Colombia enjoys a Constitution from 1991, operating in concert with a Civil Code from 1873. This is supplemented by some of the most abundant and rich constitutional precedents on the continent. Thus, the pronouncements of Colombia's Constitutional Court are regularly the subject of study, review and analysis by legal scholars across the region. Lastly, although Brazil's Constitution of 1988 is somewhat older than the nation's Civil Code (2003), Brazil has developed strong judicial precedent on equality and non-discrimination on the grounds of sexual orientation and marital and parental matters, to which we now refer.

2 Sexual Orientation and Marriage

Let us begin by discussing a group of constitutional decisions on the role of sexual orientation in the process of recognizing the existence of family relationships. Specifically, we will look at rulings on the constitutionality of marriage restrictions for people of different sexes in Colombia, Argentina, Mexico and Chile.

The former three countries present a remarkable collection of precedents on the subject, which, in general, involve decisions handed down on the constitutionality of the laws being challenged. This is not the case in Chile, where we will comment on two judgments which contain no real, substantive pronouncements.[30]

2.1 Colombia

In the case of Colombia, a 26 July 2007[31] ruling by the Constitutional Court declared unconstitutional the expression 'a man and a woman' contained in article 113 of the Civil Code – a regulation defining marriage[32] – recognizing the absence of a contractual figure that would allow same-sex couples to formalize their union.

The court stated that: 'the members of the homosexual couple must have the option to choose, one that they do not currently have, since there is *no institution of a contractual nature* that, in their case, sets forth the legal bond that gives rise to the formal and solemn constitution of their family'. It went on:

the consideration of the rights of homosexual persons *does not contradict the constitutional recognition* of heterosexual marriage and the family originating in such a rite, nor its express protection, for the simple reason that this recognition and such protection is not diminished by the mere fact that an institution is

---

[30] We should note that the recognition of the rights of same-sex couples in the region has come from both lawmakers and the constitutional courts. Argentina and Uruguay enjoy legislation that has permitted so-called 'equal marriage' since 2010 and 2013, respectively. Brazil and Colombia, on the other hand, recognize such bonds based on judicial findings to which we will refer below. In Mexico, the situation is different, insofar as only some states have granted such recognition.

[31] C-577/11.

[32] 'Marriage is a solemn contract whereby a man and a woman unite in order to live together, procreate and support each other.'

established to formalize, as a legal bond, the relationship between two persons of the same sex.[33]

The court also stated that 'The Constitution *is not a closed and static order* and much less could it be so in an area ... subject to constant evolution',[34] urging the country's Congress to issue, prior to 20 June 2013, a law that, in a systematic and organized manner, would regulate a contractual institution as an alternative to de facto union.[35]

Lastly, the court extended the effects of this ruling to same-sex couples who, after 20 June 2013, found themselves in one of the following four situations: first, having appeared before a Colombian judge or notary, the civil marriage had been refused on the grounds of sexual orientation; second, had entered into a contract to formalize and solemnize their relationship even when the designation or legal effects of a civil marriage were absent; third, had performed a civil marriage, but the office of vital records refused to register it, and, fourth, all those persons who formalize and solemnize their relationship through civil marriage in the future.

As we can see, this ruling by; the Colombian Constitutional Court declares unconstitutional the civil regulations on marriage, notwithstanding the provision in the national Constitution itself that could bar persons of the same sex from forming that bond.[36]

---

[33] Paragraph 4.5.3.2 (emphases added). This Court had previously ruled that the system of protections in place for heterosexual couples should be applied to same-sex couples as well, finding that Law 54 of 1990, modified by Law 979 of 2005 was unconstitutional. See Sentencias C-098/96, 7 March 1996 and C-075/07, 7 February 2007.

[34] *Ibid.* (emphasis added).

[35] Regarding the deadline set forth by the court, given that the mandated legal reform had not occurred, in April 2016 the court issued a ruling aimed at: '(i) *overcoming the deficit in protection* identified in Judgment C-577 of 2011, with regard to same-sex couples in Colombia (ii) *ensuring* the exercise of the right to marry, and (iii) protecting the principle of *legal certainty* with regards to a person's *marital status*' (emphases added). Pursuant to Court Communique 17 dated 28 April 2016 regarding the case law standardization ruling on civil marriage between same-sex couples in Colombia [Case File T 4,167863 AC – Ruling SU-214/16 (28 April)], available at www.corteconstitucional.gov.co/comunicados/No.%2017%20comunicado%2028%20de%20abril%20 de%202016.pdf [accessed 5 May 2016].

[36] Article 42.1: 'The family is the fundamental nucleus of society. It is composed of natural or legal ties, based on the free decision of a man and a woman to marry or on the responsible will to create one.'

2.2 Argentina

In the case of Argentina, prior to the enactment of Law 26,618 of 21 July 2010, which enshrines so-called 'equal marriage', there were several judgments – issued both by courts of the first instance and higher courts – which ruled on the constitutionality of regulations limiting marriage to different-sex couples. While some pronouncements rejected the legality of marriages between persons of the same sex, others declared unconstitutional the civil regulations on the exclusivity of heterosexual marriage. Among the latter, the following judgments – which paved the way for legal recognition of same-sex marriage – stand out.

On 10 November 2009,[37] a protective action filed via *amparo* against the government of the City of Buenos Aires was upheld. That ruling declared the articles of the Civil Code limiting marriage to different-sex couples unconstitutional. The decision noted that denying the marriage of two persons of the same sex did not per se constitute an illegality. However, it added that the presumption of legality of the acts of the Government of the City of Buenos Aires did not imply that such actions were legitimate. In this sense, in providing the grounds for the declaration of unconstitutionality, the court stated that the decision would remove 'an *illegitimate obstacle* that limited equality and freedom, impeded the *full development of individuals and their effective participation in the political, cultural, economic and social life of the community*, and encouraged the *perpetuation of homophobic behaviour*'.[38] All of which, the court ruled, was in clear opposition to the Argentine constitutional regime.

Similarly, in a 19 March 2010 ruling, the court declared the unconstitutionality of regulations limiting marriage to different-sex couples and ordered that the marriage of two people of the same sex who had requested an appointment for a marriage ceremony be authorized:

As noted in the preceding whereas clauses, whether from the perspective of the right to the protection of personal autonomy or from that of the right to equality based on the right to non-discrimination, the regulations on the right to marry ...

---

[37] *F.A.* v. *GCBA*. Contentious-Administrative and Tax Court # 15 of the Autonomous City of Buenos Aires. Published in: LA LEY 30/11/2009.

[38] Paragraph XVIII (emphases added).

do not meet constitutional requirements insofar as they extinguish that right for the petitioners in the absence of circumstances that could make such a prohibition legally tolerable.[39]

2.3 Mexico

As for Mexico, on 3 June 2015 the National Supreme Court of Justice addressed the sexual orientation of persons wishing to marry by alluding to the regulations on procreation.

The Supreme Court ruled that the law of any federal entity that deems the purpose of marriage to be procreation and/or that defines it as being between a man and a woman, is unconstitutional. The court found that:

attempting to link the requirements for marriage to the sexual preferences of those eligible to access the institution of marriage to procreation is *discriminatory* insofar as it *unjustifiably excludes access to marriage to homosexual couples* whose situation is similar to that of heterosexual couples. The distinction is discriminatory because sexual preference is not pertinent to differentiation in the context of the constitutional imperative.[40]

This judgement consolidated certain previous precedent on the topic and provides a solid foundation for the recognition of marriage by same-sex couples across Mexico.[41]

2.4 Brazil

In Brazil, homosexual unions are currently recognized as a family unit and same-sex marriage is available.

This situation began to consolidate after 5 May 2011 when the Brazilian Supreme Court accepted two declaratory actions of unconstitutionality and recognized homoaffective unions as family entities with the same

---

[39] *C., M. y otro* v. *GCBA*. Contentious-Administrative and Tax Court # 13. Paragraph 10. Published in: DFyP 2010 (May) (emphasis added).

[40] Paragraph 157 (emphases added). Tesis Jurisprudencial 43/2015. Décima Época. Núm. de Registro: 2009407. Instancia: Primera Sala.

[41] Previously, as was the case in Colombia, this tribunal had ruled that certain provisions that in practice discriminated against same-sex couples were unconstitutional. Thus, in a ruling dated 29 January 2014, the court found that the implicit exclusion of same-sex couples from health and maternity insurance in the context of regulations on social security was unconstitutional (Amparo en Revisión 485/2013 of 29 January 2014).

rights and duties as stable heterosexual unions.[42] In this judgment, the court applied paragraph 2 of Article 5 of the Federal Constitution which states: 'The rights and guarantees expressed in this Constitution do not preclude others from arising from the regime and the *principles* adopted thereby, or from the *international treaties* to which the Federative Republic of Brazil is party.' Insofar as the possibility of interpreting Article 1,723 of the Civil Code in a discriminatory fashion, the court deemed it necessary to resort to the technique of '*interpretation according to the Constitution*' (emphases added).

Since then, precedent has allowed the transformation of stable unions into marriage.[43] Subsequently, on 25 October 2011,[44] the Supreme Court of Justice granted unfettered authorization to marry.

2.5 Chile

In the case of Chile, we will review two rulings: the former relates to the constitutionality of the provision that defines marriage as a contract between a man and a woman; the second deals with the dissolution of marriage on special grounds, to wit, the homosexual conduct of the respondent spouse.

On 3 November 2011,[45] the Chilean Constitutional Tribunal ruled on a petition regarding the alleged unconstitutionality of Article 102 of the Civil Code.[46] This action was prompted by the Court of Appeals of Santiago upon hearing a remedy filed against an alleged violation of the right to equality before the law. The breach of this right was alleged to have

---

[42] STF, ADI 4.277 e ADPF 132, REl. Min. Ayres Britto, j. 05/05/2011. The effects of this ruling were binding and *erga omnes*. The decision served to reaffirm previous subject matter-related findings, such as a 2001 decision that recognized same-sex unions as a family for the first time in the context of inheritance rights (Rio Grande do Sul, TJRS, AC 70001388982, 7°C. Cív., Rel. Des. José Carlos Texeira Giorgis, j. 14/03/2001). Previously, the Supreme Court had recognized the existence of a de facto partnership for persons joined in same-sex union (STJ, Resp 148.897/MG, 4° T., Rel. Min. Ruy Rosado de Aguiar, j. 10 /02/1998). Moreover, in 2010, that Court had allowed a same-sex couple to adopt two children (STJ, REsp 889.852/RS, 4°T., Rel. Luis Felipe Salomao, j. 27/04/2010).

[43] TJRS, AC 70048452643, 8°C.Civ., Rel. Ricardo Moreira Lins Pastl, j. 27/09/2012.

[44] STJ, REsp 1.183.378-RS, 4° T., Rel. Min. Luis Felie Salomao, j. 25/10/2011.

[45] Case number 1881-10.

[46] The statute reads: 'Marriage is a solemn contract whereby a man and a woman are presently and indissolubly united for life, to live together, procreate, and support each other.'

occurred after a civil registry official refused both to grant an appointment for two men to marry and to authenticate two same-sex marriages performed abroad, one in Argentina, the other in Canada.

The Constitutional Tribunal rejected the petition on grounds of form, noting that the matter at issue was in fact a complex legal provision: marriage. Specifically, the court argued that an 'exclusion of law' prevented it from ruling on this matter because the Constitution itself sets forth that laws are 'a matter of civil codification'[47] and 'any other provision of a general and obligatory nature that sets forth the essential foundations of the legal order'.[48] The Tribunal found that the regulation of marriage – given its nature as a general, mandatory provision of enormous social statute – qualified as a part of the fundamental underpinnings of the civil legal order and therefore, a matter of law, not the Constitution.

As to the grounds for divorce based on homosexual conduct, on 10 April 2014[49] the Constitutional Tribunal issued a ruling rejecting the request for inapplicability on the grounds of unconstitutionality of Article 54, number 4 of the Civil Marriage Law.[50] In effect, the inapplicability of that provision was alleged in a for-cause (*culpa*) divorce proceeding in which the wife accused her husband of homosexual conduct.

The Tribunal noted that the spouse's alleged wrongdoing was an *act or activity* involving homosexual conduct, not one of mere externalized affection or preference towards a person of the other or the same sex. The Tribunal further ruled that the provision in question looks to the serious transgression of the duty of fidelity inherent to marriage as the grounds for divorce. The court also noted, moreover, that in this case, it was the conduct or actions of one of the spouses with persons of the same or different sex–involving sexual contact or significant external manifestations of affection inherent to a marriage– that was at issue. In sum, the Tribunal ruled that the provision did not represent an arbitrary differentiation with respect to other grounds of for-cause (*culpa*) divorce, since all of them – at least on the surface – involve a violation of the duty of conjugal

---

[47] Article 63, # 3 of the Political Constitution of the Republic of Chile.
[48] Whereas clause 5.   [49] Case number 2435-13.
[50] The statute reads: 'A petition for divorce may be filed by one of the spouses as a result of the culpable conduct of the other, so long as such conduct stands as a serious violation of the rights or obligations that marriage imposes, or of the rights and obligations relating to the children, that makes life together intolerable ... This cause may be invoked, among other cases, when any of the following occurs ... 4. Homosexual behaviour.'

fidelity, notwithstanding the fact that any such conduct could furthermore be a criminal offence.

3 Gender Identity

In relation to gender identity, we will address some of the most salient rulings from Colombia and Mexico.[51]

3.1 Colombia

In the case of Colombia, the Constitutional Court has issued three important decisions over the past five years. This case law is particularly relevant as it incorporates the children's rights approach and calls upon the executive to take special measures to protect children's best interests.[52]

First, in a judgment dated 16 July 2013,[53] the court reviewed a case in which a newborn baby's intersex status had not been recorded on the corresponding birth certificate (the space for 'live birth, sex' had been left blank). This flaw prevented the child from being registered with the office of vital records and, consequently, from receiving benefits from the subsidized social security system.

The court stated that: 'the requirement to indicate the male or female gender of the new-born in the generic part of the birth certificate is *legitimate and necessary*'; but that '*The indeterminacy of sex must not*

---

[51] The authors should note that Argentina enjoys one of the most advanced laws in the world on this topic. That legislation acknowledges gender identity from a comprehensive perspective and allows for name and sex changes without the need for medical evidence, treatment or surgery and provides a series of guarantees to that end (Law 26,743 of 9 May 2012). In Chile there is currently no constitutional precedent or legislation on gender identity. However, an initiative is pending in Congress aimed at regulating this field holistically (Boletín 8924-07).

[52] The first judgment (T-477/95) handed down by this court on the topic was on 23 October 1995 and circulated widely across the region. This ruling dealt with the case of a child whose sex had been adjusted at the age of 6 months, after a dog bite severed his male genitalia. The court affirmed that, in light of human dignity, free development of personality and the right to identity, the express, informed consent of the patient is indispensable to any sex change medical treatment and ordered protection to be granted to the child in the form of comprehensive physical and psychological treatment, following informed consent, and confirmed the order instructing the office of vital records to retain the masculine name with which the boy was initially registered.

[53] T-450A/13.

pose an obstacle to the exercise of the right to legal personality', there being no '*constitutional reason to justify that infants and children whose sex cannot be identified at birth, are not registered and remain hidden from the State and society*'. The court continued:

> The *tension*, on the one hand, between the interest of the State in *identifying and recording citizens* for the purpose of locating them in society and within the family, and ensuring respect for all of their rights and, on the other, the right to an *identity and to a sexual identity for intersexual or genitally ambiguous persons* who are not classified at the time of their birth as men or women, must be *resolved by the legislator without losing sight of the best interest of the child*.[54]

In sum, the court ruled that the denial of healthcare or unjustified delay by the system in meeting the needs of children, especially intersexual youth, is reprehensible, ignores their fundamental rights and is unconstitutional when based on an absence of birth records.

Second, in a decision dated 28 August 2014, the court issued a judgment[55] addressing the situation of a newborn who, according to the medical diagnosis, presented 'sexual ambiguity'. The baby was initially registered as a female. At the age of 5, his parents had managed to change his name to a male one and at 6 years of age went through proceedings to change the child's sex to male, seeking surgical intervention, with which the child allegedly agreed. The court was asked to intervene in light of the delay by public health authorities in authorizing that operation.

The court concluded that the child enjoyed autonomy and that his preferences were required to be taken into consideration. As such, the consent of the parents in his stead for the operation was not pertinent. Nonetheless, the court ruled that the minor child's consent alone was not sufficient grounds upon which the court could *order* a healthcare agency to perform the sex modification or allocation surgery. The court maintained that for such an order to be issued, a correct diagnosis – absent in the instant case – should exist. Therefore, the court affirmed that the healthcare system had violated the child's right to a sexual identity, to healthcare – the right to a diagnosis – and to a dignified life, ruling against the agency for 'failing to *prioritize* the evaluation of the instant case and failing to take the timely and *necessary steps* to ensure that the

---

[54] Paragraphs 4.5.3, 4.6.1. and 4.6.2 (emphases added).   [55] T-622/14.

process of sex reassignment sought by the minor child met the requirements of informed, qualified and continuing consent'.[56]

Lastly, on 13 February 2015,[57] the court addressed the nature of the procedures required to correct an individual's gender identity. In this case, a person who had undergone sex change surgery had requested a name and sex change in existing birth records and other identity documents. The court was asked to intervene insofar as said petition was filed with administrative rather than judicial authorities.

The court stated that the administrative authorities had instituted a practice in which a transgender person could only request a change of sex through a judicial process (voluntary jurisdiction). The court further noted that this 'can pose an *additional obstacle* to the ones transgender people already face in their efforts to be recognized and accepted by the rest of society'. Insofar as the judicial process requires that a person act through counsel, the requirement poses a barrier to access, adding that such a prerequisite 'constitutes discriminatory treatment as compared to cisgender persons whose petitions for similar changes are granted by means of public deed'.[58]

The court concluded that although the measure adopted in this case might have pursued a legitimate constitutional purpose, that is, to provide security and certainty to the changes made by the office of vital records, such requirements were unnecessary considering other means that did not create hardship or discrimination, including changes introduced by means of public deed signed before a civil law notary public.

3.2 Mexico

In the case of Mexico, we will comment on a judgment dated 8 January 2009[59] regarding the case of a person who requested the modification to the name and gender on his birth certificate. The individual had been raised, educated and legally registered as a male, although at birth he presented with ambiguous external sexual organs. However, over the years, the person's secondary sexual features had developed and presented as those of a woman.

---

[56] Paragraph 2.6.4.1 (emphases added).   [57] T-063/15.
[58] Paragraphs 7.2.3–7.2.4 (emphases added).
[59] Amparo directo civil 6/2008. Related to: facultad de atracción 3/2008-PS.

In response to the petition, the court of first instance ordered the civil registry office to amend the corresponding birth record by means of an annotation in the margin and to note a new, female name and gender for the petitioner. The judge did not, however, deem it necessary to modify the original records or to order any publication or certification of the status of the petitioner.

The petitioner, in turn, filed a direct writ of protection via *amparo*, alleging the unconstitutionality of Article 138 of the Federal District's Civil Code which sets forth the procedure for corrections to birth records by means of annotations in the margin.

The Supreme Court noted that although some of the very personal rights involved in this case, such as sexual identity and intimacy, were not explicitly set forth in the Mexican Constitution, they 'implicitly emerge from international treaties signed by Mexico, and, therefore must be construed as rights derived from the recognition of the *right to human dignity*, for only through full respect thereof can we speak of a human being in all his dignity'.[60]

Based on these elements, the court declared the provision unconstitutional. The Tribunal further noted that even though the statute provided a means of amending the birth certificate in terms of name and sex – to bring it into line with reality – the fact was that, by limiting such corrections to an annotation in the margin – given the public nature of such a change – the law constituted 'an intrusion upon the petitioner's privacy and private life, since – the court stresses – the party would in many day-to-day activities be required to reveal his previous status, which, in turn, could lead to discrimination against him in employment or social relations'.[61]

Lastly, on 5 February 2015, a decree was issued that amended and added various provisions to the Civil Code and the Code of Civil Procedure of the Federal District of Mexico with the purpose of legally recognizing gender identity. This law requires that the change be documented on the original birth record and that a new birth certificate be issued reflecting the modified information only. The original record is then kept under seal and may not be published or issued unless so ordered by a court of law or government ministry.

As we can see, this Mexican case is an outstanding example of the impact that constitutional rulings can have on legal reforms.

---

[60] Page 90 (emphasis added).   [61] Pages 98 and 99.

4 Children's Rights to Family Relations

Lastly, we would like to address a set of salient rulings handed down regarding the rights of children in their family relationships. Let us again clarify that due to space constraints we are unable to address every issue associated with these rights and relationships. Thus, we will comment solely on certain judgments involving the constitutionality of provisions on filiation by birth (Chile, Mexico, Colombia and Argentina), adoption (Colombia), caregiving relations (Chile) and multi-parenting (Brazil). In our view, these rulings all reflect the tensions between civil law and the reality of family composition in Latin American today.

4.1 Filiation by Birth

On the topic of filiation by birth, we will comment on a few decisions on the constitutionality of provisions on the causes of action in kinship cases, that is, petitions seeking to establish the identity of the child with respect to his/her biological parents. In Mexico, Chile and Colombia, existing regulations maintain strong language and protections for biological bonds. At the time these laws were enacted, the legislator prioritized the so-called 'biological truth', thus allowing unfettered investigation of paternity and maternity by means of any type of evidence. This approach was in reaction to the original nineteenth-century Civil Code statutes, which allowed for filiation inquiries to be made solely regarding children born in wedlock. Over time, material reality has come to supersede this reliance on biological and/or genetic links, placing an accent on affective and social bonds whose preservation is more relevant than the 'biological truth' revealed by means of a DNA test.

In fact, this information only identifies the person formally (formal identity) and fails noticeably in reflecting other individual and social aspects (material identity). We will refer below to this process of revision of the formal and binary principles of filiation in the context of the discussion of some Brazilian rulings on multi-parenting.

4.1.1 Chile

In the case of Chile, some judgments on the constitutionality of certain filiation-related statutes have been issued. Unlike the experience with the legal reservation the Tribunal has alleged on marriage-related issues (as noted above), in this case the court has agreed to review the substantive aspects of the provisions at hand.

First, the Chilean Constitutional Tribunal has addressed the provisions regulating a claim of filiation against the heirs of a deceased alleged biological parent. In fact, most of the Tribunal's rulings have to do with this cause of action. The first ruling on the unconstitutionality of regulations pertaining to filiation dates to 2009.[62] In that judgment, the non-applicability of Article 206 of the Civil Code was resolved. The literal wording of the statute limits the possibility of filing a kinship claim against the heirs of the deceased alleged father or mother to cases in which there is a posthumous child, or the father or mother passes away within 180 days of the birth and, moreover, sets a deadline for filing such action.[63]

While we seek to avoid using numerical criteria regarding the rulings that confirm or reject the provision's legitimacy vis-à-vis the Constitution – a count that could lead us to erroneously believe that this question is settled – we note that the Constitutional Tribunal has, in general, used arguments based on fundamental rights such as equality and identity and has invoked principles such as security and legal certainty. The discussion on this question is not fully elucidated at the constitutional level, since there are majority and minority votes that, on both sides of the argument, accept or reject the allegations of unconstitutionality of the aforementioned provision of law.[64]

Regarding the application of *res judicata* in proceedings involving actions of filiation, in a ruling dated 25 July 2014 the Tribunal rejected a petition for unconstitutionality on an alleged violation of the right to identity.[65] Specifically, the petitioner's mother had maintained an intimate

---

[62] Case number 1340-09, 29 September 2009.
[63] 'If the child is posthumous, or if one of the parents dies within one hundred and eighty days following the birth, the action may be directed against the deceased father or mother's heirs, within a period of three years, counted from the death or, if the child lacks standing, from the time child has reached full competency.'
[64] Ruling in case number 1563-09, 30 August 2011; Case #1537-09, 1 September 2011; Case #1656-09, 1 September 2011; Case #2035-11, 4 September 2012; Case #2105-11, 4 September 2012; Case #2215-12, 30 May 2013; Case #2333-12, 11 June 2013; Case #2195-12, 18 June 2013; Case #2200-12, 18 June 2013; Case #2303-12, 2 July 2013; Case #2408-13, 6 March 2014; Case #2690-14, 25 July 2014; Case #2739-14, 6 August 2015.
[65] Case #2690-14, 25 July 2014.

relationship with the petitioner, and, as a result, became pregnant with the petitioner. Given that the alleged father refused to recognize the child, the mother had omitted an indication of paternity when recording the birth with the civil registry. Nonetheless, the mother had subsequently filed a motion on behalf of her minor son. That motion had been rejected in 2005. The petitioner, who had been aware of these events all his life, upon attaining the age of majority and acquiring active personal standing to sue his biological father, filed a claim for non-marital filiation. In his response, the alleged father filed an objection of *res judicata*, invoking the effects produced by the final and enforceable judgment handed down in the civil courts that had rejected the motion when first filed.

In this case, the Tribunal left the matter somewhat open. Although the court was reluctant to apply the rules of *res judicata* which the defendant invoked, it did reject the petition, stating that 'the question of a possible conflict between *res judicata* in the matter of filiation and the recognition of the human right to identity, when a second lawsuit is filed even after the first suit has been resolved, is a topic that resides at the *level of ordinary justice*, as a matter of *legality* or, at the most, of conventionality'.[66] In this way, the court avoided resolving the question of unconstitutionality.

4.1.2 Mexico

In the case of Mexico, the trend is for greater propinquity between the right to preserve identity and the right to know who the biological parents are. This follows from the line of authority outlined below.

The first judgment in this area is dated 18 October 2006,[67] in which the Supreme Court heard arguments on a theory of contradictory case law. On the one hand, a lower court had ruled that in a paternity investigation suit, the requisite genetic sample could not be taken coercively with the assistance of law enforcement; on the other hand, a separate court found that the right of the minor child to be able to establish his identity prevailed over the right of his parent to refuse to voluntarily provide a blood sample.

In this case, the Supreme Court ruled in favour of the use of force on the grounds of the best interests of the child and the child's right to

---

[66] Clause 8 (emphases added).
[67] Case theory conflict: 154/2005-PS. Novena Época. Núm. de Registro: 20018. Instancia: Primera Sala.

information on biological origin and the identity of their biological parents. In effect, the court stated:

The importance of this fundamental right to identity lies not only in the possibility of knowing the name and biological origin (ancestry), but rather that, based on that knowledge, firstly the child's right to a nationality can be ascertained and, furthermore, the minor child's constitutional right pursuant to Article 4 to have his/her needs for *food, health, education and healthy recreation, and comprehensive development* met.[68]

Subsequently, in a ruling dated 28 May 2014,[69] the Supreme Court confirmed its position in hearing arguments on a new contradiction of law. The complainant court asserted that the existence of a record containing a filiation posed no obstacle to the admission of genetic testing. The respondent court, however, argued that such evidence was not admissible insofar as paternity had previously been recognized. Were the evidence to be admitted, the court argued, the existing paternity would have to be deemed null and void to ensure that the respondent's rights would not be irreparably be harmed. In sum, the case brought two countervailing rights to the forefront: the right of the child to an identity and the right of the father to privacy.

In this case, the Supreme Court ruled that: 'Within a family it is imperative that a person know who he is, what his name is, what his origin is, who his parents are, in order to exercise *his right to biological identity*', adding that: 'This means that when the reality of a biological bond is not reflected at the legal level, the right of the person (whether a minor child or an adult) to a family must be recognized in keeping with their *blood ties*.'[70]

Lastly, the ruling is categorical as to the impossibility of having two paternities:

In cases in which the petitioner seeks to establish a new legal affiliation, it should be noted that where the provisions of law themselves do not allow or recognize the division and distinction of this set of legal relationships, legal certainty and the best interests of the child require that *only one father–child bond exist.* In other words, there could be *no case of two simultaneous legal paternities.*[71]

---

[68] Clause 5, Section I (emphases added).
[69] Case theory conflict: 430/2013. Décima Época. Núm. de Registro: 2007454. Instancia: Primera Sala.
[70] Paragraphs 75–6 (emphases added).
[71] Paragraph 84 (emphases added). This issue was confirmed in a judgment of 8 August 2011 (Contradiction Thesis 355/2011, Tenth Period. Circuit Courts), referring to the case of a

This position is in opposition to the approach taken in some Brazilian judicial rulings we will examine towards the end of this section (see section 4.4).

4.1.3 Colombia

In the case of Colombia, in a Constitutional Court judgment dated 10 November 2010,[72] we can observe the prevalence of 'substantive' criteria versus 'adjective' (or procedural) criteria in facilitating the processing of a filiation request by redefining the concept of the 'present interest' of the petitioner. Thus, the court ruled that the right to legal personality 'confers on the holder *the power to demand that true filiation prevail over purely formal or fictional filiation*'.[73] In this case, the petitioner had been told in the context of a suit questioning paternity, that his cause of action was doomed to fail on the grounds that he lacked present interest to sue, despite having filed the petition within the twenty-day term after obtaining the results of a DNA test that suggested that it was highly unlikely that the female child he had recognized was in fact his.

The court indicated that while the case could be resolved on grounds of a legally admissible interpretation, violations of fundamental rights could ensue if the statute were construed to mean '*conferring less than optimal effectiveness* on the right to freely decide on the number of children, legal personality, filiation and access to the administration of justice'.[74] Thus, the court indicated that the reasonable interpretation of the tolling [starting of clock for purposes of limitation of action] for 'present interest' in a paternity challenge commenced when the first doubt about the existence of such a filial bond arose once the person had been recognized as a child.

Furthermore, the Colombian Constitutional Court has referred to the tolling of challenges to filiation – although from opposing camps – based on the proportionality of the interpretation of the provision of law. Thus, in a judgment dated 15 February 2012[75] the court found that the constitutionally valid interpretation of a provision 'is one in which the *tolling of the challenge to paternity shall be counted as of the date upon which certainty*

---

father who, after having voluntarily recognized his son and performed his functions as such for over eleven years, affirmed that the child was not his son and filed suit against the mother to contest paternity. This request was denied by the trial court, but granted on appeal, leading the mother to seek relief at the Supreme Court.
[72] Ruling T-888/10.   [73] Paragraph 14 (emphasis added).
[74] Paragraph 24 (emphasis added).   [75] Ruling T-071/12.

was obtained by means of a DNA test showing that [the petitioner] was not the biological father'.[76]

In the opposite sense, in a judgment of 28 June 2013,[77] the Colombian Constitutional Court stated that:

> in the specific case, although there is evidence that the petitioner is not the progenitor of the child Juan Diego, his inactivity over the course of eight years suggests that he accepted his role as father of said minor child'; And that 'when confronted with the potential presence of a substantive defect by ignoring the constitutional mandate that states that substance should take precedence over form regarding the law ... *in this case, effectively, the declaration of the tolling of the action is not disproportionate* ... [since] The application of this provision is intended *to protect legal certainty and preserve the stability of ties of kinship.*[78]

4.1.4 Argentina

In Argentina, a judgment of 16 April 2008[79] declared unconstitutional Article 259, paragraph 2, of the Argentine Civil Code in force at the time as it limited the term in which a husband could contest paternity to one year from the date of birth, unless he was unaware of said birth. In the latter case, action would be time-barred at the one-year marker of his becoming aware of the existence of the child.[80] In this ruling, the challenge to paternity within wedlock was admitted, stating that there was no biological bond of parentage between father and daughter.

---

[76] Paragraph 9.2.2.1 (emphasis added). [77] Ruling T-381/13.
[78] Paragraph 7.3 (emphases added).
[79] Family Court 2, Córdoba. *G., D. E.* v. *F. N. O. y otra*. Published in: Lexis # 70053706.
[80] It should be noted that this provision was repealed with the entry into force in 2015 of the new Civil and Commercial Code of the Nation. Article 590 of the new regulations states:

> Challenging filiation presumed by law. Legitimation and expiration. The action to contest the filiation of the spouse of the person giving birth can be exercised by him or her, by the child, by the mother and by any third party who invokes a legitimate interest.
>
> The child may initiate such action at any time. For other right holders, the action expires if one year elapses from the inscription of the birth or since it was known that the child could not be the child of the person the law presumes him/her to be.
>
> In the event of the death of the direct right holder, the heirs thereto may challenge the filiation if the death occurred before the term established in this article expired. In such case, the action expires for them once the term that commenced during the life of the right holder has expired.

The judgment sets forth that 'the restrictions imposed on individual rights, in the case of the right to establish true filiation, *have a substantial limit that stems from the principles of reasonableness and proportionality*',[81] and stated that the aforementioned article contained an unreasonable limitation that violated the right to know the biological truth, which is a component of the right to personal identity, together with the right to establish legal ties of filiation between persons related by biology, and the right to prove true family status (the dynamic aspect of the right to identity).

4.2 Filiation by Adoption

In Colombia, in a judgment dated 19 February 2016[82] the Constitutional Court settled the case of a woman identified as *Y* who was born as the result of an extramarital relationship between *YSA* and *GCZ*. *AAL* and his spouse *ACZ* had provided for her since, at the time of her birth, her biological mother *(YSA)* was a minor. *Y*'s biological father, *GCZ*, was the brother of her 'foster father' *(ACZ)* and her biological uncle, but had never assumed his parental role. After coming of age, *Y* and *ACZ* decided to legalize their kinship through adoption.[83] While that application was initially rejected by the family court, it was subsequently accepted by another court. The problem arose when the latter ruling provided for *Y*'s surname to be changed to that of her 'social father' and simultaneously ordered the name of the biological mother on the birth record stricken, thereby eliminating the filial and family bond with her mother. In response, *Y* appealed and requested that suppression of the name of her biological mother with whom she had 'carried out normal relations as mother and daughter' be revoked. However, the appellate court reaffirmed the decision, ruling that one of the effects of full adoption is the extinction of all previous blood relationships.

In a noteworthy interpretation, the Constitutional Court stated that the preceding judicial resolutions that thwarted the adoption should have interpreted existing regulations on the adoption of a person of legal age

---

[81] Section II. 1 (emphases added).   [82] Ruling T-071/16.
[83] Article 69 of the Colombian Children and Adolescent Code (2006) allows for the adoption of adults if the adopted party was under the care of the adopting party and that both had lived together for at least two years prior to the adoptee's eighteenth birthday.

more systematically and more harmoniously, particularly since it was never the parties' intent to extinguish the parental bonds between the daughter and the biological mother. The court also noted that 'the adoption sought to recognize a *real bond* that had formed over the years between adoptee and adopter' that would reward '*the love, affection and support* the adopting father had provided to her in her formative years in his efforts to fulfil the obligations of parenting'.[84]

In addition to opening up the idea of social kinship and underscoring the validity of affection-based relationships as a source of civil effects, this decision also calls for a review of the classic impacts of one of the institutions with the strongest groundings in family law: adoption. In this sense, the court established that it cannot disproportionately affect the right to identity and the right to family life, by erasing previous bonds. This element could open the way for the reincorporation of some types of adoption repealed in several Latin American legal systems, under which the legal ties between a child and his/her biological parents (simple adoption) persist.

4.3 Caregiving Relationships

On the topic of the personal care of a child, prior to reforms introduced in 2013, the Chilean Civil Code gave preference to the mother in determining the personal care of children in all cases in which the parents lived apart. In the authors' opinion, that statute ran contrary to the principles of the best interests of the child and to parental equality and, in effect, was subsequently modified by means of Law 20,680 of 2013. That reform corrected this arbitrary discrimination, replacing the provisions of Article 225, paragraph 1 with language that takes into consideration the de facto place of residence of the child, that is, with which parent the child is residing at the time of the separation.

Following the entry into force of Law 20,680, the Constitutional Tribunal has had occasion to rule on the constitutionality of the new language of Article 225 of the Civil Code.[85] Specifically, the Tribunal has

---

[84] Paragraph 66 (emphases added).
[85] If the parents live apart, they may jointly determine that the personal care of the children belongs to the father or the mother or to both in shared form. Such agreement shall be recorded by public deed or a record issued by any official of the Civil Registry and shall be sub-inscribed in the margin of the birth record of the child within thirty days of issuance.

considered the possibility of establishing shared personal care in the absence of agreement in this regard between the parties. In a ruling on a possible violation of due process and the right to defence, the court stated that the determination of shared personal care is not a matter to be settled by the courts: 'whereas the *imposition of shared personal care is not a matter that falls to the courts to resolve*, insofar as the legislature rightly reserved the topic for situations in which there is agreement between the parents, it is not a matter that can be resolved in an anticipatory judicial proceeding'.[86]

The Tribunal's interpretation in this case is open to debate, given that in 2013 the legislature did not expressly preclude the courts from regulating shared personal care at the request of a party. Considering that parental co-responsibility is not only one of the founding principles of this reform, but also that the new provisions have provided further content to guidance on the best interests of the child in these matters – by repealing 'indispensability' and making application more objective – it would appear that, at the very least, it would be appropriate for a judge hearing a case to order caregiving, should

---

This agreement shall establish the frequency and freedom with which the father or mother who does not have the personal care will maintain a direct and regular relationship with the children and may be revoked or modified by means of the same solemnities.

Shared personal care is a way of life that seeks to stimulate the co-responsibility of both parents living separately in the upbringing and education of their children in common, through a system of residence that ensures their adequate stability and continuity.

In the absence of the agreement of the first paragraph, the children will continue under the personal care of the father or mother with whom they are living.

In any of the cases set forth in this article, when circumstances require and the best interest of the child makes it appropriate, the judge may assign the personal care of the child to the other parent, or grant it to one of them, if by agreement some form of shared parenting exists. The foregoing should be understood without prejudice to the provisions of article 226.

In no case may the judge base his decision exclusively on the economic capacity of the parents.

Whenever the judge assigns the child's personal care to one of the parents, he shall establish, at his own initiative or at the request of a party, in the same resolution, the frequency and freedom with which the other parent who does not have personal care will maintain a direct and regular relationship with the children, considering their best interest, provided that the criteria set forth in article 229 are met.

Until such a time as a new sub-inscription regarding personal care is cancelled by a subsequent one, any new agreement or resolution will be unenforceable vis-à-vis third parties.

[86] Constitutional Tribunal, Case #2699-14, June 16, 2015 (emphasis added). Clause 24.

circumstances so warrant and so long as it is in furtherance of the child's well-being.

In this realm, we should note that as recently as 12 April 2016,[87] the Chilean Constitutional Tribunal ruled on a matter closely related to personal care. The case involved a petition for inapplicability by a family court judge regarding the custody of two minor children.

The family judge was hearing a request for curatorship filed by the brother of two minor girls on the grounds that they were residing with him – and were under his care – following the death of their father and mother. The judge affirmed that certain articles of the Civil Code imperatively obligated the court to grant custody to the girls' maternal grandfather, who was alive but did not maintain contact or have a relationship with them, unlike the petitioner, who did have an affective bond with them.

The Constitutional Tribunal accepted the case and, in addressing the substance of the matter, deemed that the application of the rules on curatorship would have unconstitutional effects in terms of the impact on the psychological integrity of the minor children and their right to equality before the law. The Tribunal noted that the law views the situation of children of parents who have passed away as different from that of children whose parents are alive, stating that such differentiation is unjustified insofar as they are in the same position: both need the law to identify the person responsible for caring for them. The former would be governed by provisions 'whose requirements make *no reference to the primary consideration that in such matters the best interest of the child should be given merit*, as a right, principle and rule of procedure'.[88]

Lastly, the Constitutional Tribunal suggested that the application of these provisions would profoundly affect the psychological integrity of minor children: 'The possibility of a change in the family environment and the loss of the family and emotional ties they have formed with the person who has cared for them since they were orphaned, would *be detrimental to their psychological integrity and the full development of their capabilities in the future*'.[89]

This ruling is particularly important because it raises a critique of the relevance of certain nineteenth-century civil law statutes. Due to their age, these rules appear to be inconsistent with more modern provisions that

---

[87] Case #2867-15.   [88] Clause 16 (emphasis added).   [89] Clause 40 (emphasis added).

address similar situations, such as those relating to the care of minor children if their biological parents are alive.

4.4 Multi-parenting

We will briefly comment now on a limited number of rulings in Brazil and Argentina that are paving the way for 'pluri-parenting' or 'multi-parenting'. They do not refer directly to the constitutionality of a given provision, but do open up previously unchartered dimensions of family law: admitting the possibility that a person may have more than two filial bonds, that is, a redefinition of the binary system inherent to the classic principles of the law of filiation.

In Brazil, this situation has been raised in the judicial realm. An example is the ruling of the Eighth Civil Chamber of the Court of Justice of the State of Rio Grande in 2015, in which recognition was given to 'multi-parenting' following a petition by a married trio consisting of two women and one man who had a 'pact of filiation'. By virtue of this pact, the three petitioners had reciprocally committed to the exercise of family power, inheritance, custody, visitation and sustenance obligations. In this case, the Chamber overturned the decision by the lower court rejecting the request and declared appropriate 'the request for recognition of multi-parenting with regards to the daughter, [ordering] *a correction to be made to the vital records to include the mother's wife as a progenitor, including the respective maternal grandparents*'.[90]

Unlike Brazil, in Argentina, this issue has emerged in the administrative sphere. In 2015, two cases were filed before the civil registry regarding children born by means of human reproduction techniques to two women married to each other. In this case, the person who provided the genetic material was a friend of the couple who also played the role of father; the children were raised by the three adults. In both cases, the corresponding civil registry accepted the recognition proffered by the man and issued a new birth certificate, reflecting the triple bond of filiation.[91]

---

[90] Eighth Civil Chamber of the Court of Justice of Río Grande Do Sul, styled L.P.R., R.C. and M. B.R. s/Acción civil declaratoria de multiparentalidad, 12/02/2015 (emphasis added) 12. JPOE #70062692876 (# CNJ: 0461850-92.2014.8.21.7000) 2014/CÍVEL.

[91] See M. L. Peralta, 'Filiaciones múltiples y familias multiparentales: La necesidad de revisar el peso de lo biológico en el concepto de identidad' (2014) 68 *Revista Interdisciplinaria de Doctrina y Jurisprudencia Derecho de Familia* 53-70; M. Herrera, C. Duprat and M. V.

5 Conclusions

This chapter has sought to provide an overview of the status of Latin American constitutional rulings on family relations. It is one of our main contentions that these judicial decisions reflect an embryonic process of constitutionalization of family law that seems to be emerging in some countries of this region. In particular, this process seems to be prominent in the constitutional case law of Argentina and Colombia.

As observed in this brief analysis of an array of judicial decisions on such matters as sexual orientation, gender identity and filiation, it appears that the constitutionalization of family law may be opening up innovative and far-reaching avenues for legal reform in an ever-changing area of the law. The process of constitutionalization is particularly important in the development of family law, given the strongly personal component inherent to the field. Modern family law is continually challenged to regulate family relationships in dynamic, complex, and deeply transformative social contexts. In modern societies, unlike the past, individual projects do not develop predominantly in the family. Today, people tend to fulfil their aspirations in contexts that go beyond private family life, leading the 'static' family that most of the civil codes of Latin America contemplated in the nineteenth century to be replaced by a type of family that changes constantly, adapts to the individual plans of its members, and forms part of people's conceptualization as legitimate option, but that does not totally cover or satisfy the individual projects.

These challenges require Latin American legal systems to adjust periodically, to reformulate their rules and provisions based on new founding principles. In this process, the task of the interpreter is fundamental and, especially, that of the courts called upon to declare the conformity of these provisions to the political constitution. In this context, the constitutionalization of family law could play a paramount role in the protection of human rights within family relations; a process that may contribute, among other aspects, to the progressive incorporation of international human rights standards into domestic law.

Pellegrini, 'Filiación e identidad: Principales desafíos del derecho filial contemporáneo en el Código Civil y Comercial de la Nación' (2015) 25 (special edn) *Revista Código Civil y Comercial* 93–110.

Nonetheless, the analysis of this embryonic process of constitutionalization should not be accepted indiscriminately. It is our contention that, while providing positive elements, extended neo-constitutionalism could provide a false sense of legal clarity. Under this new approach, family law only takes possession of its validity when suited or adjusted to the constitutional normativity (super-dogma). However, constitutional principles and fundamental rights are difficult to pin down and on many occasions understanding what the constitutional rules mandate in specific matters can be particularly thorny, thereby requiring further theoretical and normative development.

While family law is necessarily anchored in constitutional law, it should not hold fast to that anchor at the cost of dogmatic (theoretical) and normative laziness. Just as the criminal law has managed to respect core constitutional principles and rights while maintaining a robust doctrinal and normative development, so family law will need to provide a much more solid, precise set of legal principles and rules to justify its own dogma; a new dogma that reflects the transformations needed to spur effectiveness as well as the constitutional confines within which it is called to navigate.

6 The Nuclear Norm and the Free-Form Family
Irreconcilable Paths in Swedish Family Law?

Pernilla Leviner*

Sweden is often described as a modern, liberal and open society, often seen as a leader when it comes to different types of reforms regulating or influencing citizens' behaviour and developing society. In the World Values Survey by the Institute for Future Studies, Sweden is described as 'the world's most extreme country' in terms of the population's emphasis on individual freedom and secularised, 'non-traditional' values.[1] This phenomenon is particularly noticeable in the field of family law, in terms of children's rights and gender equality. For example, in 1979 Sweden was the first country in the world to introduce a prohibition on corporal punishment. Abortion became legal in 1975. Sweden has also been a forerunner in recognising same-sex relationships by introducing registered partnerships for same-sex couples in 1995, the right to same-sex adoption in 2003 and the right to enter into a same-sex marriage in 2009. As for gender equality, Swedish law manifests a clear tendency towards the equal division of childcare between parents. One expression of this intention is the introduction of 'daddy quotas', the individualisation of a part of the generous paid parental leave that each parent must use or lose. Another aspect is the clear political goal of ensuring that separated parents share legal and physical custody, with children alternatively living with each parent. Social engineering has been used by the Swedish state since the second half of the twentieth century to create a society based on equality.

---

* The work related to this article has been carried out in part during a guest research visit in the spring of 2016 at the Institute for European and Comparative Law, Faculty of Law and Exeter College, Oxford University.

[1] For a summary of these survey results carried out using e.g. interviews in many countries on a regular basis, see www.worldvaluessurvey.org/WVSContents.jsp?CMSID=Findings (accessed 30 December 2016).

In this endeavour, the focus has often been placed on children, parenthood and family life.

In Esping-Andersen's often-cited work, *The Three Worlds of Welfare Capitalism*,[2] and in later literature within the research area, 'varieties of welfare capitalism', the Swedish welfare system is classified as 'social-democratic'. This type of welfare system, which differs from liberal systems (in countries such as the US, Great Britain and Australia) and conservative systems (as in Germany, France and Italy), is characterised by its focus on generous, broad and non-needs-tested social initiatives for the country's citizens. Equality among people is the central theme in this type of system, and effort is put into giving citizens a relatively high degree of independence by limiting their dependence on the family and the market.

In the same spirit with which the welfare system as a whole was built, a new child protection system was developed in Sweden in the late 1970s, i.e. a dedicated social system to support and protect children and youths. The Swedish child protection system (in Swedish literally the childcare system, *barnavårdssystemet*) is regulated in the Social Services Act (2001: 452) and the Care of Young Persons Act (1990: 52), both founded on principles of voluntariness and self-determination, as well as a fundamental belief in the notion that with some degree of support, every person can achieve a good economic and social existence. In terms of the basic principles of the Swedish child protection system – and in line with the character of the welfare system as a whole – Sweden and the other Nordic countries differ from other countries in the 'western world'. In an international comparison, the Swedish system is usually categorised as family and service-orientated, while systems in countries such as Great Britain, Australia and the US are described as risk and protection-orientated.[3] In simple terms, the difference lies in the threshold for intervention: it is higher in risk and protection-orientated systems than in family and service-orientated systems. In addition, family and service-orientated systems ideally offer a broader set of voluntary measures designed to avoid compulsory care of children and out-of-home placements to the greatest degree possible.[4]

---

[2] G. Esping-Andersen, *The Three Worlds of Welfare Capitalism* (Princeton University Press, 1990).

[3] N. Gilbert, N. Parton and M. Skivenes (eds.), *Child Protection Systems: International Trends and Emerging Orientations* (New York: Oxford University Press, 2011).

[4] However, as is often the case with typologies, even in countries that at first glance seem to have similar systems, differences can be found on deeper levels, and systems of different characters can of course also have similarities. These systems also change over time. In Sweden, which

In addition to this welfare system context as a background to Swedish family law, there is a general typical 'Swedishness', which is claimed to explain the initiation of many reforms in the welfare system as a whole, but also as a reason for much of the family policy. History scholars Henrik Berggren and Lars Trädgårdh have coined the term 'Swedish state individualism', which describes the unusually strong role of the individual in Sweden.[5] In contrast to the situation in many other countries, the family in Sweden is not the most important social unit. Instead, the individual holds a clear and independent relationship with the state and authorities; this relationship is built on mutual trust. This Swedish state individualism as described by Berggren and Trädgårdh is in line with the efforts by the social-democratic welfare state to create independence for the citizens and limit dependence on family.

An interesting contradiction lies in this Swedish idea that the welfare of the individual is to be protected by the state rather than by the family. Individualism is strongly emphasised at the same time as there is a significant acceptance of control of the individual by the state. This contradiction between individualism and state control can be said to be reflected in the family policies and regulations in family law. Despite the fact that Sweden can be seen as a model country – at least in some respects – when it comes to the individual's possibilities to build a family and live a (family) life as they see fit, at the same time, some of the reforms that have taken place in other countries have not been welcomed in Sweden. For example, Swedish healthcare authorities are not allowed to assist in surrogacy arrangements, and a genetic relationship between at least one prospective parent and the child is still required if assisted reproduction via the Swedish public healthcare system is used.[6] Another

---

usually is described as an almost ideal country for a family and service-orientated system, we have seen a trend towards increased protection-orientated thinking, for example in the reforms of regulations for investigations of child welfare reports. T. Lundström and B. Vinnerljung, 'Omhändertagande av barn under 1990-talet', in M. Szebehely (ed.), *Välfärdstjänster i omvandling: Antologi från Kommittén Välfärdsbokslut* (SOU 2001: 52) (Stockholm: Fritzes offentliga publikationer, 2001) and P. Leviner, *Rättsliga dilemman i socialtjänstens barnskyddsarbete* (Stockholm: Jure förlag AB, 2011).

[5] H. Berggren, and L. Trädgårdh, Är svensken människa? – Gemenskap och oberoende i det moderna Sverige (2nd edn, Stockholm: Nordstedts, 2015).

[6] See the Genetic Integrity Act (2006:351). However, as noted below, a proposal to remove this requirement on genetic relationship to at least one prospective parent has been approved by the Parliament and will enter into force in 2019, see SOU 2016:11 *Olika vägar till föräldraskap*, 310 and Governmental Bill, Prop. 2017/18:155 Modernare regler om assisterad befruktning och föräldraskap.

example is the strong Swedish resistance to 'domestic adoptions', and to some extent, also to the transfer of guardianship to foster parents in situations where children who no longer can live with their parents have been placed in out-of-home care. Simply put, there is a reluctance to cut legal ties and an unwillingness to give up hope on reuniting parents with their children. Even if family is not – as in many other countries – viewed as the starting point for society's structure – there are nevertheless clear features of a legal priority for the nuclear family in Sweden. This is remarkable given the notion of Swedish state individualism and the nation's enthusiasm for reform in the field of family law.

This chapter examines this discrepancy between the relative freedom of individuals to start families and choose forms of cohabitation on the one hand, and the legal preference for the nuclear family on the other. Against the background of the reforms carried out in Swedish family law, and the nuclear family norm that plausibly remains entrenched nevertheless in the law, this discussion explores whether the identified preference for the nuclear family is merely an 'unreflected' remnant of an outdated view of the family and that the norm of the nuclear family is fading, or whether prioritising the nuclear family is a 'conscious' legal effort existing parallel to Swedish state individualism and the reforms carried out in recent decades. The term 'nuclear family' here refers to constellations having one or more of the following characteristics: (1) couple-based 'twoness' and 'romantic' love (i.e. monogamous relationships including sex); (2) marriage; and (3) genetic connections between parents and children.

The legal framework for parenthood and guardianship in the Swedish legal system is set out in the legislation, preparatory works, case law and legal scholarship. The family law system is examined here for examples of expressions of legal preference for the nuclear family in the form of the characteristics mentioned above. However, this is not intended to be a comprehensive review and description of all of Swedish family law. The aim is rather to sketch the situation and trends in Swedish family law today.

After this introduction the sections 'Forming the family' and 'Preserving the family' below provide analyses of how parenthood and guardianship are created and managed in Swedish law. The first section explores issues of who can be a parent, and how parenthood and guardianship are registered according to Swedish law – i.e. the legal formation of a family. The second examines the matter of society's authority to intervene in private and family life to protect children and young people, i.e. to break up a family, and the conditions under which children who have been placed in out-of-home care can/should/shall be reunited with their parents. This section also examines the legal prerequisites for the transfer of guardianship (*vårdnadsöverflyttning*) and adoption in child protection cases, i.e. the 'conclusion' of the family. After this review and search for 'nuclear family norms' in the formation and preservation of family, the final section of this chapter deals with general aspects associated with the nuclear family norm and the possibly irreconcilable paths in Swedish family law.

Forming the Family: Becoming and Being a (Nuclear) Family

Becoming a parent in itself is not a positive right in Swedish law. However, there is a negative right associated with parenthood. That is that in principle, no one can be deprived of the right to have children, at least not 'on one's own', through consensual sex leading to pregnancy or in another way without assistance from the public healthcare system. This right follows generally from the right to private and family life according to Article 8 of the European Convention for the Protection of Human Rights and the Basic Freedoms (European Convention). Under Swedish constitutional law, no person can be forced to undergo sterilisation, abortion or a similar procedures.[7] This latter protection of rights has not always existed – up to only a few decades ago, women were forcibly sterilised in Sweden,[8] and until 2013, those wishing to undergo sex reassignment surgery were first required to be sterilised.[9]

---

[7] Chapter 2 Section 6, Instrument of Government (1974:152).
[8] M. Tydén, *Från politik till praktik – de svenska steriliseringslagarna 1935–1975*, Stockholm Studies in History (2nd edn, Stockholm: Almqvist & Wiksell International, 2002). Today such measures are illegal and condemned, but the case may be that women are still compelled to a certain degree to use contraceptives, without this being given any attention by society.
[9] Governmental Bill, Ds. 2012:46 *Avskaffande av steriliseringskrav för ändrad könstillhörighet*.

Who Is Allowed to Be a Parent?

Having children through consensual sex or in other ways not involving public health or medical intervention is permitted, and perhaps even encouraged, considering the generous parental benefits, child support payments, state-financed childcare, free education, etc. For those who cannot or do not wish to have children 'on their own', a certain amount of help can be given by the Swedish public healthcare system as 'assisted reproduction'. Another alternative is to adopt a child.

When it comes to the regulation of adoption – which in Sweden is usually only applicable for the adoption of stepchildren or international adoptions – there are clear nuclear family norms in the law in the form of requirements that a couple wishing to adopt must be married or cohabitants. Until September 2018 the Children and Parents Code (1949:381) stated that 'persons other than married persons may not take custody of an adoptive child'. This has now changed so that also unmarried couples who are living together can adopt.[10] In other words, marriage or cohabitation is required for two persons to be able to adopt a child together. This means that two friends or siblings cannot adopt a child together since the law gives priority to nuclear families with two adult members who are married, or as from September 2018 cohabitants.[11] Single persons are not excluded as such from becoming adoptive parents,[12] but in practice the possibility of adoption is limited, as many countries do not allow 'their' children to be adopted by single persons (and even less so by homosexual couples), and domestic adoptions in Sweden are very rare.

Assistance for Involuntarily Childless Persons as Part of the Propagation of the Nuclear Family?

Assistance to those who are involuntarily childless to 'have a baby' instead of adopting a child can be given under certain circumstances. The Genetic Integrity Act (2006:351) regulates both assisted reproduction through insemination and *in vitro* fertilisation (IVF). Swedish law allows married

---

[10] Before Chapter 4 Section 4, and now Chapter 4 Section 6 the Children and Parents Code.
[11] According to statistics from Statistics Sweden, only one third of Swedish parents living together when having their first child are married. Statistiska Centralbyrån (Statistic Sweden), *Sambo, barn, gift, isär? – Parbildning och separationer bland förstagångsföräldrar*, Demografiska rapporter 2012:1, 2012, 27.
[12] Chapter 4 Section 1, the Children and Parents Code.

or cohabiting couples, hetero and homosexual, and, as of April 2016, single women, to obtain help with assisted reproduction from the Swedish public healthcare system.[13] Fertilisation can be carried out using the prospective parents' own gametes and/or donated gametes. However, there is still, until 2019, a requirement that either the male or female gametes must come from one of the prospective parents, i.e. that there be a genetic relationship with at least one parent.[14] This entails that single women[15] until now have been dependent upon the full functionality of their own egg cells as they must use donated sperm. As mentioned the requirement on genetic association between the child and at least one of the prospective parents will be removed as from 2019.[16]

When using donated gametes, there are additional requirements in the Genetic Integrity Act as to prospective parents. The medical, psychological and social situation of the couple or single woman must be suitable for assisted conception, and assistance may only be provided when it can be assumed that the future child will grow up in a good environment. The physician is to carry out a special suitability assessment.[17] Even though guidelines have been issued by the National Board of Health and Welfare, it is still not clear what this assessment comprises of and what factors should lead to individuals being denied assisted fertilisation with donated gametes.[18] Furthermore, there is no review or research in Sweden regarding such assessments to this author's knowledge. This means that there is no body of knowledge of what precisely constitutes 'suitability' or as to the number of persons who are refused help with assisted fertilisation with donated gametes.

---

[13] Governmental Bill, Prop. 2014/15:127 *Assisterad befruktning för ensamstående kvinnor*.

[14] Chapter 7 Section 3, the Genetic Integrity Act. A proposal has been made to remove this requirement and that genetic association no longer should be mandatory (Governmental Inquiry, SOU 2016:11 *Olika vägar till föräldraskap*). This proposal has been approved by the Parliament in 2018 and will enter into force in 2019. See Governmental Bill, Prop. 2017/18:155 Modernare regler om assisterad befruktning och föräldraskap.

[15] Given gender variations, a better term with respect to the medical discussion as to woman in this context could be a 'person with uterus' to include female-to-male and other transgender people, e.g. someone who in a legal sense has 'changed' from female to male and still has a functioning uterus.

[16] Governmental Inquiry, SOU 2016:11 *Olika vägar till föräldraskap*, 310 and Governmental Bill, Prop. 2017/18:155 Modernare regler om assisterad befruktning och föräldraskap.

[17] Chapter 6 Section 3 and Chapter 7 Section 5, the Genetic Integrity Act.

[18] Guidelines from the National Board of Health and Welfare, SOSFS 2009:32, *Socialstyrelsens föreskrifter och allmänna råd om användning av vävnader och celler i hälso- och sjukvården och vid klinisk forskning*, Chapter 4 Section 11.

Recent changes have been made with regard to the conditions for receiving help with assisted fertilisation from the Swedish healthcare system. However, certain limitations still exist – both actual and possibly also more 'practical' barriers that may be rooted in the pursuit of the nuclear family. One example is the barrier for those wishing to use a surrogate arrangement – i.e. when a woman becomes pregnant and gives birth with the expressed intent to give the child to a couple or person who cannot or does not wish to carry a child. Surrogate arrangements are prohibited in Sweden – i.e. healthcare clinics are not allowed to assist in surrogate arrangements. The same governmental inquiry proposing the removal of requirements for genetic association between the child and at least one of the prospective parents (see above) also investigated the desirability of allowing altruistic surrogate arrangements in Sweden. However, the conclusions reached by the inquiry were that the prohibition should remain and that no changes should be made in the *mater est* principle in the Children and Parents Code, i.e. that the woman giving birth to a child automatically receives status as the child's mother. Specific reasons given in this governmental inquiry against allowing surrogate arrangements included the risks of women being coerced into becoming pregnant and bearing a child for someone else, commercialisation and the threat posed to women's autonomy and bodily integrity. The basic view is that the state 'has the right' to decide that such arrangements are not suitable or good, irrespective of what women may think about carrying and bearing a child for another person. Another argument put forward in the governmental inquiry is that surrogate arrangements can result in a view of children as goods to be bought and sold, and that there is a knowledge gap when it comes to the living conditions and well-being – both in the short or long term – of children born in such arrangements.[19] None of the arguments against allowing surrogate arrangements in the governmental inquiry can be interpreted as explicit support for the preservation of the nuclear family. However, there might be a resistance against such arrangements below the surface as they are viewed in conflict with the image of a 'real family', including a mother who either has given birth to the child or through adoption has at least 'rescued' a child and 'helped' another mother who was unable to care for her own child.

Another example of potential 'nuclear family preservation' can be traced in the practical application of the regulations on assisted fertilisation with donated gametes. To receive assisted fertilisation care, it seems that

---

[19] Governmental Inquiry, SOU 2016:11 *Olika vägar till föräldraskap*, 445ff.

a couple must have a loving relation including sexual intercourse. The very term used – 'involuntarily childless' – indicates that assisted fertilisation is only given to couples who have sex that 'normally' could produce children but who nevertheless do not 'succeed' in becoming pregnant. The general practice in the Swedish public healthcare system is that heterosexual couples must be able to demonstrate that they have tried to conceive for a certain period.[20] This therefore eliminates the possibility of IVF assistance being given to two friends or two siblings who live together without having a sexual relationship – or, for that matter, a couple living together without having sex. Another question is whether a couple who have functioning gametes could receive assisted fertilisation care for reasons other than not being able to conceive. Could assistance be given because one parent carries a less desirable genetic trait and therefore does not want to be a genetic parent? Considering the dearth of research on the suitability assessments performed by healthcare professionals, there is no thorough review of the reasons why people seek assisted reproduction, or what healthcare considers as legitimate reasons for seeking this help.

The Registration of Parenthood and Guardianship: Legal Presumptions as an Expression of the Nuclear Family Norm

In addition to observing traces of a 'nuclear family preservation' in the regulations concerning who has the possibility to have children according to Swedish law, examining who can be registered as a parent or guardian when a child is born is also relevant. Guardians are normally the same persons who can become parents. The law however also has to address who can register as parents and guardians in 'uncertain situations'. Such situations can include when it is unclear who the parents are, and when children have been born without the help of the Swedish healthcare system but not through 'natural conception', for example in home inseminations or with

---

[20] Karolinska Hospital in Stockholm, one of the largest university hospitals in Sweden, requires that applicants for treatment have unsuccessfully attempted at least one year to conceive. See the hospital website: 'Regler och grundkrav assisterad befruktning' (Rules and basic requirements for assisted conception; author's translation), available at: www.karolinska.se/for-patienter/alla-mottagningar-och-avdelningar-a-o/kvinnokliniken/ofrivillig-barnloshet/repro duktionsmedicin/vantelista-och-kotid (accessed 30 December 2016). These rules also stipulate that the couple must be stable and the two persons must have had a continuous relationship for a minimum of two years prior to treatment.

assisted fertilisation abroad without any genetic associations with the parents, surrogate arrangements, etc. Such situations are often very complex from a legal perspective and could well be the focus for a book on their own. The focus here is on situations where children have been born without the help of the Swedish public healthcare system but 'in accordance with Swedish law', and the purpose is to examine whether the nuclear family norm can be detected in these regulations.

As typical in most legal systems, there is an assumption that the woman giving birth to a child is the child's mother,[21] and is automatically registered as parent and also as guardian.[22] The same applies for the husband of the woman bearing the child. The husband is automatically registered as parent and guardian.[23] Thus there appears to be a legal 'expectation' that married women only have sex with their husbands, which can be said to express a legal nuclear family norm and a norm of a monogamous lifestyle. No special registration is needed for children born within a marriage between a man and a woman. A man who believes that he is the father of a child born to a woman married to a different man cannot petition for paternity testing. Instead, such initiative can only be taken by the Social Welfare Board in the municipality where the child lives or by the mother if she is the guardian.[24] Thus, an 'outsider' cannot 'challenge the nuclear family' which can also be said to be an expression for the protection of the nuclear family structure.

This presumption regarding parenthood and guardianship for married heterosexual spouses does not apply to unmarried men whose partners give birth to children. Nor is there such a presumption for women who are married or cohabit with another woman giving birth to a child. However, this is under review.[25] These men and women must obtain special – i.e. not automatic – registration as parents and guardians. Such registration requires the approval of the woman bearing the child.[26] For registration of paternity in this situation, the starting point is that the *genetic* father should be registered as a parent and guardian. If it is unclear whether a man is the genetic father, a DNA test can be performed. Even if the choice lies between two 'candidate fathers', of which one is suitable and willing, but not the genetic father, and the other who is the genetic father and both unsuitable and unwilling, the

---

[21] Chapter 1 Section 7, Children and Parents Code.　[22] *Ibid.*, Chapter 6 Section 3.
[23] *Ibid.*, Chapter 1 Section 1 and Chapter 6 Section 3.　[24] *Ibid.*, Chapter 3 Section 5.
[25] See SOU 2018:68 Nya regler om faderskap och föräldraskap.
[26] *Ibid.*, Chapter 1 Section 4.

latter is to be registered as the father. Social services and courts thus have no alternative to choose the 'best dad' as genetic parenthood trumps social/suitable parenthood. There are of course a number of reasons for this, of which the medical reason is perhaps the most important – it should be possible to trace genetic sources of illnesses, etc. Another reason is the child's right to know his or her origins, expressed in instruments such as Article 7 of the UN Convention on the Rights of the Child. At the same time, it can be underscored that the search to find the 'right' genetic father has not yet been viewed so important as to entail removing the presumption of fatherhood for men married to women bearing children.[27]

In addition to limitations on *who* can be registered as a parent, there are also regulations limiting *how many* parents a child may have. As noted, there is a strong legal intention to have two persons – the genetic or consenting parents – registered as parents, and social services have a far-reaching obligation to ensure that the genetic parents are located and registered. Apart from being considered important for children to have their genetic parents registered, the standpoint taken in the legislation is also that it is in the child's best interest to have *two* parents. The state interest in having two parents share the burden of care and thus lighten the economic liability of the state for the child also comes into play.

The striving for 'twoness' in parent registration is clearly expressed in a Supreme Court judgment that received considerable media attention,[28] involving a man who petitioned to have his paternity rescinded for twins born through assisted fertilisation carried out abroad, with donated eggs and sperm. The woman who bore the children – the man's ex-wife – consented to the petition and the two were in agreement that she had undergone the fertilisation without his consent by allowing *two* embryos to be implanted, when he had agreed to have only *one* embryo implanted. The man claimed that his fatherhood, which was based on consent and not a genetic relationship, but which was automatically bestowed upon

---

[27] The regulation regarding special registration, as mentioned above, also applies to a woman living together (and having an intimate relationship) with another woman who gives birth to a child. When two women have a child together, the *consent* to assisted fertilisation and not the genetic connection to the non-childbearing women, serves as the basis for parenthood (see *ibid.*, Chapter 1 Section 9). In cases where conception has taken place outside the Swedish healthcare system – for example through home insemination – the non-childbearing partner must adopt the child in order to be registered as parent and guardian.

[28] NJA 2015, 675.

him because the couple was married at the time – should be annulled for both children. However, the Supreme Court dismissed the man's petition and determined that his registration as father should remain. In support of the decision, the Supreme Court stated that the father's interest in avoiding, to the greatest possible extent, becoming father to twins cannot exceed the children's interest in having a father. Thus, it was asserted that the interests of the children would be best served by having two parents, despite the fact that the father was thoroughly unwilling to be a parent. Many people might think that the key question here is one of responsibility, not least for provision of care, but the result in Swedish family law is that nevertheless the two-parent norm is sustained, even without a genetic relationship or consent.

In the same vein, it is only possible to register two persons as parents and guardians for a child, even if the reality is that the child has additional adults who bear the responsibility for the child in different ways – if not genetically – and who have been involved in the creation and existence of the child. If two same-sex couples decide to have a child together, by using gametes from two of the four, and all four parents are equally involved in the child's care, only two of the four (the genetic producers) can be registered as parents. This can also be seen as articulating a legal nuclear family norm.

There is a significant difference between being registered as a parent[29] and (also) being a guardian. A parent has the duty of care[30] and in principle the right to contact with the child, or at least to petition for contact and to take part in care.[31] A guardian, in comparison, also has the duty to ensure that the child's needs are met, which includes an obligation to ensure that the child attends school and that the child has good contact with the other parent.[32] To be able to fulfil this responsibility, the guardian has far-reaching decision-making rights over the child, which decrease over time in correlation to the child's assumption of responsibility, as the child ages and matures, assuming his or her own right of self-determination. However, as a rule, guardians for younger children make decisions about

---

[29] Registration of parenthood must be distinguished from being registered as a donor of sex cells, where there are no legal bonds between the child and the donor – only information about the donor's identity, etc. is documented in healthcare records.
[30] Chapter 7, Children and Parents Code.
[31] *Ibid.*, Chapter 6 Sections 5 and 15, Children and Parents Code.
[32] *Ibid.*, Chapter 6 Section 1.

contact with authorities, the school the child attends, the child's name and religion, and daily care.[33]

The legal system exhibits a strong intention that both parents be guardians and participate in the legal and practical care of their children. For example, if two unmarried persons have a child together, then only one of them (usually the mother) is registered as the guardian; but if the two marry, they will automatically share guardianship.[34] Hence, marriage can be said to be 'prioritised'. Furthermore, shared guardianship remains after separation. Alternating residence between parents is strongly recommended and is a common arrangement today for children with parents not living together.[35] Only if one parent is highly unsuitable or if the parents are completely unable to cooperate with each other can one of the parents be given sole guardianship.[36]

All in all, the regulations for registration of parenthood and guardianship appear to contain clear expressions of the nuclear family norm. It is 'legally better' that the childbearing woman is married (because there then is no need to bring parenthood into question) and the determination of genetic paternity is desirable in the sense that social services has a far-reaching duty to locate and register genetic parents. In addition, a child cannot have more than two legal parents even when a family consists of more than two adults with practical responsibility for a child. A clear nuclear norm can also be observed in the strong intention of shared guardianship for parents, even after separation, and that alternating residence for children is considered the best alternative. This can be viewed as a way to maintain the nuclear family structure even after the family has split up. Anna Singer, professor in family law at Uppsala University, has the following to say about this matter:

> We now have a legal order which is directed to a large degree towards what could be called social engineering: training parents to live up to an ideal of the cohabiting nuclear family, when this family structure no longer exists.[37]

---

[33] *Ibid.*, Chapter 6 Section 11.   [34] *Ibid.*, Chapter 6 Section 3.
[35] E. Fransson, M. Bergström and A. Hjern, *Barn i växelvis boende – en forskningsöversikt* (Stockholm: Centre for Health Equity Studies), 2015).
[36] Chapter 6 Sections 2 and 5, Children and Parents Code.
[37] A. Singer, 'Gemensam vårdnad för alla föräldrar – barnets bästa eller social ingenjörskonst?' (2014) *Svensk juristtidning* 355.

The Preservation of the Family: Protecting the Nuclear Family When Children Are at Risk and Reuniting Nuclear Families after Children Are Taken into Care

The Swedish child protection system is – as have been noted above – often described as family and service-orientated, in contrast with Anglo-Saxon systems that are usually classified as risk and protection-orientated.[38] The difference lies primarily in how the intervention is carried out and legitimised. In family and service-orientated systems, authorities intervene earlier, i.e. before the situation has become very serious, with offers of support to parents and children. Intervention in risk and protection-orientated systems generally occurs later, i.e. when the situation is more serious, with the more extensive measure of placing children in care outside the home. Though a somewhat simplified description of these 'system types', this typology says something about the respective views of parental rights and the ambitions to preserve the nuclear family.

In the Swedish child protection system, placement in out-of-home care is considered the very last resort, and many measures are taken – at least in theory – to strengthen the family and avoid taking children into care, and, as an almost absolute rule, children are to grow up with their biological parents. The legal solution to this end is strong parental rights to protect families from illegitimate interventions. To a great extent, the Swedish child protection system prioritises consensual solutions, but it has been noted that this approach does not necessarily lead to choosing measures in the best interests of the child.[39]

When social services do place a child in out-of-home care, the rules state that in the first instance, the child is to be placed within the extended family or family network. However, this seldom happens in practice as most children are placed in 'professional' family homes (foster carers), and older children are often placed in various types of institutions.[40] These extrafamilial placements are possibly the result of the general approach of the Swedish welfare system and the notion of Swedish state individualism,

---

[38] Gilbert et al., *Child Protection Systems*.
[39] P. Leviner, *Rättsliga dilemman i socialtjänstens barnskyddsarbete* (Stockholm: Jure Förlag, 2011).
[40] Socialstyrelsen [National Board of Health and Welfare], *Barn och unga – insatser år 2013, Vissa insatser enligt socialtjänstlagen (SoL) och lagen med särskilda bestämmelser om vård av unga (LVU)*, 2014, 28.

as noted above, which emphasise a pursuit of individual independence from the family with respect to welfare and support. There is a general view that placement of children is the duty of the state, not the extended family. Yet another reason can be that it is considered easier to 'control' contact between parents and children when a 'professional' home provides care, and that this arrangement can offer better conditions for family reunification.

The decision to intervene in the private and family life of individuals by placing a child in out-of-home care involves a serious intrusion, with complex assessments of risk and protection factors. In the same way that it can be very difficult to make such assessments, it can also be very challenging to determine whether and when a child who has been placed in out-of-home care can and should return to the parents. The starting point for Swedish law is that children are to return to their original families as soon as possible. The legislation on the compulsory care of children and adolescents – Care of Young Persons Act (1990:52) – stipulates that extrafamilial care is to be terminated as soon as it is no longer needed (section 21), which has been interpreted to mean that children are to be reunified with their parents as soon as the circumstances leading to the out-of-home placement have ceased.[41] This means that a reunification of the nuclear family is a clear aim in the legislation.

Increased stability for children in out-of-home care has been discussed in Sweden in recent years. With this in mind, a requirement was established in 2003 requiring that social services must consider the need for the transfer of guardianship when children have been placed in foster care for three years.[42] If such a transfer is ordered, it means that reunification is no longer the goal, and that the child is to remain with the foster family for the remainder of his or her childhood. According to the Children and Parents Code, a transfer of guardianship is to be arranged if it is clearly the best solution for the child.[43] However, transfers of guardianship are still relatively unusual, and the views of the biological parents have great influence in the Social Welfare Board's assessment of whether to seek

---

[41] See Governmental Bill, Prop. 1979/80:1 *Om socialtjänsten*, 587ff. and a case from the Supreme Administrative Court, HFD 2012 ref. 35.
[42] Section 13, Care of Young Persons Act and Chapter 6 Section 6, Children and Parents Code.
[43] Chapter 6 Section 8, Children and Parents Code.

a transfer.[44] Social services quite simply seem to be reluctant to carrying out such a transfer of guardianship if there is not total agreement among all the parties that the transfer should take place. The requirement that transfer must clearly be in the best interest of the child and the basic presumption that it is best for children to grow up with their biological parents are probably the main reasons that transfers of guardianship take place only when it is clear that it is *completely unlikely* that reunification can take place. This can be viewed as an expression of a general and legally sanctioned unwillingness to split up the nuclear family, and a clear prioritisation of genetic relationships over social ones.

In this respect the downside of the nuclear family norm can be reflected in a narrow view of family life and parenthood. The Swedish legislation expresses a dichotomy between being placed in out-of-home care and not. Either the child is to be reunited with his or her original family or the child is to remain with the foster family and in this respect create a 'new nuclear family'. It can be asserted that in many cases, the ideal situation would instead be that the child could have supportive and present biological parents, but still live with a foster family. The firm position of parental rights and the reunification principle shifts focus to the preservation of the nuclear family instead of the idea that parenting can have other forms than within the nuclear family.

In line with the strong foothold of the reunification principle, and the resistance to transfer of guardianship to foster parents, adoption is not considered as an alternative or a component in the child protection system. It is therefore very unusual that children who are placed in foster families are adopted by foster parents.[45] The question of whether adoption could be a way to increase stability for children placed in family care homes was investigated recently, but the conclusion of the inquiry was that adoption would be 'going too far' – that it would not be desirable to 'cut' the legal ties between parents and genetic parents, even when it is clear that reunification cannot happen during childhood.[46] Adoption in Sweden requires the

---

[44] T. Mattsson, *Rätten till familj inom barn och ungdomsvården* (Malmö: Liber, 2010) and P. Leviner, 'När kan och bör placerade barn flytta hem – en oklar balansering mellan återförening och stabilitet i tre olika processer', in W. Warnling Nerep and A-C. Cederborg (eds.), *Barnrätt – en antologi* (Stockholm: Norstedts Juridik, 2014).

[45] Socialstyrelsen [National Board of Health and Welfare], *Nationella adoptioner av barn i familjehem*, 2014, 18.

[46] Governmental Inquiry, SOU 2015:71 *Barns och ungas rätt vid tvångsvård – förslag till ny LVU*, 674ff.

consent of the guardians, and, as a main rule, also from parents who are not involved in care (Chapter 4 Section 8, Children and Parents Code). This must be interpreted as strong support for parental rights and thus possibly also for the nuclear family.

Concluding Remarks and Discussion: the Discrepancy between Openness While Clinging to the Nuclear-Family Notion

As has been described in the introduction to this chapter, there is a 'typical Swedishness' in our insistence on freedom in how we live, without being directed by 'traditional values' involving dependence on the family. At the same time, we accept the state's control in terms of legal frameworks for our lives in the form of prohibitions against undesirable behaviours and behaviour-directing reforms intended to create greater equality, etc. The Swedish welfare system is characterised to a high degree by the pursuit of equality and equal opportunity, but also provides strong support for the weaker parties in society; in essence, the individual is allowed to do as he or she pleases, as long as no one else gets hurt. This is most likely the central reason why surrogacy arrangements are prohibited in Sweden. Even if such arrangements would give more individuals the possibility to have children, it is just not viewed as desirable with respect to the risk that women will be exploited, and children will be treated as goods to be bought and sold.

Otherwise, medical advances in assisted reproduction are accepted, but not exactly embraced by the legal system. Reforms in this field – for example regarding help with donated gametes – are ensured through requirements as to assessments of the suitability of prospective parents. That this is discriminatory in relation to unfit parents who have children despite their unsuitability has not generated much debate in Sweden. A certain sluggishness can be detected in legal developments in this area. It is somewhat 'slower' in Sweden than in many other countries, for example, in many states in the US and the UK, where assisted fertilisation has been available longer for single persons, where no genetic connection between at least one parent and the child is required, and surrogate arrangements are permitted. The situation could be described in this way: in Sweden we have greater acceptance for the idea that frameworks for our lives are set through legal reforms and 'social engineering'. In agreement with the theory of state individualism, Swedes generally trust the state and the assessments made by its authorities, as long as our individual freedom is respected in the sense that we do not need to depend on our family.

The old nuclear family norm still survives in the legal system, and signs of this norm can even be detected in the reforms carried out in recent years. As stated above, three factors are identified as defining and comprising the nuclear family norm in terms of prioritisation: (1) couple-based 'twoness' and 'romantic' love – i.e. monogamous relationships including sex; (2) marriage; and (3) genetic connections between parents and children. This chapter has shown how these factors are expressed and still given priority in the Swedish legislation regarding family formation and family preservation, although as noted above many reforms are under way.

In terms of priority for *twoness and romantic love*, this factor can be seen in the longstanding requirement stipulating that only couples can receive help with assisted reproduction from Swedish health care. The extension of this right to single persons was not adopted until the spring of 2016. One limitation for receiving assisted reproduction is that those who live together are in a 'couple relationship' based on romantic love and sex. According to Swedish healthcare practice, the prospective parents must have had a stable relationship for more than two years. Two friends or siblings who live together (and who are not 'expected to have a sexual relationship') cannot receive assisted reproduction through the Swedish healthcare system. As for adoption, single persons can adopt children,[47] but it is likely that in practice there is a requirement of being 'solitary' in the sense that the adopting person cannot live with someone else and still be considered single.

As shown here, (heterosexual) *marriage* is also given priority through the automatic registration of a man married to a childbearing woman as the father and guardian. Even if practical considerations are the main reason for this assumption, if nothing else it reproduces a view that married women only have sex with their husbands. Clear prioritisation of marriage can also be observed in adoption legislation, in which prospective adoptive parents until September 2018 have been required to be married, and now married or cohabitants. In other words, there is no legal (but perhaps practical) barrier to adoption by single persons, but

---

[47] Chapter 4 Section 1, Children and Parents Code.

if two persons wish to adopt a child mutually, they must be married or cohabitants.

The legal system also expresses the preference for *twoness* by stating that the child can have at most two parents and two guardians (normally the same persons), irrespective of how many adults are involved in the creation and care of the child. For example, even if the child lives in two families with four or more parents, only two of these can be registered as parents and guardians. The same applies to adults who live in polygamous family structures, with shared responsibility for children. The legislation is thus founded on the historical situation in which a man, a woman and their sexual intercourse were required to create a child. Today, children can be 'created in other ways', and as the requirement on a genetic relationship is successively removed, this can hardly be counted as a legitimate reason. Instead, children could benefit from having more than two parents. It could be that the pursuit of twoness is above all based on practical aspects in that it would be practically complicated to have multiple parents and guardians registered in the system. Nevertheless, it can be asserted that in this respect, the legislation propagates the nuclear family ideal and romantic notions of twoness as the norm.

In terms of *genetic relationships*, 'genetic parenthood' has been given priority through the until 2019 prevailing requirement of a genetic relationship between the child and at least one of the prospective parents. Even in terms of legislation regarding 'already existing families', there are clear signs of the nuclear family norm through prioritisation of genetic relationships, as expressed in the strong emphasis on the principle of reunification in the Swedish child protection system. The legal order evinces strong intentions to ensure that children who are placed in out-of-home care are reunited with their genetic parents if possible and as soon as possible. This intention overrides the child's need for stability and remaining in the family care home, which the child might perceive as his or her 'real' family.

At the same time that the nuclear family can be said to be 'reproduced' in the legal system in this way: it must also be mentioned that many changes have been made in recent years to enable involuntarily childless persons to have children – and these changes represent a departure from this ideal. One can say that we are in the midst of a shift *from* the nuclear family in the sense of mum–dad–kids constellations based on love, reproductive sex and genetics *to* a new way to form families and live together. Advances in medicine will most likely make the preservation of the nuclear family norm all the more difficult to maintain in the legal system. The opportunity for single women to obtain assisted reproduction and the approved lifting of requirements on a genetic relationship between at least one of two prospective parents are examples of steps in this direction. It seems likely that the assumption that married men are always the fathers of their wives' children will disappear.

Changes are underway, but a core resistance remains. Altruistic surrogate arrangements have recently been investigated as a possibility in Sweden, but have been discarded for reasons including the increased risks for women and children. Irrespective of one's personal opinion on the matter, the resistance means in practice that some persons are not getting help with assisted reproduction from the Swedish healthcare system. This applies for example to homosexual men who, because of this situation, must turn to adoption if they wish to have children. Medical limitations still exist for male childbirth, but if men could share the task in the future, for example by carrying the child in an artificial womb, it could hardly be considered reasonable not to give these men assistance if we accept that women can receive the same help.[48] If and when the Swedish legislator is confronted with this question, the 'motherhood norm' will also be challenged. This would mean that even single men could seek to have children with the help of assisted reproduction.

A change that may be difficult to bring about – and which in some ways can be seen as the last bastion of the nuclear family – is to abandon the notion that children must have two parents and that these parents must live in a monogamous romantic relationship. In the same vein, Swedish law does not seem ready to abandon the strong intention to reunite families after a child has been placed in out-of-home care. Adoption in this context, which involves the 'severing' of legal ties between child and parents, has been dismissed time and time again, even if many claim that it would offer greater stability for children and thus a more secure family life for the child. When it comes to the responsibility for 'the society's children', i.e. children in out-of-home care, it is possible that there is a dichotomy in Sweden that clearly expresses a nuclear family ideal in the pursuit of a state

---

[48] In September 2015 Swedish media reported on the first-ever child to be born through assisted fertilisation with the help of an transplanted womb – see the article in the Swedish newspaper *Expressen*, available at: www.expressen.se/nyheter/vincent-ar-unik-det-omojliga-blev-mojligt (accessed February 2018).

in which a child has only *one* family – either the 'original home' or the foster family.

Considering the new possibilities for having children as a result of medical advances and the law, it is possible that the nuclear family can be reproduced in some sense. Perhaps it is the case that increased opportunities to have children will call into question choices to live without children, and that not 'having a family' will be greeted with scepticism. Even in Swedish society, where individualism is strong, the family remains a focus through the facilitation of family life: parental insurance, subsidised day care, flexible working hours and even family-sized parking spaces at IKEA. Research has shown that being voluntarily childless in this child and family-focused society can be more problematic than in countries such as the US and Italy – countries traditionally considered less child-friendly.[49] In some ways, it is a more controversial position to decide not to have children in a child-focused society. Yet another dimension in this 'family ideology' is the pursuit of shared responsibility on the part of parents who do not live together. As Anna Singer pointed out, this can be construed as pressure to live up to the nuclear family norm, even when the nuclear family no longer exists after separation. There is an indication that a parent who does not shoulder (half) the burden of responsibility is viewed with scepticism and this could be one of the reasons for the increase in custody disputes in Sweden. Parents are quite simply expected to fight for and take responsibility for their children.

Two parallel tracks can be detected in the development of family law in Sweden. One track leads towards a loosening of the nuclear family structure, not least through choices to live in 'non-traditional' ways and the increased challenges to existing legislation. In this sense, family law legislation has not kept pace with the times; instead it is 'sluggish'. Parallel to this track is another path, which means that the nuclear family is reproduced – even in reforms designed to give more individuals the chance to have children, etc., because family constellations, twoness and genetics continue to be given priority. A problem in this respect is that both alternatives are based to a large extent on a parental perspective. Parents' right to have children and parents' right to live with their children threatens to steer the focus away from children's rights and needs. From a child's

---

[49] K. Engwall and H. Peterson, 'Är det privata politiskt? – Barnfri i ett barnvänligt samhälle' (2011) 2 *Socialvetenskaplig tidskrift* 126–43.

perspective, the loosening and even dismantling of old notions to make way for improved analyses of the child's best interest are important, because the child's best interest is not necessarily in agreement with the nuclear family norm. This raises the question of the shape and nature of the new norm – if it is not based on the more rigid nuclear family, what is its basis? One possibility is to see the family from a child's perspective, ask ourselves what is most important for children and reflect on what characterises an important relationship, while also providing legal protection for the structures providing the best conditions for a safe, secure and satisfying existence for children. It is possible that such legislation would direct more focus to parents' duties to their children. It is also possible that new legislation – and a new approach – mean that as a society and individuals, we must work together to take greater shared responsibility for children, even those of others. This has received considerable attention recently, with the arrival of many unaccompanied child refugees in Sweden from countries suffering from war, oppression and poverty. Shared responsibility for these children may require a new perspective on what a family and parents are and should be, and what they symbolise. It is clear that we are in the midst of a process, and its progress in different countries and traditions, both legal and cultural, promises to take us on an interesting journey.

7 South African Family Law and the Chimera of Diversity

Anne Louw

Introduction

The Constitution of the Republic of South Africa, 1996[1] (the Constitution) has fundamentally transformed the legal landscape of life partnerships in South Africa. New legislation has diversified the matrimonial options available to life partners. Except for these new statutes, spousal relations in South Africa are still governed by outdated legislation predating the constitutional era. The Constitutional Court, as the highest court on constitutional matters,[2] has consequently played an enormous role in developing family law in South Africa – even at the risk of overstepping the boundaries of judicial interpretation in some cases.[3] Family law in South Africa has thus increasingly become precedent-driven and the importance of the judgments of this court cannot be overestimated, as will become abundantly clear from the discussion that follows. The selection of the issues discussed in this contribution was prompted by a desire to show how family law is being transformed by this 'judicial law-making'[4] process taking place in South Africa. The contribution will focus on three main issues, namely the promotion of diversity, the recognition of unmarried life partners and the hierarchical nature of life partnerships. In the course of

---

[1] An *interim* Constitution 200 of 1993 preceded the final Constitution which came into operation on 4 February 1997.
[2] See www.concourt.org.za/index.php/about-us/role, for an explanation of the role and place of the Constitutional Court within the judicial system in South Africa.
[3] See *Laubscher N.O.* v. *Duplan and Others* 2017 (2) SA 264 (CC), para. 67 and the sources in n. 65, mentioning the 'fluid notion of separation of powers' applied by the Constitutional Court in facilitating transformative measures.
[4] See in general A. Singh and M. Z. Bhero, 'Judicial law-making: Unlocking the creative powers of judges in terms of section 39(2) of the Constitution' (2016) 19 *Potchefstroom Electronic Review/Potchefstroom Electronic Law Journal* 1, 17–18, available at https://journals.assaf.org.za/index.php/per/article/view/1504. Section 39(2) of the Constitution requires every court to 'promote the spirit, purport and objects of the Bill of Rights' when interpreting 'any legislation, and when developing the common law or customary law'.

these discussions attention will be drawn to other important features of South African family law, including the way in which the aspiration towards achieving (gender) equality has acted as a catalyst for transformation and the extent to which cultural and religious diversity is tolerated in this country. Given the selected scope of this contribution it is not intended, nor does it presume to be, a comprehensive reflection of family law, or even matrimonial law, in South Africa.

The Promotion of Diversity and Matrimonial Rainbowism

Until the Constitution became the supreme law of South Africa in 1994,[5] family law in this country was structured around a strict two-tier hierarchy of intimate relationships – married and unmarried.[6] At that stage the 'married' status could only be acquired through the conclusion of a monogamous heterosexual civil marriage solemnised by a competent marriage officer as prescribed by the Marriage Act of 1961.[7] In terms of the common law, such a marriage implies the creation of a *consortium omnis vitae* that includes a reciprocal duty of support between husband and wife. The civil marriage is by default in community of property. Should the parties wish to exclude the default matrimonial property system by means of an antenuptial contract, the accrual system will apply to the ensuing marriage out of community of property unless expressly excluded.[8] The patrimonial consequences of the marriage are regulated mainly by the Matrimonial Property Act of 1984. If a civil marriage is dissolved by death, the surviving spouse can inherit intestate in terms of the Intestate Succession Act of 1987 and/or claim maintenance in terms of the Maintenance of Surviving Spouses' Act of 1990. The only other way to dissolve the marriage is by means of a divorce order granted in terms of the Divorce Act of 1979.

As a result of the constitutional entrenchment of, inter alia, the rights to equality and dignity in the Bill of Rights,[9] the state could no longer justify a matrimonial regime that catered only for monogamous heterosexual marriages. Customary marriages, allowing for polygynous unions between

---

[5] See n. 1 above.
[6] L. Schäfer, 'Marriage and marriage-like relationships: Constructing a new hierarchy of life partnerships' (2006) 123 *South African Law Journal* 626–47, 626.
[7] Section 30(1) makes provision only for a 'husband' to marry a 'wife'.
[8] Matrimonial Property Act of 1984, s. 4.   [9] Constitution, Ch. II, ss. 9 and 10 respectively.

indigenous African people, were the first to benefit from the constitutional era, receiving full legal recognition in 2000 when the Recognition of Customary Marriages Act of 1998 (RCMA) came into operation. In 2006 South Africa became the first country in Africa and the fifth country worldwide to recognise same-sex marriages or unions in terms of the Civil Union Act of 2006 (CUA).

Although the official application of matrimonial pluralism would seem to answer to the constitutional imperatives of equality and non-discrimination on grounds of culture and sexual orientation,[10] its application in the South African context has elicited vociferous and widespread criticism and has become an increasing cause for concern on a number of levels.[11] Some authors argue that the recognition of diversity is more apparent than real if regard is had to the fact that not only customary marriages, but civil unions as well, were reconceived in the 'valorised'[12] mould of civil marriages before formally being accorded the same status.[13] The RCMA has had the (perhaps) unintended effect of assimilating customary marriages into the civil understanding of marriage,[14] rather than promoting the right to culture and diversity and harmonising the civil law with customary law. As a result, the development of the law in this regard would seem to show more signs of unification than pluralism.[15]

---

[10] South Africa became the first country in the world expressly to recognise in its Constitution sexual orientation as a prohibited ground of discrimination: see P. de Vos, 'The "inevitability" of same-sex marriage in South Africa's post-apartheid state' (2007) 23 *South African Journal on Human Rights* 432–65, 435–43.

[11] See e.g. J. Sloth-Nielsen and B. van Heerden, 'The constitutional family: Developments in South African family law jurisprudence under the 1996 Constitution' (2003) 17 *International Journal of Law, Policy and the Family*, 121–46, 140, who refer to the 'potentially dangerous proliferation of legally recognised family forms'.

[12] E. Bonthuys, 'Race and gender in the Civil Union Act' (2007) 23 *South African Journal on Human Rights* 526–42, 531.

[13] *Ibid.*, 541–2; J. Bekker and G. Van Niekerk, '*Gumede v President of the Republic of South Africa*: Harmonisation, or the creation of new marriages laws in South Africa?' (2009) 24 *SA Public Law* 206–22, 206.

[14] W. Amien, 'Reflections on the recognition of African customary marriages in South Africa: Seeking insights for the recognition of Muslim marriages' (2013) *Acta Juridica* 357–84, 366.

[15] M. W. Prinsloo, 'Pluralism or unification in family law in South Africa' (1990) 23 *Comparative and International Law Journal of Southern Africa* 324–36, 324; E. Bonthuys, 'Accommodating gender, race, culture and religion: Outside legal subjectivity' (2002) 18 *South African Journal on Human Rights* 41–58, 56–7; P. Bakker, 'Die weg vorentoe: Unifikasie of pluralisme van die Suid-Afrikaanse huweliksreg?' (2004) 67 *Journal of Contemporary Roman Dutch Law* 626–39, 626; C. Rautenbach, 'South African

These observations are supported by claims that the RCMA has effectively transformed the communal nature of African customary marriages, which traditionally represent a bond between families, into an individualistic-based nuclear unit that characterises the western approach to marriage.[16] Bakker[17] goes even further by claiming that the formally recognised customary marriage of today is in actual fact no different from a civil marriage that allows polygyny. According to the Constitutional Court in *Gumede (born Shange)* v. *President of the Republic of South Africa and Others*[18] one of the most important aims of the RCMA is to 'jettison gendered inequality within [customary] marriage and the marital power of the husband by providing for the equal status and capacity of spouses'.[19] While insulating the RCMA against a constitutional challenge, the equal status provision included in the Act contradicts the lived reality of spouses in a traditional polygynous customary marriage. For this reason a distinction is drawn between so-called 'official customary law', as applied by the courts and state bodies, and 'living customary law', represented by the current customary practices of the people whose customary law is in question.[20] There is some debate about whether and to what extent customary law has been preserved as far as the dissolution of such a marriage is concerned.[21] Since the enactment of the RCMA a customary marriage, like any civil marriage, can only be dissolved by a court order in terms of the Divorce Act.[22] Even where the RCMA incorporates traditional features of African customary marriages, it does not do so in quite a traditional manner.[23] For instance, *lobolo* or bridewealth, which is a standard feature and prerequisite for the conclusion of a valid

---

common and customary law on intestate succession: A question of harmonisation, integration or abolition' (2008) 3 *Journal of Comparative Law* 119-32, 129.

[16] Amien, 'Reflections on the recognition of African customary marriages', 366.

[17] P. Bakker, 'Chaos in family law: A model for the recognition of intimate relationships in South Africa' (2013) 16 *Potchefstroom Electronic Review/Potchefstroom Electronic Law Journal* 116-50, 122.

[18] 2009 (3) SA 152 (CC).   [19] Para. 24.   [20] See discussion of the *Ramuhovhi* case below.

[21] See C. Himonga, 'The dissolution of a customary marriage by divorce', in J. Heaton (ed.), *The Law of Divorce and Dissolution of Life Partnerships in South Africa* (Cape Town: Juta, 2014) 237-43.

[22] Under traditional African customary law, dissolution of the marriage was negotiated between the families of the spouses and not between spouses themselves (*ibid.*, 'Dissolution of a customary marriage by divorce', 238-9).

[23] Amien, 'Reflections on the recognition of African customary marriages', 366.

traditional customary marriage, is not included as a compulsory requirement in the RCMA.[24]

While the abovementioned examples are revealing, the displacement of customary law by civil law principles, in my view, is nowhere more evident than in the way the judiciary has altered the proprietary consequences of customary marriages since the enactment of the RCMA. The following discussion traces the developments in this regard.

African customary law does not traditionally include the notion of a matrimonial property regime, since property was meant to be administered for the benefit of the family.[25] When the RCMA came into operation, the Act provided that the proprietary consequences of customary marriages entered into *before* the Act ('old' customary marriages) would still be regulated by customary law.[26] The proprietary consequences of de facto monogamous customary marriages concluded *after* the RCMA ('new' customary marriages) would be treated like civil marriages – in community of property by default unless excluded by means of a valid antenuptial contract.[27] Although not relevant for purposes of this discussion, the patrimonial consequences of 'new' polygynous customary marriages in terms of the RCMA are depended on a court-approved contract that arguably can only provide for a complete separation of property.[28]

The Constitutional Court in *Gumede* held that the application of the RCMA provisions could mean that some women in 'old' *monogamous* customary marriages would be deprived of a right to family property when customary law is applied, based simply on the date on which their marriage was concluded.[29] The impugned provisions were thus declared unconstitutional and invalidated to the extent that they unfairly discriminated against such women based on their gender.[30] The order in *Gumede* has meant that the proprietary consequences of all de facto monogamous customary marriages, regardless of whether they were concluded before or after the RCMA, are the same as those of civil marriages. The proprietary

---

[24] The RCMA, s. 1, however, does include a definition of *lobolo* as 'the property in cash or in kind, whether known as *lobolo, bogadi, bohali, xurna, lumalo, thaka, ikhazi, magadi, emabheka* or by any other name, which a prospective husband or the head of his family undertakes to give to the head of the prospective wife's family in consideration of a customary marriage'.

[25] *Gumede*, para. 43.   [26] RCMA, s. 7(1).   [27] *Ibid.*, s. 7(2).

[28] *Ibid.*, s. 7(6), as discussed in J. Heaton and H. Kruger, *South African Family Law* (4th edn, Durban: LexisNexis, 2015) 224–6.

[29] Para. 34.   [30] Para. 49.

consequences of 'old' *polygynous* customary marriages were thus the only remaining marriages that would still be regulated by customary law. The court in *Ramuhovhi and Another* v. *President of the Republic of South Africa and Others*[31] has now changed this position as well. The facts of the case reveal the intersection between customary law and civil law and the impact of the RCMA on the lives of African families in South Africa.

During his lifetime and before the RCMA was enacted, the deceased entered into polygynous customary marriages with three wives of which one had already passed away at the time of his death in 2008.[32] The deceased had also entered into civil marriages with two wives.[33] One of these marriages had been terminated with the demise of the wife, while the other had been declared null and void because of the deceased's already existing customary marriages at the time of conclusion of the civil marriage.[34] The deceased died testate. In terms of his last will and testament the deceased bequeathed his estate to his respective wives, including his civil law 'wife', and all his children.[35] By the time the application came before the court, all the previous wives of the deceased and most of his children had already passed away.[36] The applicants were the surviving children born from the deceased's 'old' customary law marriages.[37] The applicants submitted that with the application of the RCMA and the applicable Venda customary law, their mothers were excluded from ownership of the estate amassed by the deceased.[38] This in turn was due to the discriminatory nature of the provisions of the RCMA, as amended by *Gumede*, which caused prejudice to the deceased's wives and children. According to Lamminga AJ who delivered the judgment, the prejudice took the form of being excluded from participating in the management of, and control in, the marital property.[39] Unlike wives in all other customary marriages who are protected in terms of matrimonial property regimes, women in 'old' polygynous customary marriages remained unprotected. Denying these women and children equal protection, in the court's view, would perpetuate their vulnerability in many respects.[40] Women who have no rights in matrimonial property are vulnerable to eviction and may find acquiring property rights challenging.[41] Lamminga AJ was also alive to the fact that

---

[31] 2016 (6) SA 210 (LT).   [32] Paras. 6 and 7.   [33] Para. 7.
[34] *Ibid*. The polygynous customary marriages created and absolute impediment to the conclusion of a subsequent civil marriage or union (RCMA, s. 3(2)).
[35] Para. 8.   [36] Para. 13.   [37] Para. 6.   [38] Para. 14.   [39] Para. 18.   [40] Para. 33.
[41] *Ibid*.

the RCMA has been an attempt to 'remedy the historical humiliation and exclusion meted out to spouses in marriages which were entered into in accordance with the law and culture of the indigenous African people of this country',[42] in accordance with the Constitution and also the principles agreed to in terms of the international and regional treaties that South Africa has ratified.[43] Apart from the fact the RCMA unfairly discriminated against women based on their gender, the provisions were also deemed discriminatory on the basis of race and/or ethnic or social origin.[44] The latter discrimination was evident from the way in which women in polygynous customary marriages were excluded from protection afforded to women in monogamous customary and civil marriages. The RCMA also differentiated between women in 'old' customary marriages and women in 'new' customary marriages by providing protection only for the latter.[45] As such the court had no problem in declaring the relevant provisions of the RCMA unconstitutional.[46] The court had far greater difficulty in coming up with a remedy to address the discrimination. The court investigated three possible options: developing the customary law, striking down the impugned provisions leaving it for the legislature to deal with it as it deems fit and, lastly, making an interim order.[47] Developing the customary law was deemed inappropriate for two reasons:

1. The Constitutional Court, as the ultimate court that would have to confirm the order, has not engaged in the incremental development of customary law; and
2. the impugned provision affects a class of vulnerable persons across various ethnic groups in significantly similar fashion, making piecemeal remedy on a case-by-case basis undesirable due to the inevitable protraction, unpredictability and legal uncertainty which would result. The

---

[42] Para. 35, reaffirming the dictum of Moseneke DCJ in *Gumede*, para. 16.
[43] Para. 34 n. 35 refers to the following treaties: 'CEDAW and its Optional Protocol; The ICCPR; Convention against Torture and Other Cruel Inhuman and Degrading Treatment; Commitments made in respect of the Beijing Declaration and Platform of Action; Protocol to the African Charter on Human and Peoples Rights on the Rights of Women in Africa; Solemn Declaration on Gender Equality in Africa and Southern African Development Addendum to the Declaration on Gender and Development.'
[44] Para. 46.   [45] *Ibid.*   [46] *Ibid.*
[47] Para. 48, following the precedent created in *Bhe and Others* v. *Khayelitsha Magistrate and Others (Commission for Gender Equality as* Amicus Curiae) 2005 (1) SA 580 (CC) para. 105.

court agreed with the *Bhe* case[48] that, in order to ensure constitutional protection of the rights of women (and children) in old polygynous marriages, a direct approach is required instead of a piecemeal, slow development of customary law.[49]

Given the dismal track record of the legislator to address the issue of the proprietary consequences of polygynous marriages, the court concluded it would be better to make an interim order pending the required legislative processes.[50] For the purpose of arriving at a just and equitable order, the court then considered the basic principles applicable to 'old' customary marriages in terms of the 'formal' customary law.[51] The option of declaring such marriages in community of property was considered but rejected in the following terms:

All of this seems like an effort to put a square block in a round hole – trying to force foreign concepts of individual ownership and matrimonial property regimes onto a traditional system which operates on a basis of communal rights, subject to the welfare of the members of the family unit and administered by the family head.[52]

In an expressed attempt to retain the core nature of polygyny[53] and to ensure that rights in property are exercised for the benefit of the family unit, the court's order would allow wives in 'old' polygynous customary law marriages to have 'equal and joint rights of management and control over and in the marital property' with their husbands[54] – similar, in fact, to the 'concurrent management' regime applicable to spouses married in community of property.[55] As far as the nature of the property itself was concerned, the court distinguished between 'house property', that must be managed and controlled jointly by the husband and the wife of the house, and 'family property' that must be managed by the husband and 'all the [customary] wives'.[56] Parties would retain exclusive rights to their personal property.[57]

The Constitutional Court[58] confirmed the high court's declaration of constitutional invalidity in November 2017. In terms of this judgment, the order of invalidity is suspended for a period of twenty-four months to

---

[48] *Bhe and Others* v. *Khayelitsha Magistrate and Others (Commission for Gender Equality as Amicus Curiae)* 2005 (1) SA 580 (CC) paras 111–12.
[49] *Ramuhovhi*, para. 52.   [50] Para. 53.   [51] Paras. 55–9.   [52] Para. 61.   [53] Para. 75.
[54] Para. 76.   [55] Matrimonial Property Act of 1984, Ch. III.   [56] *Ibid.*   [57] *Ibid.*
[58] *Ramuhovhi and Others* v. *President of the Republic of South Africa and Others* 2018 (2) SA 1 (CC).

afford Parliament time to correct the defect in the impugned provisions of the RCMA.[59] If the legislature fails to address the unconstitutionality within the period of suspension, the interim relief will be made applicable after the period of suspension. The nature of the interim relief granted by the Constitutional Court, however, differs in two significant respects from the relief granted by the high court. The order by the Constitutional Court, in the first instance, expressly extends the customary wives' rights to marital property to include rights of ownership and not merely rights of management and control.[60] Second, the order limits the retrospectivity of the declaration of invalidity by making it applicable only to marital property that has not yet been transferred.[61] Where the transfer of marital property has been completed but the heir in question was *mala fide* aware of the fact that the transfer was subject to a constitutional challenge as a result of the declaration of invalidity, the transfer can also be challenged and invalidated.[62]

The *Ramuhovhi* judgments clearly show the challenges faced by the courts in attempting to preserve customary law in a constitutionally responsible way that promotes gender equality. The cases also illustrate the tensions existing within customary law.[63] However, despite the decision to apply 'formal' customary law, the interim relief granted does seem to go beyond merely creating 'paper rights'[64] by 'ensuring that rights and protection provided for in terms of living customary law are applied'.[65]

Bringing Cohabitants 'in from the Cold'[66]

Informal life partners or domestic partners, as they are commonly referred to in South Africa, currently cannot *ex lege* avail themselves of spousal benefits. Until laws that discriminated against persons on ground of their

---

[59] Para 71. [60] *Ibid.* [61] *Ibid.* [62] *Ibid.*
[63] See e.g. Bekker and Van Niekerk, '*Gumede v President of the Republic of South Africa*', 207.
[64] *Ramuhovhi and Another* v. *President of the Republic of South Africa and Others* 2016 (6) SA 210 (LT), para. 54.
[65] *Ibid.*
[66] This heading was inspired by the title of the following chapter: P. de Vos, 'Still out in the cold? The Domestic Partnership Bill and the (non)protection of marginalised woman', in J. Sloth-Nielsen and Z. du Toit (eds.), *Trials and Tribulations, Trends and Triumphs Developments in International, African and South African Child and Family Law* (Cape Town: Juta and Company, 2008) 129.

sexual orientation could be challenged as an infringement of the constitutional right to dignity and equality, informal life partners had to regulate themselves. Based on these constitutional rights, the judiciary recognised and extended spousal benefits to same-sex domestic partners on a case-by-case basis.[67] The courts argued that since the relationship between same-sex domestic partners was no different from a marital relationship, the law discriminated unfairly against such partners by not giving them the choice to formalise their relationship in the form of a marriage. To this extent the position of a heterosexual couple was distinguishable from a same-sex couple – a heterosexual couple could choose to get married. Because same-sex domestic partners could not become 'spouses', they were entitled to equal protection of the law provided, of course, their relationship had the characteristics of a conjugal relationship.[68] In this way a suitably committed domestic partner of the same-sex, for example, was afforded the right to qualify as a dependant for purposes of the other partner's medical aid,[69] can qualify for 'spousal benefits' in terms of the Judges Remuneration and Conditions of Employment Act of 1989[70] and can claim compensation for the negligent death of a partner who was the breadwinner in terms of the common law dependant's action.[71] When a *heterosexual* surviving partner sought to be recognised as a 'survivor' for purposes of a claim for maintenance in terms of the Maintenance of Surviving Spouses Act, the high court[72] initially upheld the claim[73] but was overruled by the Constitutional Court in *Volks NO v. Robinson and Others* (*Volks*).[74] By

---

[67] Legislative recognition of domestic partnerships became common for the same reason: see e.g. the Insolvency Act of 1936, s. 20(13); the Employment Equity Act of 1998, s. 1; the Domestic Violence Act of 1998, s. 1; the Children's Act of 2005, ss. 231 and 293.
[68] In many of the cases where the interpretation of 'spouse' was extended to include a same-sex partner, the court required not only permanency in the relationship but also reciprocal duties of support.
[69] *Langemaat* v. *Minister of Safety and Security* 1998 (3) SA 312 (T).
[70] *Satchwell* v. *President of the Republic of South Africa* 2002 (6) SA 1 (CC).
[71] *Du Plessis* v. *Road Accident Fund* 2004 (1) SA 359 (SCA); *Verheem* v. *Road Accident Fund* 2012 (2) SA 409 (GNP) and *Paixão* v. *Road Accident Fund* 2012 (6) SA 377 (SCA).
[72] *Robinson and Another* v. *Volks NO and Others* 2004 (6) SA 288 (C).
[73] Davis J. (p. 299I) noted: 'For a range of reasons ... domestic partnerships are a significant part of South African family life. To ignore the arrangement ... is to undermine the dignity of difference and to render the guarantee of equality somewhat illusory insofar as a significant percentage of the population is concerned'.
[74] 2005 (5) BCLR 446 (CC).

applying the so-called 'choice argument',[75] the Constitutional Court ultimately held that treating unmarried opposite-sex domestic partners different from their married counterparts did *not* infringe on their dignity.[76] The differential treatment therefore could not be considered unfair discrimination against heterosexual partners because they had always had the option of marrying one another and yet had chosen not to do so.[77]

The unsatisfactory piecemeal recognition of *same-sex* partnerships was finally brought to a head in the case of *Minister of Home Affairs* v. *Fourie (Doctors for Life International and Others,* Amici Curiae); *Lesbian and Gay Equality Project and Others* v. *Minister of Home Affairs (Fourie).*[78] Declaring the common law definition of marriage unconstitutional,[79] the Constitutional Court gave the legislator exactly one year to remedy the situation.[80] The court was explicit in condemning any legislation that would create a 'separate but equal'[81] opportunity for same-sex couples to marry, demanding that whatever legislative remedy is chosen, it must be 'as generous and accepting towards same-sex couples as it is to heterosexual couples' and suggesting that '[i]n a context of patterns of deep past discrimination and continuing homophobia, appropriate sensitivity must be shown to providing a remedy that is truly and manifestly respectful of the dignity of same-sex couples'.[82]

A week before the expiry of the deadline and the enactment of the CUA, the Constitutional Court in *Gory* v. *Kolver*[83] was called upon to determine whether it was constitutionally acceptable for section 1(1) of the Intestate Succession Act to exclude same-sex life partners from its ambit.[84] After

---

[75] See B. C. Bester and A. Louw, 'Domestic partners and "the choice argument": *Quo vadis?*' (2014) 17 *Potchefstroom Electronic Review/Potchefstroom Electronic Law Journal* 2951–81, 2952.

[76] Para. 62.

[77] The decision was, however, not unanimous. The dissenting Justices Sachs (para. 236, Mokgoro and O'Regan, para. 132) all felt that excluding heterosexual life partners, who had entered into reciprocal duties of support during the relationship, from the benefits afforded by the Act, constituted unfair discrimination on ground of marital status.

[78] 2006 (1) SA 524 (CC).   [79] Paras. 82 and 114.   [80] Para. 156.   [81] Para. 150.

[82] Para. 153. According to B. S. Smith and J. A. Robinson 'The South African Civil Union Act 2006: Progressive legislation with regressive implications?' (2008) 22 *International Journal of Law, Policy and the Family* 356–92, 379, the drafters of the Act have paid mere lip service to the guidelines proffered by the Constitutional Court and (at 380) 'the Act appears to be a good example of bad drafting that illustrates the dangers of rushing the legislative process' to meet the deadline.

[83] 2007 (4) SA 97 (CC).

[84] The Intestate Succession Act, s. 1(1) only conferred rights on a 'spouse'.

concluding that such exclusion was indeed unconstitutional,[85] the court remedied the unconstitutionality of the provision by ordering a 'reading-in' of the words 'or partner in a permanent same-sex life partnership in which the partners have undertaken reciprocal duties of support' after the word 'spouse', wherever it appears in the section.[86] As far as the impact of this remedy was concerned, Van Heerden AJ made the following statement in the now famous paragraph 29 of the case:

> It is true that, should this Court confirm paragraph 2 of the High Court order, the position after 1 December 2006 will be that section 1(1) of the Act will apply to both heterosexual spouses and same-sex spouses who 'marry' after that date, if Parliament either fails to respond before the *Fourie* deadline or if it does enact legislation permitting same-sex couples to 'enjoy the status and the benefits coupled with responsibilities it accords to heterosexual couples'. Unless specifically amended, section 1(1) will then also apply to permanent same-sex life partners who have undertaken reciprocal duties of support but who do not 'marry' under any new dispensation. Depending on the nature and content of the new statutory dispensation (if any), there is the possibility that unmarried heterosexual couples will continue to be excluded from the ambit of section 1(1) of the Act.

This meant that, notwithstanding the enactment of the CUA giving same-sex couples (like their heterosexual counterparts) the choice to 'marry', a surviving same-sex domestic partner would still be deemed a 'spouse' for purposes of the Intestate Succession Act. The judgment thus contradicted the general assumption[87] that since the rationale for treating same-sex domestic partners differently from opposite-sex couples had now fallen away, judgments expanding the interpretation of spouse to include an unmarried domestic partner would no longer apply after the enactment of the CUA.

While some authors have defended the differential treatment of unmarried same-sex life partners and opposite-sex life partners as fair discrimination and a 'pseudo-anomaly' in our law,[88] others have described the situation as 'peculiar, ironic, paradoxical and anomalous'.[89]

---

[85] *Gory*, para. 19.   [86] Para. 66.
[87] Based on the judgment of the Constitutional Court in *Volks*.
[88] M. C. Wood-Bodley, 'Intestate succession and gay and lesbian couples' (2008) 125 *South African Law Journal* 46–62, 60, whose argument is based on the notion of substantial equality.
[89] H. Kruuse, '"Here's to you, Mrs Robinson": Peculiarities and paragraph 29 in determining the treatment of domestic partnerships' (2009) 25 *South African Journal on Human Rights* 380–91, 385–6.

In the lingering absence of legislative guidance regarding the regulation of informal domestic relationships, it was perhaps inevitable that the Constitutional Court would be called upon to decide the inheritance rights of an unmarried surviving same-sex partner once again. In the recent case of *Laubscher N.O.* v. *Duplan and Another*,[90] the deceased and his same-sex partner had lived together since 2003 without ever formalising their union in terms of the CUA.[91] The parties had during the subsistence of their relationship nonetheless undertaken reciprocal duties of support.[92] The deceased died intestate on 13 February 2015, leaving behind no descendants or adopted children.[93] The applicant and brother of the deceased, as the only surviving relative, contended that notwithstanding the decision in *Gory*, the deceased's surviving life partner could not inherit from the intestate estate since he was not a 'spouse' within the meaning of the Intestate Succession Act. The respondent, on the other hand, relied exclusively on the judgment in *Gory* to claim his right to inherit the whole estate. The majority judgment in *Laubscher* was delivered by Mbha AJ (first judgment). Froneman J. delivered a separate but concurring judgment (second judgment).

In terms of the first judgment the decision in *Laubscher* hinged on the consideration of three aspects:

1. Was the reading-in remedy in *Gory* an interim measure?
2. The interplay between the judgment in *Gory* and the CUA.
3. Are the principles stemming from *Volks* applicable in this matter?

Mbha AJ argued that it was evident from the judgment in *Gory* that the court was alive to the impending enactment of the CUA yet nevertheless employed the remedy of reading-in to cure the constitutional invalidity of the Intestate Succession Act.[94] Moreover, the judgment in *Gory* made it quite clear that the order in that case would remain operative until such time as the legislature specifically chooses to amend it.[95]

In so far as the interplay between the *Gory* order and the CUA was concerned the first judgment adopted a twofold approach – a contextual approach and an interpretative approach.[96] The contextual approach demanded an assessment of the question whether the enactment of the CUA addressed the mischief that the reading-in order in *Gory* sought to

---

[90] 2017 (2) SA 264 (CC).   [91] Para. 3.   [92] *Ibid.*   [93] *Ibid.*   [94] Para. 23.   [95] Para. 24.
[96] Para. 25.

address. The interpretative approach merely prescribed an interpretation of section 1(1) of the Intestate Succession Act.[97] The court came to the conclusion that the *Gory* order sought to address the exclusion of (all) permanent same-sex partners from the ambit of the Intestate Succession Act.[98] The CUA, in the court's view, therefore only addressed the mischief as far as *some* of these same-sex life partners are concerned, namely those who register a union in terms of the said Act. As far as the residuary category of same-sex partners who have not formalised their relationship is concerned, the reason for *Gory* did *not* fall away with the enactment of the CUA.[99]

In terms of a purely interpretative approach, section 1(1) of the Intestate Succession Act was amended by the reading-in order in *Gory* which, in the court's view, has not specifically been amended by the CUA or any other legislation.[100] The *Gory* order thus effectively legislated an amendment of the section.[101] The applicant's suggestion of an analogy between *Laubscher* and *Volks* was rejected on the basis of the facts and the law.[102] First of all, the two cases were said to concern the constitutionality of two different statutes (in *Volks* the Maintenance of Surviving Spouses' Act was under attack).[103] Second, the deceased in *Volks* died testate while the deceased in *Laubscher* died intestate.[104] Lastly, the *Laubscher* case was said not to be concerned with an equality challenge but a determination of the continued validity of the *Gory* order in the light of the enactment of the CUA.[105] In answer to a claim by Froneman J. that the first judgment avoids the import of the majority judgment in *Volks*, Mbha AJ reiterates the stance adopted by many of the previous courts extending recognition to same-sex partners that a court 'should be reluctant to revisit principles that are not within the purview of the facts of a case'.[106] The plight of unmarried heterosexual partners who will continue to be excluded from inheriting intestate from each other, in the court's opinion, therefore could not be addressed *mero motu*:

Whether to provide 'equality of the graveyard or the vineyard'[107] to permanent same-sex partners, is a matter best left to the competencies of the Legislature.[108]

---

[97] *Ibid.* [98] Para. 33. [99] Para. 36. [100] Para. 40. [101] Para. 51. [102] Para. 46.
[103] *Ibid.* [104] *Ibid.* [105] *Ibid.* [106] Para. 53.
[107] The reference is taken from *Fourie* (para. 149) and refers to the legislator's options when deciding on how to remedy the under-inclusivity of a statutory provision – total exclusion of the benefits from all unmarried life partners (also called 'levelling-down') or full inclusion or opening up of the benefits to all unmarried partners (also called 'levelling-up').
[108] Para. 55.

The second judgment delivered by Froneman J. differs on the reach of the order in *Gory* and the import of the majority judgment in *Volks*.[109] According to the second judgment, the CUA *did* in fact remedy the mischief the court was called upon to remedy, i.e. the impediment suffered by same-sex life partners of not being legally entitled to marry.[110] While acknowledging that this was not the only possible interpretation of paragraph 29 in the *Gory* case, Froneman J. nevertheless considered it a reasonable one:

> The caution against 'legislating' too widely when fashioning a reading-in remedy implies that the more restrictive of alternative reasonable interpretations of the *Gory* order should carry the day.[111]

If the CUA then remedied the wrong addressed in *Gory*, it meant that those same-sex partners who did not take advantage of the removal of the obstacle (after the enactment of the CUA) would still be excluded from intestate inheritance.[112] This, in the opinion of Froneman J., is where the significance of the *Volks* judgment comes to the fore.[113] *Volks* established the general principle that if partners decided not to marry while having the choice to do so, it was constitutionally justifiable *not* to treat them as spouses. The logic of these statements in Froneman's view 'forces one to confront directly the obstacle that the principle, as laid down in *Volks* presents'.[114] The obstacle is embodied in the fact that matrimonial law in South Africa remains 'marriage-centric'.[115] According to Froneman J.:

> This 'marriage-centric' approach is the 'bad' part, at least for some critics. It is bad because the reason for being 'marriage-centric' is unarticulated, and the unarticulated preference lies in moral choices not countenanced by the Constitution. The decision in *Volks* is said to be an example of this unreasoned moral preference.[116]

The court then addresses the other main point of criticism against *Volks*, namely that the majority in *Volks* failed to give proper recognition to the factual reality of reciprocal support between the unmarried partners.[117] Had proper recognition been given to that, the rationale for preferring the

---

[109] Para. 58. [110] Para. 59. [111] Para. 70. [112] Para. 71. [113] Para. 72. [114] *Ibid.*
[115] Paras. 80 and 84. [116] Para. 82.
[117] B. S. Smith, 'Rethinking *Volks v Robinson*: The implications of applying a "contextualised choice model" to prospective South African domestic partnerships legislation' (2010) 13 *Potchefstroom Electronic Review/Potchefstroom Electronic Law Journal* 238–300, 257. Courts in South Africa have extended recognition of a common law duty of support based on factual existence in a long line of cases, most recently in *Paixão* v. *Road Accident Fund* 2012 (6) SA 377 (SCA), where it was held that the dependant's action is to be extended to

marriage validated legal duty of support, in the court's opinion, would have been severely undermined for the following reason:

> It is a feature of this Court's jurisprudence that the existence of factual reciprocal duties of support in unmarried relationships underlies the reasoning that it is unfair to discriminate between married legal duties of support and unmarried factual duties of support. Formally they may be different, but functionally they are similar.[118]

The validity of these criticisms of *Volks*, in Froneman's view, justifies a rejection of the decision in *Volks* as 'not inclusive enough in the present social context'.[119] Unshackled from *Volks*, the second judgment concludes by directing that the CUA be interpreted in a manner that best conforms and least infringes the fundamental right to equality.[120] This means that the meaning of 'spouse' should not only include those who accept benefits by marriage formalisation but also those unmarried (same-sex *and heterosexual*) partners with reciprocal duties of support. Since the respondent fell into the latter category he should be entitled to inherit from his deceased life partner on the same basis as any other similarly situated spouse.[121]

Neither of the two judgments in *Laubscher* is entirely satisfactory. The first judgment seems to support the criticism that the Constitutional Court 'is not ready to embrace a contextual progressive approach towards adult, intimate relationships'.[122] Even though the second judgment of Froneman J. may be 'temptingly persuasive'[123] in its use of substantive reasoning to overcome the deadlock regarding the intestate succession rights of unmarried heterosexual sexual partners, it would indeed seem to have overstepped the boundaries presented by the case. There is now little doubt that the rights of unmarried heterosexual partners can only be resolved by the legislator, but more likely a challenge driven by a surviving partner of such a relationship, given the tardiness of the legislator to formally regulate domestic partnerships. Should such a challenge materialise, the second judgment could provide excellent guidance to the court. Alternatively, an approach as suggested

---

unmarried persons in heterosexual relationships who have established a contractual reciprocal duty of support.

[118] Para. 83.   [119] Para. 84.   [120] Para. 87.   [121] *Ibid.*

[122] J. Heaton, 'South Africa: Changing the contours', in E. E. Sutherland (ed.), *The Future of Child and Family Law: International Predictions* (Cambridge University Press, 2015) 427.

[123] Words used by Froneman J. (para. 58) to describe the reasoning of Mbha AJ in the first judgment.

by Smith[124] would avoid the rejection of the judgment in *Volks* and keep the principle of *stare decisis* intact. According to Smith, the 'levelling-up' process[125] could be justified by claiming that a new form of discrimination has emerged since the *Volks* judgment.[126] This discrimination is experienced by unmarried heterosexual partners and is a 'product or culmination of the positive law that has been created in the post-1994 family law dispensation'[127] – more specifically, the *Gory* judgment. The right to intestate succession is therefore 'no longer a right uniquely attached to marriage [by operation of law]'.[128] As such, a future court would be freed from the constraints of being bound by the *ratio* in *Volks*, while giving due recognition to the fact that our 'constitutional commitment to equality also entails recognising the shifting patterns of inequality'.[129] The finding that the *Volks ratio* is capable of being circumvented in the context of intestate succession would enable the court to see a surviving heterosexual partner's claim in an entirely new light, namely that the legal framework described above has created a new 'pattern' of inequality that discriminates on the intersecting grounds of marital status and sexual orientation.[130] Smith explains the argument in the following terms:

> This is because, for an opposite-sex couple to access the right to intestate succession, they would have to have been married (which constitutes discrimination against them on the basis of marital status) while, if they remained unmarried (for example due to the lack of an option to do so), they had to have been in a form of conjugal relationship (ie a same-sex life partnership) that was not in harmony with their sexual orientation (which entails discrimination on the basis of sexual orientation). Taken together, these two grounds mutually reinforce one another, and ultimately culminate in (or intersect at the point of) the discrimination experienced by B [the surviving heterosexual partner].[131]

---

[124] B. Smith, 'Intestate succession and surviving heterosexual life partners: Using the jurist's "laboratory" to resolve the ostensible impasse that exists after *Volks v Robinson*' (2016) 133 *South African Law Journal* 284–315, 305.

[125] The process of opening up the right to inherit intestate to unmarried heterosexual partners as well.

[126] Smith, 'Intestate succession and surviving heterosexual life partners', 310.

[127] *Ibid.*, 303.

[128] The *ipsissima verba* of Skweyiya J.'s judgment in *Volks*, para. 56 turned against itself (*ibid.*, 305).

[129] *Ibid.*, 306.   [130] *Ibid.*   [131] *Ibid.*

It is hoped that the residual discrimination against unmarried heterosexual partners to inherit intestate, as confirmed by the *Laubscher* judgment, will soon be addressed. This will benefit unmarried heterosexual partners by placing them in at least the same position as unmarried same-sex couples, even though it will still not guarantee them the same automatic protection spouses enjoy.

Hierarchy of Marital Relationships

Given the current range of matrimonial options available to couples as explained before, it is apparent that the two-tiered hierarchy of intimate relationships which existed in the pre-constitutional era (married and unmarried) has now simply been replaced by another, multiple-tiered hierarchy with the civil marriage still placed at the apex. The CUA has created an alternate route to marriage. It does not repeal the Marriage Act. The CUA allows for the conclusion of a civil union that, paradoxically, will not be known as a civil union. Prior to the formal solemnisation of a civil union, the authorised officer must in terms of the CUA ask the parties whether they wish to call their civil union a 'marriage' or a 'civil partnership'.[132] Although the rationale for this provision is not entirely clear, it would seem to have been an attempt to 'de-centre' marriage by creating the possibility of a 'civil partnership' as an alternative to 'marriage'.[133] Apart from the name by which the union is to be called, there is legally speaking no difference between the consequences of a civil partnership and a marriage concluded in terms of the CUA, on the one hand, and a civil marriage, on the other hand.[134] The CUA is not prescriptive insofar as the sexual orientation of the parties is concerned, but prohibits minors to conclude a civil union.[135] It has thus created the anomalous situation in

---

[132] CUA, s. 1, s.v. 'civil union'.
[133] D. Bilchitz and M. Judge, 'For whom does the bell toll? The challenges and possibilities of the Civil Union Act for family law in South Africa' (2007) *South African Journal on Human Rights* 466-99, 467-8.
[134] CUA, s. 13.
[135] The CUA, s. 1 defines a civil union as 'the voluntary union of 'two persons who are both 18 years of age or older'. Cf., however, B. S. Smith and J. A. Robinson, 'An embarrassment of riches or a profusion of confusion? An evaluation of the continued existence of the Civil Union Act 17 of 2006 in the light of prospective domestic partnerships legislation in South Africa' (2010) 13 *Potchefstroom Electronic Review/Potchefstroom Electronic Law*

terms of which adult heterosexual couples have the choice of concluding a marriage in terms of the Marriage Act or a civil union in terms of the CUA, but same-sex couples can only formalise their relationship in terms of the latter Act. This also means that provided the necessary consent is obtained, heterosexual minors can formalise their marriage in terms of the Marriage Act,[136] but gay and lesbian minors cannot formalise their relationship at all because the CUA prohibits a union between parties under the age of 18 years. Despite clearly being discriminatory on the grounds of age and sexual orientation, the CUA has not yet faced a constitutional challenge on any of its provisions. The conscientious objection clause in the CUA,[137] allowing a marriage officer to be exempted from solemnising a civil union between parties of the same-sex, based on objections derived from conscience, religion or belief, has confirmed the inferiority of at least same-sex civil unions in the eyes of some authors.[138] Moreover, since the provision curtails same-sex couples the right to enter into a civil union as freely as their heterosexual counterparts, it is seen as a violation of the equality clause and same-sex couples' right to dignity and could be considered unconstitutional.[139]

Customary marriages, originally called customary 'unions', have a history of being subordinate in status to civil marriages.[140] Before the RCMA, a customary marriage automatically came to an end when a party to a customary marriage entered into a civil marriage.[141] Despite being afforded equal status to civil marriages and civil unions, the RCMA has perpetuated the inferiority of customary marriages by, for example,

---

Journal 30–75, 51–2, who argue that wherever the CUA refers to gender it only refers to same-sex couples and it is thus uncertain whether the Act also applies to heterosexual couples.

[136] The Marriage Act must in this regard be read with the common law that sets the minimum marriageable age at 12 years for girls and 14 years for boys.

[137] CUA, s. 6.

[138] E. Bonthuys, 'Irrational accommodation: Conscience, religion and same-sex marriage in South Africa' (2008) 125 *South African Law Journal* 473-83, 476-7; H. Kruuse, 'Conscientious objection to performing same-sex marriage in South Africa' (2014) 28 *International Journal of Law, Policy and the Family* 150-76, 150.

[139] See Heaton and Kruger, *Family Law*, 208-9; Bilchitz and Judge, 'For whom does the bell toll?', 490-1.

[140] According to the court in *Gumede*, para. 16, 'Past courts and legislation accorded marriages under indigenous law no more than a scant recognition under the lowly rubric of customary "unions".'

[141] This was the position before the enactment of s. 22(1) of the Black Administration Act of 1927, which preceded and was repealed by, the RCMA.

allowing the conversion of (monogamous) customary marriages into civil marriages[142] but not vice versa.[143] On the hierarchical ladder, the customary marriage is therefore said to enjoy a form of quasi existence somewhere between the civil marriage and the civil union.[144]

Religious marriages, such as Muslim and Hindu marriages, are not yet formally recognised in South Africa. It is generally agreed that the non-recognition of religious marriages is unconstitutional because it unfairly discriminates against such 'spouses' on ground mainly of their religion, conscience, belief or culture.[145] From a sex and gender perspective, it is nevertheless arguable that Muslim marriages cannot be recognised because some features of these marriages, such as their potential polygynous nature and manner of dissolution, violate Muslim women's right to sex and gender equality and dignity.[146] These arguments, however, become less convincing when one considers the number of cases in which the courts have already recognised de facto polygynous Muslim and Hindu marriages (albeit for limited purposes).[147] It is interesting to note that the achievement of equality has not been the rationale behind the *ad hoc* recognition. According to Meyerson:[148]

The Court makes no attempt to explain the reasoning behind this concession [recognition of religious marriages], which only makes sense on the supposition that the Court regards marriage in terms of religious law as morally superior to

---

[142] RCMA, s. 10(1). [143] Bakker, 'Chaos in family law', 127.
[144] *Ibid.*, 128. Problems relating to the implementation of the RCMA seem to have overrun the debate about the inferior status of customary marriages. These problems include problems connected with the recognition and proof of customary marriages; the difficulties associated with registering customary marriages without the presence of both spouses; the role of *lobolo* under the RCMA; and the failure of the legislation to adequately regulate polygynous marriages: see e.g. R. J. Kovacs, S. Ndashe and J. Williams, 'Twelve years later: How the Recognition of Customary Marriages Act of 1998 is failing women in South Africa' (2013) *Acta Juridica* 273–91.
[145] Constitution, s. 31. [146] Heaton and Kruger, *Family Law*, 246.
[147] The most recent case being *Moosa NO and Others* v. *Harneker and Others* 2017 (6) SA 425 (WCC), in terms of which the high court declared the term 'surviving spouse' as used in s. 2C(1) of the Wills Act of 1953 unconstitutional to the extent that it did not include a spouse in a monogamous or polygynous Muslim marriage (para. 39). See other cases discussed by Heaton and Kruger, *Family Law*, 242–6 (Muslim marriages) and 249–51 (Hindu marriages). Polygyny is of course already formally recognised in terms of the RCMA as well.
[148] D. Meyerson, 'Who's in and who's out? Inclusion and exclusion in the family law jurisprudence of the Constitutional Court of South Africa' (2010) 3 *Constitutional Court Review* 295–316, 298.

other kinds of informal partnerships: religious marriage, it appears, is better than no marriage. It seems that it is this unarticulated moralistic belief that leads the Court to resort to a one-off expansion of the concept of 'marriage' beyond the *de jure* concept so as to favour religious unions. I will argue that while it is desirable to extend the protections of marriage more generously, to do so in favour of only religious unions is unprincipled. Furthermore, the Court's special solicitude towards religious unions serves to aggravate the unfairness of the Court's moralistic and exclusionary approach to other functionally equivalent relationships.

In line with this approach, some statutes (such as the Children's Act of 2005) define 'marriage' as including a marriage concluded in terms of a system of religious law and thus also treat parties to a Muslim or Hindu marriage as spouses for purposes of that particular statute. Because of the scope of legislative and judicial recognition already afforded to religious marriages, they are not relegated quite to the bottom of the hierarchy.

That position is held by domestic partnerships.[149] Despite the (disparate) ad hoc recognition afforded to these partnerships as explained in the previous paragraph, these relationships generally continue to be governed by the law of contract and the law of universal partnerships.[150]

Conclusion

While there is general consensus regarding the necessity of granting formal recognition to religious marriages and domestic partnerships, the most appropriate format for such recognition is by no means clear. The Muslim Marriages Bill of 2010 that would formally elevate Muslim marriages to the status of civil marriages has not been enacted largely due to disagreements within the Muslim community itself.[151] The Domestic Partnerships Bill that was published in 2008 for public comment[152] has not progressed past the drafting stage either. If the Domestic Partnerships Bill is enacted, the law will recognise two kinds of domestic partnerships: registered partnerships

---

[149] Bakker, 'Chaos in family law', 128.   [150] Heaton and Kruger, *Family Law*, 256–60.

[151] The bill was published for comment in 2011 (see South African *Government Gazette* no. 33946 Government Notice 37 of 2011, dated 21 January 2011). See Heaton and Kruger, *Family Law*, 241 n. 4. Since Hindu marriages could claim formal recognition on the same constitutional bases as Muslim marriages, it is reasonable to predict that a Hindu Marriages Act will follow in the wake of a Muslim Marriages Act.

[152] See South African *Government Gazette*, no. 30663, dated 14 January 2008.

and unregistered partnerships. If registered, the partnership will be recognised on almost the same basis as the other formally recognised unions and would clearly simply add to the hierarchical tapestry of marriage-clone options already available to couples in South Africa. In the case of a partnership that was never formally registered, the bill would make provision for the *ex post facto* protection of the partners by allowing them to claim certain benefits (for example maintenance and intestate succession) from each other at the termination of the partnership.

It seems the pursuit of matrimonial diversity will only come to an end when all similarly situated life partners are given some form of legal recognition and protection. While the privileged status of spouses may decline in such a dispensation, the hierarchical order of the different life partnerships will remain a problem. The hierarchy of intimate relationships does not respect diversity because it uses the civil marriage as a yardstick for all other marital institutions. Such a hierarchy violates the constitutional norms of human dignity, equality and freedom.[153] In a bid to address the objections to the law in this regard, a number of possible solutions have been tendered. The first option is to repeal either the terribly outdated Marriage Act, leaving the CUA as the more generic Act,[154] or to repeal the CUA and amend the Marriage Act by making it gender neutral so as to accommodate same-sex marriages.[155] Both these proposals envisage the enactment of new legislation to provide for the protection of domestic partners.[156] The repeal of either the CUA or the Marriage Act will, however, not address the problems endemic to the practice of polygyny and de facto dual/multiple partnerships.[157] Another option is to deregulate marriage entirely by enacting one generic act which is strictly secular by nature, to regulate all life partnerships.[158] Such an act would make it possible for the parties to choose which personal system should be applicable to their life partnership, be it civil, customary law or Muslim/Hindu religious law. Parties could negotiate monogamy or polygyny and decide what their partnership should be called – a marriage, a union or a partnership. The

---

[153] Bakker, 'Chaos in family law', 130.
[154] Bilchitz and Judge, 'For whom does the bell toll?', 497.
[155] Smith and Robinson, 'Embarrassment of riches or a profusion of confusion?', 67–8.
[156] Bilchitz and Judge, 'For whom does the bell toll?', 487 and 496–7.
[157] B. Goldblatt, 'Regulating domestic partnerships – a necessary step in the development of South Africa law' (2003) 120 *South African Law Journal* 610–29, 626.
[158] Bakker, 'Chaos in family law', 139–41.

more radical option proposed by Meyerson[159] is to abolish the state-conferred legal status of marriage altogether while extending the benefits and protection previously reserved for marriage to all comparable caregiving domestic relationships by means of legislation.[160] Whatever the case may be, it is evident that matrimonial law in South Africa is in dire need of a complete overhaul.

---

[159] D. Meyerson, 'Rethinking marriage and its privileges' (2013) *Acta Juridica* 385–408, 407–8.

[160] E. Bonthuys, 'A patchwork of marriages: The legal relevance of marriage in a plural legal system' (2016) 6(6) *Oñati Socio-Legal Series* 1303–23, 1318, available at https://ssrn.com/abstract=2891014 [last accessed 25 August 2018] goes one step further by arguing for the recognition to be extended to non-conjugal relationships such as interdependent kinship relationships.

The Post-Divorce Child Support System in China
Past, Present and Future

Lei Shi

1 Introduction

Kong and Ma Married on 15 May 2002 and had a daughter named Xiao Kong. Unfortunately, they ended the marriage and registered their divorce on 15 May 2007. They agreed that their daughter would be raised by Ma, her mother. Kong would not pay any child support, but he could visit their daughter at any time. Ma married another man in 2011 and had other two children, the elder of which died. In 2012, Ma's second husband died too. Xiao was still living with her mother. The death of her stepfather made her mother and her life miserable. Thus, Xiao filed a lawsuit in the court that her parents' divorce agreement was not effective and had no legal basis. Xiao claimed in her petition to the court that Kong should pay 1,500 RMB per month in child support from July 2007 to April 2013 and that he should also bear half of the education and medical costs. But Kong refused to pay, referring to the divorce agreement.[1]

This case is typical in post-divorce child support disputes in China. According to the present legal system in China, people can get divorced in two ways: registered divorce and divorce by litigation. Regarding registered divorce, once petitioners reach an agreement on property division and child support after divorce, they can register their divorce at the marriage registration office with their written agreement on these matters.[2] At present, registered divorce is much more popular than divorce by litigation. In 2015, 3.84 million couples divorced, 5.6 per cent higher

---

[1] See *Kong Fanmou* v. *Kong Mou* (2013) Chang Min Chu No. 7128 Civil Judgment issued by the People's Court in Changpin District in Beijing, Case Research Center of National Judges College (ed.), *China Courts Cases in 2015 (Marriage, Family and Inheritance Disputes)* (Beijing: China Legal Publishing House, 2015) 136–8.
[2] For further discussion on China's divorce system, see W. Chen and L. Shi, 'Divorce procedure in China', in J. Eekelaar and R. George (eds.), *Routledge Handbook of Family Law and Policy* (Abingdon: Routledge, 2014), 111–21.

than the previous year. Among them, 3.14 million couples chose registered divorce, while 0.69 million couples went to court to get a divorce. The crude divorce rate in 2015 is 2.8 per 1,000 couples, going up by 0.1 per 1,000 from the previous year.[3] The ratio of registered divorce is 82.0 per cent, 6.9 per cent higher than 2010.[4] The ratio of registered divorce keeps rising. From the perspective of judicial practice, although many couples registered their divorces, some of them filed lawsuits on child raising after divorce, as the above-mentioned case shows. It is, therefore, necessary to explore whether the present divorce registration system provides enough protection for children against harm or infringement of their rights. On the other hand, in relation to divorce by litigation, it is useful to explore how the judge applies the present laws to deal with child support disputes from the perspective of the child's best interests. This chapter will discuss the post-divorce child support system from both legislation and judicial practice levels, and suggest legislative proposals.

2 Evolution of the Post-Divorce Child Support System in China

The present rules on post-divorce child support are an embodiment of the principle of protecting legitimate rights of women, children and the elderly of the Marriage Law of the PRC. These rules are also important components in the divorce and parent–child relationship systems. It is necessary to look back at the evolution of the post-divorce child support system in China to find out the legislative aims and its functions.

2.1 The Post-Divorce Child Support System in the 1950s

After the establishment of the new government in Beijing in 1949, those ordinances applied in local liberated areas during the second Chinese civil war[5] were used as legal sources for post-divorce child support disputes. On 28 February 1950, the Supreme People's Court issued a Reply to the

---

[3] China's Statistical Bulletin on Social Services Development in 2015, www.china.com.cn, 11 July 2016, http://news.china.com.cn/txt/2016-07/11/content_38855906_8.htm [accessed 6 August 2016].
[4] See figure 2, Registered divorces 2003–11 (Chen and Shi, 'Divorce procedure in China', 116).
[5] The laws of the old government were completely repealed.

People's Court in Guangzhou City. This Reply named the *Instructions on Principles to Deal with Present General Matrimonial Cases* clearly stipulates in article 4 that the general principle of resolving disputes over child raising after divorce is that parents' divorce would not end the legal parent–child relationship. Generally speaking, children still breastfeeding should be raised by the mother. As regards children after the breastfeeding period, he or she can be raised by anyone or separately raised by both parents. If an agreement cannot be reached, the court will make a decision, with the first criterion being what will benefit the child. Where the children are raised by the mother, the father should bear all or part of the financial costs of raising the child and of his/her education. The people's court will determine the amount of child support obligation and for how long it lasts if both sides fail to make an agreement.[6]

Soon afterwards, the new government promulgated the first Marriage Law of the PRC (hereafter referred to as the Marriage Law 1950) on 30 April 1950, based on the Common Program of the Chinese People's Political Consultative Conference and the marriage ordinances in those local liberated areas. Post-divorce child support systems are expressly provided for. The following three key articles are found in Chapter Six of the Marriage Law 1950, entitled Child Support and Education after Divorce:

Article 20
Parents' divorce shall not end the parent and child relationship. No matter who is going to raise the children after divorce, the children are both parents' children.
   Both parents have obligations to raise and educate their children after divorce.
   Generally speaking, children still breastfeeding should be raised by the mother. As regards children after the breastfeeding period, when both sides willing to raise them have disputes over this issue and cannot reach an agreement, the court will decide based on the child's interests.

Article 21
With regard to the children raised by the mother after divorce, the father should bear all or part of the necessary raising costs and education expenses. Both parents may make an agreement on the amount of child support payment and on how long the payment lasts; the court will determine these issues if they fail. The child support can be paid by money or chattels, or labour of farming the land allocated

---

[6] X. P. Zhang, *History of China's Marriage Law Legislation* (Beijing: People's Publishing House, 2004) 202.

to the child, etc. The agreements on child support and education costs or the judgments over these issues made when divorcing shall not preclude the child from making a petition to any parent for more child support exceeding the original amount agreed by both parties or judged by courts.

Article 22
After the mother is married again, if the new husband would like to bear all the living expenses and education costs of the original child born to his wife in her first marriage or some of them, the child's biological father's burden of child support may be reduced or waived as appropriate.

The Marriage Law 1950 also added some new rules concerning ways of child support payment and remarriage of the mother.

The Industrial Revolution from as early as the eighteenth century up to the twentieth century not only brought great change in societal and economic levels in many countries, but also prompted marriage and family law reforms which gradually reduced patriarchal influence on marriages and families. Women began to leave families and enter into the labour market. Family cohesion was weakened. Fathers' rights were increasingly restricted, both administratively and judicially.[7] Meanwhile, women's rights movements made great progress. Take England and Wales as an example. From the second half of the nineteenth century to the first twenty years in the twentieth century, feminist movements in England and Wales campaigned on issues such as independent legal status for married women and rights of married women. The independent legal status of women and the expansion of their rights fundamentally changed the divorce system, which reflected the traditional ideology of a male-dominated and male-centred family.[8] Likewise, the women's liberation movement in China began with women leaving their families and entering into the labour market. But unlike other countries, the liberation of China's women was gradually achieved by abolishing semicolonial and semifeudal private ownership, making and implementing relevant laws on protecting women's rights and reforming the old social institutions that oppressed and exploited women.[9] Enacting and implementing the Marriage Law 1950

---

[7] S. Q. Chen, *Research on the Post-Divorce Parent–Child Relationship System* (Beijing: China Social Science Press, 2011) 55.

[8] L. Shi, *Research on the Modern Divorce System in England and Wales* (Beijing: Qunzhong Press, 2015) 24–5, 30.

[9] S. L. Yue and G. Y. Wei (eds.), *Research on Socialist Feminist Theory with Chinese Characteristics* (Beijing University Press, 2014) 144.

was part of the national task of abolishing the old system and establishing a new one. From this perspective, the main task of the law was to abolish feudal marriage and family laws and to implement a new democratic marriage and family laws.[10] However, the Marriage Law 1950 encountered resistance in implementation. In the first two years of implementing the Marriage Law 1950, traditional feudal thinking still existed here and there. Young males and females were not allowed to find their partners freely. Some held that women got too many advantages under the new marriage law, more than they deserved. While others held that divorced women were 'wicked' and divorce should not be granted upon request.[11] Such old patriarchal views led to the new marriage law not being strictly observed. As a result, in applying the post-divorce child support rules in judicial cases the rights and interests of women and children were not well protected. In March 1953 the government organized and carried out a national public campaign to publicize and ensure the implementation of the Marriage Law 1950. The central government established the Office of Publicizing and Checking the Implementation of the Marriage Law. Implementing Marriage Law Movement Committees were set up in local authorities. This top-down marriage law reform ensured the successful implementation of the Marriage Law 1950. It led to greater public acceptance of the need to protect the rights of women and children in the post-divorce child support system, as provided of the Marriage Law 1950.

2.2 The Post-Divorce Child Support System in the 1980s

The second marriage law after the founding of the new government was the Marriage Law of the PRC promulgated on 10 September 1980, effective on 1 January 1981(hereafter referred to as the Marriage Law 1980). In 1978, the convening of the Third Plenary Session of the 11th CPC[12] Central Committee marked the start of the era of reform and opening up. Impetus for the legal system was ushered in when, after two years of preparation, the Marriage Law 1980 was finally introduced. This law is more perfect than the Marriage Law 1950 from the perspective of legislative process.

---

[10] N. L. Xue, *Is It the Shackles and the Bible? Discussion of Chinese Women and Law* (Beijing: China Renmin University Press, 1992) 78.
[11] P. T. Zhang, *Historical Data of Marriage Reform and Judicial Reform in New China: Selected Archives of Southwest of China* (Beijing University Press, 2012) 10–11.
[12] Communist Party of China.

Before the final promulgation of the Marriage Law 1980, it went through three stages: extensive research, discussion of the draft, and revision and improvement.[13] Of the Marriage Law 1980, the post-divorce child support system and the post-divorce property and life rules, which had been separately stipulated at Chapters 5 and 7 of the Marriage Law 1950, were finally merged in the chapter on Divorce. This made the system more concise.

The post-divorce child support system of the Marriage Law 1980 can be found in Articles 29 and 30. It includes the following rules.

First, with regard to the parent–child relationship after divorce, it is provided that parents' divorce does not put an end to the parent–child relationship. Regardless of whether the children were to be raised by the father or the mother after divorce, they were still the children of both parents. Both of the parents have the rights and duties to raise and educate their children. Second, regarding with whom the children would live, it was provided that, generally speaking, breastfeeding children would be raised by their nursing mothers. For those parents who cannot agree on child support after divorce if their children are beyond the breastfeeding period, the people's court shall decide on the basis of the rights and interests of the children and the specific circumstances of both parents. Third, as regards child support payment, where the child is raised by one party after divorce, the other party shall bear all or part of the educational and living costs of the child. Both parents can make an agreement on the amount of child support payment and on how long the other party shall pay. In the event of failure to reach an agreement, the people's court shall issue a judgment. Further, any agreements or judgments concerning the costs of living and education of their children after divorce do not preclude the child from making reasonable demands to the parent, if necessary, for extra money exceeding that stipulated in the agreement or judgment.

In comparison with the Marriage Law 1950, the new law revised the following rules. First, it added new considerations when the people's court heard cases concerning child support after divorce for those children beyond breastfeeding. Namely, that 'the special circumstances of both parties' apart from the child's rights and interests should be considered. Second, the stipulation on the ways of paying child support

---

[13] See L. Li (ed.), *Review and Reflection of the Legal System in New China* (Beijing: China Social Science Press, 2004) 308.

was deleted. Third, article 22 of the Marriage Law 1950 was also deleted. That concerned whether the child's father's obligation to pay child support may be reduced or exempt because of the mother's marriage to a third party.

On the one hand, these amendments reflect the legislative guiding ideology of the Marriage Law 1980: that is, that this legislation was to be simple rather than complex, so that it would be concise and easy to understand.[14] On the other hand, these amendments also reflect the needs of judicial practice. The reason for adding the new consideration of 'the special circumstances of both parties' probably lies in difficulties of judging what the child's rights and interests are in some custody dispute cases. Regarding the second change of deleting ways of paying child support, it did not change the nature of paying child support, which is an essential liability for parents. Meanwhile, this revision made this new law more concise. In addition, the deletion of article 22 of the Marriage Law 1950 actually helped to clarify the idea that the relationship between parents and children after divorce would not change essentially just because the step-parent pays the living and educational costs of the child.

In summary, the promulgation and implementation of the Marriage Law 1950 marked that the marriage and family system in China had become a new one, suitable for a new society, emphasizing freedom of marriage and divorce and rejecting the traditional approach of a semicolonial and semifeudal society. However, the existence of feudal remnants of old male-centred views, some mistakes in the development of China as well as temporary difficulties caused by natural disasters from 1959 to 1961 resulted in a rise in feudal thinking. The new marriage and family system under the Marriage Law 1950 seemed to be useless and some old, outworn and objectionable habits reappeared.[15] Therefore, the Marriage Law 1980 still had to take up the task of rejecting feudal outdated thinking on marriage and the family. The promulgation of the Marriage Law 1980 consolidated and developed the achievements made by the Marriage Law 1950, which was conducive to raising public awareness and moral values

---

[14] C. Z. Wu and Y. L. Xia, 'Evolution of the marriage law in thirty years since opening-up and reform policy came out', in W. Chen (ed.), *Review and Outlook of the Research on the Marriage, Family and Succession Law in China: Thirty Years after Opening-up and Reform Policy (1978–2008)* (Beijing: China University of Political Science and Law Press, 2010) 4.

[15] Y. L. Xia, *New Regulation on the Marriage and Family Relationship in the 21st Century* (Beijing: China Procuratorate Press, 2001) 192.

and strengthening the legitimate rights and interests of women and children. Revising the post-divorce child support system, with the aim of emphasizing and safeguarding the lawful rights and interests of the minor children, also fits in with the wider the legislative purposes.

2.3 The Post-Divorce Child Support System in the Twenty-First Century

Entering the twenty-first century, China amended the Marriage Law 1980 in 2001 (hereafter referred to as the Marriage Law Amendment 2001). The post-divorce child support system was amended and stipulated in articles 36 and 37 of the Marriage Law Amendment 2001. Article 36 uses new terms of directly supporting children, stipulating that regardless of whether the children would be directly supported by the father or the mother after divorce, they are still the children of both parents. Other parts of the post-divorce child support system remain unchanged. This amendment emphasizes once again that the parent–child relationship is not eliminated by divorce. Even if the children live with one parent, this would not terminate the other parent's rights or obligations of supporting his/her children. From the perspective of the legislative logic and consistence, this provision is consistent with paragraph 2 in article 36, which stipulates that parents still have rights of raising and educating children after divorce.

3 The Content of the Present Post-Divorce Child Support System

3.1 Common Elements of Rules in this System

3.1.1 Time Requirements

The post-divorce child support system regulates the parent–child relationship after divorce, while the parent–child relationship during a marriage is regulated by articles 21–24 of the Marriage Law Amendment 2001. For those parents without a marriage, such a parent–child relationship is regulated by article 25 of the Marriage Law Amendment 2001. A child in this situation could be one born out of wedlock, one born to a married woman, but fathered by a man who is not her husband, or a child born in a void marriage or a voidable marriage but declared void. In other words, only where parents register their divorce or divorce by litigation, can the post-divorce child support system be applied to regulate the parent–child relationship.

The *Opinions on Child Support When People's Courts Hearing Divorce Cases* (hereafter referred to as the *Child Support Opinions 1993*) issued by the Supreme People's Court in 1993 stipulates in article 11 that the child support payment obligation would generally end when a child reaches 18 years old. Where a child over 16 and less than 18 years old and can make a living mainly by their own legitimate income and maintain a general standard of living in the local area, parents may stop paying child support. However, article 12 further explains that where an adult child[16] who has not yet lived by themselves is in any of the following circumstances, parents still have obligations to pay child support: (1) the child is incapacitated or unable to work, or has not completely lost their ability to work but can only achieve a meagre income and cannot maintain themselves; (2) the child is still studying at school; (3) the child is unable to live independently. It is safe to conclude that generally speaking, the child support obligation would be terminated when the child reaches 18. However, there are exceptions where the adult child cannot live independently and parents have the ability to support their child. In this scenario, parents shall continue to pay child support. It should be noted that the current judicial interpretation regarding situation (2) above adopts a narrow approach to limit its application, and the stipulation that the child who cannot live independently refers to adult children being accepted into education in high school or inferior education, or unable to maintain livelihood due to non-subjective reasons such as loss of ability to work or reduced ability to work.[17]

3.1.2 Who Has Responsibility for Raising a Child?

Basically, divorced parents have obligations to raise their child, which includes biological parents with a blood relationship with their children, who are raising them, and adoptive parents, who have an established legal adoption relationship with their adoptive children. But, China's law does not extend these obligations to step-parents.

---

[16] Anyone 18 years old is an adult under Chinese law.
[17] Article 20 in the *Interpretation No. I of the Supreme People's Court on Several Issues in the Application of Marriage Law of the People's Republic of China 2001*.

Regarding the step-parent–stepchild relationship, article 13 in the *Child Support Opinions 1993* stipulates that if the step-parent and the birth parent get divorced and the step-parent is not willing to support the stepchild after divorce, the stepchild shall be raised by his/her birth parents. In this scenario, if the step-parent is not willing to continue to support the stepchild, or if the step-parent is willing to do this while the birth parent does not agree, the parent–child relationship legally formed by raising and educating the stepchild shall be ended at the time of divorce.

As regards to legally established adoption, the adoption shall be agreed by both parents. So, once the adoption is established, the end of the adoptive parents' marriage has no negative legal effect on the adoptive parent–child relationship. The adoptive children shall be the children of both adoptive parents. Adoptive parents still have obligations to raise and educate their adoptive children.

3.2 Separate Elements of the Rules in this System

3.2.1 The Parent–Child Relationship after Divorce: Continuation of Child Support for Minor Children

Article 36 of the Marriage Law Amendment 2001 stipulates that the relationship between parents and children shall not come to an end at the time of divorce. After divorce, whether the children are directly supported by the father or the mother, they shall remain the child's parents. Divorce only terminates the personal relationship and the property relationship between parents, not between parent and children. Therefore, after divorce, both parents shall still have the right and duty to bring up and educate their children. It is the embodiment of the fundamental principle of both the Constitution of the PRC, and the Convention on the Rights of the Child that 'children are protected by the state'.

3.2.2 Who Can Live with the Child after Divorce: Focus on Rearing and Educating Minor Children

Paragraph 3, article 36 of the Marriage Law Amendment 2001 further stipulates that in principle, a breastfed infant shall live with the mother after divorce. If an unresolved dispute arises between both parents over the custody of their child who has been weaned, the People's Court shall make a judgment in accordance with the rights and interests of the child and the actual conditions of both parents. This is the principle used to deal with child support disputes according to the child's age. Apart from this stipulation, articles 1 to 6 in the *Child Support Opinions 1993* are still effective. In accordance with articles 1 and 2, a child less than 2 years old generally lives with the mother. The child may live with the father where the mother is in one of the following situations: (1) the mother has been suffering from infectious diseases or other serious diseases for a long time and these diseases have not been cured; (2) the mother can rear the child but fails to do so and the father wants the child to live with him; (3) the child cannot live with his/her mother due to other rational reasons. Where parents reach an agreement that the child under 2 years old would live with the father and this would have no adverse effects on the child's healthy growth, the court can give effect to this agreement. Article 3 provides ways to deal with child support where the child is over 2 years old. For children under the age of 2, if both parents would like to live with the child, one party in the following circumstances may be given priority: (1) one party has undergone sterilization surgery or has lost fertility due to other reasons; (2) one party has lived with the child for a longer time, and changing the child's living surroundings would be obviously disadvantageous to the child; (3) one party has no children while the other party has other children; (4) living with one party is more advantageous to the child while the other party has been suffering from infectious diseases or other serious illnesses for a long time and these diseases have not been cured, or the other party has other circumstances not beneficial to the child's physical and mental health and it is not suitable that the child live with them. This judicial interpretation also provides in article 4 particular considerations, in a case where both parents would like to live with the child and they have similar conditions to support the child. That is, if the child has actually been living with one party's parents for quite a long time and these grandparents want the child to live with them, and the grandparents have the ability to rear the child, then the court can make a judgment that the child shall live with this party. Article 5 concerns the child's right to participation, which states that in the case that parents are unable to agree on with whom the child should live, if the child is over the age of 10, the child's opinion shall be taken into account. Article 6 further stipulates that where both parents agree to take turns to raise their child and that is a beneficial arrangement, which protects the child's rights, the court can make an order effecting their agreement.

It is not difficult to conclude from the foregoing provisions that to determine whom the child shall live with much depends on an assessment of what is the best way to raise and educate the child. It is expressly stated that the relevant considerations are the child's interests and both parents' situations. It is worth noting that the most important consideration is the child's interests. However, the specific situation of both parents is also an important consideration. Parents play a critical part in the parent–child relationship. As long as the child's interests are protected, balancing the child's interests and both parents' situations is a good way to work out a practical arrangement. This is not only an important means to solve child custody disputes, but also provides a favourable basis for both parents to reach an agreement on raising and educating their children and successfully negotiating with each other how to share this common obligation. Surely it is desirable to reconstruct the parent–child relationship after divorce, if possible. In the final analysis, these rules are designed to protect the child's interests.

3.2.3 Paying Child Support after Divorce: Encouragement of Negotiation, Supplemented by Intervention of Public Power

After divorce, the party living with the child can fulfil the parent's child-raising obligation by taking care of their daily lives, while the other party is usually unable to fulfil his/her responsibility in this way. Therefore, the law requires them to pay child support after divorce. This requirement not only alleviates the economic pressure on the parent with whom the child lives, it also safeguards the child's welfare. Further, it is an important means for the paying party to realize his/her parenting responsibilities.

In accordance with article 37 of the Marriage Law Amendment 2001, after divorce, if one parent lives with the child, the other parent shall bear part or all of the child's necessary living and educational expenses. The two parents shall seek agreement regarding the amount and duration of such payment. If they fail to reach an agreement, the people's court shall make a judgment. Apart from this provision, the *Child Support Opinions 1993* sets out more detail on this. Article 7 in the *Child Support Opinions 1993* stipulates that the amount of child support payment can be determined based on the actual needs of the children, the wealth of both parents and the actual living standards of the local community. Where the other parent has a fixed income per month, child support can be paid at a rate of 20 to 30 per cent of the total monthly income. If two or more children need to be raised, the proportion shall be increased appropriately, but generally not more than 50 percent of total monthly income. If the other parent has no fixed income per month, the amount of child support payment can be calculated on the basis of the obligor's total income of that year or the industry average income with reference to the foregoing proportion. This ratio can be increased or decreased appropriately as the court may think fit. In judicial practice, the court needs to balance three factors: the actual needs of their children, the affordability of both parents and the actual living standards of the local community. These three factors have the same weight when deciding the amount of child support payment. The court will strive to find an optimal solution after balancing these factors, in order to resolve child support disputes.

In addition, the *Child Support Opinions 1993* made clear the ways to pay child support. Article 8 stipulates that the child support should be paid on a regular basis, or paid in a lump-sum payment if possible. Article 9 adds that in the event that the parent due to pay child support has no income or his/her whereabouts are unknown, his/her property may be used to offset the payment of child support.

It is worth noting that although the law provides the freedom of negotiation over child support payment to both parties, the agreement finally reached must abide by the principle of protecting the legitimate rights and interests of children. Article 10 in the *Child Support Opinions 1993* stipulates limitations on this: Parents can agree that the child lives with one parent and this parent bears all the costs in raising this child. But where the court confirms that this parent obviously cannot guarantee to meet the child's needs thus it is disadvantageous to the child's development, the court can reject this agreement. Where the child is over 16 years old and can live independently and maintain the general living standard in the local community, parents can stop paying child support (Article 11 in the *Child Support Opinions 1993*).

3.2.4 Change of Child Support and Child Custody after Divorce: Based on the Child's Interests

Change of child support and child custody is a mechanism for divorced families to cope with changing realities. After divorce, the original child support payment or educational expenses reached by both parents or judged by the people's court might be not enough for the child's reasonable needs due to rising prices or increases of reasonable educational costs etc. Relevant articles on this problem can be found at article 27 of the Marriage Law Amendment 2001. Paragraph 2 of article 27 stipulates that if necessary, the child can petition for a reasonable increase of child support exceeding the original child support payment or educational expenses reached by both parents or judged by the people's court.

Other relevant articles are stipulated in the *Child Support Opinions 1993*. Article 17 of this judicial interpretation provides where both parents agree to change the child custody, the court shall give effect to their agreement. While article 15 adds that if one party requests a change of child custody or the child requests more child support, they can make a separate petition.

Two points need to be clarified here. First, article 27 of the Marriage Law Amendment 2001 makes clear that if there is a necessary and reasonable increase of living and education costs, the people's court may support a petition to increase the payments due. Article 18 in the *Child Support Opinions 1993* explains that in the event that the child petitioning for an increase of child support faces the following situations and the other parent has the ability to pay, the people's court can support such claims. (1) The amount of the original child support payment is not sufficient for the child to maintain the local standard of living; (2) the original child support cannot meet the child's actual needs due to his/her medical bills or educational expenses; (3) there are other rational reasons. In other words, these rules aim to better protect the child's rights and interests.

Second, regarding change of child custody, Article 18 in the *Child Support Opinions 1993* further explains that one parent requesting change of child custody faces the following circumstances, the people's court can support his/her petition. (1) The parent living with the child cannot continue to support their child due to this parent's serious illnesses or injuries or disability; (2) the parent living with the child fails to fulfil his/her child-rearing obligation and abuses the child, or his/her lifestyle has adverse effects on the child's physical and mental growth; (3) the child over 10 years old is willing to live with the other parent and this parent has the ability to support their child; (4) there are other rational reasons.

Apart from the foregoing rules, the present system has more articles on failing to support their children. Article 19 in the *Child Support Opinions 1993* stipulates that parents shall not refuse to pay child support only because their children change their surnames. If the father or the mother, without negotiation with the other parent, changes the surname of the child to the stepmother's or the stepfather's surname, the court will order the child's original surname to be restored. Article 20 in the *Child Support Opinions 1993* stipulates that where both parents are not willing to support their children during the divorce litigation, it can be ordered that one parent shall raise the children temporarily. Article 21 provides remedies for failure to fulfil child support obligations. That is, the people's court may, in accordance with Article 102 of the Civil Procedure Law of the PRC, impose compulsory measures on the parties refusing to perform child support obligations or other persons obstructing others in fulfilling child support obligations stipulated in judgments, orders or mediation agreements.

From the development of the post-divorce child support system, it is safe to conclude that the amendment in 2001 does not change this system substantially. Instead, this new amendment only changes some legal terms. The important judicial interpretation on child support after divorce, i.e. the *Child Support Opinions 1993*, is still effective. The next section of this chapter explores whether this system operates well in practice.

4 Exploration of Judicial Practice of the Post-Divorce Child Support System

In judicial practice, the post-divorce child support system in China faces the following questions.

First, in registered divorce, if both parents agree that the parent not living with the minor children should not pay child maintenance (hereafter referred to as no-payment agreement) and register this divorce agreement, is that agreement legally binding? In accordance with article 31 of *the* Marriage Law Amendment 2001, the parties who wish to divorce may do so by means of registration. For registration, they need to submit a divorce registration agreement to the marriage registration office. It must be stated in this agreement that the parties have agreed on child support and division of property. Once registered, the agreement is legally binding on both parties unless there are situations which make the agreement invalid.[18]

---

[18] W. CHEN and L. SHI, 'Divorce procedure in China' in J. Eekelaar and R. George (eds.), *Routledge Handbook of Family Law and Policy* (Oxford: Routledge, 2014) 112.

Therefore, generally speaking, even if both parents agree that the parent not living with their children does not pay child support, such an agreement is legally binding on both parties. Our recent survey shows that divorce agreements having such a stipulation account for 31.52 per cent among those registered divorces involving children.[19] However, regarding this agreement's effectiveness, judges differ.[20]

We maintain that the post-divorce child support system aims for protecting the child's rights to life and education. The rights to life and education enjoyed by the minor children is essentially different from the spouse's right to division of property when divorcing.[21] The agreement on child support reached by both parents when divorcing concerns how to share both parents' responsibilities between themselves. It is not legally binding on the minor children.[22] That said, because the minors do not have full capacity, the parent living with the children usually act as the agent to manage their properties. Therefore, it is extremely difficult in practice to distinguish the property of one parent and the property of the child. In registered divorce, lots of divorcees hold that if one spouse gets more properties than the share he or she deserves, the more properties acquired should be regarded as the child support paid by the other spouse in a lump-sum payment. This is why people are always worried that, if both parents agree that the parent with whom the child does not live should not pay child support but then the court supports the other parent's petition of child support, this violates the principle of good faith in the civil law. So, to determine whether a no-payment agreement is effective, we need to

---

[19] W. Chen, L. Shi and W. L. Zhang, 'Empirical research on protection of children's rights and interests in registering divorce in China' (2016) 18 *Journal of Southwest University of Political Science and Law* 119.

[20] Some judges would support the child support claim, i.e. such an agreement is invalid. See Case Research Center of National Judges College (ed.), *China Courts Cases in 2013 (Marriage, Family and Inheritance Disputes)* (Beijing: China Legal Publishing House, 2013) 104–6. While some judges would not support this claim if the agreements stipulated such that the other party do not pay child support. See Case Research Center of National Judges College (ed.), *China Courts Cases in 2015 (Marriage, Family and Inheritance Disputes)* (Beijing: China Legal Publishing House, 2015) 136–8.

[21] In China, the statutory matrimonial property regime is the common property regime which means that any property acquired by one spouse during the marriage shall be regarded as the common property owned by both spouses. Therefore, at the time of divorce, each spouse has the right to get his/her share in the common properties.

[22] For similar arguments, see L. P. Wang, *Research on the Parent-Child Law* (Beijing: Law Press, 2004) 135; Chen, *Research on the Post-Divorce Parent-Child Relationship System*, 212.

examine the effectiveness of the divorce agreement. Where there are circumstances such as deceit and coercion, which invalidate the divorce agreement, the court can declare this agreement null and void. In the absence of such circumstances at the time of reaching such a divorce agreement and there has been no significant change in both parents' economic situations which could greatly affect the child's rights to life and education, this agreement should be legally binding on both parents. On the contrary, if the parent living with the child encounters misfortune resulting in difficulties in raising the child, the court shall support the child's child support claims based on the changes in circumstances. Likewise, once the parent has proved any of the circumstances stipulated in article 18 in the *Child Support Opinions 1993*, he or she can request to increase child support.

Second, for those choosing to divorce by litigation, how does the court determine who shall have the custody of a child over the age of 2? Since the late 1970s, China has been implementing its family planning policy, i.e. one child–one family. The direct effect of this policy is that there is only one child in many families in China. Therefore, in many families, both sides litigate for the child to live with them.[23] A recent survey shows that among the four circumstances stipulated in article 3 in the *Child Support Opinions 1993*, dealing with cases where the child is under the age of 2, the 'status quo' factor (i.e. the second circumstance) has become the primary factor and been applied more than other factors in practice. The court usually has no time to further investigate other factors due to heavy caseloads for these judges of first instance. In 245 investigated child custody cases, 111 judgments show that the children were ordered to live with the parent with whom they have been living at the time of the hearing, meaning the status quo was following in 45 per cent. That survey also indicates that these children's status quo usually involved their grandparents. For example, in some cases, the children's parents went out as migrant workers, and the child was raised by his/her grandparents. The court usually decides that the child shall live with the parent whose parents did raise and live with the

---

[23] As China's ageing population is growing rapidly, it has become an ageing society. Accordingly, on 29 October 2015, the Fifth Plenary Session of the 18th CPC Central Committee decided to adopt a new family planning policy allowing all couples to have two children. This problem might disappear soon.

children before divorce litigation.[24] This may lead to another disturbing situation where both parents seeking to win child custody kidnap the child and live with him/her for a period of time so as to gain support from the court in child custody cases. Unsurprisingly, some judges have criticized this behaviour.[25] However, other judges did not consider that kidnapping hurts the child and unexpectedly supported those kidnapper parents' claim based on the status quo.

Judicial practice also reflects an unavoidable fact that judges of first instance face great pressures resulting from heavy caseloads and a shortage of judges in lower courts. In resolving child custody disputes, judges certainly will consider those preferred circumstances first. But for those without these circumstances, judges usually give parents' voice more weight when determining child custody, with the aim of settling the disputes. The function of protecting the child's rights provided by the post-divorce child support system is weakened to some degree. For instance, another survey discovers that 56 per cent of divorce cases were settled by mediation among those divorce cases involving child support. Unfortunately, an investigation of the parent's child-rearing ability and his/her health cannot be made in these divorce mediation agreements.[26]

These problems might be caused by the fact there is no explicit stipulation of the child's best interests principle in the family law of China. Generally speaking, the child's answers to the judge's questions are easily influenced by their parents. Considering the heavy caseload borne by the judge, they usually do not have time to investigate what the child really thinks. Instead, they are inclined to make settling disputes the top priority. The child involved in these child custody disputes are an important stakeholder, but their voices are weaker compared with their parents. Even if their rights are infringed, they probably cannot petition for protection due to their limited competence.[27] The direct result is that their voice is not being heard by the court.

The third question is on the limitation of action regarding child support arrears. At present, there are some disputes over whether an action to

---

[24] L. Zhao and Y. Ding, 'Problems and countermeasures on child custody in divorce cases' (2016) 1 *Journal of China Women's University* 27, 32.

[25] Ibid.

[26] W. Chen and Q. L. Zhang, 'The juridical practice of child-rearing questions in divorce proceedings and its improvement proposals' (2015) 1 *Hebei Law Science* 13-33.

[27] China does not have independent litigation agents for children in these cases, although some lawyers argued for it.

recover unpaid child support arrears should be subject to the general two-year limitation. Some argue that since there is no specific rules on the limitation on these actions, the general two-year limitation should be applied. That means any claim for unpaid child support arrears beyond the two-year limitation would be rejected. Some point out that the child-raising obligation is the common responsibility of both parents. Where one parent has fulfilled this obligation, the child has no right to claim unpaid child support arrears beyond the limitation of action. Others argue that the right to collect child support arrears comes from the parent–child relationship. It is a special personal right. The child support obligation aims for protection of the child's right to life. This right always exists until the child reaches adult age. From this perspective, the general rule on limitation of action should not apply in these circumstances.

We maintain that child support claims should not be subject to the general rule on limitation of action. First, from the purposive approach, the post-divorce child support system aims for protecting the legitimate rights and interests of minor children. Child support claims are critical for the children's right to life, and minor children are in a weak position, in need of special legal protection. Therefore, the rules in this system should be applied and explained in a way which is conducive to realization of child protection. Second, common views on limitations of action hold that these limitation stipulations should not be applied to claims concerning personal relationships.[28] Although claims for maintenance, support or alimony, etc. concern monetary payments, these claims are usually significant for the recipient's standard of living. Without such payments, it would be difficult for them to keep their heads above water. Public order would also be threatened. Therefore, the general stipulations on limitations of action should not be applied in child support claims in order to protect the child's basic human right to life.[29]

It should be noted that once a minor becomes an adult, the post-divorce child support system is not applied. Therefore, if the child has reached 18 and petitions for child support before such age (i.e. he or she actually does not need child support anymore), the general limitation of action shall be

---

[28] L. M. Wang (ed.), *The Civil Law* (5th edn, Beijing: China Renmin University Press, 2010) 144.

[29] X. M. Xi (ed.), *The Supreme People's Court's Understanding and Application of Judicial Interpretation of Limitation of Action in Civil Cases* (Beijing: People's Court Press, 2008) 53.

applied. The child support action must be filed no later than the twentieth birthday of the child. But unless the obligor invokes this rule as a defence, the court shall not invoke this stipulation directly. In addition, it would not stop expiry of the time limit if the obligor who knows this stipulation intentionally waits for the twentieth birthday. But if the obligor deceives the obligee and prevents him/her from exercising the right to claim child support explicitly violating the principle of good faith, the defence of expiry of the time limit cannot be supported.[30]

5 Suggestions on Improving the Post-Divorce Child Support System in China

Child protection in family is an important part of child's rights protection. It has a basic position to protect a child's physical and mental health and cultivate them as citizens, which cannot be replaced with other forms of protection. The rupture of a child's family has a profound effect on them. The establishment of a perfect system of child support after divorce is the proper duty of the state to fulfil its obligations in accordance with the provisions of the Convention on the Rights of the Child. And it is also one of important measures to properly handle divorce disputes and minimize the harm of divorce to minor children. At present, China is making marriage law an integral part of the Civil Code. To solve these problems arising in practice, we suggest that the marriage law should be improved in the following aspects so as to prepare for legislation of the Civil Code.

5.1 Stipulating the Agreement of Non-Payment of Child Support Prohibited

The end of marriage does not mean the end of the parent–child relationship. On the contrary, even if some parents are not recognized as the children's legal parents, once the blood relationship of parent and child is established by birth, it is irreversible. Considering the troubles caused by the agreement of non-payment of child support, we suggest that an amendment should be added that prohibits agreements of non-payment of child support. Instead, divorce agreement should be required to state

---

[30] J. J. Ma and T. M. Yu, *The Civil Law* (3rd edn, Beijing: Law Press, 2007) 247.

explicitly the level of child support. Even if one parent would like to make in a lump-sum payment, they should expressly agree that some particular property should be held or transferred as child support. In this way, this property is legally considered as the child's property. This would be easier for both the marriage registration office and the people's court to complete the related tasks, paperwork formalities, etc. The child's rights would be more easily protected and child support disputes accordingly be reduced.

5.2 Explicitly Stipulating the Child's Best Interests Principle

We suggest that the principle of child's best interests should be added to the considerations made when resolving parental disputes over children.[31] General considerations also need to be amended. Lawmakers should stipulate more detailed regulations on implementing the dual-track system of common custody (also referred to as rotational child-raising) and single custody. Theoretically speaking, common custody after divorce is beneficial for both parents and the child to keep their appropriate intimate relationships. Meanwhile, sharing child support obligations after divorce between parents undoubtedly minimizes the unfavourable consequences of divorce to the child and reduces the financial burden of raising the child by one parent. When parents need to decide a child's important matters, it is easier for them to negotiate where the common custody mode is adopted. Surely this would be conducive to easing the tensions between parents and ultimately turn the parents' divorce into a positive lifestyle change in the child's eyes. It is in line with the child's best interests principle stipulated in the Convention on the Rights of the Child. Therefore, for those parents who can reach a common custody agreement such as cases where the father's home and the mother's home are nearby, and where both want their children to grow up healthily and are willing to play a positive role in his/her growth etc., the people's court shall do its best to help them reach such a common custody agreement. If necessary and possible, social workers, counsellors and other third-party organizations can be invited to help

---

[31] See X. M. Wang, 'Research on the best interests principle of child's rights protection (1)' (2002) 4 *Global Law Review* 493–7; X. M. Wang, 'Research on the best interests principle of child's rights protection (2)' (2003) 1 *Global Law Review* 108–19; W. Chen and J. J. Xie, 'Establishing the child's best interests principle in China' (2005) 5 *Studies in Law and Business* 38–42; H. Wang, 'On the principle of best interests of the child' (2003) 6 *Modern Law Review* 34.

them. Besides, considerations to decide the child's best interests should also be perfected. Apart from the above-mentioned favourable considerations to decide with whom the child shall live as per article 3 in the *Child Support Opinions 1993*, other unfavourable considerations should be added. For example, if one parent has engaged in the following behaviour, the child should live with the other parent: kidnapping minor children to gain custody; gambling; having drug addiction problems; or committing serious domestic violence; and other behaviour unfavourable to the child's interests. Regarding children over 10 years old, the use of the social care system should be promoted.[32] Establishing channels for children to express their voices would definitely help the court to determine with whom children should live.

5.3 Explicitly Stipulating the General Time Limit of Actions Not Applied in Child Support Claims

As mentioned, we suggest that it should be expressly stipulated that the general time limit of actions should not be applied in child support claims, so that the child's best interests principle can be better enforced and vulnerable minors as well as direct child-raising parents better protected.[33]

---

[32] See also D. Y. Zhao *et al.*, 'Research on family cases on child supporting and visiting heard in juvenile court' (2015) 4 *Juvenile Delinquency Prevention Research* 23.

[33] Fortunately, this suggestion was adopted by the legislature, and article 196(3) of the General Rules of the Civil Law promulgated in 2017 clearly states that the provisions on time limit of actions do not apply to claims of child support. Children still have the right to claim for child support due even when they become adults. From this perspective, child protection law has clearly been improved.

The Problem with Personal Law in India   9

Farrah Ahmed*

Introduction

Family law in India is largely based on a system of religious laws, commonly referred to as 'personal laws'. The term 'personal law' is thought to have been used to distinguish laws that apply to people based on their religious affiliation from territorial laws.[1] It is also thought that the laws were 'personal' because they regulated the 'private' sphere of family life. From at least 1772, the British in India used personal laws based on religious doctrine to decide questions of family law.[2] This practice

---

* The author gratefully acknowledges the excellent research assistance provided by the Law Research Service at Melbourne Law School, and the work of Cate Read in particular. The author thanks Jarrod Hepburn for comments on a previous draft. This chapter draws on earlier work including: F. Ahmed, 'Personal autonomy and the option of religious law' (2010) 24 *International Journal of Law, Policy and the Family* 222-44; F. Ahmed, *Religious Freedom under the Personal Law System* (New Delhi: Oxford University Press, 2016); F. Ahmed, 'Remedying personal law systems' (2016) 30 *International Journal of Law, Policy and the Family* 248-73.

[1] See A. Bhattacharjee, *Muslim Law and the Constitution* (2nd edn, Calcutta: Eastern Law House, 1994) 9; J. Derrett, *Religion, Law and the State in India* (Delhi: Oxford University Press, 1999) 39; I. Jaising, 'Gender justice: A constitutional perspective', in I. Jaising (ed.), *Men's Laws, Women's Lives: A Constitutional Perspective on Religion, Common Law and Culture in South India* (New Delhi: Women Unlimited, 2005) 23; *Parbati Kumari v. Jagadis Chunder* ILR 29 Cal 433 (PC) 452; A. Parashar, *Women and Family Law Reform in India: Uniform Civil Code and Gender Equality* (London: Sage, 1992) 46. It is also thought that the laws were 'personal' because they regulated the 'private' sphere of family life. See also F. Agnes, 'The hidden agenda beneath the rhetoric of women's rights', in M. Dutta, F. Agnes and N. Adarkar (eds.), *The Nation, the State, and Indian Identity* (Delhi: Popular Prakashan, 1996) 68-94; C. Mackinnon, 'Sex equality under the Constitution of India: Problems, prospects and "personal laws"' (2006) 4(2) *International Journal of Constitutional Law* 181, 196; D. Washbrook, 'Law, state and agrarian society in colonial India' (1981) 15(3) *Modern Asian Studies* 649, 652.

[2] See Bengal Regulation 1772 (Plan for the Administration of Justice). For text and history, see C. Ilbert, *The Government of India: A Digest of the Statute Law Relating Thereto* (2nd edn, Oxford: Clarendon Press, 1907) 249-50; H. Westra, 'Custom and Muslim law in the Netherlands East Indies' (1939) 25 *Transactions of the Grotius Society* 151, 153-6; *State of Bombay v. Narasu Appa Mali* AIR 1952 Bom 84 [23] (Gajendragadkar J.); A. Fyzee and T.

stemmed from a variety of considerations including respect for the religious sentiments of Hindus and Muslims, the social instability that they feared would result from offence to these sentiments[3] and the limited effect these laws were thought to have on commercial dealings.[4] Today, those whom the state identifies as Hindus, Buddhists, Sikhs, Jains, Muslims, Parsis,[5] Jews[6] and Christians in India continue to be governed by personal laws that regulate matters relating to the family.[7] Generally, their presumed religious identity determines which personal law – ostensibly based on the religious doctrine and the norms of their religious community[8] – will apply to them.[9]

As the personal law system governs much of family law in India, it will be the focus of this chapter. Section I offers an overview of the Indian family law regime, including both personal laws and general family laws. Section II offers an account and an assessment of how Indian family law responds to cultural and religious diversity. Section III outlines the gender-

Mahmood, *Outlines of Muhammadan Law* (New Delhi: Oxford University Press, 2008) 43) (citing the Charter of George II, 1753).

[3] See Fyzee and Mahmood, *Outlines of Muhammadan Law*, 42.

[4] See Jaising, 'Gender justice', 3.

[5] The term 'Parsi' here refers to the ethnic-religious group (also sometimes called 'Parsi Zoroastrian') governed by personal law in India. The religion underlying the personal law group is called 'Zoroastrianism'. See M. Sharafi, 'Bella's case: Parsi identity and the law in colonial Rangoon, Bombay and London, 1887–1925' (PhD dissertation, Princeton University, 2006) for a discussion the difference.

[6] There is not much literature on Jewish personal law in India, but see F. Agnes, *Family Law Volume I: Family Laws and Constitutional Claims* (New Delhi: Oxford University Press, 2011) and J. Derrett, 'Jewish law in Southern Asia' (1964) 13 *International and Comparative Law Quarterly* 288–301, 288.

[7] The personal laws also regulate aspects of the law relating to property, religious trusts and other miscellaneous matters, but they primarily regulate family matters.

[8] See Agnes, 'Hidden agenda', 68–94. It is often argued that many of the personal laws that purport to be based on 'religious tradition' are often distorted versions of the 'religious tradition' that they seek legitimacy from. See, for example, M. Anderson, 'Islamic law and the colonial encounter in British India', in D. Arnold and P. Robb (eds.), *Institutions and Ideologies: A SOAS South Asia Reader* (Richmond, UK: Curzon, 1993) 165; T. Mahmood, *The Muslim Law of India* (Allahabad: Law Book Co., 1980) 49–94; *A Yousuf Rawther* v. *Sowramma* MANU/KE/0059/1971 [7] (VR Krishna Iyer J.); J. Derrett, 'The administration of Hindu law by the British' (1961) 4 *Comparative Studies in Society and History* 10.

[9] Bhattacharjee, *Muslim Law and the Constitution*, 10; M. Galanter and J. Krishnan, 'Personal law and human rights in India and Israel' (2000) 34 *Israel Law Review* 101; Jaising, 'Gender justice', 324; G. Larson, 'Introduction: The secular state in a religious society', in G. J. Larson (ed.), *Religion and Personal Law in Secular India: A Call to Judgment* (Delhi: Social Science Press, 2001) 1; J. Redding, 'Human rights and homo-sectuals: The international politics of sexuality, religion, and law' (2006) 4 *Northwestern University Journal of Human Rights* 436.

related implications of the personal law system, highlighting its discriminatory and unjust aspects. Section IV offers an account of the potential for party autonomy under Indian family law, and makes a proposal for reform.

I Overview

Personal Laws

The system of personal laws is complex. It applies personal law to those that it identifies as members of certain religious groups. These groups will be referred to here as 'personal law groups' to indicate that the groupings made by the personal law system do not necessarily correspond to the way individuals or religious groups self-identify. The content of each of the laws that applies to each of the personal law groups is derived from diverse sources, including religious texts, commentaries on religious texts, case law interpreting religious doctrine, statutes codifying personal law and general statutes that affect, for example, the situations in which personal law, as opposed to the general civil law, will apply.

The personal laws are typically gender-differentiated, so that a person's legal rights and duties are a function of not only their personal law group but also their gender (on which, see section II). It is neither always clear which personal law group the system will assign people to nor how it will treat people who fall into the 'gaps' between the personal law groups. The multiplicity of the sources of personal law and the relative paucity of settled case law on key legal questions mean that many legal questions of personal law are difficult to ascertain.

A General Family Laws

In addition to the personal laws, there are general family laws that govern some of the matters that the personal laws traditionally dealt with. It is difficult to discern any principle that explains when these general laws apply to people instead of (or in addition to) the personal laws. Much of what follows is therefore only *generally* true; however, it illustrates how complicated and unpredictable movement between the personal laws and general family laws can be.

There is currently some uniformity, at least, in institutional arrangements with respect to family law – the Family Courts Act 1984 sets up a system of courts looking into family law disputes. But the most significant general family law is the Special Marriage Act 1954, an ostensibly secular enactment,[10] which allows the registration of marriages solemnized according to both civil and traditional or religious ceremonies.[11] The Special Marriage Act allows two people of the same or different faiths to marry,[12] does not recognize polygamous marriages,[13] does not grant men a more expansive power of divorce than it does women[14] and gives courts the power to grant alimony or maintenance to the woman.[15] In another move towards more uniform marriage laws, in 2005 the Supreme Court directed the central and state governments to provide for the registration of all marriages, regardless of personal law.[16] But the Special Marriage Act 1954 has major limitations. Only those marriages registered under the Act are governed by its provisions.[17] The Act has not been well-publicized, and only a small number of marriages are actually registered under it.[18] Agnes notes:

---

[10] But the Special Marriage Act 1954 s. 21A creates an exemption from the general rule that those marrying under the Act will be governed by the Indian Succession Act 1925. Instead, if a 'marriage is solemnized under [the] Act [by] any person who professes the Hindu, Buddhist, Sikh or Jain religion with a person who professes the Hindu, Buddhist, Sikh or Jain religion', religious personal law would govern instead of the secular law. The object of this exemption is to protect coparcenaries. It has been argued that it is discriminatory and intended to act as a disincentive to Hindus who wanted to marry a person from another personal law group. It also leaves such Hindus without the power to choose not to be governed by the Hindu personal law of succession. See F. Agnes, *Law and Gender Inequality: The Politics of Women's Rights in India* (New Delhi: Oxford University Press, 1999) 98–9.

[11] See Special Marriage Act 1954 ss. 4, 12(2).

[12] Typically, people can only marry others of a particular faith under personal laws. However, Muslim men can marry Christian or Jewish women under the Muslim law.

[13] See Special Marriage Act 1954 s. 4(a).   [14] Ibid.   [15] Ibid., s. 37.

[16] See *Seema v. Ashwini Kumar* (2005) 4 SCC 443. There has been some opposition: see e.g. M. Ali, 'Muslims object to marriage registration proposal', *The Hindu* (New Delhi, 22 April 2014), available at www.thehindu.com/todays-paper/tp-national/tp-newdelhi/muslims-object-to-marriage-registration-proposal/article5935659.ece [accessed 10 September 2018].

[17] Special Marriage Act 1954 s. 21.

[18] See Agnes, *Family Law Volume I*, 97; G. Mahajan, 'Can intra-group equality co-exist with cultural diversity? Re-examining multicultural frameworks of accommodation', in A. Eisenberg and J. Spinner-Halev (eds.), *Minorities within Minorities: Equality, Rights and Diversity* (Cambridge University Press, 2004) 105–6.

Though the Act has been in existence for a long time, it is the least publicized legislation and is shrouded by misconceptions. The most common misconception which prevails is that this law is to be used only in cases of inter-religious or inter-caste marriages, or 'love' marriages, which term refers to marriages of choice contracted against parental wishes. The fact that anyone, including those belonging to the same religion, can opt to get married under this Act has not been sufficiently highlighted.[19]

Besides a lack of awareness about the existence of this enactment, there are serious practical difficulties in having a marriage solemnized under the Act.[20] One account of an attempt to register a marriage under the Act suggests that it was impossible to do so without identifying the religion(s) of the couple.[21] The provisions of the Act, and their implementation, make it difficult for people who wish to marry against the wishes of their families to do so.[22] Moreover, if a Hindu marries someone identified by the personal law system as non-Hindu under the Act, his property rights might be adversely affected.[23]

When people marry or register their marriage under the Special Marriage Act, they are also automatically governed by the Indian Succession Act 1925,[24] except if they are both considered 'Hindu' by the system.[25] Thus, the Indian Succession Act can, like the Special Marriage Act, only be described as *ostensibly* secular.[26] There are also general family laws that apply to people without their having to opt out of the personal law system or explicitly choose general family laws. Maintenance may be claimed from a person by his parents, minor children, wives and ex-wives[27] under

---

[19] See Agnes, *Family Law Volume I*, 92.
[20] See C. Kapoor, 'Act of Vigilantism', *Indian Express* (18 April 2007), available at www.indianexpress.com/news/act-ofvigilantism/28598 [accessed 10 September 2018].
[21] 'When I presented my daughter's fiancé's documents with the column for religion left blank, the marriage officer took great offence and snapped that he had never heard of anyone doing such a thing in all his years' (Kapoor, 'Act of Vigilantism').
[22] See V. Venkatesan, 'Inconsistencies in Special Marriage Act', *Frontline* (21 August 2013), available at www.frontline.in/cover-story/inconsistencies-in-special-marriage-act/article5037686.ece [accessed 10 September 2018].
[23] See Special Marriage Act 1954 ss. 19, 21A.   [24] *Ibid.*, s. 21.   [25] *Ibid.*, s. 21A.
[26] 'The Indian Succession Act contained separate sections for Parsis and non-Parsis ... Although applicable primarily to Christians, this statute could be deemed a residuary law since it was also applicable to person contracting a civil marriage' (Agnes, *Family Law Volume I*, 66–7).
[27] If the ex-wives are Muslims married under Muslim personal law, the Muslim Women (Protection of Rights on Divorce) Act 1986 applies. See *Danial Latifi* v. *Union of India* (2001) 7 SCC 740 and *Shabana Bano* v. *Imran Khan* AIR 2010 SC 305 for the way this

the Code of Criminal Procedure 1973, which therefore applies almost uniformly. The Guardians and Wards Act 1890, which deals with guardianship of minors, is applicable regardless of one's personal law group.[28] In 2006, an amendment to the Juvenile Justice (Care and Protection of Children) Act 2000 allowed people of any personal law group to adopt.[29] However, this provision is restricted to children who are orphaned, abandoned, neglected or abused.[30] Before this, only Hindus had the power to adopt.[31]

II Cultural and Religious Diversity in Family Law

Diversity under the Personal Law System

Personal laws are based on an understanding of these religions that glosses over even strong differences in interpretation of religious doctrine.[32] For

enactment operates. In Agnes' words (F. Agnes, 'Shah Bano to Shabana Bano', *Indian Express* (15 December 2009), available at www.indianexpress.com/news/shah-bano-to-shabana-bano/554314/0 [accessed 10 September 2018]): 'first, a divorced Muslim woman's right to maintenance (or economic settlement) from her husband is not extinguished upon divorce; second, she has dual claims – under s. 125 for recurring maintenance, or for a lump-sum settlement under MWA [Muslim Women Act]. Third, while the jurisdiction for MWA is in magistrates' courts, where family courts have been set up, divorced Muslim women are entitled to claim maintenance in family courts.' See also, *Sabra Shamim* v. *Maqsood Ansari* 2004 (9) SCC 616.

[28] This has at least one exemption – a relatively minor one – for Hindus (s. 21 of the Act).
[29] See s. 41, Juvenile Justice (Care and Protection of Children) Act 2000; *Shabnam Hashmi* v. *Union of India & Ors* (2014) 4 SCC 1; M. Ali, 'Ruling does not interfere with Muslim personal law', *The Hindu* (23 February 2014), available at www.thehindu.com/todays-paper/tp-national/tp-newdelhi/ruling-does-not-interfere-with-muslim-personal-law/article5717980.ece [accessed 10 September 2018]. A recent judgment of the Bombay High Court found that even Hindu parents who have adopted under the Hindu Adoptions and Maintenance Act 1956 can adopt further children under the Juvenile Justice (Care and Protection of Children) Act 2000 (*Vinay Pathak and his Wife* v. *Unknown*).
[30] Section 41(2) of the Act clarifies that '[a]doption shall be resorted to for the rehabilitation of such children as are orphaned, abandoned, neglected and abused through institutional and non-institutional methods'.
[31] Under the Hindu Adoptions and Maintenance Act 1956 s. 7.
[32] See M. Galanter, 'The displacement of traditional law in modern India' (1968) 24 *Journal of Social Issues* 65–91, 65). All those associated with these religions have this single state-endorsed interpretation applied to them. See M. Kishwar, 'Codified Hindu law: Myth and reality' (1994) 29 *Economic and Political Weekly* 2145–61, 2145. Some have argued that this homogenizing trend in the personal laws was motivated by Hindu and Muslim nationalism.

instance, the personal law system's understanding of the Hindu religious doctrine is applied even to those who dissent from this understanding. The Hindu Adoptions and Maintenance Act 1956 recognizes a particular form of adoption known as *dattaka*, in preference to other customary forms of adoption practised by Hindus.[33] But these customary forms of Hindu adoption allow married women to adopt in their own right. The Act does not permit such adoptions, except in unusual circumstances.[34] Furthermore, there are customary Hindu forms of adoption that allow the adoption of an unlimited number of children, while the Hindu Adoptions Act permits the adoption of only two children.[35] Similarly, the courts have interpreted the Hindu Marriage Act, 1955 to mean that *saptapadi* (i.e. the taking of seven steps by the bridegroom and the bride jointly before the sacred fire) and *datta homa* (invocation before the sacred fire) must be performed in order to validate a Hindu marriage. However, these ceremonies are not customarily performed in many Hindu communities.[36]

Even more surprising is that Sikhs, Buddhists and Jains[37] – who generally do not think of themselves as Hindus – are regarded as such by Hindu personal law.[38] They are also, therefore, governed by this state-sanctioned interpretation of Hindu law even though they have religious beliefs quite distinct from Hindus.[39] Some Sikhs, as well as Hindus, who disagree with

---

[33] See Kishwar, 'Codified Hindu law', 2153.
[34] See the Hindu Adoptions and Maintenance Act 1956, s. 8(c).
[35] A Hindu cannot, under the Act, adopt a boy if he already has a son, or adopt a girl if he already has a daughter.
[36] See F. Agnes, 'Hindu men, monogamy and Uniform Civil Code' (1995) 30 *Economic and Political Weekly* 3238; W. Menski, *Comparative Law in a Global Context: The Legal Systems of Asia and Africa* (Cambridge University Press, 2006) 253; *Nagalingam* v. *Sivagami* AIR 2001 SC 3576 ('it has been held that if the parties to the second marriage perform traditional Hindu form of marriage, "Saptapadi" and "Datta Homa" are essential ceremonies and without there being these two ceremonies, there would not be a valid marriage'). This latter reading, however, is a questionable interpretation of the Act (W. Menski, 'The Uniform Civil Code Debate in Indian Law: New Developments and Changing Agenda' (2008) 9 *German Law Journal* 211, 286–8).
[37] See *Shuganchand* v. *Prakash Chand* AIR 1967 SC 506; *Bal Patil* v. *Union of India*, available at indiankanoon.org/doc/502741 [accessed 10 September 2018] on Jains as a minority; R. Sen, 'The Indian Supreme Court and the quest for a "rational" Hinduism' (2010) 1 *South Asian History and Culture* 86–104.
[38] See Hindu Marriage Act 1955 s. 2; Hindu Succession Act 1956; Hindu Adoptions and Maintenance Act 1956.
[39] However, some tribal people are exempted from Hindu law (P. Saxena, *Family Law Lectures: Family Law II* (New Delhi: LexisNexis, 2007) 6–7).

the state's understanding of Hindu doctrine have requested exemptions from Hindu personal law, but so far these requests have been denied.[40]

Similarly, Muslim personal law applies regardless of 'peculiarities in belief, orthodoxy or heterodoxy'.[41] But, like Hindu law, Muslim personal law sometimes accommodates custom[42] and the courts will generally apply the law of the sect or 'school' to which at least one of the parties belongs,[43] thereby recognizing and accommodating some differences in the religious belief within a tradition. However, it is unclear what criteria, if any, would be used by courts in deciding whether to recognize a sect or school for the purpose of applying personal law. In general, 'syncretic, ambiguous or localised' identities are unlikely to receive special legal recognition, and are more likely to be subsumed under a larger, legally recognized religious sect or school.[44]

The personal law system is generally insensitive to religious diversity within a personal law group. The system also responds with uncertainty to who find themselves in the interstices of two or more personal laws. They sometimes lack legal protection, as is illustrated by the following extract from an influential case:

[Sunita] contends that she along with Jitender Mathur who was earlier married to Meena Mathur embraced Islam and thereafter got married. A son was born to her. She further states that after marrying her, Jitender Prasad, under the influence of her [sic] first Hindu-wife, gave an undertaking on April 28, 1988 that he had reverted back to Hinduism and had agreed to maintain his first wife and three children. Her grievance is that she continues to be Muslim, not being maintained by her husband and has no protection under either of the personal laws.[45]

---

[40] See Kishwar, 'Codified Hindu law', 2151; Menski, 'Uniform Civil Code Debate', 293; *Partap Singh* v. *Union of India* AIR 1985 SC 1695; Menski, *Comparative Law in a Global Context*, 250. See also, 'Centre says no to separate Sikh Marriage Act, SAD to meet PM' (*Indian Express*, 2011); 'Sikh Marriage law – Problems and remedies' (*Punjab Newsline*), available at www.sikhphilosophy.net/threads/sikh-marriage-law-problems-and-remedies.26144 [accessed 10 September 2018].

[41] See P. Diwan and P. Diwan, *Muslim Law in Modern India* (Faridabad: Allahabad Law Agency, 2000) 1; Fyzee and Mahmood, *Outlines of Muhammadan Law*, 46.

[42] See Diwan and Diwan, *Muslim Law in Modern India*, 8; Fyzee and Mahmood, *Outlines of Muhammadan Law*, 51. Hindu personal law does as well (Hindu Marriage Act 1955 ss. 5, 7).

[43] See Diwan and Diwan, *Muslim Law in Modern India*, 11; A. Fyzee and T. Mahmood, *Outlines of Muhammadan Law* (New Delhi: Oxford University Press, 2008) 54; M. Hidayatullah and A. Hidayatullah (eds.), *Mahomedan Law* (18th edn, Bombay: Tripathi, 1977) 27; *State of Bombay* v. *Narasu Appa Mali* AIR 1952 Bom 84 [20] (Gajendragadkar J.); *Rajah Deedar Hossain* v. *Ranee Zuhoornussa* (1841) 2 MIA 441.

[44] See Anderson, 'Islamic law'; Sen, 'Indian Supreme Court', 86–104.

[45] *Sarla Mudgal* v. *Union of India* (1995) 3 SCC 635.

In such cases the courts resort to a residuary rule that is found in pre-independence statutes and was endorsed by the Privy Council in *Waghela Rajsanji* v. *Shekh Masluddin*.[46] Under this rule, where there are 'gaps' in the law, the courts might decide 'according to justice, equity and good conscience'. This rule might also be applied to cases of conflicts between the personal laws, for instance, when different personal laws apply to each party to a marriage, or in cases of conversion.[47]

Assessing India's Response to Cultural and Religious Diversity in Family Law

The personal law system represents India's response to questions of cultural and religious diversity in family matters. However, as indicated above, this response poses a number of problems, leading to doubts over whether the system offers a commendable comparative example of accommodation of diversity in family law. Even the brief description of the system's features given above – including, for instance, the inability to choose which personal law group an individual falls into, or the lack of nuance in the approach to religious doctrine taken by state courts – indicates some of its problems.

Supporters of the system might offer two defences. The first is that the Indian state, in limited circumstances, allows people to choose to be governed by generally applicable secular family laws instead of religious personal laws.[48] (There are also circumstances in which people can move from one personal law group to another or are governed by more than one personal law.)[49] Some supporters of the system argue that the (limited) movement that the system allows between personal law and the secular law[50] alleviates other concerns one might have about the system's effect on autonomy.[51]

---

[46] *Waghela Rajsanji* v. *Shekh Masluddin* ILR 11 Bom 551, 561; Bhattacharjee, *Muslim Law and the Constitution*, 85–106.
[47] See *Sarla Mudgal* v. *Union of India* (1995) 3 SCC 635 [12].
[48] Some examples of such secular, generally applicable laws affecting family matters include the Indian Succession Act 1925, the Code of Criminal Procedure 1973, Guardians and Wards Act 1890, and the Juvenile Justice (Care and Protection of Children) Act 2000.
[49] Hidayatullah and Hidayatullah, *Mahomedan Law*, 287.
[50] And perhaps between the personal laws themselves.
[51] See Mackinnon, 'Sex equality', 181; Redding, 'Human rights and homo-sectuals', 436–70.

A second defence might be that since being governed by the personal law represents an additional option available to religious people in India, this enhances their autonomy. Having the option of being governed by the religious norms, they might say, gives religious people a kind of expressive opportunity – the opportunity to express their commitment to their faith – that adds to their autonomy.

Both defences are premised on the idea that individuals can choose when they engage with the system. But the existence of this choice is often elusive in practice. For one thing, the choice between general secular law and personal law is possible under the system *only* in very limited circumstances.[52] It is *not* a choice that individuals governed by the system are routinely presented with. It is also helpful to bear in mind that when the system does provide individuals with a choice between personal and general secular law, this choice can usually only be exercised once. When they have selected one or the other, they cannot later change their minds.

Moreover, in relation to the choice between personal law and general secular law, in many communities in India, if an individual chooses the secular law, this will be interpreted as a denunciation or rejection of community.[53] Other members of these communities are likely to react negatively to such a choice. Specifically, it is likely that they will: (i) think less of a member who chooses the secular law; (ii) try to convince her not to make this choice; and (iii) at least in some cases threaten her with some degree of ostracism.[54] This claim is not easily established because the system as it functions at present often does not allow a choice between general secular and personal law, and even when it does, people are often unaware of the existence of an option apart from the personal law. But anecdotal evidence, including the much-discussed reaction of one

---

[52] F. Ahmed, 'The effect of the institutional features of the Indian system of personal laws on personal religious autonomy' (M.Phil. thesis, University of Oxford, 2008), available at http://ora.ouls.ox.ac.uk, s.1.4 [accessed 11 September 2018].

[53] For the possibility that 'exit' is an indication of dissatisfaction with an association or organization, see A. Hirschman, *Exit, Voice, and Loyalty: Responses to Decline in Firms, Organizations, and States* (Cambridge, MA: Harvard University Press, 1970).

[54] F. Shaheed, 'Controlled or autonomous: Identity and the experience of the network, women living under Muslim laws' (1994) 19 *Signs: Journal of Women in Culture and Society* 997, 1004; J. Spinner-Halev, 'Feminism, multiculturalism, oppression, and the state' (2001) 112(1) *Ethics* 84. See also Agnes, 'The argument against an optional code would be that a large majority of women do not have a choice and they will be excluded from the application of this act' ('Hidden agenda', 84).

community to Shah Bano, a woman who claimed maintenance from her husband under general secular law when she was also governed by Muslim personal law,[55] supports this claim:

> In her native Indore, the 75-year-old Shah Bano was denounced by conservatives as an infidel; demonstrations were held outside her house and neighbours were asked to ostracise her. On 15 November Shah Bano succumbed to the pressure, affixing her thumb impression to a statement saying that she disavowed the Supreme Court verdict, that she would donate the maintenance money to charity and that she opposed any judicial interference in Muslim personal law.[56]

Another commentator recounts how Shah Bano was forced to state '(in a pitiful statement signed with her thumbprint) that she now understands that her salvation in the next world depends on her not pressing her demand for maintenance'.[57]

Religious communities are often a major, sometimes a primary setting in which social bonding takes place; families tend to share a religion and religious people tend to know and form bonds with people of the same religion. Religious schools, churches and community service activities all make it likely that people could find many of their social needs met by their religious communities. Under these conditions, acceptance and respect by one's religious community can constitute an important personal need. The women and other vulnerable persons living under the system may, according to the law, have a choice between general secular and personal law. However, the exercise of this power to choose in favour of the general secular law appears to attract adverse consequences for them. In particular, it harms a personal need of great importance – their social bonds. The preservation of their social bonds is clearly a reason of great weight for them to select the personal law, even when formally offered an alternative by the state. The community's behaviour in these circumstances amounts to coercive pressure, which makes autonomous decision-making impossible. The fact that these obstacles to autonomous decision-making come from religious or social communities rather than the state does not render them less coercive. As Mill reminds us in *On Liberty*, the 'the moral coercion

---

[55] *Mohammad Ahmed Khan* v. *Shah Bano Begum* AIR1985 SC 945.
[56] R. Guha, *India after Gandhi: The History of the World's Largest Democracy* (London: Picador, 2007) 581.
[57] M. Nussbaum, 'India: Implementing sex equality through law' (2001) 2 *Chicago Journal of International Law* 35, 45.

of public opinion' is also a means of 'compulsion and control' of the individual by society.[58]

The system of personal law, as a response to issues of cultural and religious diversity, thus suffers from some significant problems. Section IV offers some thoughts on how Indian family law might be improved.

III Gender and Family Law

Section II outlined several features of India's system of 'personal' laws that carry problematic gender implications. Women, in particular, often suffer extensive pressure of various kinds to conform to the demands of the personal law system. The system itself is typically gender-differentiated, so that a person's legal rights and duties are a function of not only their personal law group but also their gender. (The Appendix at the end of the chapter illustrates this feature of the personal law system, with examples of the rules pertaining to marriage, divorce, adoption and succession.)

There is good reason to believe that being governed by the personal laws is autonomy-reducing, especially for women. The personal laws show inadequate respect for individual liberty. For example, Muslims governed by Muslim personal law are denied powers of testamentary succession.[59] Since the uncodified Indian personal laws (unlike any Indian secular law) do not have to conform to constitutional rights,[60] they also freely discriminate on the grounds of both religion and sex.[61] This kind of discrimination could undermine autonomy by attacking the self-respect of those discriminated against.[62] The personal laws also show inadequate concern for the welfare of women and children, leaving them with inadequate

---

[58] J. Mill, *On Liberty* (New York: Cosimo, 1859, republished 2005) 13.
[59] Diwan and Diwan, *Muslim Law in Modern India*, 218; G. Venkata Subbarao, *Family Law in India: Hindu Law, Mahomedan Law, and Personal Law of Christians, Parsis, etc., including Law of Testamentary and Intestate Succession* (Madras: Subbiah Chetty, 1979) 400.
[60] *State of Bombay* v. *Narasu Appa Mali* AIR 1952 Bom 84; *Shri Krishna Singh* v. *Mathura Ahir* MANU/SC/0657/1981; *Ahmedabad Women Action Group (AWAG)* v. *Union of India* AIRIR 1997 SC 3614.
[61] See e.g. *State of Bombay* v. *Narasu Appa Mali* AIR 1952 Bom 84.
[62] J. Gardner, 'Liberals and unlawful discrimination' (1989) 9(1) *Oxford Journal of Legal Studies* 1.

resources for an autonomous life.[63] By giving women weaker rights to inheritance and weak powers of marriage, divorce, adoption and guardianship, most personal laws leave them with fewer options and less power over their own lives. Without such rights, women are denied valuable options, including the many options closed by a lack of money.[64]

The discriminatory nature of the personal law system is particular to this area of private law in India. When the Indian Constitution was enacted, large areas of private law were already codified and uniformly applied across India.[65] Family law, however, was not codified. The Indian Constitution's direction to the state to endeavour to secure a uniform civil code throughout the territory of India[66] therefore amounts to a direction to enact a code of uniform *family* laws to replace the personal law system.

The persistence of the personal law system in the face of the constitutional directive to create uniform family laws raises difficult questions about India's constitutional commitments to secularism, gender equality and religious freedom (questions that resonate also with other jurisdictions with personal law systems). The rules of the personal law system, for instance relating to marriage, divorce and alimony, are criticized as unjust, harmful, discriminatory against women and contrary to constitutional guarantees of gender equality.[67] Apart from gender issues, the personal law system has been further criticized for harming religious freedom, failing to recognize some religious identities, and for misrecognizing other religious identities and heterodox religious norms.[68] Moreover, the application of religious law sits uneasily with India's constitutional status as a secular state.

There is, therefore, strong support from some corners for the abrogation of personal laws and their replacement with uniform family law, as

---

[63] Z. Hasan, 'Governance and reform of personal laws in India', in I. Jaising (ed.), Men's Laws, Women's Lives, 350–73, 362.

[64] G. Cohen, 'Freedom and money' (2001) *Revista Argentinade Teoría Jurídica*, available at www.utdt.edu.ar/Upload/_115634753114776100.pdf [accessed 10 September 2018].

[65] For example, the Contract Act 1872, the Transfer of Property Act 1872, the Trusts Act 1882, the Evidence Act 1872, the Companies Acts 1956; see R. Dhavan, 'Codifying personal laws', *The Hindu* (1 August 2003), available at www.hinduonnet.com/2003/08/01/stories/2003080100521000.htm [accessed 10 September 2018].

[66] Constitution of India 1950, art. 44.

[67] Agnes, *Law and Gender Inequality*; A. Parashar, *Women and Family Law Reform in India: Uniform Civil Code and Gender Equality* (London: Sage, 1992); Jaising, 'Gender justice'. See also Appendix at end of present chapter.

[68] Ahmed, *Religious Freedom*.

directed by the Constitution. This support includes political support from the Bharatiya Janata Party, the governing Hindu nationalist party. The stated aim of this call for reform is to rectify the gender-related problems of the personal laws[69] – especially Muslim personal law – and to put an end to the system's (supposed) tendency to promote religious communalism[70] and undermine national unity.[71] However, there are also worries about the motives behind calls for uniform family laws. Calls from Hindu nationalists for uniform family laws are thought to carry a negative subtext about Indian Muslims:[72] that they are 'obscurantist and fundamentalist',[73] 'barbaric'[74] and not as committed as other groups to 'the cause of national unity and integration'.[75] Many fear therefore that supporting the enactment of uniform family laws may be read as support for Hindu nationalism and an endorsement of this negative subtext relating to Indian Muslims.[76] Others oppose uniform family laws because of concerns that they would reflect Hindu norms to the exclusion of others.[77] Many who defend the personal law system appeal to religious freedom[78] and minority group autonomy.[79] Further, for some Indian Muslims, the personal laws have become associated with group identity in such a way that calls for abolition are perceived as an attack on their identity group, and as forced assimilation;[80] this in turn leads some commentators to argue that the legal reform

[69] Bharatiya Janata Party, *Vision Document 2004* (2004), available at www.bjp.org/index.php?option=com_content&view=article&id=136&Itemid=548 [accessed 10 September 2018].
[70] The term is meant pejoratively. See R. Bajpai, 'The conceptual vocabularies of secularism and minority rights in India' (2002) 7 *Journal of Political Ideologies* 179, 184.
[71] Agnes, *Family Law Volume I*, 117.
[72] *Ibid.*, 117–18; R. Kapur and B. Cossman (eds.), *Subversive Sites: Feminist Engagements with Law in India* (New Delhi: Sage, 1996).
[73] Hasan, 'Governance and reform of personal laws in India', 350–73, 363.
[74] See the comments in Agnes, *Family Law Volume I*, 117 on the judgment of Kuldip Singh J. in *Sarla Mudgal* v. *Union of India* (1995) 3 SCC 635; see also Kapur and Cossman, *Subversive Sites*, 260.
[75] Agnes, *Family Law Volume I*, 163.
[76] Agnes, *Family Law Volume I*; Redding, 'Human rights and homo-sectuals', 436; Kapur and Cossman, *Subversive Sites*, 260.
[77] Nussbaum, 'India: Implementing sex equality through law', 35.
[78] R. Williams, *Postcolonial Politics and Personal Laws: Colonial Legal Legacies and the Indian State* (New Delhi: Oxford University Press, 2006) 100–1.
[79] Constitution of India, arts. 26, 29 and 30.
[80] Z. Hasan, 'Introduction: Contextualising gender and identity in contemporary India', in Z. Hasan (ed.), *Forging Identities: Gender, Communities and the State of India* (Oxford: Westview, 1994) xiii; G. Mahajan, *Identities and Rights: Aspects of Liberal Democracy in India* (Delhi: Oxford University Press, 1998) 107–8.

of Muslim personal law against the wishes of Indian Muslims would be an instance of Hindu oppression.[81]

Here is the dilemma: to maintain the personal law system would be to disregard a constitutional directive and perpetuate a harmful, discriminatory, unjust (and arguably unconstitutional) system; to abolish it in favour of uniform family laws would be to raise the concerns about oppressive assimilation, religious freedom, group autonomy and pejorative casting of Indian Muslims described above. This dilemma has led to an intractable stalemate that has persisted through seven decades of debate and political activism around the personal law system.[82]

IV Autonomy under Indian Family Law: a Proposal for Reform

Given the stalemate outlined below, this section proposes a novel and unexplored reform possibility, anchored in the concept of party autonomy in family matters: supplementing the enactment of uniform family laws with a well-regulated state-recognized regime of religious alternative dispute resolution (ADR). This section argues that this reform proposal has significant advantages compared to both the personal law system and uniform family laws alone, and averts the stalemate that has slowed reform of the Indian personal law system. It argues that three major problems associated with the Indian personal law system – misrecognition and non-recognition of religious identities; interference with religious freedom; and discrimination and injustice for women – would be ameliorated by the adoption of this proposal. It further argues that the reform proposal would enhance group autonomy.

A Religious Alternative Dispute Resolution

Religious ADR, as used in this section, refers to arbitration, mediation or conciliation conducted according to religious norms. ADR is already well established in India. State courts and tribunals do not currently

---

[81] J. Spinner-Halev, 'Feminism, multiculturalism, oppression, and the state' (2001) 112 (1) *Ethics* 84: 94–9; A. Noorani, 'Impossible agenda', *Frontline* (11 June 2014), available at www.frontline.in/the-nation/impossible-agenda/article6097233.ece [accessed 10 September 2018].

[82] Ahmed, *Religious Freedom*; Larson, 'Secular state in a religious society', vii.

monopolize dispute resolution. Nor is the constitutional directive to establish a uniform civil code[83] thought to preclude ADR. Private arbitration, conciliation and mediation are recognized, facilitated and encouraged in many areas of law – including, to some degree, in family law.[84] Judicial decisions reveal a range of family law disputes that have been referred to binding arbitration.[85] Members of the Parsi community, at one point, campaigned for a system of arbitration for Parsis.[86] This section argues that the existing facilities for ADR in the Indian legal system should be developed, modified and publicized so that religious ADR becomes a meaningful option for those who wish to be governed by religious norms in family law.

The debates on the accommodation of religious norms in family law in many western jurisdictions[87] have focused on religious ADR as a mode of accommodation of religious norms in family law. At the same time, religious ADR has been given very little attention in the academic and political debates on the reform of the personal law system in India,[88] despite the growth of religious ADR forums in India. As Gopika Solanki notes, in matters of marriage and divorce, 'the Indian state has adopted ... a model of shared adjudication, in which the state splits its adjudicative authority with social actors and organizations in the regulation of marriage and divorce among a section of religious and caste groups and other actors'.[89] Thus, religious ADR deserves to be taken seriously as part of any proposal for the reform of the personal law system.

[83] Constitution of India 1950 art. 44.
[84] A. Malhotra and R. Malhotra, 'Alternative dispute resolution in Indian family law – Realities, practicalities and necessities' [2010] *Journal of the International Academy of Matrimonial Lawyers* 3. *Aviral Bhatla* v. *Bhawna Bhatla* 2009 (2) KLJ 116 (SC), available at www.indiankanoon.org/doc/320406 [accessed 10 September 2018]. The *Bhatla* judgment notes how effective the Delhi Mediation Centre (www.delhimediationcentre.gov.in) was at helping the parties reach a settlement.
[85] For example, *Chiranjilal Srilal Goenka* v. *Jasjit Singh* (2000) Supp. 5 SCR 313; *Syed Ghouse Mohiuddin* v. *Syed Quadri* AIR 1971 SC 2184.
[86] Sharafi, 'Bella's case', 192.
[87] See generally R. Ahdar and N. Aroney (eds.), *Shari'a in the West* (Oxford University Press, 2010).
[88] A notable exception is R. De, 'Personal laws: A reality check', *Frontline* (19 August 2013), available at www.frontline.in/cover-story/personal-laws-a-reality-check/article5037670.ece [accessed 10 September 2018].
[89] G. Solanki, *Adjudication in Religious Family Laws: Cultural Accommodation, Legal Pluralism and Gender Equity in India* (Cambridge University Press, 2011) 10.

Religious ADR, where it exists, is generally agreed to by parties in a contract as a means of resolving a dispute. Under Indian law as in most jurisdictions, arbitration is binding on the parties to it,[90] but mediation and conciliation are normally non-binding.[91] However, even parties to a mediation or conciliation may choose to sign a settlement agreement binding them to the terms of their (otherwise) non-binding mediation or conciliation settlement; this agreement would then be legally enforceable.[92]

Religious ADR could be used to settle many disputes currently governed by the personal law system such as the terms of a divorce, disputes relating to maintenance and the division of marital property, as well as disputes relating to inheritance.[93] However, statuses such as marriage, divorce or adoption are not usually subject to ADR.[94] The contractual norms governing religious ADR – the procedure to be followed, the person(s) who will arbitrate, mediate or conciliate, and the norms by which the dispute will be resolved – can be decided privately by the parties. But the parties could also approach existing organizations that conduct religious ADR. These organizations (examples of which are discussed in the sections that follow) may have standard-form contracts which assist parties in establishing an ADR mechanism to resolve their dispute. They can also provide access to arbitrators, mediators, conciliators, legal practitioners, social workers and other state actors such as the police.[95]

B Religious ADR and Religious Identities

Religious ADR, in contrast to the personal law system, would not misrecognize religious identities. People would only use religious ADR if they wanted to. Since this would be an opt-in system, an individual would only be associated with a particular organization if they chose to. Not only would this minimize misrecognition, it might also provide a means of valuable recognition. Heterodox individuals or 'micro-

---

[90] Arbitration and Conciliation Act 1996 s. 30(2). The arbitral award is final and binding on the parties and persons claiming under them (Arbitration and Conciliation Act 1996 s. 35).
[91] N. Atlas, S. Huber and W. Trachte-Huber, *Alternative Dispute Resolution: the Litigator's Handbook* (Chicago: American Bar Association, 2000) 5–6, 309–11.
[92] Arbitration and Conciliation Act 1996 s. 73(2) and (3); s. 89(1) of the Civil Procedure Code 1908.
[93] *Chiranjilal Srilal Goenka* v. *Jasjit Singh* (2000) Supp. 5 SCR 313.
[94] *Malka* v. *Sardar* AIR 1929 Lahore 394.
[95] Solanki *Adjudication in Religious Family Laws*, 54.

minorities', such as Baha'is or tribal indigenous groups, might find in these religious ADR organizations both the locus of a religious group and a means of valuable recognition. Religious ADR as a supplement to the uniform family law, by preventing the misrecognition of religious identities, and providing the potential for valuable recognition, represents a significant advantage over the personal law system, as well as a regime of uniform family law alone.

Under the personal law system, as noted above, the state takes a 'cookie-cutter' approach to religion that applies the *state's* understanding of Hindu, Muslim, Jewish or other religious norms to those that *the state* identifies as belonging to those religious groups. In the course of this process, the state often ends up applying personal laws to those who may not endorse them. Both the personal law system and any proposed uniform family law, by obliging people to organize their lives according to certain norms, stand in the way of those who endorse other norms (usually religious norms, in this context) from organizing their lives in accordance with them. They stand in the way therefore of religious practice and expression.

On the other hand, the regime proposed here is a form of 'cultural voluntarism',[96] under which individuals always have resort to both general state law as well as religious ADR tailored to their beliefs. While the personal law system only applies (the state's version of) the norms of five defined religious groups, religious ADR would permit those who disagree with the state-endorsed version of their religious doctrine, or members of new religious movements, or those belonging to groups that are not recognized by the personal law system (e.g. Baha'is), to order their lives according to their religious beliefs. They could use religious ADR to ensure that their disputes are settled according to their own religious norms, and, furthermore, settled by people that they trust to interpret those norms. Further, those who reject religion or have no religious beliefs would be free to make ADR arrangements based on other norms, or indeed to follow uniform family laws. Thus, supplementing uniform family laws with religious ADR gives an opportunity to practise religion in family law matters to those who want it. This would allay the concerns about oppressive assimilation that are often raised against the enactment of uniform family law.

---

[96] J. Eekelaar, 'From multiculturalism to cultural voluntarism: A family-based approach' (2010) 81 *Political Quarterly* 344–55.

C Religious ADR and Women

There is reason to think that religious ADR would be better for women than the personal law system. The establishment of the All India Muslim Women's Personal Law Board, sharia courts and 'jamaats' run by women across the country, and the involvement of Muslim women's NGOs such as Bharatiya Muslim Mahila Aandolan and Awaaz-e-Niswan[97] in developing gender-just interpretations of religion for religious ADR are promising signs.[98] One scholar offers this account of the activities of a women's religious ADR group:

> [they] arbitrate in cases of marital disputes and custody matters and assist with legal aid. They challenge the clergy in their orthodox interpretation of Islam and help women obtain *faskh* or *khula* [types of divorce] through *qazis* [clergy] who are known to hand down women-friendly judgments. The committee also participates in various campaigns to work towards legal reforms. These groups draw on their own ideas of [religious] law.[99]

The emergence of these new religious ADR providers also opens up a 'competition' between religious ADR organizations offering different visions of religious doctrine – including between patriarchal and gender-just organizations.

Despite the development of these gender-just ADR organizations, it is important to acknowledge the danger that religious ADR might use norms which disadvantage women. Critics of religious ADR might point to religious norms that deny women equal inheritance rights,[100] that make it difficult for them to get a religious divorce[101] or that treat them as the wards of men. To prevent this possibility, it is important to introduce

---

[97] Aawaaz-e-Niswaan, 'Our work' (2011), available at www.niswaan.org/our-work.html [accessed 10 September 2018].

[98] De, 'Personal laws'; see also R. Ilangovan and S. Dutta, 'Taking on patriarchy', *Frontline* (21 August 2013), available at www.frontline.in/cover-story/taking-on-patriarchy/article5037878.ece [accessed 10 September 2018]; A. Rashid, 'City's first sharia court for women gets off to a modest start', *Indian Express* (3 October 2013), available at http://indianexpress.com/article/cities/pune/citys-first-sharia-court-forwomen-gets-off-to-a-modest-start [accessed 10 September 2018].

[99] Solanki *Adjudication in Religious Family Laws*, 291–2.

[100] Under Islamic inheritance law, male heirs in the same relationship to the deceased as female heirs inherit more (Fyzee and Mahmood, *Outlines of Muhammadan Law*, 316).

[101] Jewish women, for instance, have approached courts in relation to the get. See e.g. T. Rostain, 'Permissible Accommodations of Religion: Reconsidering the New York Get Statute' (1987) 96 *Yale Law Journal* 1147–71.

safeguards that would prevent the enforcement of such discriminatory norms. Muslim women in India are already campaigning for the expansion of legal recognition of religious ADR.[102] This legal recognition could be coupled with threshold requirements for the recognition or enforcement of the outcome of a religious ADR process. Indian law already requires that that ADR processes that seek legal recognition follow natural justice[103] and that their outcome not be contrary to public policy.[104] Indian law should require still more of ADR processes (including religious ADR processes) in family law. For instance, in the Canadian case *Miglin* v. *Miglin*,[105] the Supreme Court, faced with a spousal separation agreement, assessed not just whether the agreement was entered into freely but also the substance of the agreement, including the extent to which the agreement was in compliance with the objectives of Canadian family legislation. The Court thus acknowledged the need to:

recognize economic advantages or disadvantages to the former spouses arising from the marriage or its breakdown; apportion between the former spouses any financial consequences arising from the care of any child of the marriage over and above any obligation for the support of any child of the marriage; relieve any economic hardship of the former spouses arising from the breakdown of the marriage; and in so far as practicable, promote the economic self-sufficiency of each former spouse within a reasonable period of time.[106]

If it were a condition for the enforcement of every ADR agreement, including a religious ADR agreement, that it be substantially compliant with conditions such as those identified by *Miglin*, then agreements which are unfair or discriminatory are highly unlikely to be enforced.

Beyond introducing the safeguards already discussed, the Indian state could also accredit or license religious ADR organizations such as the Bharatiya Muslim Mahila Aandolan who operate on gender-just principles, so that the outcomes of their processes are readily recognized and enforced by state courts. Equally the state could refuse to accredit or license religious ADR organizations that do not operate on gender-just principles. The state could also offer free or subsidized professional development courses to religious ADR organizations that educate arbitrators, conciliators and

---

[102] See Bader Sayeed's work, discussed in Ilangovan and Dutta, 'Taking on patriarchy'.
[103] Arbitration and Conciliation Act 1996 s. 34(2)(a)(iii). [104] *Ibid.*, s. 34(2)(b)(ii).
[105] *Miglin* v. *Miglin* [2003] 1 SCR 303.
[106] *Ibid.* [20]; Divorce Act 1985 (Canada) RSC 1985 c 3 (2nd Supp) s. 17(7).

mediators on the requirements of Indian family law, including the safeguards proposed above, and the threshold requirements ADR processes must meet for their outcomes to be enforced in India. Additionally, the state could subsidize and provide funding to gender-just religious ADR organizations, and publicize the availability of their services. This will give all religious ADR organizations an incentive to provide gender-just ADR services to those who use them.

If the state supports gender-just religious ADR organizations, if courts develop a robust jurisprudence ensuring that religious ADR outcomes in family law matters are only enforced when they are substantively just, and if safeguards ensure that the ADR processes are entered into freely, religious ADR has the potential to deliver better outcomes for women than the personal law system currently does. It also has the potential to deliver better outcomes than a regime of uniform family law alone. Given the pressure that women in India have traditionally faced to support personal laws,[107] there is a danger that in the absence of accessible religious ADR, women would be coerced into unofficial informal forms of dispute resolution[108] which operate 'under the radar' of state law and may well be unjust and harmful.

D Religious ADR and Group Autonomy

The personal law system is sometimes thought of as a form of autonomy for religious groups.[109] Group autonomy is the ideal of a group governing itself and shaping its own path. Group autonomy is diminished when a group is coerced or dictated to by an outside force such as the state, a person or another group.[110] While a group does not need to be perfectly democratic in order to be autonomous, it does need to have to be minimally representative and deliberative. In other words, group autonomy is

---

[107] F. Ahmed, 'Personal autonomy and the option of religious law' (2010) 24 *International Journal of Law, Policy and the Family* 222–44.
[108] V. Bader, 'Legal pluralism and differentiated morality', in R. Grillo (ed.), *Legal Practice and Cultural Diversity* (Farnham, UK: Ashgate, 2009) 50–3.
[109] A. Lijphart, 'The puzzle of Indian democracy: A consociational interpretation' (1996) 90 *American Political Science Review* 258, 260–1.
[110] For a similar definition, see C. Wellman, 'The paradox of group autonomy' (2003) 20 *Social Philosophy and Policy* 265, 266.

'something that can be exercised by a collective *as a whole*, rather than individually by persons in a group'.[111]

There are many reasons why the personal law system does not, in fact, promote group autonomy. First, the personal laws are applied by state courts and, generally speaking, administered by state officials. Under the personal law system, the state, rather than the religious group, decides on who qualifies as a member.[112] The personal law system thus does not allow groups to decide on the boundaries of their own membership, which is a necessary precondition for group autonomy.[113] Second, the state, not the group, decides which norms the personal law system applies to religious groups. If group autonomy means anything, it surely means that the group should decide for itself the norms by which it is governed. But the personal law system ossifies the *state's* interpretation of each religion into law. Third, unlike *millet*-style arrangements,[114] India's personal law system does not recognize representatives or leaders from amongst the recognized religious groups. Nor is there a process for choosing leaders. It is true that there are those who claim to speak for minority groups and that their opinion has been taken as the opinion of the group by the Indian state in debates about the future of the personal law system. But the personal law system itself does not recognize them as group leaders. In any case, a group is not autonomous when group leaders are identified by the *state*, rather than the group itself.[115] Leaders whose positions are dependent on the state's identification of them as such are less likely to represent the group's interest, especially if it involves challenging the state. Since under the personal law system, religious groups do not benefit from control of the boundaries of their membership, their norms or representative leaders, it is difficult to argue that the system promotes group autonomy.

Religious ADR, meanwhile, does have the potential to enhance group autonomy. When a religious group has members that consent to ADR arrangements, it can be said to govern itself or be autonomous at least over matters amenable to ADR. By enhancing group autonomy, religious ADR organizations have the potential (but only the potential) to benefit

---

[111] Wellman, 'Paradox of group autonomy', 273. [112] Ahmed, *Religious Freedom*, ch. 2.
[113] D. Réaume, 'Justice between cultures: Autonomy and the protection of cultural affiliation' (1995) 29 *UBC Law Review* 117, 121.
[114] W. Kymlicka, 'Two models of pluralism and tolerance' (1992) 14 *Analyse & Kritik* 33.
[115] R. Ahdar and I. Leigh, *Religious Freedom and the Liberal State* (Oxford University Press, 2005) 338–46.

their members through better representation. This can occur at two levels.[116] The first is at the level of the religious group as a whole. That is, religious ADR organizations representing each religion could develop into organizations of governance. Religious ADR also has the potential to enhance group autonomy at a second level by providing a locus for smaller groups, or movements within larger religious groups.[117]

By providing religious groups with control over the boundaries of membership and the norms which it will apply to its members, as well as over who resolves disputes, religious ADR organizations have the potential to enhance group autonomy. The Indian state could nurture this potential by accrediting or certifying religious ADR organizations that have the potential to enhance group autonomy and offering these organizations subsidies or state funding. Besides promoting group autonomy, such support could relieve the significant case load pressures on the Indian court system.

This section has proposed that religious ADR should supplement uniform family laws. It should be open to people to use religious ADR to decide those family law matters which can be resolved using ADR – e.g. financial terms of a divorce, disputes relating to maintenance and the division of marital property, as well as disputes relating to inheritance.[118] Meanwhile, uniform family laws would apply to statuses such as marriage, divorce or adoption, which are not usually subject to ADR.

V Conclusion

India's personal law system, on its face, appears to provide recognition for religious identities. But in fact, a major problem with the system is that it treats individuals with misrecognition and non-recognition.[119] Charles Taylor explains the harm that misrecognition and non-recognition cause:

our identity is partly shaped by recognition or its absence, often by the *mis*recognition of others, and so a person or group of people can suffer real damage, real

---

[116] F. Ahmed, 'Religious norms in family law: Implications for group and personal autonomy', in J. Eekelaar and M. Maclean (eds.), *Managing Family Justice in Diverse Societies* (Oxford: Hart, 2013).
[117] Ahmed, 'Religious norms in family law', 41–2.
[118] *Chiranjilal Srilal Goenka* v. *Jasjit Singh* (2000) Supp. 5 SCR 313.
[119] Ahmed, *Religious Freedom*, 111–13.

distortion, if the people or society around them mirror back to them a confining or demeaning or contemptible picture of themselves. Non-recognition or misrecognition can inflict harm, can be a form of oppression, imprisoning someone in a false, distorted, and reduced mode of being.[120]

Non-recognition and misrecognition are, as Taylor's remarks suggest, damaging, disrespectful and among the most grating insults to which we could subject a person. Non-recognition comes in many forms. Treating a person as if they did not exist, as if they were invisible or as if they made no mark on the world can certainly have a devastating effect on them. Failing to recognize the very existence of people and treating them as if they were invisible is perhaps an extreme case of misrecognition – of failing to recognize the truth about their existence or some aspect of their selves.

The personal law system shows little regard for how people identify themselves and what their understanding of their religion really is. It often identifies people in terms different from the terms in which they identify themselves.[121] By applying a single, state-endorsed religious interpretation to all those whom the state identifies as belonging to a particular religious group, it ignores the fact that the religious interpretations of many people within this group may well deviate from that of the state. Despite the fact that a person's understanding of their religion may be central to their identity and self-perception, under the personal law system it is simply not important enough for the state to take the trouble to do more than paint everyone in one personal law group with the same brush.

The dominance of the personal law system within Indian family law therefore carries numerous consequences for Indian responses to cultural and religious diversity, for gender issues, for the privileged position of marriage and for the role of party autonomy in family matters. This chapter has sought to outline the potential and actual negative effects of the system that pervade Indian family law, while also offering a possible path towards reform.

---

[120] C. Taylor, 'Multiculturalism and the politics of recognition', in C. Taylor, A. Gutmann and J. Habermas (eds.), *Multiculturalism: Examining the Politics of Recognition* (Princeton: Princeton University Press, 1994) 25.

[121] Ahmed, *Religious Freedom*, ch. 6.

	I. Hindu	II. Muslim	III. Christian	IV. Parsi	V. Jewish
Marriage	M: May have only one spouse at a time.[1] F: May have only one spouse at a time.[2]	M: May have up to four spouses at a time.[3] F: May have only one spouse at a time.[4]	M: May have only one spouse at a time.[5] F: May have only one spouse at a time.[6]	M: May have only one spouse at a time.[7] F: May have only one spouse at a time.[8]	M: May have only one spouse at a time.[9] F: May have only one spouse at a time.[10]
Divorce	M: May be granted by a court on grounds listed in statute.[11] F: May be granted by a court on grounds as available to a man, or on four additional grounds.[12]	M: Effected by formal performative utterance following attempts at reconciliation with arbitrators. Must show reasonable cause for divorce.[13] F: May be granted (by a court) on the grounds listed in statute.[14]	M: May be granted by a court on grounds listed in statute.[15] F: May be granted by a court on grounds as available to a man, or on three additional grounds.[16]	M: May be granted by a court on grounds listed in statute and on one ground not available to the wife.[17] F: May be granted by a court on grounds as available to a man, and on one additional ground.[18]	M: Divorce effected by the husband giving a bill of divorcement or a 'get' to the wife, or by order of the court.[19] F: Divorce effected by the husband giving a bill of divorcement or a 'get' to the wife, or by order of the court.[20]

(cont.)

M and F refer to male and female. A different version of this table originally appeared in Ahmed, *Religious Freedom*.

[1] Hindu Marriage Act 1955 s. 5(i).   [2] *Ibid.*
[3] Hidayatullah and Hidayatullah, *Mahomedan Law*, 285; Fyzee and Mahmood, *Outlines of Muhammadan Law*, 74.
[4] *Ibid.*   [5] Indian Christian Marriage Act 1872 s. 60(2).   [6] *Ibid.*
[7] Parsi Marriage and Divorce Act 1936 ss. 4 and 5.   [8] *Ibid.*
[9] *Mozelle Robin Solomon v. Lt Col RJ Solomon* MANU/MH/0220/1968.   [10] *Ibid.*
[11] Hindu Marriage Act 1955 s. 13.   [12] *Ibid.*
[13] *Shamim Ara v. State of U.P. & Anr* (2002) 7 SCC 518; *Dagdu S/O Chotu Pathan, Latur v. Rahimbi Dagdu Pathan, Ashabi* 2003 (1) Bom CR 740 [26]; Solanki, *Adjudication in Religious Family Laws*, 134–5. For older position, see Hidayatullah and Hidayatullah, *Mahomedan Law*, 280; Fyzee and Mahmood, *Outlines of Muhammadan Law*, 120.
[14] Dissolution of Muslim Marriage Act 1939. However, there seems to be some question about how this Act affects a woman's ability to terminate the marriage without recourse to the courts (Fyzee and Mahmood, *Outlines of Muhammadan Law*, 150).
[15] Indian Divorce Act 1869 s. 10.   [16] *Ibid.*
[17] Parsi Marriage and Divorce Act 1936 ss. 32 and 32B.   [18] *Ibid.*
[19] However, it appears that the court will not order the husband to give the wife the 'get' (*Mozelle Robin Solomon v. Lt Col RJ Solomon* MANU/MH/0220/1968; J. Derrett, 'Jewish Law in Southern Asia' (1964) 13 *International and Comparative Law Quarterly* 288–301; *David Sassoon Ezekiel v. Najia Noori Reuben* (1931) 33 BOMLR 725, 728).
[20] As n. 19 above.

(cont.)

	I. Hindu	II. Muslim	III. Christian	IV. Parsi	V. Jewish
Alimony/ Maintenance	M: May apply for maintenance from spouse.[21] The order for maintenance may be affected by the fact that 'he has had sexual intercourse with any woman outside wedlock'.[22] F: May apply for maintenance from spouse.[23] The order for maintenance may be affected by the fact that 'she has not remained chaste'.[24]	M: No provision to apply for maintenance from spouse. F: May apply for maintenance from spouse.[25]	M: No provision to apply for maintenance from spouse.[26] F: May apply for maintenance from spouse.[27]	M: May apply for maintenance from spouse.[28] The order for maintenance may be affected by the fact that 'he has had sexual intercourse with any woman outside wedlock'.[29] F: May apply for maintenance from spouse.[30] The order for maintenance may be affected by the fact that 'she has not remained chaste'.[31] The court may settle part of the property of an adulterous woman on her children.[32] Further, a woman may not receive maintenance payments directly, but through a court-appointed guardian.[33]	M: No provision to apply for maintenance from spouse. F: May apply for maintenance from spouse in certain circumstances.[34]

[21] Hindu Marriage Act 1955 s. 25. [22] Ibid., s. 25(3). [23] Ibid., s. 25. [24] Ibid., s. 25(3).
[25] Muslim Women (Protection of Rights on Divorce Act) 1986. Divorced Muslim women alone cannot claim maintenance under the otherwise generally applicable Code of Criminal Procedure 1973 s. 125. But in *Daniel Latifi* v. *Union of India* (2001) 7 SCC 740 the Supreme Court claims to have interpreted the Act in a way that made it a 'reasonable and fair substitute' for s. 125.
[26] Indian Divorce Act 1869 ss. 36–38. [27] Ibid.; Code of Criminal Procedure 1973 s. 125.
[28] Parsi Marriage and Divorce Act 1936 s. 40. [29] Ibid., s. 40(3). [30] Ibid., s. 40.
[31] Ibid., s. 40(3). [32] Ibid., s. 50; Agnes, *Family Law Volume I*, 83. [33] Ibid., s. 41; ibid.
[34] Indian courts granted a Jewish woman a decree of judicial separation entitling her to be maintained by her husband in *Mozelle Robin Solomon* v. *Lt Col RJ Solomon* MANU/MH/0220/1968, 38.

Succession	M: According to statute, with no significant distinctions made between sons and daughters.[35] In general, may bequeath all assets.[36]	M: In general, male heirs in the same relationship to the deceased as female heirs inherit more.[39] In general testamentary power is limited; men cannot bequeath more than one-third of their assets.[40]	M: In general, according to statute with no significant distinctions made between sons and daughters.[43] In general, may bequeath all assets.[44]	M: According to statute with no significant distinctions made between sons and daughters.[47] In general, may bequeath all assets.[48]	M: In general, according to statute with no significant distinctions made between sons and daughters.[51] In general, may bequeath all assets.[52]
	F: According to statute, with no significant distinctions being made between sons and daughters.[37] In general, may bequeath all assets.[38]	F: In general, male heirs in the relationship to the deceased as female heirs inherit more.[41] In general, testamentary power is limited; women cannot bequeath more than one-third of their assets.[42]	F: According to statute, with no significant distinctions made between sons and daughters.[45] In general, may bequeath all assets.[46]	F: According to statute, with no significant distinctions made between sons and daughters.[49] In general, may bequeath all assets.[50]	F: According to statute, with no significant distinctions made between sons and daughters.[53] In general, may bequeath all assets.[54]

(cont.)

---

[35] Hindu Succession Act 1956 ch. II. [36] *Ibid.*, s. 30. [37] *Ibid.*, ch. II. [38] *Ibid.*, s. 30.
[39] Thus, a son inherits more than a daughter and a brother inherits more than a sister (Fyzee and Mahmood, Outlines of Muhammadan Law, 316).
[40] *Ibid.*, 442.
[41] Thus, a son inherits more than a daughter and a brother inherits more than a sister (*Ibid.*, 316).
[42] Fyzee and Mahmood, Outlines of Muhammadan Law, 442.
[43] Indian Succession Act 1925, pt V. Following *Mary Roy v. State of Kerala* 1986 AIR 1011, this Act applies also to communities formerly governed by the Travancore Christian Succession Act.
[44] Indian Succession Act 1925 pt VI. In *John Vallamattom v. Union of India* 2003 AIR 2902, the Supreme Court struck down s. 118 of this Act, which formerly prohibited bequests made for religious or charitable purposes by Indian Christians with living relatives, unless the bequest was provided for by will at least a year before death.
[45] Indian Succession Act 1925 pt V. [46] *Ibid.*, pt VI.
[47] *Ibid.*, pt V ch III, except the case of heirs of predeceased children: see s. 53.
[48] *Ibid.*, pt VI; see especially ss. 58(2) and 59.
[49] *Ibid.*, pt V ch III, except the case of heirs of predeceased children: see s. 53.
[50] *Ibid.*, pt VI; see especially ss. 58(2) and 59. [51] *Ibid.*, pt V. [52] *Ibid.*, pt VI.
[53] *Ibid.*, pt V. [54] *Ibid.*, pt VI.

(cont.)

	I. Hindu	II. Muslim	III. Christian	IV. Parsi	V. Jewish
Adoption and Guardianship	M: Has the power to adopt under the personal law, but if married his wife's consent is required.[55] Has primary power of guardianship of any children, above that of the mother.[56] F: No power to adopt if married. May adopt otherwise.[57] Has power of guardianship of any children secondary to that of the father.[58]	M: No power to adopt under the personal law.[59] Has primary power of guardianship of children, above that of the mother.[60] However, may adopt under general law.[61] F: No power to adopt under the personal law.[62] Has power of guardianship of any children secondary to that of the father.[63] However, may adopt under general law.[64]	M: No power to adopt under the personal law.[65] Has primary power of guardianship of children, above that of the mother.[66] However, may adopt under general law.[67] F: No power to adopt under the personal law.[68] Has power of guardianship of any children secondary to that of the father.[69] However, may adopt under general law.[70]	M: No power to adopt under the personal law.[71] Has primary power of guardianship of children, above that of the mother.[72] However, may adopt under general law.[73] F: No power to adopt under the personal law.[74] Has power of guardianship of any children secondary to that of the father.[75] However, may adopt under general law.[76]	M: Unlikely that Indian courts would recognize adoptions under Jewish law.[77] Has primary power of guardianship of children, above that of the mother.[78] However, may adopt under general law.[79] F: Unlikely that Indian courts would recognize adoptions under Jewish law.[80] Has power of guardianship of any children secondary to that of the father.[81] However, may adopt under general law.[82]

55 Hindu Adoptions and Maintenance Act 1956 s. 7.
56 Hindu Minority and Guardianship Act 1956 s. 6; *Geeta Hariharan v. Reserve Bank of India* AIR 1999 SC 1149; K. Kusum and P. Saxena, *Family Law Lectures: Family Law I* (3rd edn, New Delhi: LexisNexis Butterworths, 2008) 303–4.
57 Hindu Adoptions and Maintenance Act 1956 s. 8.
58 Hindu Minority and Guardianship Act 1956 s. 6; *Geeta Hariharan v. Reserve Bank of India* AIR 1999 SC 1149; Kusum and Saxena, *Family Law Lectures: I*, 303–4.
59 Unless it can be proved that custom recognizes such an adoption: Shariat Application Act 1939 ss. 2 and 3; Agnes, Family Law Volume I, 99–100.
60 Kusum and Saxena, *Family Law Lectures: I*, 305–6.
61 *Shabnam Hashmi v. Union of India & Ors* (2014) 4 SCC 1.
62 Unless it can be proved that custom recognizes such an adoption (Shariat Application Act 1939 ss. 2 and 3; Agnes, Family Law Volume I, 99–100).
63 Kusum and Saxena, *Family Law Lectures: I*, 305–6.
64 *Shabnam Hashmi v. Union of India & Ors* (2014) 4 SCC 1.
65 Kusum and Saxena, *Family Law Lectures: I*, 334.

66 'The father, under every system of law is a natural guardian of a minor child' (*Sushilaben Dhulubhai Solanki v. Ramakant Dehyubhai Parmar* (1994) 2 GLR 1260 [5]; *Jacob Mathew v. Mrs Maya Philip Alias Annama* AIR 1999 Ker 192 [67]–[68]).
67 *Shabnam Hashmi v. Union of India & Ors* (2014) 4 SCC 1.
68 Kusum and Saxena, *Family Law Lectures: I*, 334.
69 'The father, under every system of law is a natural guardian of a minor child' (*Sushilaben Dhulubhai Solanki v. Ramakant Dehyubhai Parmar* (1994) 2 GLR 1260 [5]; *Jacob Mathew v. Mrs Maya Philip Alias Annama* AIR 1999 Ker 192 [67]–[68]).
70 Ibid.   71 Ibid., 333.
72 *Sushilaben Dhulubhai Solanki v. Ramakant Dehyubhai Parmar* (1994) 2 GLR 1260 [5]; Guardians and Wards Act 1890 s. 19.
73 *Shabnam Hashmi v. Union of India & Ors* (2014) 4 SCC 1.
74 But there is a customary form of adoption, by which the widow of a childless Parsi can adopt a child on the fourth day of her husband's death for the purpose of performing religious ceremonies. This child, however, acquires no property rights (Kusum and Saxena, *Family Law Lectures: I*, 333).
75 *Sushilaben Dhulubhai Solanki v. Ramakant Dehyubhai Parmar* (1994) 2 GLR 1260 [5]; Guardians and Wards Act 1890 s. 19.
76 *Shabnam Hashmi v. Union of India & Ors* (2014) 4 SCC 1.
77 Two of the books that the Indian courts have consulted in Jewish law cases (Kaduishin's *Code of Jewish Jurisprudence* and Mielziner's *The Jewish Law of Marriage and Divorce in Ancient and Modern Times*) do not appear to discuss adoption. Thus, much depends upon which text of Jewish law the courts decide to look into, as the question appears to have no precedent in Indian courts. Many texts praise those who raise the child of another person, especially if this child is an orphan. But the law does not treat this child as it would a 'natural' child. In the absence of a will, the adopted child does not inherit from his adoptive parents; the adopted son does not free his mother from *chalitzah* in case her husband dies without issue (A. Cohen, *Halacha and Contemporary Society* (New York: Ktav Publishing, 1985) 31; D. Pollack *et al.*, 'Classical Religious Perspectives of Adoption Law' (2004) 79 *Notre Dame Law Review* 101.
78 *Sushilaben Dhulubhai Solanki v. Ramakant Dehyubhai Parmar* (1994) 2 GLR 1260 [5]; Guardians and Wards Act 1890 s. 19.
79 Ibid.   80 See n. 78 above.
81 'The father, under every system of law is a natural guardian of a minor child' (*Sushilaben Dhulubhai Solanki v. Ramakant Dehyubhai Parmar* (1994) 2 GLR 1260 [5]; *Jacob Mathew v. Mrs Maya Philip Alias Annama* AIR 1999 Ker 192 [67]–[68]).
82 *Shabnam Hashmi v. Union of India & Ors* (2014) 4 SCC 1.

10 The Postcolonial Fallacy of 'Islamic' Family Law

Abdullahi Ahmed An-Na'im

I Introduction

All Muslims today live with a set of norms and institutions which is commonly called family/personal law, but since it is enacted and enforced by the state, this field of state law does not qualify as being 'Islamic' by any clear and verifiable criteria of what it means to be Islamic. This set of norms and institutions are simply secular state law, and not immutable divinely ordained sharia. They are enacted and enforced through the political authority of the state, and are subject to amendment and changed in the same way; which is fundamentally different from how sharia norms and institutions are established and complied with by believers in their communities. Stealing is both a sin and a crime, but it is not a sin because it is a crime and it is not a crime because it is a sin. Confusing the two will have drastic consequences for both the religion of a people and the legal system of their state.

The problem with this process as it applies to the field of family law throughout the Muslim world is calling its outcome 'Islamic' family or personal status law (*al-Ahwal ash-Shakhsiya* in Arabic),[1] because it is the same as any other state legislation in the rest of the legal system. By using reference to sharia as a legitimising framework, Muslim reformists are defeating their presumed purpose of facilitating social and legal reform in their societies. This critique applies whether Muslims are a so-called majority or minority, living in self-proclaimed 'Islamic states' like Iran and Saudi Arabia, or in constitutionally identified secular states like Senegal and India. Reference to the postcolonial in this chapter title indicates the sources of tension and paradox in this subject, namely colonial formations

---

[1] J. J. Nasir, *The Islamic Law of Personal Status* (3rd edn, Dordrecht: Kluwer Law International, 2002) 34–43.

of the nation state and specialisation of so-called Islamic family law. The notion of 'Islamic family law' (hereafter IFL) is a colonial fabrication that falsely invoked the religious authority of Islam in this field while at the same time displacing the historical practice of sharia in Islamic societies by European codes and institutions.[2]

It is true that some principles of sharia, as mediated through local customary practices, have traditionally governed family relations among other fields of human concerns, but those principles were integral to a comprehensive religious normative system that was constantly adapting to changing social and economic conditions.[3] By initiating a discrete field of so-called 'Islamic family law', while displacing sharia in every other aspect of the legal systems of colonised Muslims, European colonial administrations created an isolated island of archaic family law norms and institutions in a sea of dynamic social and economic change.[4] My purpose in exposing this fallacy is to contribute to opening up the field of family law among Islamic communities to genuine enlightened reform, away from the intimidation and confusion of religious discourse.

Contrary to common current perceptions, family law regimes among Muslims around the world today are in fact the secular law of the state, and not immutable norms of sharia. Muslims in their communities may practise what they believe to be binding sharia, but they do so as a matter of religious compliance with a communal *normative system* among believers, beyond any possibility of adjudication or enforcement by state courts or administrations. In contrast, modern postcolonial nation states seek to enforce their own regulation of social relations of marriage, divorce, custody of children and inheritance. This is necessary for all states to do fairly and without any discrimination on such grounds of race, sex and religion, as mandated by their human rights obligations. Although state legislation and regulation should reflect the religious/cultural values and practices of the communities they govern,

---

[2] N. J. Coulson, *A History of Islamic Law* (University of Edinburgh Press, 1964) 149–62; N. Anderson, *Law Reform in the Muslim World* (University of London, Athlone Press, 1976) 1–2, 33; H. Liebesny, *The Law of the Near and Middle East* (State University of New York Press, 1975) 56.

[3] W. B. Hallaq, 'Can the shari'ah be restored?', in Y. Haddad and B. Stowasser (eds.), *Islamic Law and the Challenges of Modernity* (Walnut Creek, CA: Altamira Press, 2004) 21–53.

[4] See generally, A. A. An-Na'im, ed., *Islamic Family Law in a Changing World: A Global Resource Book* (London: Zed Books, 2002).

that must be with due regard to constitutional and human rights requirements of equality and non-discrimination. I have extensively discussed tensions regarding constitutional and human rights issues elsewhere.[5] The problem with claiming that state family law has the quality of being 'sharia' is to insulate that field from critical reflection and development. In that way, the most vital source of justice and human dignity in our most intimate social relationships is isolated as an island of stagnation and regressive values in a sea of social and economic change.

Sharia norms defy codification or legislative enactment because that would change the religious nature of the norm and deny Muslims the inherent religious freedom of choice among different interpretations of the Quran and Sunna (reports of the exemplar of the Prophet) established by traditional Sunni or Shi'a schools of jurisprudence. Since Muslims are religiously accountable for compliance with sharia, they must have the freedom and responsibility to decide which interpretation of the sources and methodologies of sharia they accept. In contrast, arbitrary and harsh outcomes are bound to follow when the rich diversity of views among Muslim scholars is reduced to the extreme selectivity of the language of codification of the positive law of the modern state. The claim of ruling elites of monarchies or republics alike to exclusively specify which sharia norms shall be applied by state authorities to the entire Muslim population of their countries violates freedom of religion for Muslims and inhibits possibilities of positive social change in their communities.

Another objection to claims of IFL is that the high degree of selectivity by which modern family law statutes have been drafted and enacted by human political authorities, without due regard to the authoritative methodology of established schools of jurisprudence, which are supposed to legitimise such legislation. The mechanisms of the enactment of state law are problematic from a sharia perspective because religious validity can neither be determined by a despotic ruler with his few advisers nor through majority rule in parliamentary politics. Theoretical improvement in the status and rights of Muslim women through political legislative process, for example, is unlikely to be realised in practice because it is promised by

---

[5] See, for example, my book *Muslims and Global Justice* (University of Pennsylvania Press, 2011), chs. 2–4 and 6.

the state by reinforcing the authority of conservative religious scholars over family law among Muslims.[6]

Sharia has been the product of community-based practice of intergenerational consensus around historically established founding scholars and their traditional schools of jurisprudence. Norms and principles became part of sharia for believers over time because generations of Muslim communities accepted them, and not because a religious or civil authority enacted them. The same community-consensus process applied to change and adaptations of local interpretations of sharia over the century, but the flexibility and dynamism of that tradition is now lost to rigid and arbitrary legislation based on political expediency of ruling elites and their partners. More broadly, 'state judges and other officials lack the religious authority and technical competence to interpret and apply religious norms. State enforcement of religious norms will distort the meaning, abuse the methodology and weaken the moral authority of these norms, and ultimately starve them to death by cutting them off from their religious foundations and sources of communal development.'[7]

Assuming my argument is plausible, it may seem problematic for Muslims to 'suspend' the practice of sharia norms and institutions of family life. This concern is more apparent than real for several reasons.

First, the argument is against enforcement of sharia by the state, and not personal and communal compliance outside state courts and institutions. In fact, my argument is in favour of voluntary personal and communal compliance with whatever Muslims believe to be sharia.

Second, it is not true that sharia requires enforcement of its norms and institutions by the state, or that it even addresses the state as a political institution. In fact, the Quran and Hadith never describe or prescribe any form or type of state, which is to be expected since those sources of Islam do not address political institutions that are incapable of religious belief and accountability.

Third, Muslims throughout the world are *already* living with non-enforcement of what they accept as clear aspects of sharia that can only be applied by the state, like conducting jihad for the propagation

---

[6] See, for example, E. Fawzy, 'Law No. 1 of 2000: A new personal status law and limited step on the path to reform', in L. Welchman (ed.), *Women's Rights and Islamic Family Law: Perspectives on Reform* (London: Zed Books, 2004) 58–94.

[7] A. A. An-Na'im, 'Religious norms and family law: Is it legal or normative pluralism?' (2011) 25(2) *Emory International Law Review* 787.

of Islam or the regulations of non-Muslims. Regardless of whether one accepts or rejects such traditional interpretations of sharia today,[8] my point is about the fact that the vast majority of Muslims who still accept these principles to be binding aspects of sharia are living without their enforcement by the state.

As the following review of the main principles of sharia regarding family law will show, it is possible for Muslims to comply with almost all sharia family law principles without enforcement by the state. This review may also help explain the temptation of assuming that the systematic normativity of sharia principles can easily be transformed into state legislation. My argument is that this temptation must be resisted because the religious nature of the authority of sharia principles is drastically different from the authority of state legislation. Recalling the opening statement of this chapter, stealing is a sin and a crime, but it is not a sin because it is a crime and it is not a crime because it is a sin. It is problematic to confuse the religious normativity of family principles and the legal authority of state family law because of the difference in the normative basis and consequences of the two types of characterisations of the issue in question.

II Traditional Normativity of Sharia and the Family

I am using the term 'normativity of sharia' in this section's heading to avoid the implication that sharia norms as such can be the positive law of the state. Subject to this caveat, I will use the term 'family law' due to its familiarity as the exceptional field for the application of sharia principles in the modern legal systems of some forty Muslim-majority countries,[9] in addition to many Muslim minorities in countries like India and Israel.

Possible reasons for the exception of family law from displacement by colonial European codes include the high level of specific family principles provided for in the Quran and Sunna, and their stronger significance for the moral sensibilities of Muslims in general, especially regarding issues of sexual propriety, legitimacy of children and so forth. Another possible

---

[8] For a discussion of coherent and systematic reinterpretation of sharia on such issues see my book, *Toward an Islamic Reformation: Civil Liberties, Human Rights and International Law* (New York: Syracuse University Press, 1990).

[9] I prefer the term 'Muslim-majority' to 'Islamic' country or society because the former formulation focuses on the self-identity of people.

reason for the persistence of IFL in modern legal systems may have been that this field was irrelevant to the economic and political interests of colonial administration. That is, colonial administrations may have either not cared which law applied to family issues, or did not wish to arouse political opposition in matters that were marginal to their colonial objectives. Whatever the reasons may have been, family law remained the exceptional aspect of sharia that successfully resisted displacement by European codes during the colonial period and continues to be the primary sharia field for Muslims, whether they are the majority or minority of the population. IFL has become the symbol of Islamic identity for most Muslims, the hard, irreducible core of what it means to be a Muslim today.

To appreciate the underlying tension of the application of IFL within secular legal systems, we need to first understand the main principles of IFL as stated in traditional sharia sources, and how those principles were incorporated into modern state law, mainly through statutes, as illustrated in the next section. Since it is not possible to present a comprehensive review of this vast and complex field of sharia, this review will be limited to the main principles of the Hanafi madhhab (the most globally widespread among the main Sunni schools of Islamic jurisprudence).

The following factors influenced the formation of traditional IFL:

1. Pre-Islamic customary practices with which Islamic norms had to cope from the start in Arabia and as Islam spread across Africa and Asia over several centuries. This factor was particularly influential in shaping foundational assumptions about the nature of the family and gender family relations, duties and obligations of spouses and parent–child relations, and related matters.
2. Cultural and contextual factors continued to influence the development and elaborations of IFL throughout the formative stages of sharia. In particular, IFL was intended to regulate issues of marriage, divorce, etc., as matters of concern for extended families and community, rather than of the individual spouses alone.
3. The religious ethics of sexuality and sexual propriety from a normative Islamic perspective and their implications for paternity and upbringing of children. For the vast majority of Muslims, it is inconceivable to engage in any sexual relationship outside marriage, and being born out of wedlock remains extremely stigmatised today.

4. The contractual paradigm constructed by early Muslim jurists for the formation and termination of marriage, and the tendency to take legal analysis to its logical, legalistic conclusion. Though obviously aware of the human nature of matrimonial relations, Muslim jurists focused on elaborating the legal relationship and its formal implications.
5. While IFL issues are covered in more detail in the Quran and Sunna than other fields, it is misleading to cite specific verses of the Quran or texts of Hadith as the direct source of any principle or rule of IFL because the system evolved through the specific methodology (*usul al-fiqh*) of each of the schools of Islamic jurisprudence. In particular, that methodology regulated in great detail the relationship between Quranic texts of general and specific application, and between those texts and Hadith. It would, therefore, be necessary to account for a wide range of inter-related applicable texts as the 'source' of a principle or rule of IFL, which is not possible to do in the present limited space.

In light of these factors, we now turn to a brief review of a sample of sharia principles regarding family relations.

Sharia Principles of Marriage

The key to marriage and all its consequences under IFL is that *it is a contract*. Early Muslim jurists developed separate doctrinal categories of 'named' contracts (*al-uqud al-musama*), rather than a unified doctrine of contract. The contract of sale was the paradigmatic model, but each type of contract had its own characteristic features. The contract of marriage therefore shared some of the common requirements of a valid contract, in addition to its own characteristic features as a specific type of contract. As Hallaq explains:[10]

Marriage [*nikah*], then, rests on an indefinite contract that may be written or oral, but in all cases must involve at least two contracting parties, two witnesses, and a guardian. The foundational elements *(arkan)* necessary to affect a valid marriage must involve a language *(sigha)* of offer by one party and acceptance by the other. The guardian represents the woman in concluding the contract, and the witnesses attest to it as a legal fact, but their function is also to advertise that fact in society so

---

[10] W. Hallaq, *Sharī'a: Theory, Practice, Transformations* (Cambridge University Press, 2009) 272–3.

as to preclude any suspicion of *zina*. The witnesses thus fulfill the requirement of social sanction, since it is this sanction that marks the difference between secretive, illicit acts and lawful behavior.

Accordingly, a marriage contract must satisfy the following essential 'pillars' of a valid contract, namely:

1. the *concurrence* of an offer and acceptance;
2. between two legally competent parties who are qualified to be married to each other;
3. exchanged through a clear and categorical formulation (*sigha*) that affirms the mutual consent of the parties; and
4. in the presence of at least two competent witnesses to attest to and publicise the fact that the marriage contract was validly concluded.
5. A marital gift (*mahr*) must be paid by the man to the woman, a sort of 'obligatory gift', but this is a necessary consequence of marriage, and not a requirement of the validity of the marriage contract.

While a marriage contract is traditionally concluded between two agents of the spouses to be, the contract is between the man and the woman who are to become husband and wife. All the principles of all forms and types of contracts apply to every marriage contract: e.g. requirements of legal competence to conclude a contract, the clarity and unequivocal nature of the language or formula, that an offer cannot be withdrawn once accepted, but the consensual nature of the contractual obligation must be ensured, i.e. the parties clearly understood and freely consented to the formation of a contact of marriage in particular.

The requirement of competent and qualified parties (2., above) includes that the man and woman are not already related to each other in any of the ways that preclude the possibility of marriage. These legal bars to marriage can be either permanent or temporary. The reasons for a *permanent* bar to marriage include certain specific blood relations, such as mother/father (including grandparents), aunt/uncle on either side, sister/brother (whether half or full). Being cousins (son or daughter of an aunt or uncle) is not a legal bar to marriage, and tends to be socially and economically desirable in traditional settings. A peculiar aspect of IFL is that all types of blood relations are also attributed to fostering relationship – called 'milk child or sibling', i.e. when a child is breastfed by a woman other than his or her biological mother, that woman becomes the child's mother for all purposes of prohibition of marriage due to blood relations. That is, the woman's husband becomes the father of the milk-child and her children become the child's milk-brothers and milk-sisters. Consequently, any relationship that bars marriage from blood relations applies equally to relations based on such fostering relations.

There are five grounds of *transient* bar to marriage, i.e. marriage can become permissible once the temporary bar ends. Situations of temporary prohibition include:

1. A man cannot marry a married woman or during her waiting period (*idda*)[11] after divorce or death of her husband, but can marry her once the waiting period ends.
2. A man cannot be married to sisters at the same time, but can marry one after the termination of his marriage to her sister.
3. A man cannot be married to more than four wives, but can marry again when one of those marriages is terminated.

The legal consequences of marriage can be summarised as:

1. The wife is entitled to the dower gift (*mahr*) according to the terms agreed with the husband or decreed by court or arbitration, if necessary. For instance, if no amount was agreed, each school of Islamic jurisprudence has rules for determining the amount and conditions for its payment to the wife. This gift is the exclusive property of the wife personally, and she is not required to spend any of it on maintaining the household.
2. Each spouse is entitled to inherit from the estate of the other upon death, according to the applicable rules of inheritance.
3. The wife is entitled to maintenance (food, shelter, clothing and other material support) by the husband, without spending any of her own property. In exchange, the husband is entitled to obedience by his wife. These mutual obligations are interdependent, so that the husband is not entitled to obedience if he fails to provide appropriate maintenance, and the wife is not entitled to maintenance if she refuses to be obedient to the husband.

---

[11] *Idda* is the waiting period a wife must observe before she can remarry. *Idda* is normally three months after termination of marriage and four months and ten days after death of husband.

The preceding is a very general overview of Sunni IFL principles, and there are many variations and differences of opinion among schools of Islamic jurisprudence and individual jurists on almost every single principle. Still, the following general comments may be true of Sunni Muslims' view of marriage.

First, the focus of Muslim jurists on the careful 'legal' consequences of mutual contractual rights and obligations of the spouses can be misleading if taken to represent the exclusive nature of the relationship, within their personal and social networks. The vast majority of marriage relationships tend to run their normal course in mutual love and respect, and the usual tensions of matrimonial life are resolved through mediation within the extended family and community. Still, the legalistic aspects of the contractual relationship tend to be more visible and controversial because they are normally contested when a marriage fails or runs into difficulties.

Second, dower (*mahr*, also called *Sadaq*) is a sum of money or other property which becomes payable by the husband to the wife as an effect of marriage, a sort of required gift upon marriage. It is misleading to call it 'bride-price' because it is the exclusive entitlement of the wife herself, and not any other person. The fact that dower is a consequence of marriage, and not a condition of validity of the contract of marriage, does not diminish the wife's entitlement to it. *Mahr* is implied into the contract even if it is not expressly stated. There is unanimous agreement among Muslims scholars that any property can be paid as dower. There is also unanimous agreement that there is no upper limit to a valid dower, but no agreement on the minimal amount of dower. Although the practice of payment of excessive dower can inhibit prospects of marriage by most young men, any restriction on the maximum amount that can be paid is commonly seen as violation of sharia principles.[12]

Third, although Sunni jurists are unanimous in rejecting 'temporary marriage' (*muta*), the issue should be noted here because of its controversial nature. To Sunnis (and Ismaili Shia), the Prophet prohibited any explicit or implicit time limit on marriage, but Twelvers Shia accept the validity of temporary marriage because they reject the reports (Hadith) of that prohibition. In Twelvers Shia jurisprudence, the duration of cohabitation in a temporary marriage contract must be fixed (could be a day, a month, a year or number of years), and the dower must be specified. The

---

[12] Nasir, *Islamic Law of Personal Status*, 83–6.

wife is entitled to full dower if the temporary marriage is consummated and half the dower if the marriage was not consummated, but she is not entitled to maintenance. There are no mutual rights of inheritance between the man and woman, but children conceived during the temporary marriage are legitimate and entitled to inherit from both parents.[13]

Sharia Principles of Termination of Marriage

The term 'termination of marriage' refers to the variety of ways in which marriage can end, some of which do not fit the modern notion of divorce. As a general rule of the Sunni jurisprudence and subject to many significant disagreements among schools and scholars on various aspects of this process, marriage can be terminated in any of the following main ways:

1. Unilateral repudiation by the husband (*talaq*); or by the wife under delegation by the husband (*talaq al-tafwid*). Once given, the husband cannot revoke such delegation unilaterally, and if exercised by the wife, it results in a final irrevocable termination of the marriage.
2. Mutual agreement on termination of marriage upon payment of compensation by the wife to the husband (*khul*).
3. By judicial decree, which can be based on a wide range of grounds, e.g. annulment (*faskh, tafriq* or *tatliq*) for legal reasons like defects in the contract, lack of social compatibility (*kafaa*) between the spouses, inadequacy of dowry (*mahr*), or legal cause like failure of the husband to provide maintenance, causing harm or incompatibility of the spouses. Recall that there are significant disagreements among schools and scholars on almost all these causes of judicial termination of marriage.

The first form of dissolution of marriage, namely, this structure of repeated repudiations by the husband, may be summarised as follows:

Talaq 1: becomes final only after *idda*, unless unilaterally revoked before then. This is minor finality, which permits the parties to remarry with a new contract;

Talaq 2: same consequences;

---

[13] *Ibid.*, 59–61.

Talaq 3: same consequences, except that after *idda*, this becomes major finality of termination of marriage, with no possibility of remarriage between the two parties, unless the woman marries another man and that marriage runs its normal course.

The second form of dissolution of marriage noted above is known as *khul* (literally to take off or remove), which is a way for a wife to pay her way out of a marriage she no longer wishes to keep. The compensation the wife pays to the husband in exchange for his consent to terminate the marriage can be the return of her bridal gift (*mahr*), or forfeiting the balance of that gift which was postponed at the time of contracting marriage (*muakhar al-sidaq*). In this way, the bridal gift can either provide the wife with some financial security in the case of divorce or death of the husband or enable her to negotiate ending an unhappy marriage. Hallaq explains the consequences of this form of dissolution of marriage: 'If the husband accepts the offer, he will then repudiate his wife once, considered to be an irrevocable utterance *(bain)*. The finality of the single utterance stems from the fact that payment renders the repudiation contractual, thus making the acceptance of the offer binding upon conclusion of the session – which is not the case in unilateral, non-contractual *talaq*.'[14]

Child Paternity and Custody

IFL principles of paternity, suckling, moral upbringing and supervision of property affairs of the child can be summarised as follows.

Muslim jurists gave particular care to questions of paternity not only because all legal rights and obligations of the child for the rest of her or his life depends on paternity but also because of the strong social stigma of illegitimacy. Paternity is established through the application of several principles.

First, there is a very strong but rebuttable presumption that a child is the legitimate offspring of the marriage, if the apparent parents were married at the time of conception of the child. Some scholars of sharia sought to maintain the application of this presumption by extending the minimum and maximum possible duration of pregnancy, from six months to up to

---

[14] Hallaq, *Sharī'a*, 284.

four years. This exaggerated view of possible duration of pregnancy was intended to avoid a charge that the mother is guilty of the capital crime of extramarital sexual intercourse (*zina*). If the wife cohabited with her husband at any time during that extended period of possible pregnancy, then the husband's paternity of the child is assumed.

Second, if the presumption of legitimacy is totally untenable in that the spouses could not have had intercourse within the framework of such extended duration of possibility of pregnancy, the father may still claim the child as the offspring of the marriage, provided he does not admit that the child was born of illicit sexual intercourse.

Third, if a child cannot be deemed the offspring of a valid marriage either by date of birth in relation to the consummation of the marriage or by the husband claiming the child to the marriage, then the child is deemed to be illegitimate. In that case, the child belongs to the mother alone.

The modern legal concept of custody does not exist under traditional IFL, and the material and moral care of the child is divided into material care for the child (*hadana*), and moral upbringing and supervision of property/financial affairs (*wilaya*). Material care (*hadana*) from birth up to a specific age is determined by each school (e.g. 7 for boys and 9 for girls, according to some scholars). After the specified age, the material care of the child shifts to the father. However, 'Child custody laws in Saudi Arabia, Iran, Syria, Iraq, Kuwait and Jordon show that no matter which school of *Fiqh* is predominant, no fixed age of custody is uniformly followed in these countries and the majority of the laws and trends of courts show that courts have the power to extend child custody to mothers beyond the age stated in texts, depending upon the circumstances of the case'.[15]

The moral well-being of the child and supervision over his or her property/financial affairs (*wilaya*) always belongs to the father, even while the child is still under the material care (*hadana*) of the mother. The father has the authority to supervise (*wilaya*) the property/financial affairs of the child, but the child has her own legal capacity (*ahliya*) to conclude contracts, own and dispose of property, etc. Such issues of legal personality and capacity are governed by a series of presumptions based on the age of the child when the right or obligation is acquired. For instance, every child has a right to parentage, inheritance or receiving a gift even before she or

---

[15] A. Rafiq, 'Child custody in classical Islamic law and laws of contemporary Muslim world (an analysis)' (2014) 4(5) *International Journal of Humanities and Social Science* 273.

he is born, e.g. if the father dies before birth and the child is actually born alive. From birth up to a set age, 7 according to some scholars, a child can acquire some rights and obligations, e.g. he owns what he purchases (or is purchased for him by his guardian), and has the obligation to pay restitution for what he destroys. Generally, the child progresses in her or his rights and obligations, but always subject to supervision (*wilaya*) until the age of puberty or majority.

IFL is particularly concerned that every person has a clearly defined legal personality from viable pregnancy to death, with carefully specified relationships determining the person's rights and obligations for the full duration of her life. The same concern with precise legal determination of rights and obligations is also reflected in sharia principles of property and contacts. In addition to the obligations of the husband/father for the maintenance of his wife and children, sharia also set a maintenance obligation among members of the wider family and other relatives. This obligation depended on such factors as the degree of relationship and material status of relatives, whereby the obligation is most strongly owed to parents and destitute relatives and weakest for distant relatives or those who have no need for assistance. Whether the state provides legal remedies for failure to provide extended family support, the obligation under sharia remains binding.

Sharia family law principles are usually enacted by statute in the context of modern state legal systems in most Muslim-majority countries today.[16] This is not problematic per se because every society is entitled to decide on its own laws as a matter of self-determination. What is profoundly problematic, I argue, is the fact that such state legislation tends to be called 'sharia family law', instead of simply ordinary legislation.[17] This is misleading because in such enactment, the language of the statute is the law, and it is the law by virtue of the political authority of the state, and not by virtue of the sharia principle as such. In fact, the extreme diversity of interpretations of sharia by various schools of Islamic jurisprudence means that it is the state as a political institution that decides which views are to be enacted into law and which views are to be excluded. Moreover, the legislative organs of the state have the sole authority to amend, add or remove

---

[16] See generally, A. A. An-Na'im (ed.), *Islamic Family Law in a Changing World: A Global Resource Book* (London: Zed Books, 2002).
[17] See generally Nasir, *Islamic Law of Personal Status*.

provisions from these statutes. It is therefore clear that the so-called IFL is nothing more than secular state legislation presented as sharia to promote its legitimacy among Muslims and insulate it against criticism.

III From Traditional Practice to Postcolonial Transformation

The primary question for this chapter is the relationship of traditional IFL principles to modern legal systems of the postcolonial nation state. This question emerged out of the rise of so-called territorial nation states during European colonial rule over most Muslim communities in Africa and Asia, including the transformation of the legal system and public administration of the emerging states. The magnitude and consequences of those changes can be appreciated in light of the following brief review of the processes of administration of justice in traditional Islamic societies.

Traditional Practice of Sharia

Whatever court system or manner of resolution of disputes in the precolonial era no longer exists or has been subjected to fundamental change in our time.[18] We should understand the premodern practice of sharia in terms of the political and social context when Muslim societies did not operate on the bureaucratic organisation of modern political regimes. In premodern states, the caliphs and sultans had absolute military and political power and authority that was based on 'personal loyalty rather than obedience to abstract, impersonal regulations'.[19] At the same time, caliphs and sultans needed the legitimising authority of scholars and religious leaders of the communities because legitimacy was seen as 'the preserve of religion, erudition, ascetic piety, moral rectitude, and, in short, in the *persons* of those men who had profound knowledge of, and fashioned their lives, after, the example of the Prophet and the exemplary forefathers'.[20]

The political and legal history of Muslim societies can therefore be seen as a constant interaction and negotiation between the rulers and the

---

[18] K. S. Vikor, *Between God and the Sultan: A History of Islamic Law* (Oxford University Press, 2005) 140.
[19] Hallaq, *Sharī'a*, 147.   [20] *Ibid.*, 131.

scholars/jurists. The rulers needed the legitimacy of the knowledge and interpretation of sharia by the Muslim scholars/jurists, who in turn needed the political authority of the rulers to implement sharia. That mutual dependency required both sides to observe a traditional form of what could be called 'checks and balances'. Rulers had to curtail their impulse to seek to co-opt or influence the scholars, and scholars had to resist co-optation or influence to maintain the 'dance of power and knowledge'. Rulers needed to respect the integrity and autonomy of scholars to preserve their legitimising competence, and the scholars needed to protect their integrity and autonomy to maintain their moral standing among their communities. As a result, the worst charge for scholars in Islamic societies up to the present time is to be called *ulama' al-Sultan* (scholars of the state).

The structural safeguard of the integrity and autonomy of the founding Muslim scholars of sharia was first ensured by the independence of the informal educational system of 'circles of learning' (*halaqas*) that usually convened in mosques where Muslims came to pray five times a day. Throughout Muslim history, these informal circles of learning remained the established forum of legal education and retained their autonomy by not receiving endowments from the ruling elites.[21] In addition, however, more institutionalised colleges (*madrasas*) emerged at the end of the eighth century when endowments and salaries began to be paid to professors.

It was through the funding of these institutions that the ruling elites gradually co-opted scholars/jurists and influenced the legal profession. Madrasas did not substitute halaqas; they 'rather bestowed on the *halaqa* an external legal framework that allowed pedagogical activity to be conducted under the auspices of endowments'.[22] By the seventeenth century, unfortunately, most jurists were employed by the state, and those who insisted on maintaining their autonomy 'had to function within a diminishing "moral community" created by the financial and material dependence of their less independent peers on the ruling powers'.[23] The decline in the autonomous role of sharia and its scholars started before the rise of European colonialism in Africa and Asia.

The central role in the daily practice of sharia was that of the jurist/scholar (mufti) whose task was to consult a whole host of sharia sources, according to his training and affiliation with one of the schools of Islamic jurisprudence (madhhab) to produce a legal opinion (fatwa), which

[21] *Ibid.*, 140.   [22] *Ibid.*   [23] *Ibid.*, 151.

becomes the basis of rulings by judges (qadis) in specific cases. The authority of the mufti was based on his reputation as a learned and pious scholar, while the authority of judges was drawn either from official appointment or voluntary submission by individual litigants. The fatwa established the connection between relevant principles of sharia and the particular case, and was in theory valid only for the case for which it was formulated. Judges were not obliged to seek a fatwa for every case they had to decide, and could seek it only when unsure of the legal basis for determining the case or if he felt the need for stronger authority for his ruling due to the nature of the case or public attention it attracted.

The role of both judge and *mufti* was confined to identifying and interpreting the law for application to specific cases, but never to create the law. The tasks of a judge (qadi) included resolving conflicts (tahkim), adjudicating rights and obligations (qada) and representing the community (hisba). To duly perform his functions, a judge was supposed to investigate not only the facts of the case, but also information about the integrity of the litigating parties and the history of their interactions. He had to take into account social customs and strive to resolve the dispute in ways that preserved social harmony and stability.[24]

Transition to Nation State Legal Systems

Whatever the nature and manner of the role of sharia in the daily administration of justice in Islamic communities from West Africa to Central and Southeast Asia may have been, that role has been drastically transformed by European colonialism even for parts that were not formally colonised like the Arabian Peninsula and Iran. European colonialism has been spectacularly successful not only in its scale and scope, but more importantly in transforming the political and legal institutions of the colonised societies as well as the global economic and trade system. Those transformations were first prompted by the attempts of the Ottoman Empire to modernise its political and legal institutions during the nineteenth century to meet the challenge of rising European powers. The symbolic significance of the Ottoman concessions to rising European powers culminated in the

---

[24] For clear explanation of the traditional practice of sharia prior to its displacement by colonial legal systems in the nineteenth and twentieth centuries, see Vikor, *Between God and the Sultan*, chs. 8–9.

abolition of the caliphate (symbol of Islamic unity and sovereignty) by 1924. This event marked the irreversible shift to European models of the state and its legal system that came to prevail throughout Ottoman regions in the Middle East and North Africa. Concurrent processes were taking place in Iran and South Asia, which culminated in similar outcomes.

Thus it was a combination of colonial European challenge and accommodation and adaptation by Islamic societies in the nineteenth and first half of the twentieth centuries that resulted in the establishment of 'nation states' from North and West Africa to South and South East Asia. When Islamic societies of Central Asia were finally released from the grip of Russian/Soviet colonialism by 1991, they also opted for the nation state formation that had become the established global order. The same dynamic process resulted in the total incorporation of all Islamic societies into the global state-centric economic, political and security systems of today. As openly secular state courts applied European statutes during the colonial era and since independence in almost all Islamic societies, the domain of sharia became limited to the family law field. Even in the family law field, the state continued to regulate the role of sharia as part of broader legal and political systems of government and social organisation within the framework of postcolonial European models.

While this process unfolded in different ways among Islamic societies, the experience of the late Ottoman Empire has probably had the most far-reaching consequences. The concessions made by the Ottoman Empire to European powers during the nineteenth century set the model for the adoption of western codes and systems of administration of justice. The Ottoman Majallah was promulgated over a ten-year period (1867–77), to codify the rules of contract and tort according to the Hanafi school, combining European format with sharia content. This major codification of sharia principles simplified a huge part of the relevant principles and made them more easily accessible to litigants and jurists.

The Majallah acquired a position of supreme authority soon after its enactment, partly because it represented the earliest and most politically authoritative example of an official promulgation of large parts of sharia by the authority of a modern state, thereby claiming to transform sharia into positive state law in the modern sense of the term. Moreover, the Majallah was immediately applied in a wide range of Islamic societies throughout the Middle East and North Africa, and continued to apply in some parts into the second half of the twentieth century. The success of the

Majallah was also due to the fact that it included some provisions drawn from sources other than the Hanafi school, thereby expanding possibilities of 'acceptable' selectivity of legislative enactment from within the Islamic tradition. The principle of selectivity (*takhayyur*) among equally legitimate doctrines of sharia was not new within Muslim communities, but it was never before done in statutory enactment for centralised and bureaucratic administration of the justice by the state.[25]

This trend towards increased eclecticism in the selection of sources and the synthesis of Islamic and western legal concepts and institutions was also carried further and became irreversible. The most influential work in this regard is that of the Egyptian jurist Abd al-Razzaq al-Sanhuri (died 1971),[26] who used this approach in the drafting of the Egyptian Civil Code of 1949, the Iraqi Code of 1951, the Libyan Code of 1954 and the Kuwaiti Code and Commercial law of 1960, among others.[27] Those developments made the entire corpus of sharia principles more available and accessible to judges and policymakers in the process of the incorporation of those principles into modern legislation. This was also often done by mixing some general or partial principles or views from one school of sharia (madhhab) with those derived from other schools, without due regard to the methodological basis or conceptual coherence of any of the schools whose authority was being invoked.

The accessibility of sharia principles highlighted the complexity and diversity of the broad Islamic tradition, and highlighted the strong disagreement among and within Sunni and Shia schools. This is particularly significant in view of the fact that Sunni and Shia communities sometimes coexist within the same country, as in Iraq, Lebanon, Saudi Arabia, Syria and Pakistan, with each community following a different school, regardless of the official status of those schools in relation to state law. Judicial practice may not necessarily be consistent with the school followed by the majority of the Muslim population in the country. For example, the courts of Egypt and Sudan followed the official Ottoman preference for the Hanafi

---

[25] J. L. Esposito, 'Perspectives on Islamic law reform: The case of Pakistan' (1980–1) 13 *New York University Journal of International Law and Policy* 236.

[26] See, generally, G. Bechor, *The Sanhuri Code, and the Emergence of Modern Arab Civil Law (1932 to 1949)* (Leiden: Brill, 2007).

[27] N. Saleh, 'Civil codes of Arab countries: The Sanhuri Codes' (1993) 8(2) *Arab Law Quarterly* 161–7.

school, while popular practice continued to observe the Shafi'i and Maliki schools.

The legal and political consequences of these developments were intensified by the significant impact of European colonialism and postcolonial influence in the fields of general education and professional training of state officials, business leaders and other influential social and economic actors. Changes in educational institutions not only dislodged traditional Islamic education but also introduced a range of secular subjects that tend to create a different worldview and expertise among young generations of Muslims. Moreover, the monopoly held by Islamic scholars of intellectual leadership in societies that had very low literacy rates has been drastically eroded by the fast growth of mass literacy and growing higher education in secular sciences and arts. Regarding legal education in particular, the first generations of lawyers and jurists took advanced training in European and North American universities and returned to teach subsequent generations or to hold senior legal and judicial offices.

More generally, the establishment of the European model for Muslim-majority countries as part of a global system based on the same model has radically transformed political, economic and social relations throughout the region. By retaining these models at home and participating in them abroad after independence, Islamic societies have become bound by the national and international obligations of membership in a world community of states. All Islamic societies today live under national constitutional regimes and legal systems that require respect for certain minimum rights of equality and non-discrimination for all their citizens. Even where national constitutions and legal systems fail to expressly acknowledge and effectively provide for these obligations, a minimum degree of practical compliance is ensured by the present realities of international relations. These transformations also affected the situation of Muslim minorities living in other countries, including Western Europe and North America, who continued to assume the Islamic religious and cultural authority of the Middle East and North Africa.

Wael Hallaq examines this process in terms of 'modernizing the law in the age of nation-state', in relation to such modernist projects as nationalism and law reform, except for family law.[28] Whatever may have been the rationale or justification of the exception of IFL from displacement by

---

[28] Hallaq, *Sharī'a*, 445.

European codes, the point for our purposes here is that despite the popular perception that IFL remained 'an authentic and genuine expression of the *fiqhi* [of Islamic jurisprudence] family law, the fact of the matter is that even this sphere of law underwent structural and foundational changes that ultimately resulted in its being severed from both the substance of classical *fiqh* and the methodology by which *fiqh* had operated'.[29] Devices deployed in this process included the principles of necessity (*darura*), the procedural device of administrative discretion (*siyasa shar'iyya*) and eclectic selection and amalgamation (*takhayyur* and *talfiq*) of any views not only from within any school, but also from other schools. 'The product thereof was entirely new, because the opinions now combined had originally belonged to altogether different, perhaps incongruent, premises.'[30] Other devices included new forms of free interpretation (neo-*ijtihad*) and the notion that any law that does not contradict sharia is lawful.[31]

Postcolonial Legislative Reforms

To conclude this review of traditional community-based practice of sharia and its postcolonial transformation, I emphasise that my purpose is not to offer a general discussion of IFL in Muslim-majority countries. In particular, I am not in the least suggesting or implying a critical evaluation of the reforms that IFL statutes have introduced in the various countries. On the contrary, my objection to the fallacy of calling these statutes 'Islamic' is intended to facilitate and promote future prospects of such reforms away from any inhibition or confusion of pretending to comply with sharia standards. As I have tried to briefly explain at the beginning of this chapter, sharia norms and institutions lose their religious Islamic quality when enacted into and enforced as positive law of the state. Acknowledging this reality, I argue, releases the social and political dynamics of family law reform, and facilitates the contributions of social science scholars, civil society organisations and other concerned actors.

According to unanimous traditional practice of sharia, 'any departure from the legal doctrine (*madhhab*) as stated in these sources renders his

---

[29] Ibid. 446–7. [30] Ibid., 448.
[31] For more elaborate explanation and illustrations of these devices and their outcomes, see Anderson, *Law Reform in the Muslim World*, 42–82.

[jurist/*mufti*] opinion suspicious if not altogether void'.[32] It should also be recalled that traditional practice was the realm of scholars, muftis and judges, and was never codified by any state in thirteen centuries of Islamic history. This methodological inconsistency and the arbitrary outcomes of recent reforms are profoundly problematic for the integrity and cohesion of sharia as a comprehensive religious normative system in two primary ways.

First, state determination and enforcement of supposedly sharia norms undermine the integrity of the whole system. Second, arbitrary selectivity fails to account for the normative and social cohesion of each school in its broader social context. In each school, the rule of inheritance, for instance, operates in the same context as the rules of maintenance during marriage or consequences of termination of marriage. Whether one agrees or disagrees with the principles that were the outcome of traditional methodologies, each set of rules is integral to the normative and sociological system of each school as a whole.

Turning now to a brief review of postcolonial legislative reforms,[33] by being the first codification of sharia principles, the Ottoman Majallah of the 1870s already indicated a major departure from traditional Islamic juridical practice. The Majallah 'was based on principles derived from the Shari'a. Instead, however, of adopting the dominant doctrine in the *Hanafi* school in all particulars, this code comprised a selection of opinions from among those which had found any sort of recognition in that school (although some of them originated, in fact, in one of the other schools).'[34] That compounded deviation from traditional sharia practice was soon followed by more drastic departures by the use of 'an amalgamated selection (*takhayyur*) from several traditional doctrines held by a variety of schools. Even weaker doctrines within an individual school, inadmissible in the traditional system, have been rejuvenated

---

[32] W. B. Hallaq, *A History of Islamic Legal Theories: An Introduction to Sunni Usul al-Fiqh* (Cambridge University Press, 1997) 209.

[33] Although the Ottoman heartland was not occupied and colonised as such, the Ottoman state was acting in a postcolonial mode already during the second half of the nineteenth century. That functional postcolonial mode operated from mimicking European military and administrative organisation to copying European codes. After all, colonialism is a state of mind of the colonised as well as the coloniser.

[34] J. N. D. Anderson, 'Modern trends in Islam legal reform and modernisation in the Middle East' (1971) 20 *International and Comparative Law Quarterly* 2.

and bestowed by a legitimacy equal to that enjoyed by the "sound" (*sahih*) doctrines.'[35]

As noted earlier, the Ottoman Law of Family Rights (1917) was the first major state legislation that employed such dubiousness in the name of sharia. It was followed first in Egypt,[36] and then in Ottoman provinces of the Middle East and North Africa, as they gradually became independent states. Examples of this include the Jordanian Law of Family Rights in 1951 (replaced by the Jordanian Law of Personal Status in 1976), the Syrian Law of Personal Status in 1953, the Tunisian Law of Personal Status of 1956, the Moroccan Code of Personal Status in 1958 and the Iraqi Code of Personal Status of 1959.[37] Family law codes in Arab countries took the arbitrary reformist methodologies further 'to include Shi'ite doctrines, a step previously unthinkable. Moreover, the reformers resorted to the so-called *talfiq* according to which part of a doctrine of one school is combined with a part from another.'[38] The methodological expedience of selectivity, *takhayyur*, was extended in Egypt 'first, to *any* opinion ... within the orthodox schools, held in the past in some extinct school, or attributed to some early jurist ... to views culled from one of the "heterodox" schools of the *Shi'is* or *Ibadis*; and finally to the combination of part of the opinion of one school or jurist with part of the opinion of another school or jurist'.[39]

Similar reform strategies to arbitrary or inconsistent outcomes were deployed in the Indian subcontinent. For instance, the Indian Dissolution of Muslim Marriages Act of 1939, relied on the Maliki madhhab (school of Islamic jurisprudence which is dominant in North and West Africa) in expanding grounds for termination of marriage beyond the three accepted under the Hanafi madhhab (school of Islamic jurisprudence). While the expanded grounds were supposedly based on the Maliki madhhab, the outcome was different from what that school provided for:

---

[35] Hallaq, *History of Islamic Legal Theories*, 210.
[36] B. A. Venkatraman, 'Islamic states and the United Nations Convention on the Elimination of All Forms of Discrimination Against Women: Are the shari'a and the Convention compatible?' (1995) 44 *American University Law Review* 1986-7.
[37] For a discussion of these reforms in regional comparative perspectives, see L. Welchman, 'The development of Islamic family law in the legal system of Jordan' (1988) 37 *International and Comparative Law Quarterly* 871-86.
[38] Hallaq, *History of Islamic Legal Theories*, 210
[39] Anderson, 'Modern trends in Islam legal reform', 13.

Maliki law utilized judicial repudiation (*talaq*) whereas the Dissolution of Muslim Marriages Act adopted judicial recision [rescinding] (*faskh*). There is a significant and very practical difference between these two forms of divorce. *Talaq* is a revocable repudiation which only becomes final after ninety days, *i.e.*, the end of the '*iddah*, or waiting period. The purpose of this waiting period, provided by the Qur'an, is to provide a time for possible reconciliation as well as to establish paternity. *Faskh* bypasses these procedures for it is a decree which becomes final upon its issuance by the court.[40]

Although such reform methodologies are implemented in the name of upholding sharia rule, they are in fact an affront to the very essence of sharia as a normative system because they fail to respect and protect the internal rationality and consistency of the various schools. To the founding scholars and their successors in schools of Islamic jurisprudence, the principles of property, contact, financial capacity and competence, inheritance, marriage and its termination, custody of children, etc., are all designed to serve an integrated holistic social and economic system. Modern reformers may disagree with some aspects of the integrated system supported by early schools, but the opportunistic selectivity of modern reformers to serve their alternative view of the social and economic system of their societies is profoundly offensive to the theological and methodological integrity of the same schools of Islamic jurisprudence modern reformers claim to be supportive of their family law legislation as 'Islamic'. If modern reformers think that the internal consistency and cohesion of the traditional schools are no longer important or relevant, it would then be intellectually dishonest and hypocritical to invoke the names of the same schools to legitimise the reform outcomes, without even acknowledging their disagreement with the founding scholars of those schools.

IV Concluding Remarks

In conclusion, the religious nature of sharia and secular nature of state law requires differentiation of the two normative systems, while the methodological and normative similarities between sharia and state law indicate possibilities of interaction and cross-fertilisation between

---

[40] Esposito, 'Perspectives on Islamic Law Reform', 230–1.

the two.[41] Although sharia evolved among independent Muslim scholars and their communities, completely outside state institutions, the methods those scholars used for developing sharia principles and rules are similar to modern techniques of textual construction and reasoning by analogy and precedent.[42] Normative similarities between sharia and state law can be seen in such fields as property, contracts and civil liability for damage or misappropriation of property.[43]

We should also appreciate the difference between the religious and moral nature of marriage and family relations and the legal regulation of such relationships by the state. Human relationships of love and compassion are both the objective and the daily norm, to varying degrees, in the vast majority of family relations. This human norm includes possibilities of negotiations among the spouses and mediation by extended family advisers as well as communal sanction against offending spouses. Still, the enforcement of legal regulation must remain available as a last resort. However, that framework can cope only when severe family discord is the exception, and not the daily norm. This social and legal framework became more complex as modern states assumed more responsibilities through bureaucratic processes.

For instance, a marriage or divorce could be valid from a sharia point of view but most Muslim-majority countries today require it to be officially registered to be recognised by state courts and civic administration. Thus, official registration of marriage or divorce has become a prerequisite condition for obtaining judicial remedy or determination of any dispute regarding issues of marriage, divorce, and maintenance and custody of children. Official registration is also required for recognition of the marriage by administrative agencies of the state for such purposes as pension, social security payments, tax status or other consequences of marriage.

In practice, however, the requirement of registration tends to unfairly penalise vulnerable women who have little opportunity to comply with it in the first place. A Muslim woman who accepts to enter into a polygamous marriage without satisfying the conditions set by the state may believe herself legitimately married under IFL, but her marriage simply 'does not

---

[41] A. A. An-Na'im, 'The compatibility dialectic: Mediating the legitimate coexistence of Islamic law and state law' (2010) 73 *Modern Law Review* 1–29.
[42] Hallaq, *Sharī'a*.
[43] *Ibid.*, 239–45 on sharia principles of contracts, and 296–306 on property.

exist' for state courts and administrative agencies. This will not only deny her any of the entitlements of a wife under state law, but also leave her in an untenable position of neither being married for all official purposes nor unmarried from a religious point of view so that she can marry someone else.

The IFL reforms reviewed above may indeed be appropriate for exploring possibilities of reform in the enactment or interpretation of statutory law of the state. My objection is not only to the pretence that the outcome is valid and legitimate sharia, but also to reinforcing the misconception that family law reform is necessarily confined to the realm of historical Islamic jurisprudence. Stated slightly differently, the issue is not the precise nature and value of the reforms so introduced, but it is the defective methodology that is bound to lead to more complications for the presumably enlightened outcome, for instance, by reinforcing the belief that so-called Islamic institutions, like al-Azhar in Egypt, should hold the exclusive authority to approve or reject future reforms.[44]

---

[44] Fawzy, 'Law No. 1 of 2000', 58–94.

Index

Abortion in US, 56
Adoption
   China, child support in, 211, 212
   in Colombia
      overview, 131
      filiation by adoption, 151–152
   in Germany
      overview, 83
      forced adoption, 93
   in India
      dattaka (form of adoption), 230–231
      neglected and abused children, 230
      under personal laws, 230–231
   in Sweden, 173–174
Ahmed, Farrah, 2–3, 4, 5–6, 7–8
Alimony or maintenance
   decline of, 11–12
   in Germany, 101–102
      overview, 12, 97
      after separation, 100–101
      "community of accrued
         interests," 97–98
      criticisms of, 98–99
      during marriage, 99–100
      pension rights, 97
   in Islamic family law, 262
   in US, 11–12
Alternative dispute resolution (ADR)
   autonomy as reason for, 7–8
   Canada, religious ADR in, 8, 244
   complexity as reason for, 7
   cost as reason for, 7
   in England and Wales, promotion of
      family mediation, 41–42
   India, religious ADR in
      overview, 7–8, 239–241
      autonomy and, 239, 245–247
      criticism of, 243–244
      religious identity and, 241–242
      women and, 243–245
   in Islamic family law, 8
   reluctance to use, 9
   unequal bargaining power and, 8

An-Na'im, Abdullahi Ahmed, 6, 8
Argentina
   Civil Code of 1876, 134, 150
   constitutionalisation of family law in,
      134, 156
   filiation by birth in, 150–151
   gender identity in, 141
   marriage in, 135, 137–138
   multi-parenting in, 155
   National Civil and Commercial Code, 134,
      150
   same-sex marriage in, 137–138
Assistive reproductive technologies (ARTs)
   in England and Wales, Sweden compared,
      174–175
   in Germany, 83–84
   in Latin America, 130–131
   National Board of Health and Welfare, 164
   in Sweden
      attempt to conceive as prerequisite,
         165–166
      England and Wales compared, 174–175
      gamete donation, 163–164
      reluctance to embrace, 174–175
      restrictions on, 165–166
      surrogacy, 165, 174, 177
      US compared, 174–175
      womb transplantation, 177
   in US
      overview, 65–66
      Sweden compared, 174–175
Australia
   overview, 106–109
   Australian Council of Social Service,
      115–116
   Australian Institute of Family Studies,
      119, 124
   Australian Law Reform Commission, 106,
      113
   autonomy in, 16
   de facto relationships in, 108, 109
   dependent children in, 108

divorce in
    empirical evidence of effects of, 114
    gender equalisation, 3
    women and children, effects on, 114–118
Family Law Act 1975 (Cth)
    overview, 108–109
    de facto financial disputes under, 125
    judicial discretion under, 110
    "just and equitable" requirement under, 111–112, 113–114
    lawyers, application by, 123
    property division under, 121
    separate property regime under, 109–110
gender in
    divorce, equalisation in, 3
    pay gap, 118
"just and equitable" requirement
    overview, 111–112
    factors considered, 113
    lack of definition, 113–114
legal aid in, 107
NASTEM Income and Wealth Report, 117–118
Productivity Commission, 112–113
property division in
    overview, 12
    adjudicated cases, 124–126
    contributions versus need, 110–111, 118
    de facto financial disputes, 125
    definition of property, 109–110
    diversity in, 126
    factors affecting, 120–121
    fairness, perception of, 122–123
    high-asset versus moderate-asset cases, 125
    informal agreements, 119–122
    judicial discretion, 110
    lawyers, role of, 123–124
    separate property regime, 109–110
    statistics, 119
    uncertainty in, 126
reform proposals in
    consensus, difficulty in achieving, 126–127
    historical background, 112–113
    limitations of, 127
    need for, 127
    research, need for, 126

Sweden compared, 159
Women's Legal Service Victoria, 107
Autonomy
    ADR, as reason for, 7–8
    in Australia, 16
    in China, 14
    in England and Wales
        overview, 40
        family mediation, promotion of, 41–42
        pre-nuptial agreements, 42–44
    in Germany
        overview, 15–16, 102–103
        divorce and, 103
        pre-nuptial agreements and, 103–104
        same-sex marriage and, 103
        unequal bargaining power and, 103
    in India
        group autonomy, 245–247
        personal laws and, 234
        religious ADR and, 239, 245–247
    individualisation and, 14–15
    judicial discretion and, 16
    in Latin America, 15
    in Sweden, 15
    true extent of choice, 13–14
    in US
        overview, 13
        contracts and, 62
        increases in, 48–50

Bakker, P., 183
Beck-Gernsheim, Elisabeth, 14–15
Berggren, Henrik, 160
Bonthuys, E., 202
Brazil
    Civil Code, 134
    Constitution, 134, 139
    constitutionalisation of family law in, 134
    marriage in, 135, 138–139
    multi-parenting in, 155
    same-sex marriage in, 138–139

Canada, religious ADR in, 8, 244
Child care and rearing
    in Chile, 152–155
    China, preference for maternal child-rearing in, 206, 208, 212–213
    England and Wales, equalisation of gender roles in, 3
    equalisation of gender roles, 3
    Germany, equalisation of gender roles in, 3

282　Index

Child care and rearing (cont.)
　in Latin America, 132
　Sweden, equalisation of gender roles in, 3
Child custody or arrangements
　in Chile, 154–155
　in China
　　changes in, 216
　　determinations of, 212–214
　　litigated divorce and, 219–220
　in England and Wales, consideration of domestic violence, 38–40
　in Germany
　　Cochemer Model, 89
　　contact rights, 90–91
　　50:50 shared care, 89–90
　　"high-conflict parents," 89
　　joint parental responsibility model, 87
　　post-separation parental responsibility, 88–89
　　unwed biological fathers and, 87–88
　in Islamic family law, 266–267
　in US
　　gender-based presumptions, 67
　　historical background, 66–67
　　shared custody, 67–68
Child endangerment in Germany
　forced adoption, 93
　progressive measures regarding, 91–93
Children's rights
　in China, 18
　in Latin America, 18
Child support
　in China
　　overview, 203–204
　　adoption and, 211, 212
　　amount of, 214–215
　　best interests of child standard, 215–216, 220, 223–224
　　changes in, 215–216
　　continuation of parent-child relationship and, 208, 212
　　factors considered, 214–215
　　limitations of actions, 220–222, 224
　　method of payment, 215
　　negotiated agreements, 214, 215
　　in 1950s, 204–207
　　in 1980s, 207–210
　　non-payment of, 216–217, 222–223
　　post-divorce obligations, 205–206, 208
　　recommendations regarding, 222–224
　　registered divorce and, 217–219
　　remarriage, effect of, 206, 208–209
　　step-parents and, 211–212
　　termination of obligation, 210–211
　in Germany, 102
　in Islamic family law, 267
　in US
　　filial responsibility statutes, 69–70
　　financial burdens of, 69
　　financial inequality and, 70–71
　　freedom of choice, 68–69
Chile
　child custody in, 154–155
　child-rearing in, 152–155
　Civil Code, 134, 139, 146, 152–153, 154
　Civil Marriage Law, 140
　Constitution, 134, 140
　constitutionalisation of family law in, 134
　filiation by birth in, 145–147
　gender identity in, 141
　marriage in, 139–141
　same-sex marriage in, 139–141
　shared personal care in, 152–154
China
　adoption, child support and, 211, 212
　autonomy in, 14
　child custody in
　　changes in, 216
　　determinations of, 212–214
　　litigated divorce and, 219–220
　children's rights in, 18
　child support in
　　overview, 203–204
　　adoption and, 211, 212
　　amount of, 214–215
　　best interests of child standard, 215–216, 220, 223–224
　　changes in, 215–216
　　continuation of parent-child relationship and, 208, 212
　　factors considered, 214–215
　　limitations of actions, 220–222, 224
　　method of payment, 215
　　negotiated agreements, 214, 215
　　in 1950s, 204–207
　　in 1980s, 207–210
　　non-payment of, 216–217, 222–223
　　post-divorce obligations, 205–206, 208
　　recommendations regarding, 222–224
　　registered divorce and, 217–219
　　remarriage, effect of, 206, 208–209
　　step-parents and, 211–212
　　termination of obligation, 210–211

Civil Code, 222
Civil Procedure Law, 217
Common Program of the Chinese People's Political Consultative Conference, 205
common property regime in, 218
Communist Party Central Committee, 207
Constitution, 212
divorce in
  litigated divorce, 219–220
  registered divorce, 203–204, 217–219
family planning policy in, 219
General Rules of the Civil Law, 224
Implementing Marriage Law Committees, 207
Instructions on Principles to Deal with Present General Matrimonial Cases, 204–205
Marriage Law Amendment 2001
  changes in child support under, 216
  continuation of parent-child relationship under, 210, 212
  effect of, 217
  enactment of, 210
  maternal child-rearing, preference for, 212–213
  negotiated agreements for child support under, 214
  registered divorce under, 217
Marriage Law 1950
  child support, post-divorce obligations, 205–206
  continuation of parent-child relationship under, 205
  enactment of, 205
  general provisions, 206
  implementation of, 207
  Marriage Law 1980 compared, 207–210
  maternal child-rearing, preference for, 206
  remarriage, effect of, 206
  resistance to, 206–207
Marriage Law 1980
  child support, post-divorce obligations, 208
  continuation of parent-child relationship under, 208
  enactment of, 207–208
  Marriage Law 1950 compared, 207–210
  maternal child-rearing, preference for, 208
  remarriage, effect of, 208–209

Office of Publicizing and Checking the Implementation of the Marriage Law, 207
  step-parents, child support and, 211–212
  in 21st Century, 210
  women in, 206
Civil partnerships or unions
  in England and Wales
    overview, 10
    evolution of, 20
    future of, 20–21
    heterosexual couples, 21–22
    review of, 21
    statistics, 20
  in South Africa
    overview, 182
    defined, 197–198
    in hierarchy of marital relations, 197–198
    marriage versus, 10
Cohabitation
  England and Wales, property division in, 31–33
  in Germany, 96
  marriage versus, 9–10
  in South Africa
    in hierarchy of marital relations, 200–201
    inheritance rights and, 190–191, 192–197
  in US
    changing demographics, 52
    contracts, use of, 61–62
Colombia
  adoption in
    overview, 131
    filiation by adoption, 151–152
  Children and Adolescent Code, 151
  Civil Code, 134, 135
  Constitution, 134, 136
  constitutionalisation of family law in, 134, 156
  filiation by birth in, 149–150
  gender identity in
    intersex children, 141–142
    sex change surgery, 143
    sexual ambiguity, 142–143
  marriage in, 135–136
  same-sex marriage in, 135–136
Constitutionalisation of family law
  in Argentina, 134, 156
  in Brazil, 134

Constitutionalisation of family law (cont.)
  in Chile, 134
  in Colombia, 134, 156
  in Germany, 77, 81
  in Latin America, 128–129, 156–157
  in Mexico, 134
Contraception in US, 56
Convention on the Rights of the Child
  overview, 131–132
  child support and, 212, 222, 223
  genetic testing and, 167–168

Deech, Ruth, 30
De Vaus, Davis, 116–117
Dewar, John, 126
Diduck, Alison, 41
Divorce or dissolution
  in Australia
    empirical evidence of effects of, 114
    gender equalisation, 3
    women and children, effects on, 114–118
  in China
    litigated divorce, 219–220
    registered divorce, 203–204, 217–219
  in England and Wales
    amicable post-separation arrangements, undermining of, 23–24
    fabrication, incentives for, 23
    grounds for, 22
    judicial consideration of facts, lack of, 23
    no-fault divorce, calls for, 24
    review of, 24
  gender, equalisation of, 3
  in Germany
    overview, 95
    alimony, 101–102
    autonomy, 103
  in Islamic family law
    judicial decree, 264
    khul (mutual agreement), 264, 265
    registration of, 278–279
    talaq (unilateral repudiation), 264–265
  marriage, effect on, 10
  South Africa, dissolution of customary marriage in, 183
  in US
    alimony, decline in, 11–12, 58–59
    changing demographics, 52
Domestic partnerships. *See* Cohabitation
Domestic violence
  child contact and, 13
  complexity of, 13
  in England and Wales
    overview, 34
    child arrangement cases, consideration in, 38–40
    criminalisation of, 34–36
    forced marriage and, 34–36
    funding of response to, 12–13
    public law crisis regarding, 37–38
    statistics, 36, 37
  in Germany, 91
Dworkin, Ronald, 133

Egypt
  Civil Code of 1949, 272
  family law reform in, 276
  Sunni-Shia conflict in, 272–273
England and Wales
  overview, 19, 47
  access to justice in, 44–46
  ADR in, promotion of family mediation, 41–42
  Anti-Social Behaviour, Crime and Policing Act 2014, 35
  assistive reproductive technologies (ARTs) in, Sweden compared, 174–175
  autonomy in
    overview, 40
    family mediation, promotion of, 41–42
    pre-nuptial agreements, 42–44
  child care in, equalisation of gender roles, 3
  Children Act 1989, 38
  Children and Families Act 2014, 37
  Civil Partnership Act 2004, 20, 22
  civil partnerships in
    overview, 10
    evolution of, 20
    future of, 20–21
    heterosexual couples, 21–22
    review of, 21
    statistics, 20
  divorce in
    amicable post-separation arrangements, undermining of, 23–24
    fabrication, incentives for, 23
    grounds for, 22
    judicial consideration of facts, lack of, 23
    no-fault divorce, calls for, 24
    review of, 24
  domestic violence in

overview, 34
child arrangement cases, consideration in, 38–40
criminalisation of, 34–36
forced marriage and, 34–36
funding of response to, 12–13
public law crisis regarding, 37–38
statistics, 36, 37
Family Justice Review, 37, 38
Human Rights Act 1998, 21
Labour Party, 32, 34
Latin America compared, 130–131
Law Commission, 26, 30, 31–32, 44
legal advisers, 24
Legal Aid, Sentencing and Punishment of Offenders Act 2012, 46
Legal Aid Agency, 46
legal aid in, 45–46
Marriage Act 1949, 24–25
Marriage (Same-Sex Couples) Act 2013, 20
marriage in
overview, 19–20
forced marriage, 34–36
formalities of, 24–26
"non-marriage,"25–26
pre-nuptial agreements, 42–44
Sharia Councils, 26–28
Matrimonial Causes Act 1973, 20, 22, 110–111
pre-nuptial agreements in, 42–44
private law crisis in, 44–46
property division in
overview, 28
cohabitation and, 31–33
rules versus discretion, 28–31
uncertainty in, 29–31
women allegedly favoured by, 29–31
reasonable ordinary parent standard in, 16–17
religion in
freedom of choice, 6
overlap with family law, 4
Serious Crime Act 2015, 36
Sharia Councils, 26–28
Southall Black Sisters, 27
Sweden compared, 159
women in
expansion of rights, 206
property division allegedly favouring, 29–31

Espejo Yaksic, Nicolás, 3–4, 15, 18
Esping-Andersen, G., 159
European Convention on Human Rights (ECHR)
civil partnerships and, 21
German Basic Law and, 80, 86, 87–88
Sweden, right to parenthood in, 162

Family violence. *See* Domestic violence
Fehlberg, Belinda, 3, 12, 16, 120
Fish, Stanley, 127
Fisher, Hayley, 114–115, 117

Gamete donation in Sweden, 163–164
Gender. *See also* Women
in Australia
divorce, equalisation in, 3
pay gap, 118
change in gendered roles, 2
child care, equalisation of gender roles, 3
discrimination against women, 2–3
divorce, equalisation in, 3
in India
personal laws, gender differences in, 227
personal laws and, 236–237
religious ADR and, 243–245
Latin America, equalisation of gender roles in, 3
US, gender-based presumptions in child custody in, 67
Gender identity
in Argentina, 141
in Chile, 141
in Colombia
intersex children, 141–142
sex change surgery, 143
sexual ambiguity, 142–143
Germany, transsexuals in, 78
intersex children and, 3–4
in Latin America
overview, 141
intersex children and, 3–4
Mexico, sexual ambiguity in, 143–144
Genetic testing
in Germany, 80
parenthood and, 17
in Sweden, 167–168
Germany
overview, 77, 81–82
adoption in

Germany (cont.)
  overview, 83
  forced adoption, 93
  alimony in, 101–102
  assistive reproductive technologies (ARTs) in, 83–84
  autonomy in
    overview, 15–16, 102–103
    divorce and, 103
    pre-nuptial agreements and, 103–104
    same-sex marriage and, 103
    unequal bargaining power and, 103
  Bürgerliches Gesetzbuch (Civil Code)
    alimony under, 101–102
    child arrangements under, 88, 90
    child endangerment under, 92–93
    genetic testing under, 80
    maintenance under, 99–101
    unwed biological fathers under, 86
  child arrangements in
    Cochemer Model, 89
    contact rights, 90–91
    50:50 shared care, 89–90
    "high-conflict parents," 89
    joint parental responsibility model, 87
    post-separation parental responsibility, 88–89
    unwed biological fathers and, 87–88
  child care in, equalisation of gender roles, 3
  child endangerment in
    forced adoption, 93
    progressive measures regarding, 91–93
  children born out of wedlock in, 78
  child support in, 102
  cohabitation in, 96
  constitutionalisation of family law in, 77, 81
  divorce in
    overview, 95
    alimony, 101–102
    autonomy, 103
  domestic violence in, 91
  fatherhood in
    mixed principles, 84
    social father versus genetic father, 84–86
    unwed biological fathers, 79–80, 86, 87–88
  gender identity in, transsexuals and, 78, 104–105
  genetic testing in, 80
  Gewaltschutzgesetz (Protection against Violence Act), 91
  Grundgesetz (Basic Law)
    overview, 77, 78
    autonomy under, 102–103
    child endangerment under, 91, 92–93
    divorce under, 95
    ECHR and, 80, 86, 87–88
    marriage under, 95
    personality under, 80–81
    rights of children under, 93–94
    social father versus genetic father under, 84
    transsexuals under, 104–105
  human rights in
    overview, 81
    autonomy and, 15–16
    children born out of wedlock and, 78
    same-sex marriage and, 79
    transsexuals and, 78
    unwed biological fathers and, 79–80
  maintenance in
    overview, 12, 97
    after separation, 100–101
    "community of accrued interests," 97–98
    criticisms of, 98–99
    during marriage, 99–100
    pension rights, 97
  marriage in
    overview, 95
    same-sex marriage, 96, 103
  Ministry of Family Affairs, Senior Citizens, Women and Youth, 98
  motherhood in
    birthmother dogma, 82–83
    co-mothers, 83–84
    by sperm donation, 83–84
  Nichtehelichengesetz (Law of the Status of Children Born out of Wedlock), 78
  parenthood in
    genetic testing and, 17
    as status, 82
  pre-nuptial agreements in, 103–104
  rights of children in, 93–94
  role of children in legal proceedings, 94
  same-sex marriage in, 79, 96, 103
  transsexuals in, 78, 104–105
  Transsexuellengesetz (Act on Transsexuals), 104
Glennon, Theresa, 11–12, 13, 14, 18

Hallaq, Wael, 260–261, 265, 273–274
Heiderhoff, Bettina, 3, 12, 15–16
Hetherington, David, 118
Homosexuals. *See* Civil partnerships or unions; Same-sex marriage
Human rights
  in Germany
    overview, 81
    autonomy and, 15–16
    children born out of wedlock and, 78
    same-sex marriage and, 79
    transsexuals and, 78
    unwed biological fathers and, 79–80
  Islamic family law and, 255–256
  in Latin America, 130
Hunter, Rosemary, 3, 6, 8–9, 10, 12–13, 14, 123

India
  overview, 226–227
  adoption in
    dattaka (form of adoption), 230–231
    neglected and abused children, 230
    under personal laws, 230–231
  All India Muslim Women's Personal Law Board, 243
  autonomy in
    group autonomy, 245–247
    personal laws and, 234
    religious ADR and, 239, 245–247
  Awaaz-e-Miswan, 243
  Bharatiya Janata Party, 238
  Bharatiya Muslim Mahila Aandolan, 243, 244
  Code of Criminal Procedure 1972, 229–230, 233
  Constitution, 237–239
  Dissolution of Muslim Marriage Act 1939, 276
  Family Courts Act 1984, 228
  gender in
    personal laws, gender differences in, 227
    personal laws and, 236–237
    religious ADR and, 243–245
  general family laws in, 227–230, 233–236
  Guardians and Wards Act 1890, 230, 233
  Hindu Adoptions and Maintenance Act 1956, 230–231
  Hindu Marriage Act 1955, 231
  Indian Succession Act 1925, 228, 229, 233
  Islamic family law in, 232, 234–235, 236, 238–239, 243
  Juvenile Justice (Care and Protection of Children) Act 2000, 230, 233
  marriage in
    datta homa (invocation ceremony), 231
    under general family laws, 227–230
    under personal laws, 231
    saptapadi (seven steps ceremony), 231
    solemnization, difficulties in, 229
  Muslim Women Act, 229–230
  Parsis in, 226, 229, 240
  personal laws in
    adoption under, 230–231
    autonomy and, 234
    Buddhists under, 231–232
    chart, 249–252
    Constitution versus, 237–239
    distortion of religious traditions in, 226
    freedom of choice under, 234–235
    gender and, 236–237
    gender differences in, 227
    general family laws versus, 227–230, 233–236
    historical background, 225–226
    intra-group religious diversity, insensitivity to, 232–233
    Jains under, 231–232
    marriage under, 231
    misrecognition under, 247–252
    nonrecognition under, 247–252
    opting out of, 227–230, 233
    outside of family law context, 226
    "personal law groups," 227
    problems with, 233, 247–252
    Sikhs under, 231–232
  religion in
    application of rules, 5–6
    assignment of, 2–3
    coercion regarding, 235–236
    general versus specific rules, 5–6
    overlap with family law, 4
  religious ADR in
    overview, 7–8, 239–241
    autonomy and, 239, 245–247
    criticism of, 243–244
    religious identity and, 241–242
    women and, 243–245
  Special Marriage Act 1954, 228–229
  women in
    personal laws and, 236–237
    religious ADR and, 243–245

Industrial Revolution, 206
Inheritance rights
  in Islamic family law, 262
  in South Africa
    cohabitation and, 190–191, 192–197
    of same-sex couples, 190–191, 192–197
Institute for Future Studies, 158
Intersex children. *See also* Gender identity
  in Colombia, 141–142
  in Latin America, 3–4
Iraq
  Code of 1951, 272
  Code of Personal Status of 1959, 276
  Sunni-Shia conflict in, 272
Islamic family law. *See also specific country*
  overview, 254–258
  child custody in, 266–267
  child support in, 267
  as colonial fabrication, 254–255
  colonialism, impact of, 270–271
  constitutional norms and, 255–256
  divorce or dissolution in
    judicial decree, 264
    khul (mutual agreement), 264, 265
    registration of, 278–279
    talaq (unilateral repudiation), 264–265
  eclecticism in, 271–272
  England and Wales, Sharia Councils in, 26–28
  factors influencing development of, 259–260
  fatwas (legal opinions), 269–270
  halaqas (circles of learning), 269
  Hanafi Madhhab, 259
  Hanafi School, 271–273, 275–276
  human rights and, 255–256
  in India, 232, 234–235, 236, 238–239, 243
  inheritance rights in, 262
  madrasas (colleges), 269
  mahr (dower), 262, 263
  maintenance in, 262
  Maliki School, 272–273, 276
  marriage in
    capacity of parties, 261–262
    contractual nature of, 260–261, 263
    registration of, 278–279
    temporary marriage, 263–264
    transient bar to, 262
  modernization of, 273–274
  moral versus legal aspects, 278
  muftis (scholars), 269–270
  nation-states, emergence of, 271
  paternity in
    overview, 265
    illegitimacy and, 266
    presumptions regarding, 265–266
  post-colonial legislative reforms, 274–277
  qadis (judges), 269–270
  religious ADR in, 8
  religious versus legal aspects, 278
  Shafi'i School, 272–273
  sharia
    community consensus regarding, 257
    departure from, 274–275
    historical background, 268–270
    interaction with state law, 254, 259, 277–278
    misconceptions of, 267–268, 279
    as normative system, 255, 258
    persistence of, 258–259
    problems with codification of, 256
    state enforcement of, problems with, 6, 257–258, 275
  state law
    European model, 273
    interaction with *sharia*, 254, 259, 277–278
    selectivity of, 256–257
  Sunni-Shia conflict in, 272
Italy, Sweden compared, 178

Jordan
  Law of Family Rights of 1951, 276
  Law of Personal Status of 1976, 276

Kapoor, C., 229
Keidan, Charles, 21
Kuwait, Code and Commercial Law of 1960, 272

Lathrop Gómez, Fabiola, 3–4, 15, 18
Latin America. *See also specific country*
  overview, 128–129, 156
  assistive reproductive technologies (ARTs) in, 130–131
  autonomy in, 15
  biological parenthood, departure from, 130–131
  broad model of family in, 129
  child-rearing in, 132
  children's rights in, 18
  constitutional courts in, 133–134

constitutionalisation of family law in, 128–129, 156–157
emerging jurisprudence of family law in, 129–132
England and Wales compared, 130–131
equalisation of gender roles in, 3
filiation by birth in, 145
gender identity in
  overview, 141
  intersex children, 3–4
human rights in, 130
intermediate model of family in, 129
international human rights law and, 130
judicial decisions, precedential value of, 133
marriage in, 135
neo-constitutionalisation in, 133–134
restrictive model of family in, 129
rights of children in, 131–132
same-sex marriage in, 135
Lawyers
  Australia, role in property division in, 123–124
  challenges facing, 1–2
Lebanon, Sunni-Shia conflict in, 272
Leviner, Pernilla, 3, 11, 15
LGBT persons
  civil partnerships or unions (*See* Civil partnerships or unions)
    same-sex marriage (*See* Same-sex marriage)
    South Africa, same-sex couples in
  "choice argument" and, 189–190
  heterosexual couples versus, 188–190, 191, 197–198
  inheritance rights of, 190–191, 192–197
  marriage, 182, 190
Libya, Code of 1954, 272
Louw, Anne, 6–7, 10
Low, Hamish, 114–115, 117

Maintenance. *See* Alimony or maintenance
Marriage
  in Argentina, 135, 137–138
  in Brazil, 135, 138–139
  in Chile, 139–141
  cohabitation versus, 9–10
  in Colombia, 135–136
  divorce, effect of, 10
  in England and Wales
    overview, 19–20

  forced marriage, 34–36
  formalities of, 24–26
  "non-marriage," 25–26
  pre-nuptial agreements, 42–44
  Sharia Councils, 26–28
in Germany
  overview, 95
  same-sex marriage, 96, 103
in India
  datta homa (invocation ceremony), 231
  under general family laws, 227–230
  under personal laws, 231
  saptapadi (seven steps ceremony), 231
  solemnization, difficulties in, 229
in Islamic family law
  capacity of parties, 261–262
  contractual nature of, 260–261, 263
  registration of, 278–279
  temporary marriage, 263–264
  transient bar to, 262
in Latin America, 135
in Mexico, 135, 138
nature of institution, 10
parenthood, effect of decline on, 17
in South Africa
  access to, 9
  "choice argument" and, 189–190
  civil unions in hierarchy of marital relations, 197–198
  civil unions versus, 10
  cohabitation in hierarchy of marital relations, 200–201
  conscientious objection clause, 198
  customary marriage in hierarchy of marital relations, 198–199
  minimum age, 198
  non-married persons versus, 181
  pluralism, criticism of, 182–184
  recommendations regarding, 201–202
  religious marriages, 199, 200
  same-sex marriage, 182, 190
in Sweden
  alternatives to, 11
  preference for, 175–176
in Uruguay, 135
in US
  access to, 9
  changing demographics, 51
  diminishing financial support from, 55, 58–59
  discouragement of, 11
  inter-spousal contracts, 61

Marriage (cont.)
　　non-marital relationships, 57–58
　　restrictions on, 57
　　same-sex marriage, 57, 65
Merkel, Angela, 79
Mexico
　　Constitution, 134
　　constitutionalisation of family law in, 134
　　Federal Civil Code, 134
　　Federal District Civil Code, 144
　　Federal District Code of Civil Procedure, 144
　　filiation by birth in, 147–149
　　gender identity, sexual ambiguity, 143–144
　　marriage in, 135, 138
　　same-sex marriage in, 138
Meyerson, D., 199–200
Mill, John Stuart, 235–236
Morocco, Code of Personal Status of 1958, 276

On Liberty (Mill), 235–236
Ottoman Empire
　　colonialism and, 275
　　Law of Family Rights, 276
　　Majallah, 271–272, 275–276

Pakistan, Sunni-Shia conflict in, 272
Parent-child relationship
　　China, continuation in, 208
　　in US
　　　　overview, 62–63
　　　　assistive reproductive technologies (ARTs) and, 65–66
　　　　broadening base of, 63–66
　　　　in loco parentis, 65
　　　　non-marital parents, 63–65
　　　　presumption of, 63
　　　　in same-sex marriage, 65
　　　　state intrusion into, 66
　　　　unwed fathers, 63–65
Parenthood
　　genetic testing and, 17
　　in Germany
　　　　birthmother dogma, 82–83
　　　　co-mothers, 83–84
　　　　genetic testing and, 17
　　　　by sperm donation, 83–84
　　　　as status, 82
　　marriage, effect of decline of, 17
　　paternity (*See* Paternity)

　　relational definition of, 17–18
　　in Sweden
　　　　genetic parenthood preference, 176
　　　　genetic testing, 167–168
　　　　guardianship versus, 169–170
　　　　involuntarily childless persons, 176–177
　　　　nuclear family preference, 170
　　　　number of parents, 168–169
　　　　presumptions, 167–168
　　　　registration requirement, 166–167, 168
　　　　same-sex couples, 168
　　　　"twoness" preference, 168–169, 175, 176
Parkinson, Patrick, 112
Paternity
　　in Germany
　　　　mixed principles, 84
　　　　social father versus genetic father, 84–86
　　　　unwed biological fathers, 79–80, 86, 87–88
　　in Islamic family law
　　　　overview, 265
　　　　illegitimacy and, 266
　　　　presumptions regarding, 265–266
Pre-nuptial agreements
　　in England and Wales, 42–44
　　feminist critique of, 43
　　in Germany, 103–104
　　in South Africa, 181
　　in US, 59–61
Privacy in US
　　overview, 55
　　abortion, 56
　　constitutional protection, 56
　　contraception, 56
　　historical background, 55–56
　　same-sex marriage, 57
　　sexual relations, 56–57
Property division
　　in Australia
　　　　overview, 12
　　　　adjudicated cases, 124–126
　　　　contributions versus need, 110–111, 118
　　　　de facto financial disputes, 125
　　　　definition of property, 109–110
　　　　diversity in, 126
　　　　factors affecting, 120–121
　　　　fairness, perception of, 122–123

high-asset versus moderate-asset cases, 125
informal agreements, 119-122
judicial discretion, 110
lawyers, role of, 123-124
separate property regime, 109-110
statistics, 119
uncertainty in, 126
in England and Wales
  overview, 28
  cohabitation and, 31-33
  rules versus discretion, 28-31
  uncertainty in, 29-31
  women allegedly favoured by, 29-31
in South Africa
  in customary marriage, 184-188
  "family property," 187
  "house property," 187

Qu, Lixia, 119-121, 122

Religion
  in England and Wales
    freedom of choice, 6
    overlap with family law, 4
  in India
    application of rules, 5-6
    assignment of, 2-3
    coercion regarding, 235-236
    general versus specific rules, 5-6
    overlap with family law, 4
  Islamic family law (*See* Islamic family law)
    overlap with family law, 4-5
    religious ADR (*See* Religious ADR)
  in South Africa
    "religion free zone," family law as, 6-7
    religious marriages, 199, 200
Religious ADR
  in Canada, 8, 244
  in India
    overview, 7-8, 239-241
    autonomy and, 239, 245-247
    criticism of, 243-244
    religious identity and, 241-242
    women and, 243-245
  in Islamic family law, 8
Rhoades, Helen, 125

Same-sex marriage
  in Argentina, 137-138
  in Brazil, 138-139
  in Chile, 139-141

in Colombia, 135-136
in Germany, 79, 103
in Latin America, 135
in Mexico, 138
in South Africa, 182, 190
in US, 57, 65
al-Sanhuri, Abd al-Razzaq, 272
Sarmas, Lisa, 3, 12, 16
Saudi Arabia, Sunni-Shia conflict in, 272
Shi, David, 14, 18
Singer, Anna, 170, 178
Smith, B.S., 196
Smith, Warwick, 118
Solanki, Gopika, 240
South Africa
  overview, 180-181, 200-202
  Children's Act of 2005, 200
  Civil Union Act of 2006, 182, 190-191, 192-195, 197-198, 201
  civil unions in
    overview, 182
    defined, 197-198
    in hierarchy of marital relations, 197-198
    marriage versus, 10
  cohabitation in
    in hierarchy of marital relations, 200-201
    inheritance rights and, 190-191, 192-197
  Constitution, 180, 185-186
  Constitutional Court, 180
  customary marriage in
    overview, 188
    criticism of, 182-184
    dissolution of, 183
    in hierarchy of marital relations, 198-199
    property division, 184-188
    recognition of, 181-182
  Divorce Act of 1979, 181, 183
  Domestic Partnerships Bill (proposed), 200-201
  duty of support in, 194-195
  inheritance rights in
    cohabitation and, 190-191, 192-197
    of same-sex couples, 190-191, 192-197
  Intestate Succession Act of 1987, 181, 190-191, 192-195
  Judges Remuneration and Conditions of Employment Act of 1989, 189
  lobolo (bridewealth), 183-184, 199

South Africa (cont.)
  Maintenance of Surviving Spouses' Act of
    1990, 181, 189
  Marriage Act of 1961, 181, 197–198, 201
  marriage in
    access to, 9
    "choice argument" and, 189–190
    civil unions in hierarchy of marital
      relations, 197–198
    civil unions versus, 10
    cohabitation in hierarchy of marital
      relations, 200–201
    conscientious objection clause, 198
    customary marriage in hierarchy of
      marital relations, 198–199
    minimum age, 198
    non-married persons versus, 181
    pluralism, criticism of, 182–184
    recommendations regarding, 201–202
    religious marriages, 199, 200
    same-sex marriage, 182, 190
  Matrimonial Property Act of 1984, 181
  Muslim Marriages Bill (proposed), 200
  polygyny in
    criticism of, 182–184
    property division and, 184–188
    recognition of, 181–182
  pre-nuptial agreements in, 181
  property division in
    customary marriage, 184–188
    "family property," 187
    "house property," 187
  Recognition of Customary Marriages Act
    of 1998, 181–188, 198–199
  religion in
    "religion free zone," family law as, 6–7
    religious marriages, 199, 200
  same-sex couples in
    "choice argument" and, 189–190
    heterosexual couples versus, 188–190,
      191, 197–198
    inheritance rights of, 190–191,
      192–197
    marriage, 182, 190
  separation of powers in, 180
  sexual orientation discrimination,
    prohibition against, 182
  Wills Act of 1953, 199
Steinfeld, Rebecca, 21
Sudan, Sunni-Shia conflict in, 272–273
Surrogacy in Sweden, 165, 174, 177
Sweden
  overview, 161–162
  adoption in, 173–174
  assistive reproductive technologies (ARTs)
    in
    attempt to conceive as prerequisite,
      165–166
    England and Wales compared, 174–175
    gamete donation, 163–164
    reluctance to embrace, 174–175
    restrictions on, 165–166
    surrogacy, 165, 174, 177
    US compared, 174–175
    womb transplantation, 177
  Australia compared, 159
  autonomy in, 15
  Care of Young Persons Act, 159, 172
  child care in, equalisation of gender roles,
    3
  child protection system in
    overview, 159
    extra-familial placement, 171–172
    as family and service-oriented system,
      159–160, 171
    out-of-home care placement, 171–172
    reunification, preference for, 171–174
    risk assessments, 172
    state intervention, 171
  Children and Parents Code, 163, 165, 172,
    175–176
  England and Wales compared, 159
  formation of family in
    overview, 162
    right to parenthood, 163
  Genetic Integrity Act, 160, 163–164
  genetic testing in, 167–168
  Italy compared, 178
  marriage in
    alternatives to, 11
    preference for, 175–176
  nuclear family versus openness in
    overview, 161
    genetic parenthood preference, 176
    marriage preference, 175–176
    parenthood, nuclear family preference
      in, 170
    "reproduction" of nuclear family,
      177–179
    romantic love and, 175
    "twoness" preference, 175, 176
  parenthood in
    genetic parenthood preference, 176
    genetic testing, 167–168

guardianship versus, 169–170
involuntarily childless persons, 176–177
nuclear family preference, 170
number of parents, 168–169
presumptions, 167–168
registration requirement, 166–167, 168
same-sex couples, 168
"twoness" preference, 168–169, 175, 176
progressive policies and attitudes in, 158–159
Social Services Act, 159
Social Welfare Board, 167, 172–173
state control versus individualism in, 160–161
"Swedish state individualism," 160, 174
US compared, 159, 178
welfare system in, 159, 174
Syria
Law of Personal Status of 1953, 276
Sunni-Shia conflict in, 272

Taylor, Charles, 247–248
Technological developments, 1
Thompson, Sharon, 40, 43
The Three Worlds of Welfare Capitalism (Esping-Andersen), 159
Trädgårdh, Lars, 160
Transgendered persons. *See* Gender identity
Transsexuals in Germany, 78, 104–105
Tunisia, Law of Personal Status of 1956, 276
Turbulence in family law, 1–2

United Kingdom. *See* England and Wales
United States
overview, 48–50, 74–75
alimony, decline of, 11–12
alimony in, 11–12
assistive reproductive technologies (ARTs) in
overview, 65–66
Sweden compared, 174–175
autonomy in
overview, 13
contracts and, 62
increases in, 48–50
changing family demographics in
overview, 50–51
cohabitation, 52
divorce, 52
employment, 53–54

family complexity, 52–53
financial insecurity, 54–55
marriage, 51
multi-partner fertility, 52–53
child custody in
gender-based presumptions, 67
historical background, 66–67
shared custody, 67–68
child support in
filial responsibility statutes, 69–70
financial burdens of, 69
financial inequality and, 70–71
freedom of choice, 68–69
cohabitation in
changing demographics, 52
contracts, use of, 61–62
contracts, use of
autonomy and, 62
cohabitation, 61–62
inter-spousal contracts, 61
pre-marital agreements, 59–61
divorce in
alimony, decline in, 11–12, 58–59
changing demographics, 52
Due Process Clause, 56
Earned Income Tax Credit (EITC), 73, 74
filial responsibility statutes, 69–70
financial inequality in
overview, 48–50, 71
changing demographics, 54–55
child support and, 70–71
diminishing financial support from marriage, 58–59
employment and, 71–73
public benefits and, 73–74
Fourteenth Amendment, 56, 57
gender-based presumptions in child custody, 67
marriage in
access to, 9
changing demographics, 51
diminishing financial support from, 55, 58–59
discouragement of, 11
inter-spousal contracts, 61
non-marital relationships, 57–58
restrictions on, 57
same-sex marriage, 57, 65
Massachusetts, alimony in, 58–59
parent-child relationship in
overview, 62–63

United States (cont.)
    assistive reproductive technologies (ARTs) and, 65–66
    broadening base of, 63–66
    in loco parentis, 65
    non-marital parents, 63–65
    presumption of, 63
    in same-sex marriage, 65
    state intrusion into, 66
    unwed fathers, 63–65
  pre-marital agreements in, 59–61
  privacy in
    overview, 55
    abortion, 56
    constitutional protection, 56
    contraception, 56
    historical background, 55–56
    same-sex marriage, 57
    sexual relations, 56–57
  same-sex marriage, 57, 65
  Social Security, 57, 73–74
  Sweden compared, 159, 178
  Temporary Assistance for Needy Families (TANF), 73–74

Texas, alimony in, 58–59
Uruguay, marriage in, 135

Violence. *See* Domestic violence

Wade, John, 123
Wales. *See* England and Wales
Womb transplantation in Sweden, 177
Women. *See also* Gender
  Australia, effects of divorce on women in, 114–118
  changing social status of, 1
  in China, 206
  discrimination against, 2–3
  in England and Wales
    expansion of rights, 206
    property division allegedly favouring, 29–31
  in India
    personal laws and, 236–237
    religious ADR and, 243–245
  Latin America, equalisation of gender roles in, 3